Deviant BEHAVIOR

Deviant BEHAVIOR

CRIME, CONFLICT, AND INTEREST GROUPS

CHARLES H. McCAGHY

Department of Sociology
Bowling Green State University

MACMILLAN PUBLISHING CO., INC.
New York

COLLIER MACMILLAN PUBLISHERS
London

Macmillan Publishing Co., Inc.
866 Third Avenue, New York, New York 10022

Collier Macmillan Canada, Ltd.

Library of Congress Cataloging in Publication Data

McCaghy, Charles H
  Deviant behavior.

  Includes index.
  1. Crime and criminals.   2. Deviant behavior.
I. Title.   [DNLM: 1. Conflict.   2. Crime.
3. Social behavior disorders. WM600 M121d]
HV6025.M27   364.3   75-14131
ISBN 0-02-378400-8

Printing: 3 4 5 6 7 8   Year: 7 8 9 0 1 2

To Dawn

Preface

This opening statement is analogous to the sections entitled "To the Teacher" that I used to see in my grade school textbooks. With a mixture of curiosity and a little guilt, I occasionally scanned these in an attempt to penetrate the rarefied world of adults who knew so much. Rather than being a key to knowledge, however, those pages invariably were stuffy and incomprehensible. So I concentrated on the rest of the text, which was addressed "to the student."

The purpose of this preface—risking stuffiness and incomprehensibility—is to alert the instructor that the rest of the book is written "to the student" in the strictest meaning of that phrase. The text is not written with the intent of impressing or informing colleagues. Its goal is to provide, within the framework of interest group conflict, a basic discussion of the principal issues and research findings in the field of deviant behavior. Too many texts are encyclopedic in their attempt to provide a thorough review of the literature; their authors cite an enormous range of articles. In one recent undergraduate text, for example, twelve different sociologists' names appear on two consecutive pages. Although such a format is appropriate for highly motivated undergraduate and graduate students, the "average" undergraduate is bewildered and put off by the machine-gunning of names of contributors to the field.

In order to hold the attention of the hypothetical "average" student, I have resorted to two devices. First, I have restricted the discussion of specific articles or books to a minimum. Consequently, the only persons identified in the text are those whose theories, ideas, or research are examined in some detail. This means that reference to many excellent theoretical and research papers is missing from the text, but interested students and instructors can find them in the footnotes. Of course, the works incorporated in the text necessarily reflect my particular theoretical bias, but I have made a deliberate effort to counterbalance this bias in the notes.

The second device designed to make the book palatable to its audience is the inclusion of real life examples to illustrate points. In large degree illustrations are drawn from the mass media. True, this eliminates some of the academic luster, but I believe that sociology is more a folk science than many of us would care to admit. Journalists' comments on social behavior are often more incisive and significant than the ponderous declarations found in our scholarly journals. Because the job of this book is to teach sociology, I felt exclusiveness was an unnecessary encumbrance.

As has been said in countless prefaces, the writing of a book is rarely accomplished by the author alone. Many other persons contribute in ways great and small. I express my special appreciation to Professors Marcia Garrett, Stuart Hadden, and Stuart L. Hills, who labored through the first draft. They made many valuable suggestions and pointed out my errors and shortcomings. The errors and shortcomings that remain must be attributed to the author's stubbornness, not to a lack of excellent advice.

I also extend my thanks to Donald J. Black, R. Serge Denisoff, Karen Gilbert, Brad Larsen, Robin Room, Hal Theis, Charles W. Thomas, Ralph Wahrman, and Margaret Zahn. And for outstanding clerical assistance I acknowledge Dianna Blankenship, Lauretta Lahman, and Lynn Schmid.

C. H. M.

Contents

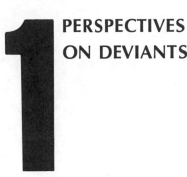

1 PERSPECTIVES ON DEVIANTS

If any single factor makes human social life possible and bearable, it is the ability of individuals to predict the behavior of others. One often hears that "human behavior cannot be predicted," but some reflection will reveal that the adage contains a bit of nonsense. In your daily activities you constantly behave on the basis of predictions; they provide sets of assumptions or expectations upon which to act. For example, you come to class assuming the instructor will be there to lecture; you take notes assuming they will be of some use in furthering your intellectual development or, at least, your grade average; and you answer test questions assuming that the instructor reads the responses and grades according to the degree your answers reflect the "truths" he or she communicated.

Should the instructor fail to meet these expectations by consistently missing classes, by posing trivial or unrelated examination questions, and by assigning grades on the basis of students' looks, you would feel cheated, put on, and generally ripped off. And all because your predictions did not materialize.

Not that all unpredictability is bad. Surprises and departures from routine are certainly welcome at times. We are concerned here with people who behave in both unexpected and unacceptable ways. What constitutes unexpected and unacceptable behavior may seem to be rather personal and individual judgments. To some extent they are, yet group life would obviously be difficult without considerable agreement among members concerning the ground rules regulating behavior. Regardless of how dedicated they may be to personal gratification, group members operate under some constraints if the group is to survive. It is difficult to imagine any viable group in which members did whatever they wished regardless of the feelings and well-being of others. If, for example, a group of free spirits formed a ruleless community in which everyone could follow any impulse, how long would it last if a member decided to enjoy some sadism followed by cannibalistic snacks, or, worse yet, refused to help with the dishes? Unless the others were extremely pliant masochists, one can safely assume that some restrictions would be shortly forthcoming.

If any group is to continue as an operating entity there must be some agreement among members upon how they shall act toward one another; obversely, there will be at least tacit consensus on what constitutes unacceptable behavior. Your ventures into the world of human relations depend on these rules and consensus toward them. You reasonably assume, generally on the basis of past experience, that such relations will be conducted according to rules as you understand them. In everyday life you are usually secure from unpleasant surprises. Although those about you are seeking to satisfy their own interests and appetites, their behavior is usually predictable and within acceptable limits. These rules governing human relations within social groups are what sociologists call *norms*. Specifically, a norm is defined as "a standard shared by members of a social group in which the members are expected to conform, and conformity to which is enforced by positive and negative sanctions." [1]

But, as we know, human relations do have their unsettling moments. Some people ignore or defy the norms. They do not conform to your expectations and are the source of an entire range of negative emotions such as irritation, disgust, suspicion, and even fear. They are people who are not on time, who deceive, who renege on promises, who take things that do not belong to them, who are inconsiderate, who cannot be trusted, and so on. In short, they are deviant.

What Is Deviant?

Offhand, this seems a simple question. A dictionary definition is consistent enough with our above discussion: "Differing from a norm or from accepted standards of society." [2] So too is a definition from an introductory sociology text: "Deviant behavior is that behavior which does not conform to social expectations." [3] But these definitions prompt us to ask, "What are the accepted standards and social expectations"? This is a considerably more difficult question to answer. You personally know what is accepted and expected within your own circle of family and friends, and this knowledge enables you to get along reasonably well. But what about "out there" in that arena called American society? To what degree do your conceptions of deviant behavior match those of the more general society?

Some years ago a sociologist, Jerry L. Simmons, conducted an interesting study involving 180 persons of various characteristics and backgrounds. He asked them to list "things or types of persons" they regarded as deviant. Concerning his results he writes:

> The sheer range of responses predictably included homosexuals, prostitutes, drug addicts, radicals and criminals. But it also included liars, career women, Democrats, reckless drivers, atheists, Christians, suburbanites, the retired, young folks, card players, bearded men, artists, pacifists, priests, prudes, hippies, straights, girls who wear makeup, the President, conservatives, integrationists, executives, divorcees, perverts, motorcycle gangs, smart-alec students, know-it-all professors, modern people, and Americans.[4]

Undoubtedly, if Simmons' study were replicated there would be several changes in the above list formulated over a decade ago. The conclusion drawn from the study probably would not change, however. Although there is wide agreement that some behaviors are deviant, many other behaviors are considered deviant by smaller numbers of people. Thus, standards and expectations concerning behavior depend less upon either universal norms or consensus over norms than upon a particular point of view.

Yet it is scarcely enlightening simply to say that deviance is relative and let the matter rest. Some deviance is definitely more relative than others. For example, the members of a society are likely to express greater agreement over the banning of murder than of spitting on the sidewalk. Even granting that under some circumstances a majority of the population might condemn expectorations before they would executions, in any society guidelines concerning the taking of human life are deemed important ones. In the United States there is disagreement over the acceptability of some killings, such as the slaying of civilians in the time of war, capital punishment, abortion, and euthanasia (mercy killing recently recoined as "death with dignity" by proponents). But evidence indicates considerable agreement over the unacceptability of more conventional murder and an assortment of other behaviors.

In 1968 John E. Conklin interviewed a sample of 266 persons in a suburb and an area of a large eastern metropolitan center.[5] In seeking to measure the degree of support for certain laws, Conklin posed specific examples such as:

> An unarmed man breaks into an unoccupied house at night and steals $100.00 in cash (Burglary).
> A man enters a bar, says he is going to kill another man, and attacks this man with a knife. He doesn't kill him, but he injures him seriously (Aggravated assault).
> A man forcibly rapes a woman (Rape).

For these and other examples Conklin asked, "In your opinion, should there be a law to punish this person?" He found that several behaviors elicited a practically unanimous response: over 95 per cent of the sample said yes for burglary, aggravated assault, rape, robbery, auto theft, murder, and larceny. There was considerably less agreement concerning other acts such as marihuana use and gambling.

It would appear from Conklin's findings that even within the highly heterogeneous environment of a metropolitan area there is nearly perfect consensus that certain actions are unacceptable. But such a conclusion is misleading without some qualification. Imagine if Conklin's examples had read:

> An American soldier breaks into a citizen's home in enemy territory and steals $100 in cash.
> A man attacks with a knife and seriously injures a homosexual who made a pass at him.
> A man forcibly rapes a woman he knows to be a prostitute.

We can be reasonably certain that the consensus of responses to these examples would be considerably less than for the original versions. It must be understood that *agreement concerning the deviant character of actions applies only when they are directed against members of one's own group or society.* Similar acts against those defined as "enemies," "strangers," "not our kind," or "deserving what they get" do not readily qualify for the same interpretation.

It should be clear by now that while deviance is behavior that departs from social norms, describing the character of such norms is not a simple matter. It is not enough to say "people are against killing and stealing." People are not against all violence that harms others, or all acts that deprive others of their properties. They are primarily concerned with protecting their own interests, and the interests of those they know, love, and respect.

Historically, most theorists have dealt with this problem by assuming that the norms of a society are embodied in its criminal law. The theorists' position was that the criminal law concerned the well-being of all and reflected the conscience of the total society regardless of the interests of various individuals or groups. Thus, for all practical purposes the deviant was the criminal—a person whose behaviors were formally forbidden by legislation and were punishable by the state.[6]

But this interpretation of criminal law is subject to criticism. The making of the law and its application are essentially political activities. Legislation is not made by all in a society, but by those with the power to do so, and power is not equally distributed. Stuart L. Hills describes the process this way:

> The unequal distribution of power and authority means that some interest groups will have greater access to the decision-making process and will use their power and influence to have legislation enacted to protect and maintain their interests at the expense of less powerful groups.
>
> . . .
>
> Criminal laws (including legislative statutes, administrative rulings, and judicial decisions) will change with modification in the interest-power structure of society. As social conditions change—altering the distribution of power and the relative fortunes of various interest groups; threatening the economic, political, religious, and status interests of dominant groups; or modifying the values and interests at stake—criminal-law definitions will change, adapting to these shifting conditions.[7]

The relationship between interest groups and criminal law will be elaborated upon later. For now, the reader should keep in mind that in the discussion immediately following the theorists are exclusively concerned with a specific type of deviant—the person designated by the state as a criminal.

The Rational Deviant—
The Classical School of Criminology

The first generally recognized school of criminology, the classical school, did not emerge until the middle of the eighteenth century. Its principal author was the Italian mathematician and economist, Cesare Beccaria (1738–1794), who was strongly influenced by the French writers Montesquieu, Rousseau, and Voltaire.[8]

A single work by Beccaria constitutes the manifesto of the classical school of criminology. Entitled *On Crimes and Punishments* (published as *Dei Delitti e delle Pene* in 1764), the book is essentially a plea for reform of the judicial and penal systems of the time, which were characterized by secret accusations, extensive use of torture, harsh penalties for trivial offenses, the application of law to implement political policy, and extreme arbitrariness by judges in levying punishments.

Because Beccaria's work was aimed at reforming the justice system, strictly speaking it did not deal directly with the question of why deviance occurs. Nevertheless, some underlying assumptions about the nature of humanity are apparent in it, and from these a kind of theory of deviant behavior does emerge.

According to Beccaria, humans are fundamentally rational and hedonistic; they possess free will and make deliberate decisions to behave based upon a calculation of the pain and pleasure involved. It is from these characteristics that society emerges. In order to avoid continual chaos resulting from total individual freedom, humans essentially enter a contract in which they relinquish part of their liberty in exchange for security under the laws of a state. Humans are basically self-serving, however. Given the opportunity they will enhance their own positions at the expense of other humans. Thus the role of the state is to reduce crime. Beccaria wrote:

> It is better to prevent crimes than to punish them. This is the ultimate end of every good legislation, which, to use the general terms for assessing the good and evils of life, is the art of leading men to the greatest possible happiness or to the least possible unhappiness.[9]

To this end Beccaria argued that the law should be clear, simple, and directed against only those behaviors clearly endangering society and individuals in it. Compliance with the law should be rewarded, and it is necessary to convince individuals that punishment for violations will be unavoidable, prompt, and in slight excess of the pleasure derived from the illegal act. Unlike the criminological theorists who were to dominate the field for the next 150 years, Beccaria perceived humans as equal, self-determining individuals whose freedom and responsibility were preeminent and unaffected by personal characteristics, extenuating circumstances, and past experiences. Because of their rationality, all humans were seen as equal before the law; Beccaria accepted literally the notion that punishment should fit the crime.

The work of Beccaria resulted in many judicial and penal reforms throughout Europe, but a viable theory of deviance never emerged from the classical school. This was a result of Beccaria's oversimplified conceptions of the nature of human behavior and almost deliberate neglect of the motivations behind behavior. For example, while he stressed the rational equality of humans he ignored the obvious inequalities of wealth and power that might contribute substantially to criminal behavior. In short, Beccaria did not recognize that some people are more equal than others.[10] Regardless, the assumptions of the classical school were eventually replaced by those of the positive school.

The Deviant as Determined—
Positivist Criminology

The nineteenth century produced several revolutionary landmarks in various branches of the physical sciences. To name but a few: the rediscovery of the atomic constitution of matter, the establishment of stratigraphic geology for dating geological formations, the founding of the science of oceanography, and the formulation of the fundamental laws of genetics. Developments in biology were particularly rapid with the publications of works by Charles Darwin. In 1859 the *Origin of Species* set forth the idea of natural selection among living things, and in 1871 the *Descent of Man* linked *Homo sapiens* with early, nonhuman animal life. The simultaneous growth and development of the scientific method and the revelation that humans had evolved from ape-like ancestors brought about a revolution in thinking about the nature of human beings and how their behavior might be interpreted. One result was what has come to be known as the positive school of criminology.

To understand the changes in criminological perspective occurring in the nineteenth century, it is important to become acquainted with two terms. The first, *positivism,* is a philosophical approach founded by Auguste Comte (1798–1857), which replaced speculation with scientific inquiry as the source of knowledge about social life. More specifically positivism is defined as:

> a philosophical approach, theory, or system based on the view that in the social as well as in the natural sciences sense experiences and their logical and mathematical treatment are the exclusive source of all worthwhile information. Introspective and intuitional attempts to gain knowledge are rejected.[11]

In short, positivism does not concern itself with the abstract and unprovable, but with the tangible and quantifiable. It involves investigating the world by objective data that can be counted or measured.

The second term, *determinism,* refers to the principle that all events, including human behavior, have sufficient causes. Specifically,

> The term *determinism* denotes a doctrine which claims that all objects or events, or all objects or events of some kind . . . are determined, that is to say *must* be as they are and as they will be [by] virtue of some laws or forces which necessitate their being so.
>
> . . .
>
> The term becomes the name of a specific doctrine when the *kind* of determinism is indicated. For instance, *economic determinism* tends to mean the doctrine that economic factors determine others, . . . *sociological de-*

terminism is likely to mean the assertion that social facts are determined, *and* that they are determined by social factors.[12]

To deal with deviance scientifically, the positivist approach shifted attention away from the rational deviant actor toward one whose behavior is determined by forces beyond the control or even awareness of the individual. The deviant is seen as compelled into behavior assaulting the sensibilities of the mass of society. These forces and the resulting behavior distinguish the deviant from everyone else—the deviant is "different," "on the fringes of society," "inadequate," and so on. Following this logic, the positivist approach requires the abolition of punishment because the behavior in question is involuntary and not a matter of choice for the offender. Instead, the forces or determinants of the behavior must be neutralized or treated.[13]

TABLE 1–1
COMPARISON OF THE CLASSICAL AND POSITIVE
SCHOOLS OF CRIMINOLOGY *

	Classical	Positive
Date developed	Eighteenth century.	Nineteenth century.
Purpose	Reform of the judicial and penal systems.	The application of scientific methods to the study of the criminal as an individual.
Definition of behavior	Crime as defined by the legal code, *nullum crimen sine lege* (no crime without law).	Rejection of legal definitions by substituting "natural crime," "anti-social behavior," "offends sentiments of the community."
Explanation of behavior	Free will, rationality; deviants and non-deviants essentially similar.	Determinism: biological, psychological, economic, genetic, etc. Deviants and non-deviants different.
Method of behavior change	Fear of punishment as a deterrent.	Scientific treatment.

* Adapted in part from Clarence Ray Jeffery, "The Historical Development of Criminology," in *Pioneers in Criminology,* ed. Hermann Mannheim (Chicago: Quadrangle Books, 1960), pp. 366–367.

Although the use of scientific methods appears superior to mere conjecture, methodology alone carries no assurance that truth is around the corner. Inaccurate assumptions, misinterpretation and misapplication of findings, and intellectual arrogance can all conspire to make the positivist approach not only misleading but dangerous. Because determinism is involved, the scientist must make some assumptions about what is doing the determining. Specific factors to be investigated as possible causes must be selected out of a great universe of factors that might differentiate the deviant from others. The selection ultimately depends upon how the scientist theorizes the nature of human behavior; is it biologically, economically, or socially oriented? If the theory of human behavior is inappropriate for the scientist's purposes, the resulting findings will be of little value.

Since there are several possible theories concerning the fundamental nature of man, it should not be surprising that since the advent of positivism every human appendage has been measured, every emotion plumbed, every social influence probed, and every bodily fluid scrutinized. As a further result of such theories social environments have been engineered, parts of the brain removed, families counseled, organs lopped off, and many sorts of chemicals injected into the human system (legally, of course). All this has been done in the apparently unlimited search for answers to the question of why some ignore or disobey others' concepts of righteous behavior.

The positivist approach has often been responsible for another, though less explicit, assumption—that the source of deviant behavior invariably can be traced to a *pathology*. Deviation in behavior can be interpreted as a departure from normality, and the positivists' research consistently indicates a presupposition that a "normal" organism in a "normal" environment would not so act. The logic here is certainly comforting. If we regard deviance as unnatural, incomprehensible, weird, and so on, everything attains an orderliness if we can conclude that the behavior is a result of imperfections or inferiorities. How often do we say when confronted with unexpected and unacceptable behavior, "She must be sick" or "What's wrong with him?"

Thus positivism can be viewed as a combination of scientific method, a search for pathology, and the application of treatment based upon scientific findings. This is a corrosive blend, however. The presumption of pathology results in the abandonment of rationality as a causal factor. This means, in turn, that because humans are viewed as not completely responsible for their behavior there is justification for taking control of deviating individuals and for applying treatment to mend them. No one is better equipped than the state for doing just that; all for the good of the individuals and society, of course.

Vold points out that the implications of positivism easily fit into the patterns of totalitarian government:

It is centered on the core idea of the superior knowledge and wisdom of the scientific expert, who, on the basis of his studies, decides what kind of human beings his fellow men are who commit crime, and who, on the basis of this knowledge and scientific insight, prescribes appropriate treatment without concern for public opinion and without consent from the person so diagnosed (i.e., the criminal). There is an obvious similarity in conception of the control of power in society between positivism and the political reality of centralized control of the life of the citizen by a government bureaucracy indifferent to democratic public opinion.[14]

The potential abuses inherent in positivism are often masked by the good will and intentions of the scientific researchers and the staffs of institutions where citizens are commited. But the facts are unavoidable. Untold numbers of people have been incarcerated on the basis of erroneous, or, at best, tentative, theories of deviance. They have had their minds and bodies tampered with by "treatments" of no proven benefit (if they have been dignified by such attention at all). For examples one can reach into the past: during the eugenic movement (to be discussed later), a four-year-old girl was committed to an Ohio institution as part of an effort to rid the community of the feebleminded, who at that time carried the burden of a great number of potential evils. In 1974, officials had no explanation of why she remained incarcerated until she died at age 103.

A contemporary example concerns persons convicted of sex crimes who are diagnosed as "sex psychopaths" (an abnormality impossible to define in objective terms), committed for indefinite periods of treatment (the effectiveness of which has never been demonstrated) to prevent further deviant sexual behavior (which there are no means to predict). The subject of compulsory psychiatric treatment for sex offenders and others will be discussed in detail later.

If we could be assured that the positivists had contributed mightily to our understanding of human behavior, some acceptance of the approach could be mustered even while keeping a careful eye on its potential dangers. In fact, however, nearly all positivist attempts to explain deviance have been disappointing. The expected differences between deviants and nondeviants rarely materialize when the evidence is carefully examined. Nevertheless, positivism remains the dominant approach among students of deviance and shows slight indication of giving way to other approaches.[15]

Despite its weakness in explanatory power, positivism continues to have appeal because:

1. It avoids the issue of possible fundamental normative conflicts within society. Normality is the status quo and it is assumed in the positivist approach that there is a high degree of consensus concerning what behavior is improper. Questions concerning social conflicts are unnecessary because the deviant is simply someone who needs to be brought back into line with everyone else.
2. It avoids the issue of choice. The normal person and the deviant are both seen as compelled to conform and deviate, respectively.

Put another way, the normal person could not possibly choose to deviate. Thus, deviation is seen as a symptom of abnormality requiring treatment. This has an added feature of being humanitarian because punishment is considered inappropriate.
3. It is scientific. The prestige of the scientific approach and technology promises that truth shall be found and remedies are forthcoming.[16]

The following sections deal with a variety of positivist approaches ranging from the constitutional to the social-psychological and the sociocultural. The purpose is not to present a comprehensive description of the multitudinous research efforts involved; for this the reader can look elsewhere.[17] Rather, it is to acquaint the student with the major theoretical positions and schools of thought, and to indicate that practically every conceivable variable that might distinguish the deviant from anyone else has been investigated with less than definitive results.

Physical Characteristics of Deviants

Of all the positivist approaches to the explanation of deviance, the investigation of a possible relationship between anatomical attributes and behavior is not only the oldest but also the most persistent. Today scarcely a year goes by without some revelation concerning the possible connection between a biological characteristic and human behavior. In fairness to the scientists of today they are generally far less sweeping in their claims than were the researchers of a few decades ago. But the probing of every nook and cranny of the human system goes on. One can only sense the public's anticipation that someday a pill or a swipe of a scalpel will put an end to thievery, homosexuality, and all sorts of behavior.

Such faith is understandable in view of the fact that it is a biological organism doing the acting, and that such an organism is far easier to measure and examine than other possible variables. Furthermore, despite admonitions that "beauty is skin deep," and "you can't tell a book by its cover," we constantly make decisions about people solely on the basis of their appearance. We also know that the way we feel affects the way we act. If a friend behaves strangely, his or her explanation, "I feel lousy," is usually sufficient.

The influence of biology on human behavior is easily overestimated and oversimplified, however. Some readers may recall that in 1966, Charles Whitman, after killing his mother and wife, climbed with six guns and provisions to the top of a tower on the University of Texas campus. From there he shot forty-six persons, killing sixteen.

His behavior was especially puzzling because he was an architectural engineering honor student and a past Eagle Scout leader, scarcely the popular notion of a homicidal maniac. In a final note complaining about tremendous headaches, Whitman requested an autopsy to determine whether he had a mental disorder. The autopsy revealed a brain tumor. Some medical experts doubted the explanatory value of the tumor, but others, the press, and evidently Whitman himself, thought his physical condition could somehow account for his behavior.[18]

There is no pretense here of offering an explanation of why Whitman acted as he did; our purpose is simply to use his case as an illustration. Whatever pressures or sensations his tumor might have caused do not satisfactorily explain his complex action of carefully arming himself, going to a practically impregnable position, and sniping at passers-by. Why did he not take a nap, commit suicide, or go duck hunting? Physical conditions may well contribute to the spontaneity of behavior, but the behavior's content is far more complex than can be explained by a particular physical condition. Sheer bursts of aggressive behavior, regardless of content, may be curbed by disposing of part of the brain; but the reason for the direction of hostilities, whether against others, animals, property, or oneself, must be sought elsewhere.

We shall return to this issue of contemporary biological explanations after reviewing the historical highlights of similar efforts.

PHYSIOGNOMICAL AND PHRENOLOGICAL APPROACHES

Physiognomical and phrenological approaches were the predecessors of the earliest attempts by positivists to explain criminal behavior. *Physiognomy* refers to the determination of individual character from features of the body, especially the face. The supporters of this approach formulated several classifications and enjoyed a measure of attention from the middle of the eighteenth century to the middle of the nineteenth.[19] Physiognomy was then replaced by a more systematic and logically constructed study known as *phrenology*—the determination of mental faculties and character traits from the configuration of the skull.[20] Readers may see a vestige of this approach hanging on the walls of fortunetellers and shops dealing in matters of the occult: a chart depicting a profile of a person's head divided into segments, each representing particular "powers" or "propensities."

According to Fink, phrenology was based on the following propositions:

First, the exterior conformation of the skull corresponded to its interior and to the conformation of the brain. Second, the mind could be analyzed into faculties or functions. Third, these faculties were related to the shape of the skull. Corollaries of these propositions held that, in general, the brain was the organ of the mind, and that certain areas of the brain contained organs to which corresponded an equal number of psychological characters, or powers.[21]

The first person to systematically develop this approach was Franz Joseph Gall (1758–1828), a famed Austrian anatomist, who toured insane asylums and prisons to investigate head shapes. (According to today's waggish criminologists, Gall was the founder of the "Bumps and Grunts School of Criminology.") Based on his findings and comparisons with the heads of noninstitutionalized persons, Gall concluded that a scientific theory of criminal nature could be developed. According to Gall and his followers the degree of development of sections of the brain corresponding to faculties could be measured by observing protuberances on the head. For example, Charles Caldwell (1772–1853), who promoted phrenology in the United States, divided the brain into thirty-four sections or "organs," three of which were related to criminal behavior: philoprogenitiveness (love for offspring), destructiveness, and covetiveness [sic].

> Concerning philoprogenitiveness it was noted that of twenty-nine females who had been guilty of infanticide the development of this organ was defective in twenty-seven. Of destructiveness it was said that when not properly balanced and regulated by superior faculties it led to murder; while of covetiveness . . . Caldwell remarked that unless restrained and properly directed it led to great selfishness and even to theft.[22]

Up to the end of the nineteenth century phrenology provided the basis for a moderate amount of theory and research on the nature of criminal beings, but in the final analysis it made no contribution to the understanding of human behavior. In the first place, the propositions underlying the approach were unsound: one cannot detect the subtle shape of the brain by examining the skull. Even more important, no single sections of the brain are completely responsible for the complex behaviors attributed to them by the phrenologists. Secondly, the research never conclusively established that criminals, a group limited by the researchers to prison populations, differed from anyone else in their cranial contours.

According to Vold, the most serious obstacle in the development of phrenology was that the intellectual community was unready for it. The implications of the approach were too deterministic, too fatalistic.[23] The major works by Gall and Caldwell were done in the early part of the nineteenth century when humans were seen by most social thinkers as directing their own lives, not being manipulated by accidents of biology. This philosophical viewpoint was to be altered, but too late for the advocates of phrenology.

CESARE LOMBROSO (1835–1909)

Lombroso has been described as "one of the best known and possibly one of the least well understood figures in criminology." [24] Without question he is the founder of the positivist school. He pursued the cause of behavior by applying scientific methods to the study of individuals. Although his notions about causative factors are not seriously considered today, his importance in spurring research on the criminal is undeniable. It is customary in American criminology to attack Lombroso solely on the basis of his biological orientation, in particular his concept of the "criminal man," later referred to as the "born criminal." In all fairness, this concept represents only a portion of his voluminous work and does not take into account modifications in his thinking. [25]

Lombroso's most important book was *L'Uomo delinquente* (*The Criminal Man*), first published in Italy in 1876. Here he presented his doctrine of evolutionary *atavism*. Criminals were seen as distinct types of humans who could be distinguished from noncriminals by certain physical traits. These traits did not cause criminal behavior, but served to identify persons who were out of step with the evolutionary scheme. Such persons were considered to be closer to apes or to early primitive humans than were most modern individuals; they were throwbacks (atavists) to an earlier stage in human development.

Lombroso was a physician trained in psychiatry and biology, and he was aware of the then dying phrenology and the recent works of Charles Darwin, who connected modern humans with a nonhuman past through his theory of evolution. Lombroso had been involved for some time in the study of physical differences between criminals and normals, but his notion of atavism as a cause of crime emerged as a bolt from the blue during his autopsy of an infamous robber, whom Lombroso found to have skull depressions characteristic of lower primates:

> This was not merely an idea, but a revelation. At the sight of that skull, I seemed to see all of a sudden, lighted up as a vast plain under a flaming sky, the problem of the nature of the criminal—an atavistic being who reproduces in his person the ferocious instincts of primitive humanity and the inferior animals. Thus were explained anatomically the enormous jaws, high cheek-bones, prominent superciliary arches, solitary lines in the palms, extreme size of the orbits, handle-shaped or sessile ears found in criminals, savages, and apes, insensibility to pain, extremely acute sight, tatooing, excessive idleness, love of orgies, and the irresistible craving for evil for its own sake, the desire not only to extinguish life in the victim, but to mutilate the corpse, tear its flesh, and drink its blood. [26]

This was decidedly someone to avoid meeting in a dark alley. In the face of extreme criticism and contradictory evidence Lombroso later de-emphasized the importance of atavism in explaining the total range of criminality. In his last publications he conceded that the born criminal probably constituted only a third of all criminals. By this time he had supplemented his approach with the idea that epilepsy might form an underlying basis for predisposing persons to crime. His final classification of criminals included: 1. the born criminal, 2. the insane criminal, 3. the epileptic criminal, and 4. the occasional criminal.

The last group represented those who were apparently unaffected by atavism or epilepsy, and whose criminal behavior was a result of any of a multitude of environmental or situational factors: climate, structure of government, corruption of police, poverty, and so on. However, even for this group Lombroso never totally abandoned his ideas that criminal individuals were different from others and that they were abnormal to some degree. In short, he never allowed for the possible existence of "normal" criminals. Many criminologists after Lombroso were less sweeping in their application of biological determinism, but the idea that at least some criminal behavior might be explained by abnormal biological factors never disappeared.

Lombroso's most famous students, Enrico Ferri (1856–1929) and Raffaele Garofalo (1852–1934), in classifying criminals broke away decisively from an exclusive concentration on physical factors. Ferri suggested five types: 1. insane criminals who act from epilepsy, imbecility, paranoia (delusions of being persecuted), and other forms of mental infirmity; 2. born criminals "whose anti-human conduct is the inevitable effect of an indefinite series of hereditary influences which accumulate in the course of generations"; 3. habitual criminals who show in an indistinct way, if at all, the marks of the born criminal, and act through moral weakness as influenced by a corrupt environment; 4. criminals of passion who act under the impulse of uncontrolled emotion on occasion during otherwise moral lives; and 5. occasional criminals who "have not received from nature an active tendency towards crime but have fallen into it, goaded by the temptation incident to their personal condition or physical and social environment." These last individuals are characterized by a lack of foresight and stimulated by factors such as age, sexuality, poverty, the weather, and so on.[27]

From the admittedly brief description given above the reader might see that Ferri was advocating a theory of multiple causation involving not only individual factors but social ones as well. Furthermore, he was substituting *heredity* for atavism in the born criminal; that is, he believed there existed a criminal type whose behavior was congenital, but stemmed from more immediate generations than implied in the notion of atavism.

Garofalo disagreed with Ferri on many counts, but not upon the hereditary basis of crime derived from recent generations. Garofalo suggested a theory of moral degeneracy. This degeneracy resulted from "retrogressive selection" and caused man:

> to lose the better qualities which he had acquired by secular evolution, and has led him back to the same degree of inferiority whence he had slowly risen. This retrogressive selection is due to the mating of the weakest and most unfit, of those who have become brutalized by alcohol or abased by extreme misery against which their apathy has prevented them from struggling. Thus are formed demoralized and outcast families whose interbreeding in time produces a true race of inferior quality.[28]

Even among writers far less sympathetic to Lombroso than were Ferri and Garofalo, heredity loomed as the major explanation of criminal behavior. Lombroso's principal critic was Charles Goring (1870–1919), who in 1902 set out to discover whether any physical attributes distinguished the criminal from the noncriminal. From a sample of 3,000 English male convicts he gathered a large number of physical measurements, items of personal history, and measures of "mental qualities." [29] For comparative purposes he obtained similar measurements from college undergraduates, hospital patients, and soldiers. Goring concluded that after allowing for variations in dimensions for all the groups, there was no evidence confirming the existence of a physical criminal type as described by Lombroso and his disciples. However, he did find that the criminal sample was differentiated from the noncriminal samples by shorter height and lesser weight. Goring speculated that in and of itself this finding did not indicate that criminals were inferior; instead, it reflected an inbreeding of the "criminal class." Goring's logic on this point is far from convincing, but went something like this. Shorter individuals have more difficulty in obtaining honest work, and are more likely to be apprehended and convicted should they commit crimes. Thus by a process of selection the slight of stature criminals are separated from the general community. They have sons who inherit their fathers' small size and who also become convicted. In the course of generations, this process leads to an inbred physical differentiation of the "criminal class."

Goring also found that mental defectiveness characterized his convict sample. After comparing various traits of fathers and sons, he concluded that not only small stature but also a proclivity for criminality must be inherited:

> A comparison of the results that have emerged from the present investigation, . . . wherein the relations of mental defectiveness, and of environmental conditions upon the genesis of crime, are presented . . . leads to two very general conclusions. The one is that the criminal diathesis[constitutional predisposition], revealed by the tendency to be convicted and imprisoned for crime, is inherited at much the same rate as are other phys-

ical and mental qualities and pathological conditions in man. The second is that the influence of parental contagion [example] . . . is, on the whole, inconsiderable, relative to the influence of inheritance, and of mental defectiveness: which are by far the most significant factors we have been able to discover in the etiology of crime.[30]

Thus the simple notions of criminal physical type and of physical traits by which the criminal could be identified were laid to rest. Not permanently, it turns out, but the efforts of many criminologists· at the turn of the century were directed toward the roles of heredity and intellect in deviant behavior.

Heredity and Mental Deficiencies

In most detailed histories of the attempts to explain deviant behavior, the attempts based upon heredity and upon mental deficiencies would not be casually thrown together. Heredity concerns the process of passing characteristics from one generation to another; mental deficiencies are specific characteristics that may or may not be seen by the theorists as inherited. One of these explanations does not, therefore, imply the other, but in practice the reader would find it difficult to separate most theorists into one or the other category. For example, Goring felt that something he called "criminal diathesis" was inherited, but in addition he felt that mental defectiveness, also believed inherited, played an important role in criminal behavior. Other theorists who considered deviance as stemming primarily from defectiveness relied heavily on heredity as a supplementary explanation.

Part of the impetus for stressing heredity as an important factor came from a book written in 1877, *The Jukes*. Juke was a fictitious name given by the author, Robert L. Dugdale, to a rural New York family whose ancestry reached back to the early colonists—truly an American family. They had lived in relative isolation in the same locality for generations. With few exceptions the group was propagated through intermarriage. Their deviance spanned the generations and extended beyond incest to all forms of assault and theft, as well as prostitution and cruelty to animals. They were so despised by others in the area that "Juke" was used locally as a common term of censure. Dugdale described their colony:

> [Their ancestors] lived in log or stone houses similar to slave-hovels, all ages, sexes, relations and strangers "bunking" indiscriminately. . . . To this day some of the "Jukes" occupy the self-same shanties built nearly a century ago. The essential features of the habitat have remained stationary, and the social habits seem to survive in conformity to the persistence of the domiciliary environment. I have seen rude shelters made of

boughs covered with sod, . . . Others of the habitations have two rooms, but so firmly has habit established modes of living that, nevertheless, they often use but one congregate dormitory.[31]

In his investigation of the family tree and criminal careers of the Jukes, Dugdale intended to suggest an explanation of the relative influence of heredity and environment on the production of crime. In his conclusions Dugdale expressed his belief that criminal behavior might be transmitted intergenerationally, though he was also convinced that environment was ultimately the controlling factor that could modify even inherited behavior patterns. But his work came at a time when evolution and genetics had caught the attention of the scientific world. Furthermore, the book appeared just a year after Lombroso's *L'Uomo delinquente* was published in Italy. With these facts in mind, it is perhaps not surprising that *The Jukes* was commonly used as proof of hereditary criminality and served to encourage other studies of similar families.

Perhaps even more popular than *The Jukes* was *The Kallikak Family* by Henry H. Goddard. The Kallikak saga began during the Revolutionary War when a young militiaman from a "respectable" family became involved with a feebleminded bargirl. Their liaison resulted in a feebleminded son and the beginning of what Goddard called "a line of mental defectives that is truly appalling." Of the son's 480 descendants, 143 were feebleminded, forty-six normal, and the remainder in doubt. Also, thirty-six were illegitimate, thirty-three "sexually immoral," twenty-four alcoholic, three epileptic, three criminal, and eight ran houses of prostitution.[32] In the meantime, the militiaman married well, and from this line came 496 descendants, none of whom were feebleminded or criminal.

From these findings Goddard concluded that feeblemindedness was hereditary and related to deviant behavior and poverty. He also suggested that Lombroso's types might have been derived from varieties of feeblemindedness that were influenced by environment to produce deviant types.[33] Between 1911 and 1914 Goddard and others tried to substantiate further the relationship between deviance and mental deficiency by conducting tests of intelligence on juvenile and adult inmates of reformatories and prisons. By 1914 Goddard concluded:

> The hereditary criminal passes out with the advent of feeble-mindedness into the problem. The criminal is not born; he is made. The so-called criminal type is merely a type of feeble-mindedness, a type misunderstood and mistreated, driven into criminality for which he is well-fitted by nature. It is hereditary feeble-mindedness, not hereditary criminality that accounts for the conditions. We have only seen the end product and failed to recognize the character of the raw material.

And:

Every feeble-minded person is a potential criminal. This is necessarily true since the feeble-minded lacks one or the other of the factors essential to a moral life—an understanding of right and wrong, and the power of control.[34]

In a lecture delivered in 1919 Goddard left no doubt as to the cause of crime:

Are the persons who commit offenses really of low mental level? The answer is no longer in doubt. . . . Every investigation of the mentality of criminals, misdemeanants, delinquents, and other anti-social groups has proven beyond the possibility of contradiction that nearly all persons in these classes and in some cases all are of low mentality. Moreover, a large percentage of all of the groups are of such low mentality as to be properly denominated feeble-minded.[35]

But the evidence contradicted Goddard's claim about the role of low mentality as a cause of criminality. During World War I the first large-scale intelligence testing program was performed on the United States draft army. Using the generally accepted criteria of what constituted feeblemindedness, 34 per cent of the cream of American youth would have had to be characterized as feebleminded. Considering only nonwhites and whites from the southern states, that percentage would have been nearly doubled. Obviously something was very wrong. Once the criteria had been modified, and the test scores of prisoners carefully compared with males among the general population, it appeared that the proportion of feebleminded among inmates was less than 5 per cent instead of the 50 per cent once suggested by Goddard. Furthermore, intelligence scores generally showed little significant difference between inmates and the general population. Thus low mental ability could no longer be maintained as an explanation of deviance.[36]

A SHORT NOTE ON EUGENICS

We briefly interrupt here the outline of deviance theories to acquaint the reader with one side effect of positivism, which occurred around the turn of the century. You will recall an earlier discussion that pointed out that the determinism inherent in positivism carried a fatalistic implication that certain human beings could not escape their predestined fates. Their genetic makeup effectively locked them into a life of crime, intemperance, and perverseness. Although environment might have a minimal influence on behavior, the fundamental cause of the behavior lay within the individual. Thus to call someone a "born criminal" or "feebleminded" was to make a firm prediction about that person's future regardless of his or her actions up to that point.

The logic of determinism was fertile ground for the growth of eugenics: a science concerned with improving the quality of human offspring, especially through the manipulation of heredity by such means as selection of parents. A eugenics movement attained some importance in the United States during the first two decades of this century. Today, much of its literature seems naive and highly moralistic.

A representative example is a handbook entitled *Eugenics*, whose title page claims that within its pages lie "important hints on social purity, heredity, physical manhood and womanhood." The contents include chapters on etiquette, hygienic bathing, ethics of the unmarried, child bearing, the dangers of "self-pollution" (masturbation— among other things it makes the eyes become glassy and permanently fall back into their sockets), and cures for a wide range of diseases. One of the hints is that:

> Over-indulgence in the sexual act . . . lowers the whole moral and physical tone of the race. Men and women lose their vitality; the children are puny, scrawny beings, many of whom in early life pass to untimely graves.[37]

The accompanying photograph shows a puny, scrawny being confined to a wheelchair. The caption reads: "Results of conception when the father was intoxicated."

Most eugenics literature was a mixture of common sense and essentially harmless hokum. But the movement had a far grimmer side. As long as deviance was believed to be inherited, either as a form of mental deficiency or as a tendency in its own right, eugenics was a logical source of a solution. What was "scientifically" found as a cause could be "scientifically" eliminated. In their extreme forms the elimination plans anticipated the mass execution methods employed by Nazi Germany during World War II. In 1901 a textbook on social problems reported on a proposal whereby "defective and confirmed criminals" would be placed in air-tight chambers and put to death by "poisonous, but not unpleasant gas." [38]

Most suggestions involved less drastic, but nevertheless serious, measures such as sterilization or castration. The latter was advocated by those who felt that mere sterilization would not curtail lustful behavior or the spread of venereal diseases. Between 1907 and 1937 a total of thirty-one states enacted laws permitting the sterilization of certain individuals without their consent. (Even before 1907 secret sterilizations had been performed on inmates of state institutions for many years.) [39] These laws were applicable to three classes of individuals: the mentally ill, the mentally deficient, and epileptics. The legacy of the eugenics movement is with us today in the form of the legal codes of twenty-six states that still permit involuntary sterilization. The mentally deficient are subject to the operation in all twenty-six states, the mentally ill in twenty-four states, and epileptics in fourteen states. Furthermore:

> Eleven states authorize the eugenic sterilization of "hereditary" criminals and seven states permit the sterilization of sex offenders, "degenerates," "moral degenerates," and syphilitics for somewhat tenuous eugenic reasons. The broadest criteria appear to be contained in the Oregon statute which covers "all persons who are feebleminded, insane, epileptic, habitual criminals, incurable syphilitics, moral degenerates or sexual perverts, and who are, or . . . will likely become, a menace to society." [40]

The fruits of positivism in the United States were not a series of purifying executions, but close to 70,000 individuals were involuntarily sterilized, and many more confined because their behavior, intellects, or backgrounds were judged by state bureaucrats to be below standards. Today, involuntary sterilization is still with us. In June 1973 two black girls—a "retarded" twelve-year-old and a "normal" fourteen-year-old—were surgically sterilized in a Montgomery, Alabama, Family Planning Clinic. At a social worker's insistence, their mother signed the permission not realizing the operation was permanent. Later investigation revealed that the clinic had performed eleven involuntary sterilizations that year: ten girls were black, seven mentally retarded, and five minors. In other parts of the country investigations disclosed instances of sterilizations coerced by social workers threatening to cut off welfare payments to entire families.[41]

The laws and the continued practice of involuntary sterilization are sobering reminders of how a theory of human behavior, whether correct or erroneous, proven or unproven, can justify the controlling of whole classes of people. Such control is covered by a mantle of science and, of course, is exercised for the "good" of everyone concerned. But however benevolent programs of "scientific treatment" or "scientific prevention" may appear, they may in fact be not only ineffectual but also dangerous to human freedom.

TWIN STUDIES

While the tracing of family backgrounds had reached its limit of usefulness after Goddard's study of the Kallikaks, the notion of hereditary criminality was far from abandoned. One study offered in support of hereditary determinism was that of Johannes Lange, a German physiologist, who published his results in 1929 in *Verbrechen als shicksal* (*Crime As Destiny*). The title is certainly not ambiguous. Lange compared the criminal records of the two types of twins: *iden-*

tical twins, those produced from a single egg, who therefore have identical genetic makeups; and *fraternal* twins, those produced from two eggs fertilized by two sperms, who therefore have dissimilar makeups. Lange reasoned that a pair of twins would experience similar environments and that any behavioral differences between twins would therefore necessarily be biologically caused. If environment were the cause of criminality, then there should be no differences between a pair of twins, regardless of whether they were identical or fraternal.

Lange then examined male inmates of a prison and a psychiatric institute to determine which were twins. The other twin was then traced to determine whether he also had been imprisoned. Lange found a group of thirteen identical twins; ten of these pairs (77 per cent) had both been imprisoned. For a group of seventeen fraternal twins, both had been imprisoned in only two instances (12 per cent).

The implications of these findings were clear to Lange and his suggestions were consistent with the deterministic philosophy:

> We should make every attempt to discover as early as possible those who must be permanently segregated if society is to be protected from grave damage. The detailed examination of all law-breakers and the thorough training of real experts in this subject are essential towards this end.
>
> Finally, and this is our most important task, we must take preventive measures. We must try to make it impossible for human beings with positive criminal tendencies to be born.[42]

Lange's work was followed by several others in the same vein but showing mixed results. Criticisms of twin studies are many and of no practical concern to us.[43] Suffice it to say that such studies considerably oversimplify the relationships between heredity, environment, and deviance-crime, which is, after all, a matter of social definition in the first place. As indicated by Mannheim, the crucial aspect of the heredity-environment controversy lies in the proposed treatment philosophies:

> It is clear that the environmentalists will put their faith more in the manipulation of the living conditions of the potential or actual criminal, while the believers in hereditary transmission will recommend eugenic programmes. Perhaps more important than this are the dangers of a fatalistic attitude so easily assumed by members of the public who are always ready to regard an offender as incorrigible because 'it is in his blood.' [44]

Physical Characteristics Revisited

BIOLOGICAL INFERIORITY

As mentioned before, attempting to explain deviance by reference to anatomical features is a venerable and long-lived pursuit tied to faith in positivist methodology. Goring's findings did not lay the matter to rest and the dead hand of Lombroso was felt many years after. Probably Lombroso's greatest latter-day champion was Earnest A. Hooton, a Harvard anthropologist, who was highly critical of Goring's research and was convinced that criminals were an "inferior" physical type. In 1926 Hooton launched a twelve-year survey of nearly 14,000 inmates of jails and prisons and, for comparison purposes, 3,200 college students, firemen, and so on. On these samples twenty-two measurements were taken of the head and body. From this incredible mass of data Hooton concluded:

> Criminal behavior is capable of considerable diversification in the manner and kind of the overt act, but . . . whatever the crime may be, it ordinarily arises from a deteriorated organism which, so far as we now know, manifests its inferiority in comparatively few and uniform ways. . . . The primary cause of crime is biological inferiority . The penitentiaries of our society are built upon the shifting sands and quaking bogs of inferior human organisms.[45]

This is not radically different from Lombroso's vision of the criminal organism emerging from the primeval slime, and it appropriately drew a barrage of criticism. Four principal reasons for rejecting Hooton's work are of interest because they—especially the first two—can often be applied to any research that attempts to distinguish between the characteristics of the "criminal" and the "noncriminal." [46]

1. Inmates of institutions do not accurately represent the population of persons who have been involved in criminal behavior. For various reasons many persons who steal, kill, rape, fail to pay alimony, and so on do not get caught. Both the highly skilled professional criminal and the one-time offender may have that much in common (not getting caught) because they are smart and lucky. Furthermore, only a portion of those caught will be found in institutions; others are spared that fate because they have a good lawyer, are "too respectable" to go to prison, or are good probation risks. Thus, researchers seeking a sample of criminals, deviants, or whatever in an institution must face the fact they are dealing with an extremely select group: those who, for a variety of reasons, were apprehended, tried, convicted, and sentenced to an institution. To further complicate the issue, many of these persons may in fact be innocent of the accused behavior.

2. The other side of the coin is that a sample of noninstitutionalized persons does not necessarily represent the population of noncriminals or nondeviants. If you sampled a number of convents and monasteries you could reasonably be assured of a "holy" but hardly representative group of noncriminals. The problem is that within practically any sample you select from the general population you will include persons who have committed acts identical to those

committed by persons who were imprisoned. Although this may be an exaggeration for some acts such as murder, kidnapping, and bank robbery; for other acts such as drug use, shoplifting, assaults, and traffic offenses the distinctions between institutionalized and noninstitutionalized samples would be less than clear-cut.

In an admittedly early study (1947) researchers administered an anonymous questionnaire to a noninstitutionalized adult population in New York City in order to obtain responses on law violations.[47] The findings indicated that 64 per cent of the males and 29 per cent of the females had committed offenses for which over a year's imprisonment was possible. The authors concluded, "Unlawful behavior, far from being an abnormal social or psychological manifestation, is in truth a very common phenomenon."

3. Classification of criminals or deviants into types is a precarious business. Hooton tried to relate particular physical traits to the offenses for which his prisoners were then incarcerated. He was scarcely unique among researchers in attempting to classify samples by current offense, although such a system is of doubtful value. Many inmates have been previously incarcerated or arrested for different offenses. Thus what type is the current burglar with a record of drug use, assault, and auto theft? Or the person convicted of robbery who, you discover, was also suspected of rape, but the charges were dropped by police because they felt the robbery was a better case? If homosexuals were considered a type, how comfortable would you be to include under that heading a female who adopts masculine demeanor and clothes, and another female who makes no effort in that direction? What is ignored in typing individuals is that the behaviors used as criteria are but portions of their total behavior patterns.

4. Differences found between deviants and nondeviants are not necessarily indications of inferiority among the deviants. You become the victim of circular reasoning if you use deviants' traits as examples of inferiority—then turn around to use those same traits in explaining how inferiority causes deviance. You must have an independent means to prove that certain traits are inferior other than their characterizing deviants. In practice this problem is seldom a real one, however. Because the distinction between deviants and nondeviants is not clear in most research, their differences are usually found to be trivial. When researchers claim significant differences, a second look usually reveals either a misinterpretation of the findings or that they have ignored the likelihood that the differences could have resulted from involvement in deviant behavior.

SOMATOLOGY

Somatology refers to the science of classifying human physical characteristics. The application of this science to the study of deviance represents the heritage of Lombroso and Hooton in its most sophisticated form. The principal proponent in the United States is *William H. Sheldon* (1899–1963) who attempted to explain juvenile delinquency by examining the relationship between body type or physique and particular patterns of mental and behavioral characteristics or temperaments.

Somatotyping individuals according to Sheldon's scheme is a complex procedure that involves assigning scores to the physique on the basis of three components. Although it is possible for someone to be described solely by a single component, most persons would be scored as a combination. Each physique component in its purest form can be characterized by a component of temperament. For any specific individual, the components of temperament vary with components of physique, according to Sheldon. The components, with their brief descriptions, are described in Table 1–2.[48]

TABLE 1–2
PHYSIQUE AND TEMPERAMENT COMPONENTS OF SOMATOTYPING

Components of Physique	Components of Temperament
Endomorphy—floats easily, soft, round, roly-poly.	*Viscerotonia*—relaxed, loves to eat, needs company and affection.
Mesomorphy—muscular, strong, hard.	*Somatotonia*—assertive, vigorous, loves action and power.
Ectomorphy—flat, fragile, lean.	*Cerebrotonia*—restrains emotions, loves privacy, apprehensive.

To complicate matters there are also "psychiatric components," but they do not coincide directly with the others. Between endomorphy and mesomorphy occurs the manic component (exuberance, expressiveness); between mesomorphy and ectomorphy is the paranoid component (reacting to events by vigilance and alertness); and between ectomorphy and endomorphy falls the hebephrenic component (withdrawal).

Sheldon's study involved the somatotyping of 200 boys who from 1939–1942 were connected with a center for "problem" children referred there by social agencies and courts in Boston. In comparison to a sample of 4,000 college males, he found the center's children to be more mesomorphic: "a little on the hefty and meaty side." [49] They also tended toward the manic and paranoid components. After presenting 200 biographies and a mass of data, Sheldon concluded that few of the youths were normal. The "varieties of delinquent youth" were generally characterized by one of the following: mental insufficiency, medical insufficiency, and psychopathy. Not surprisingly, Sheldon's commentary included words of praise for the work of Hooton and Lombroso:

[Hooton] considers it a datum of common sense that there are structurally superior and inferior human organisms, and that a relationship must exist between structural and behavioral inferiority. . . . Without question the general impression he gathered from his 15,000 criminals was similar to our impression. . . . It can be summarized in a single sentence: *Where essential inadequacy is present the inadequacy is well reflected in the observable structure of the organism.*

.   .   .

What both Lombroso and Hooton saw so clearly in their penitentiary was the spoor of insufficiency and not that of anything that needs to be called criminality. There may be no such thing as criminality, and I think it is quite possible that we will forget that concept when as a body of social scientists we at length face the meaning and the reality of human insufficiency. . . . Lombroso and Hooton were really dealing with stigmata of insufficiency.[50]

Sheldon's research and his interpretations fell prey to most of the problems of such studies mentioned above. In particular, the delinquency of the boys was frequently ambiguous, often involving merely "troublesome" or "disappointing" behavior. Furthermore, a reanalysis of Sheldon's data failed to support his conclusions about the relationship between delinquency and any of the components.[51] Thus the role of physical characteristics in differentiating deviants from nondeviants remained unproven.

The ineffectiveness of somatology does not mean that attempts to establish a relationship between physical characteristics and deviant behavior have abated. The most recent efforts have been less ambitious than those of the past, however, because they concentrate on narrower ranges of behavior such as violence or homosexuality. We will briefly discuss two such approaches to the explanation of violence: the XYY chromosome syndrome and the brain malfunction theory.

XYY CHROMOSOME SYNDROME

Human cells have forty-six chromosomes arranged in twenty-three pairs, each parent having donated one of each pair. Two of the forty-six chromosomes, labeled either X or Y because of their shape, determine sexual characteristics. Every normal cell in a woman's body contains two X chromosomes, and each cell in a male has one X and one Y. The existence of this Y chromosome is the basic distinction between men and women. However, exceptions to this genetic pattern do occur. Of interest here are the estimated .18 per cent (1 out of 550) of the males who possess an extra Y chromosome, a condition first reported in 1961.

This genetic anomaly received no public attention until 1968 when in France a defense attorney in a murder trial claimed his client possessed an extra Y chromosome and thus was not responsible for his offense. This claim was based on very limited research indicating that some chromosomally abnormal men had histories of antisocial behavior. Shortly thereafter the XYY syndrome was introduced into the trial publicity of murderers in Australia and West Germany, as well as three cases in the United States. The most publicized case was that of Richard Speck who, in 1968, murdered eight Chicago student nurses. In 1968 Speck's attorney claimed to the press that Speck had XYY chromosomes, a contention that made front page headlines. As it developed Speck was simply XY, but that finding received very little publicity.

The stage was set for a flurry of research and claims concerning the syndrome's influence on behavior.[52] It all turned out to be simply another chapter in the endless search for a link between a biological "defect" and a behavioral one. The best evidence, which is not that good in light of the sampling methods used, indicates that among incarcerated males the syndrome occurs in greater proportion than among the general population. However, evidence also indicates that these incarcerated males are not any more aggressive than XY inmates; if anything they may be less so.

The most overt feature of the XYYs is their greater average height in comparison with the general population. It has been suggested that the XYYs' overrepresentation in prison populations may be due to the height factor. It might bias police, judges, and psychiatrists toward keeping them off the streets.[53] But the principal objections to accepting the syndrome as an explanation are: 1. Even with the use of institutionalized research subjects the case for XYY as a cause of violence is ambiguous at best, and 2. It seems unlikely that an extra chromosome can be linked to most aggressive behavior that involves complex social factors. Does, for example, the chromosome arrangement explain why aggressive behavior might be directed at different objects: husband, wife, lover, professional football quarterbacks, enemy soldiers, policemen, punk kids, stupid adults, and so on? Doubtlessly, no.

BRAIN MALFUNCTION

Looking to the brain for an explanation of behavior is scarcely a recent innovation. We have already discussed the phrenologists who believed that the contours of the brain provided clues to the personality. However, systematic manipulation of the brain for purposes of *altering* behavior was not initiated until 1935 when prefrontal lobotomy was introduced by a Portuguese physician, Antonio Moniz. In this operation Moniz destroyed large sections of the frontal lobes of the brain. His subjects were twenty mental patients who had been unaffected by other treatments; according to Moniz fifteen showed some degree of improvement as a result of the operation. One lobotomized patient was later to pump five bullets into Dr. Moniz, but the operation and variations of it were widely hailed as the answer to many behavioral problems.

Moniz's lobotomies were the beginning of what is known today as *psychosurgery:* the surgical removal or destruction of brain tissue or the cutting of brain tissue to disconnect one part of the brain from another with the intent of altering behavior.[54] Between 1936 and the mid-1950s approximately 50,000 psychosurgical operations, mostly lobotomies, were performed in the United States alone. Many of the patients were returned World War II servicemen with severe emotional problems.

Such operations were not performed without a growing controversy. Although the notion that lobotomies produced placid "vegetables" was a popular one, it did overstate the case. Side effects did occur: many patients lost the ability to fantasize, to think abstractly, or to be creative. And other abuses arose:

> Some doctors performed lobotomies for mental ailments that did not require such radical treatment. Horror tales proliferated: Walter Freeman of George Washington University, who brought lobotomy to the United States from Lisbon, performed some 4,000 of the operations with an ice pick. Critics told of a Freeman lobotomy on a Peeping Tom. After the operation, the patient no longer slunk through back alleys to take his visual pleasures—he walked right up to the front windows. The operation had apparently freed him of any sense of shame, but not of his abnormal tendencies.[55]

Defenders of the operation claimed that such abuses were in the distinct minority, and that lobotomies were usually performed only as a last resort. They claimed that the alternatives were leaving patients raving or depressed in back wards of hospitals for the rest of their lives, or taking a chance on improving their condition even though their mentality might be lower as a consequence.

The controversy over lobotomies diminished as their use was eventually replaced by drugs and shock treatment. These, too, have their limitations and side effects, including the likelihood of the patient's relapse to his or her previous condition. In recent years new and more sophisticated surgical techniques have been developed that penetrate more deeply and precisely into various areas of the brain. The new methods include the use of ultrasonic beams and of tiny electrodes to electrically destroy brain cells. Along with the improved techniques have come recommendations and theories on how various forms of deviant behavior might be eliminated by psycho-surgery. Seen as likely candidates for new surgical methods are various forms of mental disorder, homosexuality, childhood behavior disorders, some narcotics addictions, and criminal behavior. We will focus our attention on the use of psychosurgery to control aggressive behavior, selecting this area because it is within the context of a plausible theoretical framework and because the research results have frequently been dramatic.

The major proponents of psychosurgery as a remedy for aggression are Vernon H. Mark and Frank R. Ervin, co-authors of *Violence and the Brain*. They claim that an appreciable percentage of persons who get involved in repeated personal violence do so because their brains do not function in a normal manner. In particular, they refer to indi-viduals characterized by a set of symptoms labeled the *dyscontrol syndrome*. These symptoms, which may include the following, are not always present at the same time:

> 1) A history of physical assault, especially wife and child beating; 2) the symptom of pathological intoxication—that is, drinking even a small amount of alcohol triggers acts of senseless brutality; 3) a history of impul-sive sexual behavior, at times including sexual assaults; and 4) a history (in those who [drive] cars) of many traffic violations and serious automobile accidents.[56]

Mark and Ervin's theory of aggression is primarily concerned with persons exhibiting this dyscontrol syndrome, but they also believe their theory will have wider application once better diagnostic tech-niques are developed. The theory is based on the following evidence: 1. animal research indicates that surgery and electrical stimulation of the limbic brain (a central portion of the brain) significantly alter the amount of aggressive or attack behavior; and 2. persons with his-tories of violent rages who show abnormal electrical activity in the limbic brain have had their aggression curbed by psychosurgery. Mark and Ervin concede that environment, culture, and social experi-ences in general do play a role in structuring aggressive behavior. But they believe that such learning principally serves a programming function; it defines the degree to which particular situations will be perceived as threatening. The retrieval of learned experiences is a memory process, hence, a brain process. As such it is subject to dis-tortion if the brain is malfunctioning:

> The kind of violent behavior related to brain malfunction may have its ori-gins in the environment, but once the brain structure has been perma-nently affected, the violent behavior can no longer be modified by manip-ulating psychological or social influences.

And:

Our past environment, once it is past, is no longer a sociological phenomenon. It is embedded in our brain and its use is dependent on the function or malfunction of the cerebral tissue.[57]

Thus Mark and Ervin do confront one of the objections leveled at most biological theories, such as the XYY syndrome, that the relationship between a defect and behavior is oversimplistic in view of the complexity of the behavior involved. Nevertheless, there still exists considerable controversy over whether the stimulation or destruction of certain areas of the human brain results in predictable changes in behavior.[58] It is still argued, in a manner reminiscent of the critiques of phrenology, that no specific and consistent human behavior results from psychosurgery, and that the practice thus leaves the results as much to chance as to scientific predictability.

Assuming that psychosurgery can become a method of obtaining predictably controlled behavior, another serious issue remains: What and whose behavior should be controlled? Mark and Ervin feel the targets should be those engaging in "unacceptable violence" (a term they admit is plagued with problems), and they urge the development of "early-warning tests for violence." Aside from the point that such predictive devices would truly be precedent-setting in regard to human behavior, this approach sounds very much like a kind of neoeugenics. As with any deterministic approach to deviance there is a potential for the more powerful in a society to define who is "unacceptable" or "dangerous" on the basis of what they might do. Just as lobotomies and drugs were used to neutralize troublesome individuals in institutions, dissidents could be subdued through psychosurgery because their brains were "malfunctioning."

Psychosurgery should not be totally abandoned, however, especially in light of its successes in treating epilepsy. But its potential for misuse should not be ignored; it could be a powerful means for changing behavior. Under serious consideration today are plans for implanting electrical relays in people's brains to provide continuous monitoring of their activities and to alter behavior.

Dr. Barton L. Ingraham of the School of Criminology at the University of California at Berkeley suggests that bugging the brain could provide not only continuous surveillance of those with "criminal tendencies" but also "automatic deterrence or 'blocking' of the criminal activity by electronic stimulation of the brain prior to the commission of the act." Dr. Ingraham concedes that the use of [electronic stimulation of the brain] would "require a Government with virtually total powers" but sees a number of things in its favor, including the fact that it would be "completely effective" and "relatively cheap." As for the economy of the matter, an electrical engineer named Curtiss Schafer agrees: "The once-human being thus controlled would be the cheapest of machines to create and operate."[59]

Ultimately citizens must decide whether a disease might not be preferable to the cure.

A Final Word on the Body and Deviance

We have come a long way between bumps on the head in the eighteenth century and brain waves in the twentieth century. Or have we? Techniques of research have certainly improved, and there have been steps in the direction of controlling or modifying some specific behaviors by drugs and surgery. But there is no evidence that we have moved any closer to finding a relationship between any component or configuration of the human body and violations of social expectations, including violence. No doubt the search will continue, as indeed it should. But the complexity and variety of deviant behavior leads one to believe that future research will continue to show that little or no biological differences exist between deviants and anyone else. As Albert K. Cohen so aptly writes:

> When we remind ourselves of what we mean by deviant behavior, or more narrowly by crime and delinquency—e.g., check forging, street fighting, income tax evasion, highway speeding, drug use, rent law violation, police corruption—we must realize that we are dealing with an enormous variety of behaviors as different from one another as filling prescriptions, selling used cars, and teaching algebra. The most reasonable expectation, it seems to us, is that the linkages of biology to the various forms of deviance will be as various, indirect, and remote as its linkages to the varieties of conforming behavior.[60]

Personality Defects and Attributes

We now turn from approaches based primarily on biological determinism to approaches based upon mental processes and characteristics; the most appropriate term embracing these approaches is *psychogenic determinism*.[61] As with the theories discussed above, the causes of deviant behavior are considered as being *in* the individual, but they are conditions of the mind or personality and, as such, are not measurable through any physical characteristic like body type, brain waves, or genetic structure. These conditions might be personality factors that directly result in deviant behavior, or simply factors that contribute to deviance whenever individuals possessing them are in particular situations or environments. Some psychogenic theories define deviant individuals as "sick," "emotionally disturbed," or "psychopathic." In any case the deviants are considered unlike nondeviants and distinguishable from them.

The beginnings of psychogenic determinism can be found in the writings of the English physician James C. Prichard (1786–1848). Prichard believed that a major portion of crime could be explained by a disorder he called *moral insanity*. This differed from ordinary insanity, which involved disorders in intellectual faculties. Moral insanity was:

> madness consisting in a morbid perversion of the natural feelings, affections, inclinations, temper, habits, moral dispositions, and natural impulses, without any remarkable disorder or defect of the intellect or knowing and reasoning faculties, and particularly without any insane illusion or hallucination.[62]

The concept of moral insanity had a long and stormy history, but of greatest interest to us here is an offshoot, which, unlike moral insanity, is still very much alive.

PSYCHOPATHY

This term was first applied to deviants in 1896 and referred to a group of individuals who apparently committed crimes upon impulse, with no motive except perhaps some satisfaction from the act itself.[63] Over time the concept has undergone considerable elaboration including a new name, *sociopathy*. (The introduction of the term *sociopathy* is not meant to confuse the reader. We mention it because the term is frequently used as a synonym for *psychopathy*. Sometimes it is considered akin to but different from psychopathy and other times one or the other term is ignored. To compound the confusion the recent edition of the American Psychiatric Association's *Diagnostic and Statistical Manual of Mental Disorders* (1968) mentions neither, although it contains an entry for *antisocial personality*, which is reminiscent of both.)

The traits attributed to the psychopath have been many; one author counted fifty-five.[64] The most careful compilation appears to be that of Hervey M. Cleckley who lists sixteen, including: superficial charm, unreliability, insincerity, lack of remorse or shame, inability to learn by experience, incapacity for love, impersonal sex life, and a lack of any life plan.[65] In practice few concepts have proven to be so vague, so confusing, and so useless as that of psychopathy. According to Michael Hakeem, a long-time critic of the psychiatric approach to criminology, "Without exception, on every point regarding psychopathic personality, psychiatrists present varying or contradictory views." Below are listed questions that Hakeem asks about the psychiatric personality and the range of answers he finds in the psychiatric literature:

1. Is psychopathic personality a clinical entity?—Yes and No.
2. Is psychopathy a serious condition?—Yes and No.

3. In what proportion is psychopathy found among criminals?—Anywhere from 0 to 100 percent.
4. What types of crimes do psychopaths commit?—Serious violent offenses are "typical;" usually the offenses are "relatively minor."
5. What causes psychopathy?—Endocrine dysfunction to cerebral trauma to blood sugar to poverty to broken homes to inadequate child training.
6. Can the psychopath be diagnosed?—Yes and No.
7. Can the psychopath be treated?—Yes and No.[66]

In general, psychopathy has served as a garbage can diagnosis. Individuals are so labeled as a matter of convenience when they do not readily fit other diagnostic categories, and a diagnosis of psychopathic more likely reflects the particular orientation of the psychiatrist rather than any peculiarity of the patient.

The whole concept of psychopathy might be lightly dismissed if it were simply a footnote in the history of attempts to explain criminality. Unfortunately, it was taken very seriously. Despite the fact that there is no agreement upon what a psychopath is, no consensus on what proportion of the criminal population is psychopathic, and a continuing debate over whether the concept is even a valid one, twenty-nine states and the District of Columbia passed special legislation directed at the psychopathic offender. Most such laws are aimed at those involved in sexual crimes and provide for indeterminate confinement and psychiatric treatment until the offender is "cured." Because the treatment is directed at a condition that may not even exist, one can easily imagine some of the serious problems that have been created. We will consider in detail the issue of the psychopath laws in a later chapter. At this point the reader may wish to consider such laws as yet another example of the dangers inherent in erroneous deterministic approaches: 1. the psychopathic approach purports to distinguish a class of individuals from "normals," and 2. on the basis of unproven claims it justifies the confinement of these individuals.

UNCONSCIOUS MOTIVATION

Anyone reading the psychiatric literature concerning criminal and/or deviant behavior will quickly discover that there are many approaches and theories, some of which seem to have little in common. Our purpose in this section is to acquaint the reader with one general theoretical approach associated with the work of Sigmund Freud (1856–1939) and a branch of psychiatry known as *psychoanalysis*. Although few unreservedly adhere to Freud's teachings today, his work provides a basis to which much of today's psychiatric writing can be ultimately traced.

The psychoanalytic approach is based upon the following propositions:

1. The human personality consists of three parts, the id, the ego, and the superego. The *id,* which is the source of all instinctual demands and drives, such as the sexual drive, forms the basis of all behavior. The id is present at birth and operates primarily below the level of awareness, that is, it is *unconscious.* The drives are unrestrained at birth and in their primitive state are not compatible with living in society. But as children grow and become more aware of their environment, they develop a means to control the id in the form of an *ego.* The ego is a kind of decision-maker that is not present in infancy but develops with awareness of one's surroundings. The ego considers both the realities of environment and the demands of the id in order to seek the greatest possible gratification without encountering painful reaction from the environment. The ego may be thought of as the conscious aspect of the personality. The *superego* develops as children begin adolescence and is the result of all the learning processes concerning morality and ethics. It acts as a restraint upon the id by calling forth the ideals and standards that the person has learned. The superego may be thought of as one's *conscience* and is partially conscious.

2. All behavior has a purpose. Much behavior is a direct result of the operation of the ego, but other behavior stems from less conscious sources. Conflicts may develop between the id and superego at the unconscious level and result in behavior that is *symbolic* of the ongoing unconscious conflicts. The most famous example of such a conflict is the Oedipus complex, which, according to Freudian theory, occurs in all males. This complex concerns the boy's id urging him to have sexual intercourse with his mother and to murder his father. The superego will have none of this, of course, and the ego feels guilty over the whole mess. If this conflict is not adequately resolved but repressed, the individual may engage in substitute behavior in an attempt to resolve the conflict. Examples here are assaulting somebody as a substitute for doing away with one's father, and committing political crimes as a means of venting hatred against a father figure (the State) without feeling guilt.[67] Generally guilt is involved somewhat differently in the psychoanalytic explanation of crime: suffering from a sense of guilt a person commits crime while unconsciously wanting to be apprehended and punished for both the crime and the desires coming from the id. In any event, criminal behavior is interpreted in terms of unconscious motivation.

3. All behavior can be ultimately explained in terms of early life expe-

riences. Since the heart of the psychoanalytic approach lies in the development of the ego and superego and their ability to restrain the id, the cause of deviant behavior is presumed to stem from conflicts initiated during that development. To ascertain the nature of these events, psychoanalysts ask patients to relate very early experiences; the psychoanalysts then, in turn, document the cause of the behavior by interpreting those experiences.

Of the three propositions outlined above only the specific references to the id, the ego, and the superego may not be immediately evident in contemporary psychoanalytic literature concerning deviance. The assumption concerning unconscious motivations stemming from guilt over mental conflicts is very much in evidence. It is on this very issue that psychoanalysis is most vulnerable to criticism. Although its practitioners claim that psychoanalysis is a science, the fact that it depends upon unconscious factors, symbolic behavior, and the interpretation of someone else's recalled events places the approach beyond the boundaries of scientific demonstration. There is no assurance that a given life story will produce the same interpretation from differing psychoanalysts—the interpretations are subjective hence nonscientific.[68] If psychoanalysis is not a science what is it? A religion? A philosophy? Regardless of the answer, many who profess it control the destinies of humans.

Aside from the above criticism, the concentration on conflict-producing experiences, especially early ones occurring in the family context, to the exclusion of other learning, weakens the psychoanalytic case. Although psychiatrists vary in the weight they assign to social factors, the emphasis remains on experiences resulting in psychic conflict. The following hypotheses dealing with sex offenders illustrate this emphasis in the psychiatric approach:

1. There is a specific kind of psychosexual trauma, occurring at some point in the early developmental experience of the individual, that makes a satisfactory, adequately pleasurable, adult heterosexual adjustment impossible. As a result, these individuals turn to other, less mature, or variant sexual patterns of behavior, in their attempts to seek sexual gratification.
2. There is a failure or distortion of the mechanisms of conscience formation that permits these individuals to act out their aberrant sexual patterns, rather than use some other method of handling the sexual conflicts, such as fantasy or sublimation [diverting the energy of impulse to acceptable behavior].[69]

What is completely ignored here is that all behavior, whether it involves homosexual activity or singing an operatic aria, requires learning experiences, including the acquiring of rationales justifying the behavior. *How* to behave and *why* to behave are often far too complicated to be attributed solely to some subconscious proddings.

PERSONALITY MEASURES

All of us recognize and understand the phrase, "It takes a particular kind of person to do that," whatever that might be: entering an occupation, leaving a religion, quitting school at midsemester, or taking up birdhouse building. And we have all experienced the blind date described to us as "Not real good-looking, but has a good personality and everybody in the dorm likes him (or her)." *Kind of person* and *personality* are terms we use in acknowledging the fact that people are seldom alike in the way they react to certain situations, in their moods, in their self-assurance, in their concern over the feelings of others, and in their readiness to openly display their emotions.

It seems logical that if personality plays an important role in every-day living it should at least be a factor in being deviant. Some formidable problems stand in the way of ascertaining the exact nature of that role, however. Personality cannot be encompassed by a single phrase. You would not be satisfied to describe yourself or your friends in that fashion, preferring instead to list a number of attributes or traits. So too researchers in the area of personality must deal with an often bewildering number of traits, only some of which may prove to be key variables in explaining certain kinds of behavior. Furthermore, these same researchers must find ways to measure those traits, a difficult problem in itself. In practice, no researcher would claim to have an instrument for measuring personality in all of its possible facets. Instead the researcher relies upon tests to measure a limited number of traits considered to be relevant for the purpose at hand.

In 1950 Karl Schuessler and Donald Cressey published a survey of research that had attempted to distinguish, by means of personality tests, between persons found guilty of delinquencies or crimes and persons who were noncriminal and non delinquent. As we have pointed out, this type of comparison is based on the questionable assumption that deviants and nondeviants really differ in their behavior. The survey covered the period from 1925 to 1948 and examined 113 studies using a total of thirty different tests. The latter figure will give you some idea of the variety of ways to approach personality traits.

The authors found that only 42 per cent of the studies showed any difference between the two groups. They concluded:

> The evidence favored the view that personality traits are distributed in the criminal population in about the same way as in the general population. . . . This overlap makes it impossible to predict individual delinquent behavior from an individual test score.

One other conclusion is worthy of mention because of its applicability to any studies attempting to interpret personality differences as causes of behavior:

The results of this method do not indicate whether criminal behavior is the result of a certain personality trait or whether the trait is the result of criminal experiences. In other words, whether a given trait was present at the onset of a delinquent career or whether the trait developed during that career is not shown.[70]

Thus with any deviant or group of deviants, their personality traits, their attitudes, and their beliefs may not have contributed to their behavior but rather may have resulted from their experiences as deviant. This would seem to be particularly pertinent to those involved in the behavior over a long time who have undergone reactions to their behavior from family, friends, police, treatment practitioners, and so on. This is not to say that such traits, attitudes, or beliefs necessarily do not exist prior to involvement in a particular form of behavior, but the reader should view with caution any claims about their predisposing individuals to deviance.[71]

A similar survey of research between 1950 and 1965 was conducted by Gordon P. Waldo and Simon Dinitz. This consisted of ninety-four studies using twenty-nine different tests, only four of which had been represented in the Schuessler-Cressey survey. Eighty-one per cent of the studies reported finding differences between groups, compared with the previous 42 per cent. Although this result appears to be an improvement, the authors express considerable caution, particularly regarding the instrument that most consistently finds differences between delinquents and nondelinquents: the Minnesota Multiphasic Personality Inventory (MMPI). Originally designed to aid diagnosis in psychiatric clinics, the MMPI does not provide an adequate theoretical explanation of delinquency nor is it clear what it measures.[72]

These problems plus the continuing use of samples inappropriate to locating predisposing factors, lead Waldo and Dinitz to conclude:

> Although the results appear more positive than they did a few years ago, in terms of the number of studies showing differences between criminals and noncriminals, the findings are far from conclusive. The conflict over the role of personality in criminality has not been resolved.[73]

A FINAL WORD ON PERSONALITY AND DEVIANCE

We have scarcely touched upon the multitude of theories suggesting relationships between psychogenic factors and deviant behavior. For example, there are elaborations on the theme of psychopathy: Harrison Gough sees that concept as a matter of the degree to which persons learn to take into account the feelings and needs of others; and Simon Dinitz and colleagues at Ohio State University are attempting to connect the concept with abnormal secretions of a hormone, epinephrine, from the adrenal glands.[74] Doubtless with each passing year new theories will be formulated and new tests constructed in an effort to determine which personality characteristics distinguish those who do not meet social expectations from those who do.

Doubtless, too, the resultant findings will continue to be far from conclusive so long as researchers ignore certain realities.

1. *Sampling problems.* As mentioned in connection with research on physical characteristics, there is no reason to assume that samples of persons officially designated as delinquent or criminal are any more deviant than persons who have no record. On the one hand you have persons convicted of various assaultive behaviors and thefts; on the other you have the unconvicted, unknown proportions of whom may have committed similar acts, may cheat on their income tax, may steal from employers, and may be involved in legitimate business that circumvents governmental regulations to make larger profits. This is not to say that specific emotional difficulties or personality characteristics do not contribute to specific behaviors. But because the definition of behavior as deviant is a social or judicial matter it appears that attempts to find differences between whole categories of delinquents and nondelinquents are doomed to failure.

Even for specific behaviors, however, differing contexts may alter the definition of a given act from deviant to conformist. For example, the calculated killing for profit of strangers who are no threat to you will vary in definition depending on whether you are acting as a mafia hit man or a bombardier dropping bombs on a nation not at war with your own.

Two psychological researchers, Starke R. Hathaway and Elio D. Monachesi, who pioneered use of the MMPI as a predictor of delinquent behavior, were well aware of this problem of relative definition. They point out the fallacy of attempting to explain such behavior by personality alone:

> What is and what is not called delinquent behavior varies with social values—even killing and pillage have been condoned in some cultures. Men in our culture have been called heroes for killing other men and for destruction of property when such acts were committed in conduct of war. Acts like these are endemic in all cultures and even though we may deplore them, the fact remains that in our society, policemen carry guns and shoot to kill, ardent proponents of causes may destroy property, and organized crime, if not officially accepted, at least gives a subcultural sanction to violence. Our teen-agers live with conflict and contrasts. . . . There are many adults whose antisocial behavior provides examples for uncritical emulation by young people. . . . Often the family itself approves of behavior among its members that the surrounding society considers to be objectionable. . . . The delinquent behavior for many of the youngsters studied probably occurred so naturally that no specifically characteristic personality pattern existed as a precursor.[75]

2. *Cause and effect problem.* Theorists who support explanations of biological inferiority and heredity can at least assume that the cause they suggest occurred prior to the behavior. Personality characteristics found to be associated with deviance may be an effect, not a cause, however. That is, certain personality traits may develop as a consequence of being involved in the behavior, or of being identified and treated as a deviant. The only way to satisfactorily resolve this problem is to begin with individuals before their involvement, and conduct the research on a longitudinal or chronological basis to discover the traits describing those who eventually become involved in deviant behavior. Obviously, this is a very costly and time-consuming procedure. Still it may neglect a tangle of contributory factors such as opportunity and other experiences that may override or alter the effect of personality variables.

Conclusions

In this opening chapter we have briefly considered one level of positivist theories attempting to explain behavior not conforming to social expectations. The underlying assumption of these otherwise diverse theories is that the cause lies within the individuals and that it distinguishes them from normal members of society. Put another way, persons involved in deviant behavior are characterized by physical or mental abnormalities. Although nearly all the theorists do concede the possible influence of outside factors, such factors are generally viewed as merely supplemental or secondary to the causal internal factors.

Research based on this assumption has been fruitless for all practical purposes, which is not surprising in view of the research procedures and the simplistic interpretations of deviance. As a general approach to explaining deviance, all of these theories have been a failure. Yet their underlying assumption remains crucial to the determinism characterizing many present-day programs of incarceration and treatment in the United States. As we shall see in later chapters, some contemporary theorists modify this assumption when searching for predisposing factors that pertain only to limited forms of behavior (e.g., heroin addiction, alcoholism, homosexuality) and are highly dependent upon other factors for the behavior to result. While this is a more promising approach, the results remain mixed.

Overall, there is to date no need to qualify David Matza's statement that:

> The history of positive criminology is in large part an elaboration of specific sets of determinants, a questioning of the efficacy of those factors, an

abandoning of them, a period of indecision, and then a substitution of a new theory based on another set of determinants.[76]

NOTES

1. Julius Gould and William L. Kolb, *A Dictionary of the Social Sciences* (New York: Free Press, 1964), p. 472. For a detailed discussion of types of norms and their various aspects, see Ephraim H. Mizruchi and Robert Perruci, "Norm Qualities and Deviant Behavior," in *The Substance of Sociology: Codes, Conduct and Consequences,* ed. Ephraim H. Mizruchi (New York: Appleton-Century-Crofts, 1967), pp. 259–270.

2. *The American Heritage Dictionary of the English Language* (Boston: American Heritage Publishing and Houghton Mifflin), 1973, p. 361.

3. Jerry D. Rose, *Introduction to Sociology* (Chicago: Rand-McNally, 1971), p. 298.

4. J. L. Simmons, *Deviants* (Berkeley, Calif.: Glendessary Press, 1969), p. 3. See also: J. L. Simmons and Hazel Chambers, "Public Stereotypes of Deviants," *Social Problems,* **13** (Fall 1965), pp. 223–232.

5. John E. Conklin, "Criminal Environment and Support for the Law," *Law and Society Review,* **6** (November 1971), pp. 247–265.

6. For a discussion of the nature of law see Stephen Schafer, *Theories in Criminology: Past and Present Philosophies of the Crime Problem* (New York: Random House, 1969), pp. 17–96.

7. Stuart L. Hills, *Crime, Power, and Morality: The Criminal-Law Process in the United States* (Scranton, Pa.: Chandler Publishing, 1971), pp. 4–5.

8. For more detailed discussions of early approaches and writings concerning criminology see: George B. Vold, *Theoretical Criminology* (New York: Oxford University Press, 1958); Hermann Mannheim, ed., *Pioneers in Criminology* (Chicago: Quadrangle Books, 1960); Schafer, *Theories in Criminology;* and Sawyer F. Sylvester, Jr., ed., *The Heritage of Modern Criminology* (Cambridge, Mass.: Schenkman Publishing Co., 1972).

9. Cesare Beccaria, *On Crimes and Punishments,* trans. Henry Paolucci (Indianapolis, Ind.: Bobbs-Merrill, 1963), p. 93.

10. For a discussion of the contradictions in classical theory see Ian Taylor, Paul Walton, and Jock Young, *The New Criminology: For a Social Theory of Deviance* (London: Routledge & Kegan Paul, 1973), pp. 1–7.

11. Gould and Kolb, *Dictionary of the Social Sciences,* pp. 520–521.

12. Ibid., pp. 194–195.

13. For detailed discussions of the assumptions of the positive school see: David Matza, *Delinquency and Drift* (New York: John Wiley, 1964), pp. 1–27; and Taylor, et al., *The New Criminology,* pp. 10–40.

14. Vold, *Theoretical Criminology,* pp. 35–36.

15. A survey of research published in major sociological journals between 1940 and 1970 indicates that this is definitely the case regarding delinquency studies. John F. Galliher and James L. McCartney, "The Influence of Funding Agencies on Juvenile Delinquency Research," *Social Problems,* **21** (Summer 1973), pp. 77–90.

16. Taylor, et al., *The New Criminology,* pp. 31–33.

17. Schafer, *Theories in Criminology*, and Hermann Mannheim, *Comparative Criminology* (Boston: Houghton Mifflin, 1965) are especially thorough. Also see textbooks in criminology such as: Don C. Gibbons, *Society, Crime, and Criminal Careers*, 2nd ed. (Englewood Cliffs, N.J.: Prentice-Hall, 1972); Elmer Hubert Johnson, *Crime, Correction, and Society*, 3rd ed. (Homewood, Ill.: Dorsey Press, 1974); Richard D. Knudten, *Crime in a Complex Society: An Introduction to Criminology* (Homewood, Ill.: Dorsey Press, 1970); and Edwin H. Sutherland and Donald R. Cressey, *Criminology*, 9th ed. (Philadelphia: J. B. Lippincott, 1974).

18. For an example of medical experts presuming causal link see Vernon H. Mark and Frank R. Ervin, *Violence and the Brain* (New York: Harper & Row, 1970), p. 148.

19. Of course, people still have notions of what criminals look like. For research on these notions see Donald J. Shoemaker, Donald R. South, and Jay Lowe, "Facial Stereotypes of Deviants and Judgments of Guilt or Innocence," *Social Forces*, 51 (June 1973), pp. 427–433.

20. For a more detailed discussion of phrenology as it applied to criminology see: Arthur E. Fink, *Causes of Crime: Biological Theories in the United States, 1800–1915* (New York: A. S. Barnes & Co., 1962), pp. 1–19; also Vold, *Theoretical Criminology*, pp. 44–49.

21. Fink, *Causes of Crime*, pp. 2–3.

22. Ibid., p. 5.

23. Vold, *Theoretical Criminology*, p. 49.

24. Sylvester, *Heritage of Modern Criminology*, p. 63.

25. For a review and generally sympathetic evaluation of Lombroso, see Marvin E. Wolfgang, "Cesare Lombroso," in *Pioneers in Criminology*, ed. Mannheim, pp. 168–227.

26. Cesare Lombroso, Introduction, in *Criminal Man According to the Classification of Cesare Lombroso*, Gina Lombroso-Ferrero (New York: Putnam, 1911), p. xiv; quoted in Wolfgang, "Cesare Lombroso," p. 184.

27. Enrico Ferri, *Criminal Sociology*, trans. Joseph I. Kelly and John Lisle (Boston: Little, Brown, 1917), pp. 138–157.

28. Baron Raffaele Garofalo, *Criminology*, trans. Robert W. Millar (Boston: Little, Brown, 1914), p. 110.

29. Charles Goring, *The English Convict: A Statistical Study*, abridged edition (London: His Majesty's Stationery Office, 1919), p. 21.

30. Ibid., pp. 267–268.

31. Robert L. Dugdale, *The Jukes: A Study in Crime, Pauperism, Disease, and Heredity*, 4th ed. (New York: Putnam, 1910), pp. 13–14. For an interesting critique of Dugdale's data gathering methods see Samuel Hopkins Adams, "The Juke Myth," *Saturday Review*, 14 (April 2, 1955), pp. 13, 48–49.

32. Henry H. Goddard, *The Kallikak Family: A Study in the Heredity of Feeble-Mindedness* (New York: Macmillan, 1927), pp. 18–19.

33. Ibid., p. 59.

34. Henry H. Goddard, *Feeble-Mindedness, Its Causes and Consequences* (New York: Macmillan, 1914), pp. 8, 514, quoted in Fink, *Causes of Crime*, pp. 221–222.

35. Henry H. Goddard, *Human Efficiency and Levels of Intelligence* (Princeton, N.J.: Princeton University Press, 1920), pp. 71–72.

36. For detailed discussions of research on the intelligence of criminals see: Fink, *Causes of Crime,* pp. 211–239; Vold, *Theoretical Criminology,* pp. 75–89; and Richard R. Korn and Lloyd W. McCorkle, *Criminology and Penology* (New York: Holt, Rinehart and Winston, 1959), pp. 259–267.

37. T. W. Shannon, *Eugenics* (Marietta, Ohio: S. A. Mullikin, 1916), opp. p. 160.

38. Charles R. Henderson, *Dependent, Defective, and Delinquent Classes: And of Their Social Treatment* (Boston: D. C. Heath, 1901), p. 317.

39. Fink, *Causes of Crime,* p. 209; and Nicholas N. Kittrie, *The Right to Be Different: Deviance and Enforced Therapy* (Baltimore: Penguin Books, 1973), pp. 312–313.

40. Kittre, *The Right to Be Different,* p. 314.

41. The discussion is based on : B. Drummond Ayres, Jr., "Racism, Ethics and Rights at Issue in Sterilization Case," *New York Times,* July 2, 1973, p. 10; Bill Kovach, "H.E.W. Head Curbs Sterilization Aid," *New York Times,* July 6, 1973, p. 54; and Edward Hudson, "Suit Seeks to Void Sterilization Law," *New York Times,* July 13, 1973, p. 43. For a discussion of racism and eugenics see Melanie Fong and Larry O. Johnson, "The Eugenics Movement: Some Insight into the Institutionalization of Racism," *Issues in Criminology,* **9** (Fall 1974), pp. 89–115.

42. Johannes Lange, *Crime As Destiny: A Study of Criminal Twins,* trans. Charlotte Haldane (London: George Allen & Unwin, 1931), p. 198.

43. For detailed criticisms see Hermann Mannheim, *Comparative Criminology,* pp. 231–235.

44. Ibid., p. 235.

45. Earnest Albert Hooton, *Crime and the Man* (Cambridge, Mass.: Harvard University Press, 1939), p. 130.

46. For specific critical evaluations of Hooton's work see: Edwin H. Sutherland, *"The American Criminal"* and *"Crime and the Man,"* in *The Sutherland Papers,* eds. Albert K. Cohen, Alfred Lindesmith, and Karl Schuessler (Bloomington, Ind.: Indiana University Press, 1956), pp. 273–278; and Vold, *Theoretical Criminology,* pp. 63–65.

47. James S. Wallerstein and Clement J. Wylie, "Our Law-Abiding Lawbreakers," *Probation,* **25** (March–April 1947), pp. 107–112.

48. William H. Sheldon, *Varieties of Delinquent Youth: An Introduction to Constitutional Psychiatry* (New York: Harper, 1949), pp. 14–16, 25–28. For a more detailed schematic arrangement see Vold, *Theoretical Criminology,* p. 71.

49. Sheldon, *Varieties of Delinquent Youth,* pp. 726–730. For a more recent study linking delinquency with mesomorphic physique see Juan B. Cortés and Florence M. Gatti, *Delinquency and Crime: A Biopsychosocial Approach* (New York: Seminar Press, 1972), pp. 44–104.

50. Sheldon, *Varieties of Delinquent Youth,* p. 752–759.

51. Edwin H. Sutherland, "Varieties of Delinquent Youth," in *The Sutherland Papers,* ed. Cohen et al., pp. 287–288.

52. For reviews of research and discussions of the legal implications see: Brian C. Baker, "XYY Chromosome Syndrome and the Law," *Criminologica,* 7 (February 1970), pp. 2–35; Theodore R. Sarbin and Jeffrey E. Miller, "Demonism Revisited: The XYY Chromosomal Anomaly," *Issues in Criminology,* 5

(Summer 1970), pp. 195–207; National Institute of Mental Health, *Report on the XYY Chromosomal Abnormality* (Washington, D.C.: Government Printing Office, 1970); Richard G. Fox, "The XYY Offender: A Modern Myth?" *Journal of Criminal Law, Criminology and Police Science,* **62** (March 1971), pp. 59–73; Menachem Amir and Yitzchak Berman, "Chromosomal Deviation and Crime," *Federal Probation,* **34** (June 1970), pp. 55–62; and Barbara J. Culliton, "Patients' Rights: Harvard Is Site of Battle over X and Y Chromosomes," *Science,* **186** (November 1974), pp. 715–717.

53. Sarbin and Miller, "Demonism Revisited," pp. 202–204; and Fox, "The XYY Offender," pp. 69–70.

54. Bertram S. Brown, Louis A. Wienckowski and Lyle W. Bivens, *Psychosurgery: Perspective on a Current Problem* (Washington, D. C.: Government Printing Office, 1973), p. 1.

55. Lee Edson, "The Psyche and the Surgeon," *New York Times Magazine,* September 30, 1973, p. 79; see also Kittrie, *The Right to Be Different,* pp. 305–306.

56. Mark and Ervin, *Violence and the Brain,* p. 126.

57. Ibid., pp. 7, 31–33, and 141.

58. Edson, "The Psyche and the Surgeon," pp. 88–89; and Brown et al., *Psychosurgery,* p. 8.

59. David M. Rorvik, "Bringing the War Home," *Playboy,* **21** (September 1974), p. 114.

60. Albert K. Cohen, *Deviance and Control* (Englewood Cliffs, N.J.: Prentice-Hall, 1966), p. 54.

61. Don C. Gibbons, "Psychogenic Approaches" in his *Society, Crime, and Criminal Careers,* pp. 150–179.

62. James Cowles Prichard, *A Treatise on Insanity and Other Disorders Affecting the Mind* (London: Sherwood, Gilbert and Piper, 1835), quoted in Fink, *Causes of Crime,* p. 48.

63. Fink, *Causes of Crime,* p. 33.

64. Hulsey Cason, "The Psychopath and the Psychopathic," *Journal of Criminal Psychopathology,* **4** (January 1943), pp. 522–527.'

65. Hervey M. Cleckley, *The Mask of Sanity,* 2nd ed. (St. Louis: C. V. Mosby, 1950), pp. 355–356.

66. Michael Hakeem, "A Critique of the Psychiatric Approach to Crime and Correction," *Law and Contemporary Problems,* **23** (Autumn 1958), pp. 668–676.

67. Mannheim, *Comparative Criminology,* p. 327.

68. For articles debating the pros and cons of psychoanalysis as a science see Sidney Hook, ed., *Psychoanalysis, Scientific Method and Philosophy* (New York: New York University Press, 1964).

69. Bernard C. Glueck, *Final Report: Research Project for the Study and Treatment of Persons Convicted of Crimes Involving Sexual Aberrations, June, 1952 to June, 1955* (New York: n. pub., n. date), pp. 23–24.

70. Karl F. Schuessler and Donald R. Cressey, "Personality Characteristics of Criminals," *American Journal of Sociology,* **55** (March 1950), pp. 483–484.

71. For a detailed consideration of problems of causal order in research see Travis Hirschi and Hanan C. Selvin, *Delinquency Research: An Appraisal of Analytic Methods* (New York: The Free Press, 1967).

72. Gordon P. Waldo and Simon Dinitz, "Personality Attributes of the Criminal: An Analysis of Research Studies, 1950–1965," *Journal of Research in Crime and Delinquency,* **4** (July 1967), pp. 185–202.

73. Ibid., p. 202.

74. Harrison G. Gough and Donald R. Peterson, "The Identification and Measurement of Predispositional Factors in Crime and Delinquency," *Journal of Consulting Psychology,* **16** (June 1952), pp. 207–212; Gough, "Theory and Measurement of Socialization," *Journal of Consulting Psychology,* **24** (February 1960), pp. 23–30; Simon Dinitz, Harry Allen, Harold Goldman, and Lewis Lindner, " 'The Juice Model': A New Look at Sociopathy," *et al.,* **3**:1 (1972), pp. 20–27; and Harry Allen, Lewis Lindner, Harold Goldman, and Simon Dinitz, "Hostile and Simple Sociopaths: An Empirical Typology," *Criminology,* **9** (May 1971), pp. 27–47.

75. Starke R. Hathaway and Elio D. Monachesi, *Adolescent Personality and Behavior: MMPI Patterns of Normal, Delinquent, Dropout, and Other Outcomes* (Minneapolis: University of Minnesota Press, 1963), pp. 99–100.

76. David Matza, *Delinquency and Drift* (New York: John Wiley, 1964), p. 12.

2

PERSPECTIVES ON DEVIANCE

With the decline of the free will position of Beccaria and the classical school, the determinist position was to emerge in the form of two fundamental approaches to the study of deviance. One, generally first associated with the work of Lombroso, sought the cause within the individual deviant; the goal was to discover individual characteristics contributing to involvement in behavior. The other approach stressed the importance of social factors as causes of deviance; the goal was to explain both the existence of deviant behavior and its distribution in society. In short, the first approach concerned the deviant; the second concerned the varying amounts of deviance within given population groupings.

Although belief in the connection between anatomical features and deviant behavior dates back several centuries, the first scientific study of deviance came not from Lombroso but grew out of social determinism. The researchers in this case were a French lawyer, Andre-Michel Guerry, who in 1833 published the first known scientific work in criminology, and a Belgian mathematician and astronomer, Lambert A. J. Quetelet.

Today's writers in criminology and deviance classify Guerry and Quetelet under such various headings as "moral statisticians," "cartographic school," and "human ecology." These terms reflect research analyzing official statistics on variables such as suicides, educational levels, illegitimate births, crimes committed, age and sex of criminal offenders, and so on, within given geographic areas for specific time periods.[1] From such analyses both Guerry and Quetelet noted two phenomena: first, types and amount of deviance vary according to geographic region; and second, annual recorded deviance within a specific area varies little from one year to another. These findings led Quetelet to speculate that an "annual budget of crime" exists:

> This remarkable constancy with which the same crimes appear annually in the same order, drawing down on their perpetrators the same punishments, in the same proportions, is a singular fact. . . . I have never failed annually to repeat that there is a *budget* which we pay with frightful regularity—it is that of prisons, dungeons, and scaffolds. . . . We might even predict annually how many individuals will stain their hands with the blood of their fellow-men, how many will be forgers, how many will deal in poison pretty nearly in the same way as we may foretell the annual births and deaths.[2]

Quetelet denied that a particular individual's future conduct could be so predicted, just as you cannot predict his or her death from a table of mortality rates for age groups. But mortality tables do provide accurate estimations of the number of persons annually who will die within a group. The regularity and predictability of group behavior such as crime rates, suicide rates, and so on, presumably placed that behavior beyond the realm of purely individual conduct. While better known for his claims concerning the effects of climate and seasons on crime, Quetelet also found that age, sex, occupation, alcohol use, and heterogeneity of population were related to a "propensity" toward crime.

But Quetelet believed that the blame for crime lay ultimately with society. While humans may have free wills, those wills become neutralized in society and behavior emerges as a product of that society. Quetelet argued that fluctuations in rates of deviance will occur as a result of substantial changes in basic social, economic, and political conditions.

> Society includes within itself the germs of all the crimes committed, and at the same time the necessary facilities for their development. It is the social state, in some measure, which prepares these crimes, and the criminal is merely the instrument to execute them. Every social state supposes, then, a certain number and a certain order of crimes, these being merely the necessary consequences of its organization.[3]

Thus arrived *social determinism* as an explanation of deviance. Throughout the nineteenth century, however, enthusiasm for this approach was never overwhelming; eventually it was to be the biological determinism of Lombroso that provided the greater impact upon the intellectual climate. Social determinism's lack of popularity lay in its implication that those in power within society might play no small role in creating the conditions that cause deviance.

> This way of looking at crime as the product of society was hardly likely to be welcome, however, at a time when a major concern was to hold down the 'dangerous classes'. . . . They were made up of those who had so miserable a share in the accumulating wealth of the industrial revolution that they might at any time break out in political revolt as in France. At their lowest level was the hard core of parasites to be found in any society, ancient or modern. And closely related to this, often indistinguishable from it were the 'criminal classes.'
>
> It served the interests and relieved the conscience of those at the top to look upon the dangerous classes as an independent category, detached from the prevailing social conditions. They were portrayed as a race apart, morally depraved and vicious, living by violating the fundamental law of orderly society, which was that a man should maintain himself by honest, steady work.[4]

Nevertheless, the nineteenth century spawned two social interpretations of deviance that were to have a profound influence upon twentieth century thought. The first concerned *economic influences*, the second *anomie*.

Economic Influences

An economic interpretation of deviance was an aspect of the work of Quetelet when he, for example, considered the price of grain to be a crucial variable in the operation of society. Similar conjectures provided impetus for several studies in Europe and America that attempted to find relationships between crime and a variety of economic factors such as the prices of various grains, business cycles, and income levels of convicted persons. Just how economic conditions are related to deviance has been the subject of a multitude of interpretations.[5] For our purposes, we will consider two: the effect of economic structure as seen by Karl Marx and Willem Bonger, and the effect of pauperism as seen by Frank W. Blackmar.

KARL MARX (1818–1883)

Marx's best known works are *Communist Manifesto* (1848), co-authored with Friedrich Engels, and *Capital: A Critique of Political Economy*, the first edition of which was published in 1867. In these and other works Marx developed an economic interpretation of societies. He claimed that all social phenomena—legal codes, political institutions, religion, ethics, the arts, the family—are products of a so-

ciety's economy in the form of its *means of production*. In a capitalistic economy there is private ownership of the means of production,
distribution, and exchange of wealth; as a consequence there exists
intense competition resulting in the exploitation of the *proletariat*
(working class) by the *bourgeoisie* (owners and controllers of means
of production).

According to Marx the continual competition requires that minimal
wages be paid for labor; the bourgeoisie becomes richer and richer,
and the proletariat becomes poorer and more miserable. The conditions of poverty and continued exploitation produce all forms of social problems. Only by destroying the economic system, ultimately
accomplished by the proletariat in violent revolution, will a classless
society emerge free of economic exploitation and its attendant evils.

Marx was proposing a grand theory of the evolutionary process of
contemporary industrial society. He never actually spelled out a
theory of deviance, but inferences can be made and his writings have
been influential to students of deviance in at least two respects.

First, Marx's writings provide a basis for viewing deviance as a
product of social conflict. According to Marxian thought deviance
cannot be eliminated by adjustments within capitalist societies; deviance is inherent in capitalism and only the total destruction of the
economic substructure will provide a remedy. Marx saw capitalist society as comprised of a one-sided conflict between groups. From his
perspective deviance was an expression of a struggle in which the
economically powerless attempt to cope with the exploitation and
poverty imposed upon them. Marx's interpreters claim he portrayed
the deviant as "demoralized and brutalized by the day-to-day experience of employment (and unemployment) under industrial capitalism
. . . but still able to grasp at the necessities of life through theft
and graft." [6]

The economic class struggle did not result in the proletarian revolution predicted by Marx. Nevertheless, his conception of society as
consisting of conflicting groups remains an important contribution to
social theory. Political, military, economic, and legislative actions are
not the products of harmonious decision-making by concerned and
affected parties. Often such actions are, at best, matters of compromise; at worst they represent only the opinions of the powerful and
may be detrimental to, or against the wishes of, a sizeable segment of
the population.

Second, Marx also points to the interrelationship of the deviant
and nondeviant aspects of society. With a touch of sarcasm he points
out how deviance serves many purposes in support of the existing society. Without deviance police, judges, juries, and law professors
would have no jobs; the mechanical inventions derived from innovations in torture would be undiscovered; and the areas of locksmith-
ing, engraving of monetary instruments, and chemical methods to de-

tect illegal adulterations of products would all remain unadvanced. Furthermore:

> The criminal breaks the monotony and everyday security of bourgeois life. In this way he keeps it from stagnation, and gives rise to that uneasy tension and agility without which even the spur of competition would get blunted. Thus he gives a stimulus to the productive forces. While crime takes a part of the superfluous population off the labor market and thus reduces competition among the laborers—up to a certain point preventing wages from falling below the minimum—the struggle against crime absorbs another part of this population. Thus the criminal comes in as one of those natural "counterweights" which bring about a correct balance and open up a whole perspective of "useful" occupations.

Marx goes on to cite an English satirist, Bernard de Mandeville (1670–1733):

> 'That which we call Evil in this World, Moral as well as Natural, is the grand Principle that makes us Sociable Creatures, the solid Basis, the *Life and Support of all Trades and Employments* without exception . . . there we must look for the true origin of all Arts and Sciences; and . . . the moment Evil ceases, the Society must be spoil'd if not totally dissolved.' [7]

WILLEM BONGER (1876–1940)

The first author to suggest a grand scale Marxian theory of crime was the Dutch scholar Willem Bonger. The thrust of his argument is outlined by the following propositions:

1. Notions of what constitutes immoral behavior and crime change with changes in the social structure.
2. Behaviors prohibited by the criminal law are those harmful to the interests of the powerful. Although some laws may protect both the upper and lower classes, rarely will an act be punished if it does not injure the interest of the upper class.
3. The capitalist system is held together by force, not by the consensus of all groups. Thus relations are based on exploitation and force, not on cooperation and trust.
4. Humans are basically pleasure-seeking, but pleasures in capitalist societies require lots of money. Consequently *egoism* (selfishness) is stimulated. In their pursuit of pleasure both the bourgeoisie and the proletariat become prone to crime as they lose compassion and sense of responsibility toward others.
5. Poverty resulting from capitalism prompts crime to the extent that (a) it creates a desperate need for food, and other life necessities, and (b) economic advantage is equated with a person's intrinsic superiority.
6. Crime also results when there is a perceived opportunity to gain an advantage through illegal means, and/or when opportunities to achieve pleasure are closed off by a biased legal system.
7. Capitalism is characterized by the conditions described above. Such conditions will ultimately be eliminated by socialism. [8]

Thus, according to Bonger, capitalism with its competition and its subordinate class struggling for the necessities of life weakens "social feelings" and encourages unrestrained egoism.

> This state of things especially stifles men's social instincts; it develops, on the part of those with power, the spirit of domination, and of insensibility to the ills of others, while it awakens jealousy and servility on the part of those who depend upon them.[9]

Bonger's theory brings to our attention the importance of conflicts of interest within society as they affect both the formulation and the enforcement of law. Unrecognized by the theory is the fact that conflicts of interest are neither limited to economic matters nor restricted to a two-party struggle between those who do and those who do not control the wealth. The owners of economic power in the United States, for example, do not exercise total control over the justice system. The system is subject to varying influences by interest groups whose power does not necessarily derive from control over means of production, but over votes. Furthermore, Bonger's theory oversimplifies the sources of deviant behavior. The link proposed between egoism and deviance ignores many motivations that may not be selfish from some other standpoint. If someone commits a "deviant" act to further the interests of her or his group, it is a matter of judgment whether the act stems from egoism or altruism.

Although Bonger's theory possesses several weaknesses as an explanation of deviance, its focus on social conflict remains an important contribution. Nevertheless, the conflict perspective was not influential in American criminology during the first sixty years of this century. Although economic factors were considered important, they were seen merely as isolated problems in an otherwise healthy, congenial society. The poor were considered not victims of economic conflict, but of themselves or their station in society.

The non-Marxist social determinists of the period were analyzing society in terms of its regularity and order; they viewed deviance as a departure from normal and as representing a maladjustment in an otherwise orderly system. In one respect they were similar to the theorists discussed in the previous chapter. Deviance was seen as symptomatic of a pathology, but in this case something was considered awry not with the individual, but with society, which was good but not perfect. An example of such an interpretation can be found in the study of the Smoky Pilgrims.

THE SMOKY PILGRIMS

At the turn of the century American sociologists saw poor economic conditions as providing an undernourished environment in which goodness had difficulty thriving. A representative study is Frank W. Blackmar's investigation of a family in Kansas, which he calls the "Smoky Pilgrims." Blackmar points out that though the city is usually considered the source of deviance while the country is "free of immoral influences," rural areas have their share of "tramps and vagabonds."

> The lack of variety in life, the little time to be devoted to books and papers, and the destruction of all taste for the same bring the mind to a low status. Their spare time on the farm and when out of employment is spent in telling obscene stories, in which perpetual lying is necessary to keep up a variety in the conversation, and the use of vile language is habitual. All this tends to weakness of mind and the decline of bodily vigor and health. The youth who is so unfortunate as to listen to all this, and to be associated with such characters, is in danger of having his imagination polluted and his standard of life degraded.[10]

Acknowledging his debt to Dugdale's study of the Jukes, Blackmar describes the family as of "dusky color and their smoky and begrimed appearance" as probably the result of "negro blood in the veins of part of the family." Like the Jukes, they lived in miserable, overcrowded huts. Seekers of odd jobs, petty thieves, beggars, and prostitutes, they are characterized as "strange and irregular" and belonging to the "pauper and weak criminal class."

> Not essentially vicious in their fundmental characters, they have reached their present status in consequence of bad economic conditions. Once thrown into the struggle for existence on a low plane, they have adapted their lives to a standard which has developed pauper and criminal tendencies. . . . They have been placed, on account of conditions and characteristics, in a helpless condition.[11]

Scarcely a Marxist, Blackmar castigates the citizens of Kansas for allowing the causes of the family conditions to continue, and suggests the family be broken up; the adults should be forced to work on public farms and the older children sent to reformatories. Blackmar concludes that a principle of "social evolution" operates whereby the stronger become stronger in order to preserve social life. However, efforts of the strong can be counteracted and neutralized by the weak. "Social sanitation" is necessary; the weak must be cared for. Although he blames bad economic conditions, Blackmar is evidently convinced that a weakness of character contributes to the Pilgrims' poverty and criminality; he believed that deviance and strength of character cannot be compatible.

Although Blackmar's study is of little relevance for contemporary criminology, it does indicate the direction to be taken by twentieth century sociologists; namely, that the causes of deviance can be found in the conditions of the lower economic classes. The presumptions behind this approach are that deviance is confined primarily to such classes and that a general consensus rather than conflict of interests exists within society. It was evident that poverty alone has little explanatory power, but the principal thrust of American sociology has been to find factors related to economic class which would explain deviance. One of the most important factors was *anomie*.

Anomie

Emile Durkheim (1858–1917), a French sociologist, wrote his major works during a time when the study of deviant behavior was dominated by those who viewed deviants as the products of defective biology. As such, deviants could not be the products of society. To carry the argument of the biological positivists to its logical conclusion, deviance could be eliminated merely by the elimination of deviants. Society could be faulted only to the extent of its failure to locate and neutralize the potential troublemakers.

Durkheim argued, however, that a society without deviance is impossible.

> In a society in which criminal acts are no longer committed, the sentiments they offend would have to be found without exception in all individual consciousnesses, and they must be found to exist with the same degree as sentiments contrary to them. Assuming that this condition could actually be realized, crime would not thereby disappear; it would only change its form, for the very cause which would thus dry up the sources of criminality would immediately open up new ones.
>
> .   .   .
>
> Imagine a society of saints, a perfect cloister of exemplary individuals. Crimes, properly so called, will there be unknown; but faults which appear venial to the layman will create there the same scandal that the ordinary offense does in ordinary consciousnesses. If, then, this society has the power to judge and punish, it will define these acts as criminal and will treat them as such.[12]

Thus, short of a society of robots it is impossible to have a collection of humans so inflexible in their behavior that none will diverge to some degree from the ideal. In a society of apparently minor divergences, there will be reactions even against these infractions based on the society's consensus concerning norms—what Durkheim called the *collective conscience*. An important corollary drawn from this view will be crucial for our later discussion of recent sociological theorists. The corollary states that deviance is not inherent in any given act, but is defined by the reaction to that act:

> Thus, since there cannot be a society in which the individuals do not differ more or less from the collective type, it is also inevitable that, among these

divergences, there are some with a criminal character. *What confers this character upon them is not the intrinsic quality of a given act but that definition which the collective conscience lends them.*[13]

Durkheim further claims that deviance is not only inevitable but also necessary for the health and progress of society. Without deviance, society would be static. New ideas and approaches to problem solving would not be tolerated since the status quo would be considered beyond improvement. Thus deviance is actually useful to society:

> Nothing is good indefinitely and to an unlimited extent. The authority which the moral conscience enjoys must be excessive; otherwise no one would dare criticize it, and it would too easily congeal into an immutable form. To make progress, individual originality must be able to express itself. In order that the originality of the idealist whose dreams transcend his century may find expression, it is necessary that the originality of the criminal, who is below the level of his time, shall also be possible. One does not occur without the other.[14]

The inevitability and desirability of deviance led Durkheim to conclude that deviance is "normal" in society. This did not mean that Durkheim necessarily regarded the individual deviant as normal. Instead, he was careful to distinguish between deviance as a sociological fact and as the result of psychological factors within a given individual. The one does not necessarily imply the other. Because a person suffers from some abnormality does not imply that he or she will focus behavior in a deviant direction, nor does deviant behavior imply an actor suffering from an abnormality. From the standpoint of society, deviance is an expression of individual freedom and one of the prices to be paid for social change. Whether the behavior results from abnormality or normality of the individual depends less upon that condition than upon the context in which the behavior occurs.[15]

Durkheim's conception of deviance as normal was unique for his time and did not gain wide acceptance even among sociologists until quite recently. Instead, one other of his major contributions was elaborated upon to fit more closely the then predominant conception of deviance as a symptom of disorder in an otherwise organized society.

DURKHEIM'S ANOMIE

Durkheim first used the concept of anomie in *The Division of Labor in Society* (1893).[16] Here it played a minor role; its purpose was to signify a lack of integration and adjustment that threatens the cohesiveness of contemporary industrial societies, which, unlike hunting and agricultural societies, are characterized by a complex variety of occupations and interests.

Four years later, in his work *Suicide,* the concept was to play a larger role by designating a particular type of suicide. Durkheim was influenced by Quetelet and others who believed that the regularity of suicide rates in given geographic areas must be caused by properties of the society, not of the individuals. Durkheim noted that different social variables were related to suicide rates in different ways. He suggested therefore that there are different forms of suicide.[17] Anomic suicide was one of four types and was considered to stem from a state of "normlessness' or "de-regulation" in society. Such suicides occur because society allows its members to have unlimited aspirations, and there is no discipline imposed on notions of what may be realistically achieved. These suicides arise particularly during periods of sudden economic prosperity.

> From top to bottom of the ladder, greed is aroused without knowing where to find ultimate foothold. Nothing can calm it, since its goal is far beyond all it can attain. Reality seems valueless by comparison with the dreams of fevered imaginations; reality is therefore abandoned, but so too is possibility abandoned when it in turn becomes reality. A thirst arises for novelties, unfamiliar pleasures, nameless sensations, all of which lose their savor once known. Henceforth one has no strength to endure the least reverse. The whole fever subsides and the sterility of all the tumult is apparent, and it is seen that all these new sensations in their infinite quantity cannot form a solid foundation of happiness to support one during days of trial.[18]

Thus, Durkheim was convinced that humans are susceptible to limitless ambition. Unless society imposes regulations upon aspirations, unless there is some check upon the passions aroused by perceived undiminishing prosperity, personal crises will develop and result in suicide.

MERTON'S ANOMIE

In 1938 Robert K. Merton elaborated upon the theme of unobtainable aspirations and extended it beyond suicide to all forms of deviance. Merton's version of anomie differs from Durkheim's in two important respects. First, Durkheim felt that human aspirations are essentially limitless and in times of rapid social change they can exceed reasonable expectations; Merton argues that aspirations are products of society and limited, but that they can exceed what is obtainable through acceptable means. Second, Durkheim claimed that anomie results from a disruption of regulation, a failure to maintain limits over the aspirations of society's members; in contrast Merton suggests that anomie results from strains in the social structure, which exert pressures on individuals, pushing them toward unrealistic aspirations.

Merton's theory involves the interaction of two social components: 1. culture goals—the aspirations and aims that define success in society, and 2. institutionalized means—the socially acceptable methods and ways available for achieving goals.[19]

According to Merton, there is an overemphasis in America on success as a goal. It is the American Dream that everyone, regardless of class origin, religion, or ethnic characteristics, can succeed in acquiring material wealth. This seems fine as an egalitarian ideal, but the realities of American society do not match it. The acceptable means to attain success are in short supply, and what means exist are not uniformly distributed to all groups. It is not the mere lack of opportunity *or* the excessive emphasis on the accumulation of wealth that creates anomie; it is when both exist in the situation where all or most members of a society believe the opportunities are available to them that anomie results. In Merton's words:

> It is only when a system of cultural values extols, virtually above all else, certain *common* success-goals *for the population at large* while the social structure rigorously restricts or completely closes access to approved modes of reaching these goals *for a considerable part of the same population,* that deviant behavior ensues on a large scale.[20]

Anomie thus constitutes:

> a breakdown in the cultural structure, occurring particularly when there is an acute disjunction between cultural norms and goals and the socially structured capacities of members of the group to act in accord with them.[21]

The premium placed on financial success in the absence of opportunities creates a disjunction between the goal and the capacities or means of individuals to attain it. In American society, the competition for wealth is not satisfactory in itself; you must be a winner. The means used to compete become secondary to the victory. Attempting to stay within the bounds of the norms while faced with sure failure can create frustration and unrelieved tension. As Bonger claimed some thirty years earlier, deviance can result when economic success is seen as an indication of intrinsic superiority when one's image as a person is on the line. The alternatives are to continue playing by the rules, to undertake other means toward the goal, or to seek avenues of escape from the anomic situation.

Undoubtedly one of the most important contributions of Merton's theory is the provision of alternative behaviors that may result from the disjunction between goals and means. What Merton calls "modes of individual adaptation" are essentially the logical possible behavioral alternatives expressed in terms of the acceptance and rejection of goals and means.

		Goals	
		Accepted	Rejected
Means	Accepted	Conformity	Ritualism
	Rejected	Innovation	Retreatism

From this scheme the reader can see there are three adaptations apart from conformity that can be defined as deviant: innovation, ritualism, and retreatism. *Innovation* is the adaptation in which most property crimes would be found. It occurs when persons accept without qualification the importance of attaining the goals, and will use any means regardless of their propriety, morality, or legality to achieve those goals. In short, their philosophy can be described in the words of Vince Lombardi when he said of professional football: "Winning isn't everything; it's the only thing."

To continue in the sports vein, an excellent example of innovation occurred at the 1973 National Soap Box Derby. After the race it was discovered that the winner's car had been equipped with an electromagnetic device that gave it extra velocity at the starting point. The innovator was not the fourteen-year-old driver, but his uncle who was subsequently charged with contributing to the delinquency of a minor. There was evidence that at least thirty-four cars in the race including six of the top ten finishers had been doctored. The uncle, after a $2,000 court decision against him, declared he would sue Derby officials for singling out his nephew. Furthermore, it turns out that this adult's son had won the Derby the previous year. The 1972 car mysteriously disappeared before it could be checked, however.[22] All this flies in the face of the conformist adage: It's not whether you win or lose; it's how you play the game.

In his discussion Merton acknowledges the existence of innovation in high places, but he is primarily interested in explaining the official statistics that attribute higher rates of crime to lower economic groups. These groups, according to Merton, have accepted American success goals yet are especially lacking in opportunities for their fulfillment. It is not poverty itself, but its combination with expectations and limited opportunity that predisposes these classes toward higher rates of robbery, burglary, auto theft, and other forms of property crimes.

Ritualism is a behavioral alternative in which great aspirations are abandoned in favor of careful adherence to the available means. Early morning classes often contain ritualists—failing students who faithfully attend lectures and just as faithfully fall asleep. Attendance is not a means for them to attain success; they are there simply because they should be. Merton uses the example of persons in factories and other bureaucracies who staunchly perform their duties, but who have neither the intention nor the inclination to advance themselves. They carefully avoid rocking the boat and prefer to play it safe. There may be some argument whether such behavior is really deviant, but the lack of ambition certainly is not in keeping with the idealized American way.

Retreatism is the category containing the mentally disordered, drug addicts, alcoholics, and any other group that has apparently withdrawn from the competitive struggle. These persons do not strive for the goals that society encourages, nor do they obey the rules of how to act. They seek their own private rewards and live by rules peculiar to their style of living. Rather than coping with the frustrations of the larger society, they have simply abandoned that society.

Rebellion is yet another adaptation to anomie that does not logically fit the diagram presented above. This involves not only a rejection of the goals and means, but the intention of replacing those goals and means by altering the social structure. In his more recent publications Merton has substituted the term *nonconforming behavior* for rebellion, while *aberrant behavior* is used to include innovation, ritualism, and retreatism. Merton characterizes the two as follows:

1. The nonconformer publicly expresses his or her dissent with the norms, while the aberrant hides his or her conduct.
2. The nonconformer challenges the legitimacy of the norms while the aberrant acknowledges their legitimacy in a general way, although they may not apply to his or her specific conduct in specific instances.
3. The nonconformer tries to change the norms, the aberrant at most only tries to justify his or her particular conduct.
4. The nonconformer is often recognized by conventional society to be acting for nonpersonal reasons, while the aberrant is acting only in his or her personal interests.
5. The nonconformer claims to act in terms of ultimate values such as justice, freedom of speech, equality, liberty; the aberrant makes no such claims and seeks only to satisfy private interests.[23]

Few theories in sociology have sparked the imagination and controversy that Merton's has. His behavioral alternatives define deviance as a matter of individuals making choices in order to cope with their positions within society. Merton thus not only explains the source of rule-breaking behavior, but also suggests the motivations and forms that comprise such behavior. But as an explanation of deviance, his means-goals schema falls short of its ambitious mark. Criticisms of the theory are many and complex, but two are critical.

First, Merton, as other positivists before him, relies heavily upon the assumptions that persons officially treated as deviant accurately represent the population of those involved in similar behavior. The biological determinists used data from prison inmates. Although Merton depends on police statistics, the result is the same: a theory attempting to explain the presence of individuals in an official category that was compiled in a highly complex and selective manner.

Official statistics clearly point to the lower economic class as the primary source of delinquency, crime, alcoholism, illegal drug use, and serious mental disorder. Like Merton, most sociologists have directed their research and theoretical efforts accordingly. A favorite target is urban, lower class, slum gangs. The reader compiling a bibliography of delinquency studies in America can only conclude that such gangs constitute practically the sole origin of delinquent behavior. Many sociologists are now recognizing that official records considerably inflate the relationship between class and delinquency. Furthermore, it appears that earlier enthusiasm over explaining the lower class gang has led to premature and highly selective conclusions concerning the general nature of delinquency.

Maynard L. Erickson, for example, finds that his data do not support the impression left by official statistics:

> Scant evidence is found that would support the contention that group delinquency is more characteristic of the lower-status levels than other socioeconomic status levels. With few exceptions, the evidence shows that the tendency to violate in groups is evenly distributed across social status levels. . . . Only arrests seem to be more characteristic of the low-status category than the other categories. . . . In short, the findings not only fail to support the contention of the group nature of delinquency: they seriously put in question the importance of [socioeconomic status] and delinquency unless, of course, one is willing to define delinquency solely on the basis of aggregate official reaction—arrests, juvenile court referrals, and the like.[24]

Other studies reveal that the lower class has no monopoly on crime, alcoholism, illegal drug use, and so on. Indeed, many acts are monopolized by the upper classes but never reach the statistics: illegal corporation practices, influence peddling by politicians, and medical malpractice, for examples. In addition, nonconforming behavior is more likely to come from the middle rather than the lower class, as evidenced by campus disruptions during the Vietnam War.

Jack D. Douglas claims, on the basis of research into official categorization procedures, that official statistics are invalid, unreliable, and biased as indicators of the occurrence of behavior:

1. Officials are concerned primarily with practical problems, not with compiling scientific information.
2. Officials categorize largely in terms of rules of thumb, not by scientific criteria.

3. Great variations exist among organizations in the formal and informal definitions of categories, organizational structures, and procedures.
4. There are great variations in the tendencies of different groups to report deviance, in the official registration of members of different groups, and in the disposition of cases from different groups.
5. Great differences can exist between public statements of official policy and actual practices in handling cases.
6. Officials often manipulate statistics in order to use them for political purposes.[25]

Thus it appears that official statistics are more valuable for studying agencies that compile them than as indicators of the distribution of deviant activity.

A second criticism of Merton's theory concerns his assumptions of common culture goals and institutionalized means. The ethnic, religious, and cultural heterogeneity of America and the rapidly changing concepts of morality in many of its segments cast doubt on whether any single set of goals-means can be said to characterize the society. While there may be a success theme in America it is scarcely limited to financial or material achievement. Accomplishment is defined in many ways by many individuals and the paths to it are equally diverse. Who is "more successful" or "more American": the president of IBM, the individual who gains fame by expending all his time and personal finances lobbying for consumer protection laws, the religious leader who calls for the renunciation of materialistic goals and who draws tens of thousands to his rallies, the actress whose pornographic movie is categorized as a "must see" by New York City's social and artistic elite, or the jazz musician who is esteemed as one of America's greatest artists but who lives near poverty throughout his life? Each has succeeded in his or her own fashion and each would probably have it no other way.[26]

Because there are many conflicting moral positions in American society, there are consequently conflicting views over what constitutes success and the proper means toward that success. As a morally pluralistic society America has far fewer commonly approved goals and means than are implied in anomie theory. The result is not the disintegration of society, however. American society holds together because:

1. There is general consensus over certain values: (a) prohibition of acts against the persons and property of members of our own groups; and (b) a national identity as Americans with rights, duties, and a government that are different from and generally considered better than those of other nations.

2. There is general recognition of the separation, or at least distinc-

tion, between public and private morality. We learn to work with and get along with persons of all sorts: those with disapproved looks, clothes, and ideas. To do this we learn to hide our personal feelings and not to intrude into others' private worlds—we learn to mind our own business. In short, the existence of a morally pluralistic society depends upon *accommodation* to various moral positions.[27]

The process of accommodation includes the ability of individuals to withdraw from the public world of work, with its exposure to strangers and others of differing morals, into a private world of family, clubs, and other settings where one can interact with those of similar interests and inclinations. Yet, there is a toleration of other private worlds—so long as they do not intrude upon one's own. An example here is the often expressed American attitude: "I don't care what (fill in the blank) do, just so they don't bother me and don't move into the neighborhood."

Another aspect of accommodation is the decreasing moralism attached to public issues. As Jack D. Douglas points out:

> There are very strong moral feelings against intruding moral issues into public issues. The "moral prude" is considered immoral in most public settings, except in so-called fundamentalist groups, which are themselves morally repugnant to most members of our society. (Fundamentalists, fire-eaters, preachers, are especially morally repugnant and are considered un-civilized, uneducated, boorish, hillbilly backwoodsmen.) . . . The reason for this demoralizing of public work and issues seems simple: in a pluralistic society with little moral agreement any public work which necessitates intergroup cooperation will be disrupted by bringing in moral issues.[28]

Douglas further argues that the accommodation process is quite evident in national political decision-making where the goals are frequently so broad as to appeal to the great majority of people regardless of their moral position. If there are ultimate national goals they can be described as continued economic progress, maintenance of greater military strength relative to the communist world, and improvement of public health.[29]

It is important to recognize, however, that accommodation and the broadening of goals do not eliminate the possibility of open conflict between moral positions. Power differences do exist between groups occupying different moral positions. Under the guise of maintaining order those with greater power can and do often use coercion to control or to render impotent the less powerful. As we shall see in later chapters, the distinction between public and private morality is often blurred—it is constantly being changed and negotiated as the conflict progresses.

This constant state of conflict, whether reduced by accommodation or not, belies the underlying premises of anomie theory. American society is characterized as much by conflict as by consensus over both success goals and the means toward those goals. Further-more, the apparent preponderance of deviance among the lower class as reflected by official statistics may be more indicative of the powerlessness of that group than of its behavior.

Subcultures of Deviance

Merton's theory of anomie purports not only to locate the specific cause of deviance within the social structure, but also to explain the form that the deviance takes. Most other theories of deviance are considerably less ambitious. In this section we shall consider theories more limited in their purpose though no less significant in their con-tributions. These theories are based upon the assumption that de-viance arises from membership in a group whose beliefs and attitudes support such behavior. Although interpreted by outsiders as deviant, the behavior in question conforms to the expectations of a particular group. Such theories are usually labelled *subcultural theories,* al-though they may also be described as *cultural transmission theories* [30] or as *cultural deviance theories.* [31]

Exactly what constitutes a subculture has not been completely re-solved in the sociological literature, but the following are generally considered as distinguishing characteristics:

1. A special vocabulary or argot, usually concerning the activities that differentiate the group from those around it. For example, urban lower-class heroin users possess a jargon practically incomprehen-sible to those unfamiliar with the activities involved.
2. A set of shared beliefs and norms, which contrast in direction or emphasis with the norms of other groups, such as the larger soci-ety.
3. Contacts between members through which behavior is learned and membership in the group is confirmed.
4. Sometimes a specialized way of dressing and acting that, like argot, serves to distinguish the members from those of other groups and to assist in identifying members to one another.

Obviously, not all subcultures are necessarily deviant in a narrow, negative sense. The Amish, for example, can be described as a sub-culture as a result of their religious beliefs that isolate members from the general community, require the wearing of plain black clothing, and forbid the use of motorized vehicles. Although characterized as a deviant subculture, the Amish rarely break the criminal code and are highly respected for their industriousness and honest dealing.

In a pluralistic society many groups, ethnic, religious, and political, could be characterized as subcultures by one or more such criteria.

Therein lies the problem when comparing any group with the larger culture. Sociologists, when suggesting the existence of deviant subcultures, usually begin with a particular form of behavior and then attempt to ascertain whether individuals involved receive support for the behavior and/or instruction from others.

The contribution of a subculture to deviance can be twofold. First, it can be viewed as the *source* of the behavior; the individual enters the group, usually though not necessarily by birth, and there acquires the knowledge and values that prompt him or her to behave in ways defined by outsiders as deviant. In short, the subculture teaches the individual to be deviant. This is usually the sequence suggested by the subcultural theories of delinquency, which we will consider briefly in a moment.

The second way in which a subculture can contribute to deviance is by providing *support* for deviant behavior. The individual is already defined by others (or by her or himself) as a deviant and as a consequence gravitates toward groups that share common interests. Admission to such groups provides the individual with a more positive image and, in all likelihood, with greater opportunity to engage in deviance. At the same time the group provides support and opportunities for deviance, it also insulates the individual from influences that might alter the deviant career path. This sequence is often associated with the homosexual subculture—the web of acquaintances, cliques, bars, argot, and life-style that frequently accompany a commitment to the gay life. The individual is not likely to first become oriented toward homosexuality in the subculture; rather, involvement in the subculture probably comes only after experience with homosexuality.

Unquestionably, subcultures as sources of deviance and as supports for deviance are interrelated notions. If a subculture has been instrumental in introducing someone to the rationales and techniques of a behavior, that person must continue to rely upon the reinforcement that only the subculture can provide; once a person has entered the subculture, the deviance becomes necessary in order to adhere to the norms of the subculture. In this case the subculture serves both as a support and as a source of behavior.

CLIFFORD R. SHAW (1896–1957)

We have already mentioned Quetelet who in the early nineteenth century utilized census statistics in an attempt to explain group influence upon rates of deviance. However, after a few years such studies were overshadowed by the influence of Charles Darwin:

> The importance of Darwinism in the late nineteenth century can hardly be overestimated. Evolution and natural selection [survival of the fittest] were concepts adopted and adapted wholesale in almost every field of intellec-

tual inquiry from biology to sociology. . . . Studies of motivation were more attractive partly because they came nearer to the vitality of human behavior, and partly because by existing at a lower level of abstraction they required less intellectual effort, a fact which led to the vulgarisations of popular pseudo-science, the notion of the 'born criminal' being a case in point.[32]

Ironically, although Darwin influenced the development of Lombrosianism, his work also was later to advance the study of the ecology of deviance pioneered by Quetelet. According to Amos Hawley, human ecology is indebted to Darwin for his conceptions of:

1) the web of life in which organisms are adjusted or are seeking adjustment to one another, 2) the adjustment process as a struggle for existence, and 3) the environment comprising a highly complex set of conditions of adjustment.[33]

It was the application of such ideas to human relationships within cities that sparked the studies of Clifford Shaw, who attempted to explain the geographic distribution of crime and delinquency. Basing his approach upon ecological theories of the time, Shaw viewed the "adjustment process" of city growth as involving a segregation into "natural areas" in which the inhabitants possess similar qualities, interests, and cultures. In time, these areas take on the character and quality of the people living there; characteristics of the community thus reflect social processes occurring among its members.

Another aspect of city growth treated by Shaw was the threat of encroachment by industry upon residential areas, thus creating a "zone of transition." This zone, immediately adjacent to the central business district, is characterized by deteriorating buildings, falling rental costs but rising land values resulting from speculation, and decreasing population. The social characteristics of this zone are recent immigrant groups, poverty, high crime and delinquency rates, and a highly heterogeneous mixture of the young, the aged, the down-and-outers, the aspiring, students, freethinkers, professional criminals, and so on. The growth of the city thus affects and is affected by both physical and social conditions.

Utilizing the records of juvenile probation agencies, courts, and the Cook County Jail, Shaw reached the following conclusions:

1. There is great variation between areas (square mile units) as to the proportions of residents having records of truancy, delinquency, and crime. Some areas show very high rates and others very low.
2. Generally, the closer the areas toward the city center the higher the rates of truancy, delinquency, crime, and repeated delinquency (recidivism).
3. Areas with high rates of delinquency also show high rates of truancy and crime.

4. The highest rates of truancy, and so on, occur in areas of physical deterioration and declining population.
5. Areas with these high rates have been characterized by high rates for at least thirty years, regardless of what ethnic or racial groups lived there.[34]

The concentration of deviance in areas undergoing the process of transition from residential to industrial use is indicative of a process of social disorganization, according to Shaw. When industry invades the community the standards of the "conventional" society weaken. Resistance to deviance is lower and the behavior is progressively more tolerated. Furthermore, the influx of recent European immigrants or rural blacks with different values also helps break down whatever community forces act to control behavior.

> In this state of social disorganization, community resistance is low. *Delinquency and criminal patterns arise and are transmitted socially just as any other cultural and social pattern is transmitted.* In time these delinquent patterns become dominant and shape the attitudes and behavior of persons living in the area. Thus the section becomes an area of delinquency.[35]

Shaw's concept of social disorganization had limited utility,[36] and in a 1942 work with Henry D. McKay, *Juvenile Delinquency and Urban Areas,* the concept was replaced by "differences in social values." In this later work the authors implicitly reject the notion of consensus within society by arguing that high delinquency areas contain competing economic value systems: legitimate business and illegitimate business, as represented by criminal gangs and the rackets. These areas provide opportunity and incentive for deviance. Although people in the community may be aware that wealth and prestige can be obtained legally, illegal means can often appear more relevant and tangible:

> A boy may be found guilty of delinquency in the court, which represents the values of the larger society, for an act which has had at least tacit approval in the community in which he lives. It is perhaps common knowledge in the neighborhood that public funds are embezzled and that favors and special considerations can be received from some public officials through the payment of stipulated sums; the boys assume that all officials can be influenced in this way. They are familiar with the location of illegal institutions in the community and with the procedures through which such institutions are opened and kept in operation; they know where stolen goods can be sold and the kinds of merchandise for which there is a ready market; they know what the rackets are; and they see in fine clothes, expensive cars, and other lavish expenditures the evidences of wealth among those who openly engage in illegal activities.[37]

A more provocative concept than social disorganization emerges from Shaw's 1929 work—the notion that certain areas contain values supportive of deviance and that these values are transmitted as are any other cultural values. This is not to imply that Shaw was the first social thinker to suggest that deviant behavior results from learning, but his work heralded the emerging sociological emphasis upon the importance of the learning process in explaining deviance.

It should be noted here that a major sequel to Shaw's studies was a series of works concerning the subculture as an explanation of the existence and activities of urban, lower class, male, gang delinquency. As was mentioned earlier, it appears that the importance of such delinquency has been exaggerated. Nevertheless the literature on the subcultures of gang delinquency represents some of the most imaginative, insightful work to be found in sociology. It is most worthy of the reader's attention.[38]

DIFFERENTIAL ASSOCIATON THEORY

In 1890 a French magistrate, Gabriel Tarde (1843–1904), published an attack upon Lombroso and his followers. In *Philosophie Pénale* Tarde argued that the explanation of crime lay not in biology but in the social world, and that crime is transmitted through intimate personal groups.

> The true seminary of crime must be sought for upon each public square or each crossroad of our towns, whether they be small or large, in those flocks of pillaging street urchins who, like bands of sparrows, associate together, at first for marauding, and then for theft, because of a lack of education and food in their homes. Without any natural predisposition on their part, their fate is often decided by the influence of their comrades. . . . The child who was the most normally constituted [could] be more influenced by half a score of perverse friends by whom he is surrounded than by millions of unknown fellow-citizens.[39]

Tarde went on to insist that persons learn crime just as they learn a trade—regardless of what characteristics one has at birth, one must learn to become criminal by association with and imitation of others.

A far more systematic and carefully formulated theory concerning the learning of crime was presented in 1939 by the American criminologist Edwin H. Sutherland (1883–1950).[40] Sutherland agreed with both Tarde and Shaw that criminal behavior patterns are transmitted within a cultural setting. But he felt that crime involved more complex learning processes than the mere imitation of others, and that social disorganization was not responsible for high rates of deviance within sections of the population. He argued that the United States is comprised of diverse cultures and that conflict between such cultures is an essential aspect of crime causation. Crime rates result, therefore, not from disorganization but from differential group organization: some groups are organized for criminal activities and some are organized against these activities.

Consistent with the concept of differential group organization is Sutherland's theory of *differential association,* the process by which conflicting norms influence the behavior of individuals.

> The formal statement of the theory indicates, for example, that a high crime rate in urban areas can be considered the end product of criminalistic traditions in those areas. . . . The important general point is that in a multigroup type of social organization, alternative and inconsistent standards of conduct are possessed by various groups, so that an individual who is a member of one group has a high probability of learning to use legal means of achieving success, or learning to deny the importance of success, while an individual in another group learns to accept the importance of success and to achieve it by illegal means.[41]

Sutherland's statement of differential association theory takes the form of nine propositions concerning the process by which individuals come to engage in criminal behavior:

1. Criminal behavior is learned. [It is not inherited nor is it the result of low intelligence, brain damage, and so on.]
2. Criminal behavior is learned in interaction with other persons in a process of communication.
3. The principal part of the learning of criminal behavior occurs within intimate personal groups. [At most, impersonal communications such as television, magazines, and newspapers, play only a secondary role in the learning of crime.]
4. When criminal behavior is learned, the learning includes (a) techniques of committing crime, which are sometimes very complicated, sometimes very simple; (b) the specific direction of motives, drives, rationalizations, and attitudes.
5. The specific direction of motives and drives is learned from definitions of the legal codes as favorable or unfavorable. [This acknowledges the existence of conflicting norms. An individual may learn reasons for both adhering to and violating a given rule. For example, stealing is wrong; that is, unless the goods are insured, when, of course, nobody really gets hurt.]
6. A person becomes delinquent because of an excess of definitions favorable to violation of law over definitions unfavorable to violation of law. [This is the key proposition of the theory. An individual's behavior is affected by contradictory learning experiences, but the predominance of pro-criminal definitions leads to criminal behavior. It is important to note that the associations are not necessarily only criminal *persons* but also definitions, norms, or patterns of behavior. Furthermore, in keeping with the notion of a learning theory, the proposition can be rephrased: A person becomes nondelinquent because of an excess of definitions unfavorable to violation of law.]
7. Differential associations may vary in frequency, duration, priority, and

intensity. [Frequency and duration are self-explanatory. Priority refers to the time in one's life when exposed to the association. Intensity concerns the prestige of the source of the behavior pattern.]

8. The process of learning criminal behavior by association with criminal and anticriminal patterns involves all of the mechanisms that are involved in any other learning. [Again, there is no unique learning process involved in acquiring deviant ways of behaving.]

9. While criminal behavior is an expression of general needs and values, it is not explained by those general needs and values, since noncriminal behavior in an expression of the same needs and values. [A "need for recognition" can be used to explain mass murder, running for president, or a .320 batting average, but it really explains nothing since it apparently accounts for both deviant and nondeviant actions.] [42]

Sutherland's theory has been subject to much research and controversy. Its most ardent defenders concede that it is too imprecise and oversimplified to satisfactorily explain how normative conflicts within society become translated into individual behavior. Furthermore, there is the seemingly insurmountable problem of testing such concepts as excess of definitions, priority, and intensity.[43] Despite these difficulties, however, no other theory has proven so consistent with the findings of research concerning the prediction of deviant behavior; [44] and attempts to find relationships between deviant behavior and associations with deviant behavior patterns have met with moderate success.[45] Thus extensive attempts have been made to modify the theory and make it more suitable for testing.

Among the more recent of such attempts is that of Melvin DeFleur and Richard Quinney who used set theory to reformulate the propositions. Sutherland's sixth proposition, "A person becomes delinquent because of an excess of definitions . . ." becomes:

Overt criminal behavior has as its necessary and sufficient conditions a set of criminal motivations, attitudes, and techniques, the learning of which takes place when there is exposure to criminal norms in excess of exposure to corresponding anticriminal norms during symbolic interaction in primary groups.[46]

This formulation clarifies the point that the associations are not simply with persons in primary groups (face-to-face relationships in small groups, which are relatively permanent, e.g., family, gang, and play groups), but also with the motives, attitudes, and techniques transmitted by those groups. It also makes clear that the learning of these motives precedes the commission of the first criminal act. Thus excluded from the theory are behaviors that might be the products of opportunity and social-psychological pressures; in these cases the attitudes and motivations might develop to justify continuation of the behavior. As DeFleur and Quinney point out:

In the Sutherland theory, opportunity is assumed; motives, attitudes, and techniques must be developed as prerequisites; and overt action results when these have been sufficiently developed through the differential association process. In an alternative theory, opportunity would be a necessary condition for crime, but some psychological or social pressure would be required to trigger the first overt action, and *attitudes and motivations* would follow as means for handling resulting anxieties, guilt, or other disturbances of the personality system. . . . Sutherland's theory, then, may not fit all crime. . . .[47]

In another reformulation, Ronald Akers rephrases the propositions in terms of reinforcement theory. Akers states the sixth proposition thusly:

The probability that a person will commit deviant behavior is increased in the presence of normative statements, definitions, and verbalizations which have acquired discriminative value for behavior in the process of differential reinforcement of such behavior over conforming behavior.[48]

We have no intention of delving into the complexities of reinforcement theory here. Risking misinterpretation through oversimplification, we suggest that the Akers proposition can be interpreted as an increased probability that a person will commit a deviant act if she or he has learned that participating in the behavior will be more rewarding than will be abstaining from it.[49] More important for our purposes are the other implications of Akers' approach. First, the primary group emphasized by Sutherland is not the sole source of influence on behavior; instead the "normative statements, definitions, and verbalizations" may also come from imaginary groups or persons portrayed in the mass media or from formal organizations such as a corporation, a school, a government, and so on. Second, Akers emphasizes more than Sutherland the importance of verbal justifications for behavior. These are excuses by which individuals can counteract the accusations and disapproval of others. Such excuses are important for dealing not only with past behavior but also, and even especially, with future behavior. They allow the individual to overcome obstacles in advance. As Akers sums it up: "The more a person defines behavior as a positive good or at least as justified, the more likely he is to engage in it.[50]

Verbalized Motives

Regardless of which interpretation of differential association one prefers, all are in agreement that a substantial proportion of deviant behavior is the normal behavior of normal individuals. Deviants are not driven by inner forces or by circumstances; they are responding to learning processes that involve reasons for behavior.

In learning deviance, we learn not only *how* to act, that is, how to shoplift or to talk an aged woman out of her life savings; we also learn reasons, stated in so many words, *why* we should act in such a manner. The expression of these reasons is most likely to arise only when one is challenged to explain his or her conduct if it has been subject to criticism.[51] For example, a person caught shoplifting might claim that the store was scarcely harmed because goods were both overpriced and insured. Now it is possible that in this particular case the individual may lie—the expressed reason was not the real one for his or her behavior. What is more important, however, is that the expressed reason or verbalized motive is apparently viewed by the shoplifter as an appropriate one. Somewhere, somehow, he or she has learned that this is a justification for shoplifting. As such, it is seen as acceptable for past, present, and future shoplifting, unless the person is convinced otherwise.

There are many types of verbalized motives of varying degrees of sophistication. Those expressed by persons whom Merton called non-conformers may be elaborate discussions concerning the immorality of the existing type of government, and how the norms enforced by that government must be directly challenged in order to cause its downfall. On the other hand, reasons may be as simple as, "I was too drunk to know what I was doing." Yet both have a ring of sincerity and seem to be understandable, if not necessarily acceptable. The point is that *reasons for deviance do exist in a society* and these reasons are met with varying degrees of acceptance depending upon the group that judges them.

For example, statements such as "I was drunk" or "I was high" may make perfect sense to you and your friends for explaining practically anything short of cannibalism and murder. In court, a judge will take a dim view of these reasons, but this does not necessarily diminish their effectiveness as motives for behavior. All of us can think of appropriate sets of circumstances and reasons for all sorts of sinful, illegal, and immoral acts. Our television shows, movies, and literature are rife with instances of persons who construct their own rules to match a particular situation, or who take the law into their own hands.

The most thorough attempt to catalog the range of possible verbalized motives for deviance is provided by Marvin Scott and Stanford Lyman:

1. Excuses—verbalized motives that admit the inappropriateness of the behavior while denying full responsibility.
   (a) Accident—victim of circumstances and human frailty. "Things happened too fast." "I was clumsy."
   (b) Defeasibility—mental processes were ineffective either be-

cause of lack of information or because they were impaired. "I didn't know they would get so upset." "I was too drunk." "I must have been crazy."

   (c) Biological Drives—victim of biological forces. "Men are like that." "It was too tempting."

   (d) Scapegoating—the fault lies primarily with the actions of others. "He got me into trouble." "She asked for it."

2. Justifications—verbalized motives that emphasize the positive aspects of actions in certain circumstances.

   (a) Denial of Injury—the harm from the action was nonexistent or trivial. "I just borrowed the car." "It was only a prank."

   (b) Denial of Victim—the victim of the action deserved what he/she got. "He was a queer." "She's a whore." "The store is a big rip-off." "The buyer should beware."

   (c) Condemnation of Condemners—the accusers are seen as hypocritical, spiteful, or stupid. "Why don't you cops quit bugging me and get back to collecting your payoffs?"

   (d) Appeal to Loyalties—sacrifices are made in favor of one's family, gang, business, or country. "I didn't do it for myself." "You never let down your family." "General Electric pays my salary." "My country—right or wrong."

   (e) Sad Tale—a dismal, depraved past is highlighted. "My father was a drunk and mother pushed cocaine." "If you came from the kind of neighborhood I did . . . ."

   (f) Self-fulfillment—the behavior is part of attaining completeness as a human being. "Acid expands the consciousness." "I didn't know love until I turned gay." [52]

The reader may have noticed that these motives are all very personal and make little reference to ultimate values or to challenging the existing values. Concern over values would characterize the arguments of nonconformers when they are asked to explain their behavior. Their reasons generally fall into the following categories:

1. Immorality of the rule—the behavior should not be questioned because the norm prohibiting it is not a legitimate one. "What someone does with his or her body is his or her own business."

2. Immorality of the system—because the government and its associated industrial-military complex are seen as both exploitive and as the makers of laws, challenges to the system may often involve violations of those laws. The stealing or destruction of corporation property is seen as both symbolic and useful in bringing the system to its knees.

From these brief descriptions it is apparent that the process of differential association involves, in part at least, the transmission of *normative definitions of situations* in the form of verbalized motives. Verbalized motives are expressed opinions about why certain situations provide opportunities and reasons for behavior otherwise forbidden. The motives can thus either facilitate the commission of acts, or can serve as explanations if and when those acts are called into question.

It is also apparent that the mere fact that someone learns and accepts the validity of a verbalized motive scarcely explains the occurrence of deviant behavior. When a person tells us, for example, that his or her behavior was an accident, there is at least an implied allegiance to the violated norm. Although the motive temporarily suspends acceptance of the norm and even excuses possible future accidents, this is not to say that the motive forces the individual into commission of an act—the motive simply allows the act.

Even when the motive involves a full-blown ideology contradicting the morality of a rule or the system imposing that rule, the motive causes behavior only to the extent that it is a critique of the power structure and an expression of intent. Verbalized motives do not drive or compel a person to shoplift or to rob a bank; they merely serve to free the individual from norms that might otherwise constrain her or his behavior in particular situations.[53]

The Situational Element

Verbalized motives constitute only a single component contributing to deviance. Another component that should be mentioned, though it is an obvious one, is opportunity. Horse theft is rare in Manhattan, as is auto theft in Timbuktu, Mali. To some extent the array of open counters and the scarcity of personnel in discount stores contribute to shoplifting. Even assuming the existence of opportunity, however, the situation also contributes to the likelihood deviance will occur, and it may be as important as verbalized motives.[54]

Consider the case of someone discovering an expensive automobile with keys in the ignition and parked in an unprotected area. To take the car rather than ignoring the situation or reporting it to the police, one must have learned that this is an opportunity to be used to one's own advantage. In this regard we are referring to the role of verbalized motives. As an admittedly extreme example here, the nonconformist may see such a situation as a chance to strike a blow against the power structure by ripping off the capitalist who obviously owns the car. But even this potential act of theft may not occur. The individual well-equipped with motives may pass by the opportunity for a variety of reasons—too busy today, just don't feel like it, and so on.

The point is that the immediate situation may contribute positively or negatively to deviance by providing pressures toward or away from the behavior. In the previous example, the situation was not "right" for theft to occur. But consider the case of a male who, desperate for a means to impress a girl friend, comes upon an identical opportunity. He may find this a fortuitous answer to his problem, imagining the reaction when he wheels up to her apartment.

Automobile theft or any deviant act may be a response to situational pressures. It may be seen as a way of dealing with circumstances; it may be considered necessary in order to prove a point to someone; or it may simply be a means to obtain needed funds. As an example, Don Gibbons points out that some acts of violence represent a combination of what we have called verbalized motives and situational factors:

> The experience of growing up in a subcultural setting where violence is a common theme is a precondition for violent acts, but . . . specific instances of aggression and homicide do not occur until other events transpire, such as a marital dispute while drinking. . . . The available research evidence indicates that forcible rapists are usually working-class males from a social situation where exploitative and aggressive themes regarding females are commonplace. But, only a small number of those males who regard sexual intercourse as something to be done *to* rather than *with* a female, or who express similar attitudes, become involved in forcible rape. One of the most important factors . . . increasing the likelihood that forcible rape will occur, may be the situational one of sexually provocative interaction between a male and female during an evening of drinking.[55]

Other examples of situational pressures contributing to deviance include non-shareable problems that lead to violations of financial trust and the general situational context in which vandalism develops. In the first instance, it has been found that misuse of entrusted funds is preceded by financial problems that individuals feel they cannot reveal to anyone else.[56] Juvenile vandalism has been found to include a high degree of pressure to involve everyone in the group once the destruction begins.[57]

The means by which situational elements precipitate and influence deviance have not been systematically studied. Therefore, the importance of these elements relative to other components, such as verbalized motives and opportunity, can only be hinted at through the use of specific examples, as above. Clearly, however, any attempt to explain violations of norms must consider the context in which the violations occur.

Conclusion

In the first chapter we dealt with explanations concerning what type of person is deviant. The theorists introduced in that chapter had all attempted to discover how deviants could be distinguished from nondeviants in order to answer the question, "Why do persons with X characteristic act that way?" The present chapter has shifted the focus toward *deviance as a group product*. The reader probably has already recognized that the change did not significantly alter the question asked, "Why do persons in X-type of class (or society, subculture, and so on) act that way?"

Whether we ask about brain damage, disjunction between goals and means, or verbalized motives, we are asking about factors determining behavior. We are still dealing with deviants as a distinct class of persons whose characteristics or experiences are detectably different from those of us who adhere to the path of goodness and righteousness. Although it is probably true that we are closer to an understanding of deviant behavior than we were half a century ago, the state of our knowledge is far from satisfactory.

Much of the difficulty lies in the single-minded attempt to explain the deviant's behavior. There is, as we discussed, the problem of bias in official statistics that makes the identification of deviants complicated at best. But detection and recognition of deviants are only part of the issue. Nearly all the approaches discussed so far rest on the critical but doubtful assumption that concensus exists over what behavior is socially expected, and that therefore the distinction between deviant and non-deviant behavior is obvious.

Sutherland and others have pointed out that whether persons adhere to rules depends upon the meanings that the rules have. People do differ in their evaluation of the appropriateness of particular rules for themselves as well as for others. We can, of course, continue to ask how people learn negative opinions toward some rules and why they persist in holding such opinions, but we then avoid dealing with the nature of the rules themselves. By concentrating on the individual and his or her behavior we ignore a fundamental issue. *What makes the behavior itself deviant?* It follows that if there is conflict over the appropriateness of rules, the distinction between deviant and non-deviant behavior is not obvious. To understand the nature of such behavior, it is necessary to consider perspectives other than those focusing exclusively upon either individuals or rates of behavior.

NOTES

1. For discussions of early ecologists see: Harwin L. Voss and David M. Petersen, eds., *Ecology, Crime, and Delinquency* (New York: Appleton-Century-Crofts, 1971), pp. 1–4; Leon Radzinowicz, *Ideology and Crime* (New York: Columbia University Press, 1966), pp. 29–38; Terence Morris, *The Criminal Area: A Study in Social Ecology* (London: Routledge & Kegan Paul, 1957), pp. 44–52; and Hermann Mannheim, *Comparative Criminology* (Boston: Houghton Mifflin, 1965), pp. 95–98.

2. Lambert A. J. Quetelet, *A Treatise on Man and the Development of His Faculties*, a facsimile reproduction of the English translation of 1842 (Gainesville, Florida: Scholars' Fascimiles & Reprints, 1969), p. 6.

3. Ibid., cf., p. 108.

4. Radzinowicz, *Ideology and Crime*, pp. 38–39.

5. George B. Vold, *Theoretical Criminology* (New York: Oxford University Press, 1958), pp. 159–182; Stephen Schafer, *Theories in Criminology: Past and Present Philosophies of the Crime Problem* (New York: Random House, 1969), pp. 255–290; and Leon Radzinowicz, "Economic Pressures," in *Crime and Justice, The Criminal in Society*, Vol. 1, eds. Leon Radzinowicz and Marvin E. Wolfgang (New York: Basic Books, 1971), pp. 420–442.

6. Ian Taylor, Paul Walton, and Jock Young, *The New Criminology: For a Social Theory of Deviance* (London: Routledge & Kegan Paul, 1973), p. 218. For a detailed discussion of Marxian thought on deviance, see pp. 209–221.

7. Karl Marx, *Theories of Surplus Value* (Moscow: Foreign Languages Publishing House, n.d.), pp. 375–376; reprinted in *Monthly Review*, **22** (December 1970), pp. 38–40.

8. Based upon Austin T. Turk, Introduction, *Criminality and Economic Conditions*, William Bonger, abridged by Austin T. Turk (Bloomington: Indiana University Press, 1969), pp. 7–12.

9. Bonger, *Criminality and Economic Conditions*, pp. 194–195.

10. Frank W. Blackmar, "The Smoky Pilgrims," *American Journal of Sociology*, **2** (January 1897), p. 489.

11. Ibid., p. 499.

12. Emile Durkheim, *The Rules of Sociological Method*, 8th ed., trans. Sarah A. Solovay and John H. Mueller (Glencoe, Ill.: Free Press, 1938), pp. 67–69.

13. Ibid., p. 70 (italics mine).

14. Ibid., p. 71.

15. Richard R. Korn and Lloyd W. McCorkle, *Criminology and Penology* (New York: Holt, Rinehart, and Winston, 1959), pp. 276–278.

16. For a detailed history of the development of the concept of anomie see Marshall B. Clinard, "The Theoretical Implications of Anomie and Deviant Behavior,'" in *Anomie and Deviant Behavior: A Discussion and Critique*, ed. Marshall B. Clinard (New York: Free Press, 1964), pp. 1–56.

17. For a critique of Durkheim's work see Jack D. Douglas, *The Social Meanings of Suicide* (Princeton, N.J.: Princeton University Press, 1967), pp. 3–76.

18. Emile Durkheim, *Suicide: A Study in Sociology*, trans. John A. Spaulding and George Simpson (Glencoe, Ill.: Free Press, 1951), p. 256.

19. Robert K. Merton, "Social Structure and Anomie," *American Sociological Review*, **3** (October 1938), pp. 672–682. For a revised discussion see Merton, *Social Theory and Social Structure*, revised and enlarged ed. (Glencoe, Ill.: Free Press, 1957), pp. 131–194.

20. Merton, *Social Theory and Social Structure*, p. 146.

21. Ibid., p. 162.

22. *New York Times*, August 25, 1973, p. 25; October 6, 1973, p. 21; and October 24, 1973, p. 15.

23. Robert K. Merton, "Social Problems and Sociological Theory," in *Con-*

temporary Social Problems, 3rd ed., eds. Robert K. Merton and Robert Nisbet (New York: Harcourt Brace Jovanovich, 1971), pp. 829–831.

24. Maynard L. Erickson, "Group Violations, Socioeconomic Status and Official Delinquency," *Social Forces*, **52** (September 1973), p. 51. See also: Paul Lerman, "Gangs, Networks, and Subcultural Delinquency," *American Journal of Sociology*, **73** (July 1967), pp. 63–72; and LaMar T. Empey and Steven G. Lubeck, *The Silverlake Experiment: Testing Delinquency Theory and Community Intervention* (Chicago: Aldine, 1971), pp. 119–133.

25. Jack D. Douglas, "Deviance and Order in a Pluralistic Society," in *Theoretical Sociology: Perspectives and Developments*, eds. John C. McKinney and Edward A. Tiryakian (New York: Appleton-Century-Crofts, 1970), p. 373.

26. For detailed critiques see: Clinard, *Anomie and Deviant Behavior;* Taylor, et al., *The New Criminology*, pp. 92–110; and Edwin M. Lemert, *Human Deviance, Social Problems, and Social Control*, 2nd ed. (Englewood Cliffs, N.J.: Prentice-Hall, 1972), pp. 26–61.

27. This discussion draws heavily upon Jack D. Douglas, "Deviance and Order in a Pluralistic Society," pp. 392–399.

28. Ibid., p. 397.

29. Ibid., pp. 397–398.

30. Albert K. Cohen, *Deviance and Control* (Englewood Cliffs, N.J.: Prentice-Hall, 1966), pp. 93–97.

31. Travis Hirschi, *Causes of Delinquency* (Berkeley: University of California Press, 1969), pp. 11–15.

32. Terence Morris, *The Criminal Area: A Study in Social Ecology* (London: Routledge & Kegan Paul, 1957), p. 41.

33. Amos H. Hawley, *Human Ecology: A Theory of Community Structure* (New York: Ronald Press, 1950), pp. 5–6, as quoted in Voss and Petersen, *Ecology, Crime, and Delinquency*, p. 9.

34. Clifford R. Shaw, *Delinquency Areas: A Study of the Geographic Distribution of School Truants, Juvenile Delinquents, and Adult Offenders in Chicago* (Chicago: University of Chicago Press, 1929), pp. 198–204.

35. Ibid., pp. 205–206 (italics mine).

36. For a critique of social disorganization as a concept see Marshall B. Clinard, *Sociology of Deviant Behavior*, 3rd ed. (New York: Holt, Rinehart and Winston, 1968), pp. 41–44.

37. Clifford R. Shaw and Henry D. McKay, *Juvenile Delinquency and Urban Areas* (Chicago: University of Chicago Press, 1942), pp. 166–167.

38. Some of the milestones in theories of gang delinquency are: Frederic M. Thrasher, *The Gang* (Chicago: University of Chicago Press, 1927); Solomon Kobrin, "The Conflict of Values in Delinquency Areas," *American Sociological Review*, **16** (October 1951), pp. 653–661; Albert K. Cohen, *Delinquent Boys: The Culture of the Gang* (Glencoe, Ill.: Free Press, 1955); Richard A. Cloward and Lloyd E. Ohlin, *Delinquency and Opportunity: Theory of Delinquent Gangs* (New York: Free Press, 1960); Lewis Yablonsky, *The Violent Gang* (New York: Macmillan, 1962); and James F. Short, Jr. and Fred L. Strodtbeck, *Group Process and Gang Delinquency* (Chicago: University of Chicago Press, 1965). See also David J. Bordua, "Delinquent Subcultures: Sociological Interpretations of Gang Delinquency," *The Annals of the American Academy of Political and Social Science*, **338** (November 1961), pp.

120–136; and Paul Lerman, "Individual Values, Peer Values, and Subcultural Delinquency," *American Sociological Review,* **33** (April 1968), pp. 219–235.

39. Gabriel Tarde, *Penal Philosophy,* trans. Rapelje Howell (Boston: Little, Brown, 1912), pp. 252–253.

40. Edwin H. Sutherland, *Principles of Criminology,* 3rd ed. (Philadelphia: J. B. Lippincott, 1939), pp. 4–9. For a discussion of the evolution of the theory see *The Sutherland Papers,* eds. Albert K. Cohen, Alfred Lindesmith, and Karl Schuessler (Bloomington: Indiana University Press, 1956), pp. 5–43.

41. Edwin H. Sutherland and Donald R. Cressey, *Criminology,* 9th ed. (Philadelphia: J. B. Lippincott, 1974), pp. 88–89.

42. Ibid., pp. 75–77.

43. A thorough review of the state of the theory will be found in Donald R. Cressey, "Epidemiology and Individual Conduct: A Case from Criminology," *Pacific Sociological Review,* **3** (Fall 1960), pp. 47–58.

44. Daniel Glaser, "Differential Association and Criminological Prediction," *Social Problems,* **8** (Summer 1960), pp. 6–14.

45. Ronald L. Akers, *Deviant Behavior: A Social Learning Approach* (Belmont, Calif.: Wadsworth Publishing, 1973), pp. 41–42.

46. Melvin L. DeFleur and Richard Quinney, "A Reformulation of Sutherland's Differential Association Theory and a Strategy for Empirical Verification," *Journal of Research in Crime and Delinquency,* **3** (January 1966), p. 7.

47. Ibid., p. 21.

48. Akers, *Deviant Behavior,* p. 46.

49. For discussions of reinforcement theory as applied to differential association see: Akers, *Deviant Behavior,* pp. 45–61; Robert K. Burgess and Ronald L. Akers, "A Differential Association-Reinforcement Theory of Criminal Behavior," *Social Problems,* **14** (Fall 1966), pp. 128–147; and Reed Adams, "Differential Association and Learning Principles Revisited," *Social Problems,* **20** (Spring 1973), pp. 458–470.

50. Akers, *Deviant Behavior,* p. 287.

51. This discussion draws upon C. Wright Mills, "Situated Actions and Vocabularies of Motive," *American Sociological Review,* **5** (December 1940), pp. 904–913; and Donald R. Cressey, *Other People's Money: A Study in the Social Psychology of Embezzlement* (Belmont, Calif.: Wadsworth Publishing, 1971), pp. 93–138. See also: Marvin B. Scott and Stanford M. Lyman, "Accounts," *American Sociological Review,* **33** (February 1968), pp. 46–62; and Scott and Lyman, "Accounts, Deviance, and Social Order," in *Deviance and Respectability: The Social Construction of Moral Meanings,* ed. Jack D. Douglas (New York: Basic Books, 1970), pp. 89–119.

52. The classification system is found in Scott and Lyman, "Accounts"; some of the examples were drawn from there and from Gresham M. Sykes and David Matza, "Techniques of Neutralization: A Theory of Delinquency," *American Sociological Review,* **22** (December 1957), pp. 664–670.

53. The role of verbalized motives generally and techniques of neutralization particularly are subject to intense debate. See Travis Hirschi, *Causes of Delinquency* (Berkeley: University of California Press, 1969), pp. 23–26; and Taylor et al., *The New Criminology,* pp. 175–188.

54. Situational pressures toward deviance are discussed by Don C. Gibbons, "Observations on the Study of Crime Causation," *American Journal of Sociology,* 77 (September 1971), pp. 262–278.

55. Ibid., pp. 274–275.

56. Cressey, *Other People's Money,* pp. 33–76.

57. Andrew L. Wade, "Social Processes in the Act of Juvenile Vandalism," in *Criminal Behavior Systems: A Typology,* eds. Marshall B. Clinard and Richard Quinney (New York: Holt, Rinehart and Winston, 1967), pp. 94–109.

3 WHY IS BEHAVIOR DEVIANT?

Although it may seem logical to probe the reasons why people do not always act the way we would prefer, we must realize that our preferences spring from a particular perspective, namely, our personal view of what the world should be. Whether we call something deviant out of fear, loathing, envy, or disgust, we are making a judgment that the behavior is disagreeable. But even when behavior does not meet our personal notions of social expectations, this does not mean we are interested in actively seeking either its cause or suppression. Priorities and time limitations dictate the degree of our concern over others' behavior.

We ourselves behave in a world filled with expectations that others have of our behavior. For example, a sign telling us that the speed limit is thirty-five miles per hour is a tangible indication of a rule made by others and imposed upon us. The rule may not reflect our cautious nature and driving skills, but the rule is there—like it or not. We also know that we technically break the law by exceeding thirty-five by even a single mile. But we know, of course, that we are good drivers; it would be a source of considerable aggravation to be stopped by police for going anything less than forty miles per hour. We are aware of the law but we also know our capabilities.

None of this alters the fact that the policeman is perfectly within his authority either to warn us or to issue a ticket for traveling thirty-six miles per hour. Ticket or no, however, we are simply unwilling to accept that we are speeders in the same sense as those going fifty-five or more. If we are not "speeders" at thirty-six miles per hour, when are we— thirty-seven, forty, forty-three? At what speed do we become "serious" violators: "reckless," "irresponsible," and a "menace to the community"?

This simple example points out that expectations concerning our behavior are not always of our making, and that violations of expectations may result in a variety of reactions. Decisions are constantly being made by others about the appropriateness of our behavior. But everyone makes similar decisions about everyone else. We pass judgment on the morality, normalcy, and legality of other people's behavior every day. Furthermore, we respond toward persons according to those judgments by hollering at them, ignoring them, calling the cops, and so forth.

But our individual judgments about others and how they should be dealt with usually have little impact beyond our families and circle of friends. There are those, however, who say, "There ought to be a law"—and there is a law. Or they say, "He should be committed," or "She should go to prison,"—and it is done. These decisions have wide social consequences and have been practically ignored in the perspectives discussed so far. Decision-making about what the rules shall be, who has broken them, and what should be done about the violators is the crux of the approaches to deviance considered in the first parts of this chapter.

Labeling Perspective

The nature and consequences of rule-making and rule enforcement are the bases of a sociological approach variously known as the *labeling, societal reaction,* or *interactionist perspective.*[1] This approach, which we shall call the *labeling perspective,* deals with two fundamental problems: the social production of deviance and the effect of labeling on behavior. Unlike traditional approaches that assume deviance is simply a violation of commonly accepted norms and that offenders must be different in ways that cause deviance, the labeling perspective shifts to the audience—those who define persons and their behavior.

THE PRODUCTION OF DEVIANCE

The reaction toward deviance is a matter of decision-making. This raises a serious question. Does it make sense to call all rule-breaking behavior deviant? From the labeling perspective, the answer is emphatically no. A principal spokesman for this view, Howard S. Becker, points out that the enforcement of a rule is highly variable and problematic. Whether others will respond to rule-breaking, and the degree of that response once it comes, depend upon many circumstances including who is violating the rule, who feels they are being harmed, and the context (time, place, and so on) in which the rule-breaking behavior occurs. Consequently, argues Becker, a distinction must be made between rule-breaking and deviance.

> Deviance is not a simple quality, present in some kinds of behavior and absent in others. Rather, it is the product of a process which involves responses of other people to the behavior. . . . Whether a given act is deviant or not depends in part on the nature of the act (that is, whether or not it violates some rule) and in part on what other people do about it.
>
> Some people may object that this is merely a terminological quibble, that one can, after all, define terms any way he wants to and that if some people want to speak of rule-breaking behavior as deviant without reference to the reactions of others they are free to do so. This, of course, is true, yet it might be worthwhile to refer to such behavior as *rule-breaking behavior* and reserve the term *deviant* for those labeled as deviant by some segment of society. . . . Deviance is not a quality that lies in behavior itself, but in the interaction between the person who commits an act and those who respond to it.[2]

This distinction between rule-breaking behavior and deviant behavior lies at the heart of the labeling perspective. The distinction is not a matter of terminological quibble. Instead, it serves to shift attention away from the characteristics of persons who break rules toward persons who make and apply those rules. Thus when Becker says that deviance is "created" by society he is not saying that behavior is caused by social factors such as a disjunction between goals and means, but that:

> *Social groups create deviance by making the rules whose infraction constitutes deviance,* and by applying those rules to particular people and labeling them outsiders. From this point of view, deviance is *not* a quality of the act the person commits, but rather a consequence of the application by others of rules and sanctions to an "offender." The deviant is one to whom that label has successfully been applied; deviant behavior is behavior that people so label.[3]

To claim that social groups create deviance in this sense is to abandon the traditional positivist concern with explaining rule-breaking behavior. The reader will recall that one criticism of positivist research is focused on the assumption that persons designated as criminals accurately represent the population of those who break the criminal law. A related assumption made by the social determinists is that official rates of deviance reflect the distribution of the behavior within society. The labeling perspective recognizes that sanctions against rule-breaking are not meted out on an indiscriminate basis regardless of race, color, class, sex, intelligence, or any other characteristic. Instead of dealing with questions of why people break rules, the labeling perspective examines the reasons and circumstances under which rules are made and certain rule-breakers become the target of official action. In the words of Kai T. Erikson:

> Deviance is not a property *inherent in* certain forms of behavior; it is a property *conferred upon* these forms by the audiences which directly or indirectly witness them. The critical variable in the study of deviance, then, is the social audience which eventually determines whether or not any episode of behavior or any class of episodes is labeled deviant.[4]

The labeling perspective leans heavily upon a relativistic concept of deviance since it is assumed that the making and enforcing of rules is both inconsistent and problematic. Deviance, according to Becker, is a product of "enterprise." It is the result of efforts by persons who, perceiving a threat, act as "moral entrepreneurs" to obtain appropriate legislation and enforcement in order to bring the behavior under control. Thus the perspective provides no estimations or explanations of initial entrance into rule-breaking behavior. Official statistics are useful only as a measure of labeler's activities. According to John Kitsuse and Aaron Cicourel:

> Rates of deviant behavior are produced by *the actions taken by persons in the social system* which define, classify and record certain behavior as deviant. . . . The persons who define and activate the rate-producing processes may range from the neighborhood "busybody" to officials of law enforcement agencies. From this point of view, *deviant behavior* is behavior which is organizationally defined, processed, and treated as "strange," "abnormal," "theft," "delinquent," etc., by the personnel in the social system which has produced the rate.[5]

Because deviance is the product of "rate-producing processes" it logically follows in the labeling perspective that the amount of deviance recorded is limited by the capacity of the apparatus to handle deviants. Erikson argues that there will be only as many criminals as the efficiency of the law enforcement system will allow; there will be only as many mentally disordered as the available psychiatric diagnostic system will permit. However, these processes will not underproduce either. The definition of what is to be called deviant will expand and contract in order to maintain a more or less constant flow:

> The community develops its definition of deviance so that it encompasses a range of behavior roughly equivalent to the available space in its control apparatus—a kind of inverted Parkinson's law. That is, when the community calibrates its control machinery to handle a certain volume of deviant

behavior, it tends to adjust its legal and psychiatric definitions of the problem in such a way that this volume is in fact realized. . . . If the police should somehow learn to contain most of the crimes it now contends with, and if at the same time medical science should discover a cure for most of the mental disorders it now treats, it is still improbable that the existing control machinery would go unused. More likely, the agencies of control would turn their attention to other forms of behavior, even to the point of defining as deviant certain styles of conduct which were not regarded so earlier.[6]

Unquestionably, the labeling perspective emphasizes an easily overlooked fact: rules are the products of social definitions. What is criminal or deviant depends upon what groups decide is threatening, disgusting, and so on, and upon the ability of those groups to persuade legislators and other rule-makers. Who will be criminal or deviant is likewise a matter of decision-making by persons and agencies responsible for enforcing rules. Power relationships, rule-making processes and labeling patterns by police, courts, and other agencies are all aspects of the production of deviance.

However, the reader should be alert to recognize that the explanation of the "production of deviance" should not be confused with an explanation of the occurrence of rule-breaking behavior.[7] Durkheim argued over a half century ago that the criminal character of acts was not due to "the intrinsic quality of a given act but that definition which the collective conscience lends them." [8] And Bonger emphasized that the criminal law prohibited behaviors that the powerful regarded as most dangerous to their interests. The labeling perspective, then, scarcely tells us anything new but does serve to reacquaint us with the fact that groups deem what shall or shall not be approved behavior.

Labeling advocates rightly bring to our attention the fact that rules are not always based on the wishes of all, or even a majority for that matter. Furthermore, the interpretations of the rules are frequently arbitrary and their enforcement selective. This is most clearly evident in reference to official rules such as the criminal law. Who is subject to sanctions and the severity of those sanctions are often contingent upon such factors as the social class, sex, color, and age of the offenders rather than upon the nature of the offenses. Furthermore, persons and agencies responsible for rule enforcement do make mistakes, real or intended, whereby the guilty go free and the innocent suffer. Thus, to some extent, social control agencies produce deviants independent of the individuals' behaviors.

The fact that our courts and prisons are filled with persons of lower socioeconomic status tells us something about the character of the criminal law and the enforcement policies behind it. But the composition of the prisons and courts is also a reflection, distorted though it may be, of actual behavior. Most persons in prison probably did commit homicide, rape, robbery, drug offenses, and so on. To this extent the labeling perspective supplements, not replaces, more traditional approaches toward deviance. *The perspective is a recognition that the meaning of behavior is socially derived; although it does not deal with the source or cause of the behavior, it insists that the reaction to behavior is a topic for investigation.*

At this point the reader may be wondering whether the labeling perspective may be more applicable to some acts and persons than to others. It obviously has relevance to cases of rule-making that result from a conflict between moral positions. Cases in point would be laws regarding the use of alcohol, the use of certain drugs, participation in certain sexual practices, and involvement in gambling. In such instances, the creation of morality and the manner in which agencies enforce that morality may fly in the face of established behavior patterns and may be subject to considerable misunderstanding, if not resentment, plus disobedience among those directly affected.

On the other hand, are there not actions that involve little if any moral conflict regarding their definition? Is not deviance more inherent than conferred in some cases? In short, may not the labeling perspective be too relativistic?

This is an issue on which there is considerable debate.[9] One may try to point to certain universal values such as taboos against murder, yet in practice it is difficult to find a universal application of such values even within a single society. For example, if you lace a roommate's candy with roach killer it seems unlikely that you or anyone else will spend much time pondering whether you have committed a deviant act. Yet, whether you will be labeled deviant still remains problematic. If you can afford a good lawyer, the jury may be convinced the act was an accident or in self-defense. If you cannot afford a good lawyer you will probably be convicted as a murderer.

But, you might argue, this still begs the question about the value of human life in American society. Some people may be able to get away with murder occasionally, but murder is still seen as wrong, isn't it? The trouble is, as the labeling perspective points out, there is little consensus as to what constitutes such acts as murder, or for that matter, rape, theft, and so on. You are not supposed to feed insect killer to your friends, but tobacco companies advertise and sell products that are just as likely to result in disease and death. Many manufacturing firms ignore safety standards for their employees in the pursuit of profits. Migrant children are often expected to work in fields just sprayed with poisonous pesticides. In most states there is legally no such thing as the rape of a wife by her husband.

The list could go on but many more examples will be forthcoming in greater detail in chapters ahead. The point is that what is officially defined as deviant is tied to interest groups and power. Recognition of that fact is essential to an understanding of the contribution of the labeling perspective.

THE EFFECT OF LABELING ON BEHAVIOR

The discussion so far should not lead the reader to believe that the behavior of deviants is of no interest to the labeling perspective. To the contrary, at the heart of the perspective lies the assumption that *labeling not only involves the defining of persons and their behavior, but may also heighten the likelihood that the behavior will continue.* Note that this differs from the traditional positivist approach, which sought the cause of the original behavior. The labeling approach ignores this problem in favor of explaining how individuals become committed to deviance and how their deviant behavior becomes stabilized. Or, to put it another way: Why do people undertake *deviant careers?*

The scholar who has most thoroughly explored this aspect of labeling is Edwin M. Lemert. In 1951 Lemert introduced a distinction between *primary* and *secondary deviance.* Primary deviance is violation of norms stemming from original causes, which may be any of several social, situational, physiological, and psychological factors. An example suggested by Lemert is that of heavy drinking of liquor. Initially it may be undertaken for one or more of a variety of personal reasons: death of a loved one, feelings of failure, group pressures, and so on. So long as such deviance can be tolerated and incorporated into an otherwise nondeviant image the deviant behavior will remain primary and of little consequence for either the individual or those viewing her or his behavior. However, should the drinking precipitate an adverse reaction from others and nevertheless continue unabated, it is possible that the drinking can eventually be attributed not to the original causes, but to new problems created by the unfavorable reactions.[10] At this point the deviance becomes secondary. In Lemert's words:

> When a person begins to employ his deviant behavior or role based upon it as a means of defense, attack, or adjustment to the overt and covert problems created by the consequent societal reaction to him, his deviation is secondary.[11]

The sequence of events leading to secondary deviance is roughly as follows:

> (1) primary deviation; (2) social penalties; (3) further primary deviation; (4) stronger penalties and rejections; (5) further deviation, perhaps with hostilities and resentment beginning to focus upon those doing the penalizing; (6) crisis reached in the tolerance quotient, expressed in formal action

by the community stigmatizing of the deviant; (7) strengthening of the deviant conduct as a reaction to the stigmatizing and penalties; (8) ultimate acceptance of deviant social status and efforts at adjustment on the basis of the associated role.[12]

Howard Becker expands upon this theme by introducing the notion of a deviant career sequence, each step of which involves "career contingencies" or factors that are necessary to insure that the individual moves to the next stage in that career. According to Becker, an important contengency is the experience of being publicly accused of being deviant. This has serious consequences, not the least of which is a new public identity. Jake the plumber becomes Jake the queer. Sally the treasurer becomes Sally the thief.

Along with this new identity come revised expectations and treatment from the public. There is the possibility that both Sally and Jake will end up in prison with all of its consequences. But even without this extreme outcome, both will experience diminished participation in activities that had been natural before. Jake will no longer be involved in Boy Scouts, even though his sexual behavior may have had nothing to do with minors. Sally will find herself uninvited to parties and dates, although her misuse of funds may not have harmed any of her acquaintances. Both will now be seen as persons who cannot be trusted, as persons others do not wish to be involved with.

The results of this treatment are twofold: first, it effectively limits the deviants' contacts with the legitimate world, thus making contacts with the illegitimate appear as more acceptable alternatives; second, the images projected upon deviants may alter the self-concepts of the deviants. Sally comes to see herself as a thief, and Jake will decide he is a queer, thus accepting many of the public's views of what that term implies.

The final step in the deviant career sequence is to move into an organized deviant group, an alternative more relevant for Jake than for Sally. Forced out of the mainstream of society into the gay subculture with its organizations, bars, argot, and life-style, Jake finds both justifications for his homosexuality and other individuals sympathetic with him. As mentioned in Chapter 2, subcultures provide support for deviant behavior by giving it a positive evaluation. In the gay subculture Jake can engage in homosexuality with far less difficulty and guilt than he experienced when first entering the career sequence.[13]

Admittedly, we have oversimplified the nature of Lemert's and Becker's discussions. Nevertheless, the reader can see that a major proposition of the labeling perspective is

Rule-breakers become entrenched in deviant roles because they are labeled "deviant" by others and are consequently excluded from resuming normal roles in the community.[14]

Or, put another way:

> Societal reaction in the form of labeling or official typing, and consequent stigmatizing, leads to an altered identity in the actor, necessitating a reconstitution of the self.[15]

In neither Lemert's process of secondary deviance nor Becker's deviant career sequence is there an implication that the processes invariably result from labeling, or that eventual commitment to deviance necessarily requires such processes. At most these authors are indicating how societal reaction *can* contribute to future deviant conduct. Just how important such reaction is for explaining the extent or likelihood of career deviance is subject to much discussion and fortified by little empirical evidence.[16] Available evidence does indicate that some deviant careers (embezzlers, some check forgers, and many homosexuals) develop without the experience of labeling. On the other hand, it is obvious that many deviants must adjust their self-concepts and life-styles to cope with actual or potential societal reaction. Although there may be a core of deviants whose careers have been directly affected by societal reaction, the degree to which the labeling perspective can explain career deviance remains uncertain.

Part of the uncertainty stems from the variety of types of reactions. Official reaction is relatively easy to understand and measure. A person is arrested, incarcerated, and spends so many months "being reacted against." But the nature of the audience doing the reacting is not always the police, courts, and prison officials. Other audiences are informal: friends and family who in subtle or not-so-subtle ways indicate what they think of a person's behavior. Perhaps a real audience is not even necessary. The labeling could take place just as effectively if the audience is a representation in the actor's mind—he or she witnesses, labels, and may even punish him or herself without reference to what others actually do. Thus persons respond to potential social reaction by taking into account what others might do should the rule-breaking activity become known.

There are other issues under debate concerning the labeling perspective of which the reader should be aware:

1. By minimizing the importance of explaining initial (primary) deviance, whatever meaning the behavior originally had for the deviant is ignored as a contributor to subsequent behavior. Although societal reaction may become a crucial factor in behavior, it is questionable that whatever purpose or reward the behavior first held is invariably replaced. For example, if a person first steals for thrills, do thrills fail to be a factor once societal reaction has taken its toll?

2. The perspective ignores the deterrent effect of societal reaction. We are presented with an interesting dilemma. The very means used to discourage behavior may actually encourage it. Not surprisingly,

the question of whether reaction stifles or generates behavior remains the subject of considerable argument.[17]

3. The perspective ignores the deviant actor as capable of choice. The impression often emerging from the perspective is that once the individual has become involved in the labeling process he or she is more or less forced into further behavior compounding the problem. As Paul Schervish points out:

> There is a persistent overtone of deterministic language and imagery. The labelee is spoken of as "victimized"; he is "imputed" a label; he is under "compulsion." For example, while bowing to the fact that "reality is not wholly like that," [Elliot] Freidson explicitly maintains a perspective that "sees the individual as a pawn or victim of others' conceptions of him, and of the structure of agencies into which he happens to get pushed." [18]

Although it is true that deviants may be pawns of the powerful, this does not mean that deviants are powerless to resist, to alter their behavior, or to acquire power themselves.

Conflict Perspectives

In Chapter 2 the reader was introduced to the works of Karl Marx and Willem Bonger who first viewed deviance as the product of *economic conflict*. Marxian theory concerns how the economic organization of capitalistic societies places power in the hands of a single class, namely, the owners of the means of production. Although Marx did not deal directly with the issue, it is inferred from his writings that deviance stems from attempts by the powerless to cope with their exploitation and poverty. It was Bonger who applied Marxian theory specifically to explaining deviance. He argued that economic conflicts destroy human beings' feelings for one another. This egoism consequently causes crime among both the proletariat and the bourgeoisie. The criminal law, however, is made and enforced primarily for the benefit of the bourgeoisie in order to protect its interests.

We will now consider several conflict approaches to deviance suggested by more contemporary American authors. One of these, Richard Quinney, extends a Marxian interpretation to the United States. The others, Sellin, Vold, and Turk, agree that deviance is a product of conflict, and that criminal law emerges from groups whose ethics and interests are not necessarily those of the larger population. However, unlike Quinney, none of these latter authors view American society as split into two opposing camps: the ruling class and the powerless. Instead, Sellin, Vold, and Turk see it as being composed of many interest groups maneuvering to protect their own interests and having various degrees of influence over the government in general and the legal system in particular.

Basic to any conflict perspective is the assumption that whichever groups can exert the greatest influence on the legislative and the enforcement processes are most assured that their interests will be protected. What is illegal depends upon the outcome of struggles between concerned parties. Who is treated as criminal depends upon the bureaucratic interpretation of both law and behavior.

Defining and treating behavior does not mean, of course, the end of the conflict. From the conflict perspective the existence of behavior that is defined as deviant indicates that a struggle between interest groups is in progress. On both sides are those who, guided by norms they believe correct for their purposes, pursue interests threatening to the other side. One side, however, has an advantage of the legal means to discourage the other's actions. Perhaps there is no better example of this condition than the case of immigrants from one culture who find themselves under the control of those from the host culture.

CULTURE CONFLICT.

During the 1930s there was considerable interest among social scientists in the problems of immigrants in the United States. In 1938, Thorsten Sellin published a pamphlet, *Culture Conflict and Crime*, concerning the relationship between immigration and crime.[19] Early in this work, which was to become a milestone in the American conflict perspective, Sellin discusses the nature of criminal law. He sees the law as representing the values treasured by dominant interest groups in society, groups which may not, however, be in the majority.

He continues his discussion by pointing out that human beings are born into cultures that provide meanings to behavior, including the norms governing that behavior. As society becomes more complex an individual cannot possibly identify with or adhere to all norms, because the norms themselves will not be consistent with one another.

> A person who as a member of a family group . . . possesses all its norms pertaining to conduct in routine life situations, may also as a member of a play group, a work group, a political group, a religious group, etc., acquire norms which regulate specialized life situations and which sustain, weaken, or even contradict the norms earlier incorporated in his personality. The more complex a culture becomes, the more likely it is that the number of normative groups which affect a person will be large, and the greater is the chance that the norms of these groups will fail to agree, no matter how much they may overlap as a result of a common acceptance of certain norms.[20]

Thus, according to Sellin, it makes little sense to speak of "antisocial" behavior because it is the group and its norms which determine whether a behavior is "normal" or not.

He next deals with the question of how conflicts of norms come about. He feels that they result from two processes:

1. *Cultural Growth.* Society becomes diverse because of population growth, intermingling of cultures, competitive interests, increased technology, and so on. As a result persons living in such a society find themselves in situations governed by conflicting norms; no matter which course they take they will violate the norms of some concerned group. This process described by Sellin is consistent with the notion of moral pluralism discussed earlier. But Sellin spends little time in developing this theme. The major thrust of his discussion concerns migration of norms.

2. *Migration of Norms.* Sellin argues that conflicts of cultures are inevitable when the norms of one come into contact with those of another. These clashes may occur in any one of the following circumstances: (a) when cultural groups are in close proximity to one another; (b) when the laws of one group are imposed upon another; and (c) when the members of one group migrate into another group. These processes, according to Sellin, account for much of the crime rates by the foreign-born in the United States. In many instances the crime may simply be the result of a misunderstanding or ignorance of the law. It is in this context that Sellin provides an often quoted example of the Sicilian male who murders the sixteen-year-old seducer of his daughter. Because the immigrant had merely defended the family honor in the traditional Sicilian way, he was quite surprised to be arrested.

The migration of norms as an explanation of crime had decreasing usefulness with the decline of migration into the United States. It was not until the late 1950s that another conflict perspective emerged in American sociology—group conflict.

GROUP CONFLICT.

The next American to substantially expand upon the relationship between conflict and deviance was George B. Vold.[21] Although Vold does not mention Sellin's contribution, his group conflict theory of crime is a logical next step from Sellin.

Vold describes conflict as a "principal and essential" social process. Society, he says, consists of many groups of differing interests and power who are constantly jockeying for positions of defense and advantage. Some groups gain political power and seek the aid of the government to protect or further their interests. Law is the outcome of the greatest influence and largest number of votes.

Some crime, says Vold, can be described as "minority group behavior." For example, crime arises from groups such as delinquent gangs that neither achieve their objectives through legitimate channels nor rely upon the protection of the state. For Vold, the gang represents a unified group in conflict with an adult world whose values and power advantage threaten the gang members.

Many other criminal acts represent more direct power confrontations—what Vold calls "acts of good soldiers fighting for a cause and against the threat of enemy encroachment." [22] These good soldiers are the company police, the strikers, and the political terrorists—none believe in murder, property destruction, and torture except as applied to accomplishing "higher" goals. The following examples cited by Vold are attempts to control the very political and cultural destinies of all society or, at least, substantial portions of that society.

1. *Political Reform Conflicts.* The ultimate form here is rebellion or revolution wherein the outcome determines who shall be the criminal. But short of that there are murders, acts of sabotage, destruction of property, burglary, briberies, and general dishonesty all for the sake of winning or retaining power. In short, acts normally condemned are condoned when a political purpose is attached to them.

2. *Management-Union Conflicts.* Strikes and strike-breaking often result in clashes between workers and between workers and police. Vandalism, assault, murder, and theft are not uncommon occurrences, again seen as necessary to obtain a satisfactory settlement.

3. *Union Jurisdictional Disputes.* Struggles between unions often involve entanglement with organized crime and favoritism from industry. Intimidation and assaults as well as confrontations with police over trespassing, and so on, frequently result from instances in which all parties feel that justice is on their side.

4. *Conflicts Over Racial Segregation.* In order to upset patterns of racial segregation, illegal behavior often results. Vold's discussion is sketchy on this issue, but one can assume he would include here acts of violence and property destruction that accompany attempts by blacks, Chicanos, American Indians, and whites to assert their "rights" over each other.

In closing his discussion of group conflict theory Vold is careful to point out its limitations:

> Group conflict theory is strictly limited to those kinds of situations in which the individual criminal acts flow from the collision of groups whose members are loyally upholding the in-group position. Such theory does not serve to explain many kinds of impulsive, irrational acts of a criminal nature that are quite unrelated to any battle between different interest groups in organized society.[23]

Vold's choice of "impulsive, irrational acts" to be the exceptions to group conflict theory seems to be an understatement. Also unexplained by the theory are "deliberate, rational acts" that occur for primarily, if not purely, personal reasons. Although the conflict theory has value for understanding why an employee might destroy company property during a strike, it may fall short of suggesting why that same individual systematically steals company materials for the house he is building.

Nevertheless, Vold's approach draws attention to the political motivations behind both behavior and laws. And he emphasizes that crime is a matter of definition as well as of behavior:

> Crime always involves both human behavior (acts) and the judgment or definitions (laws, customs, mores) of fellow human beings as to whether specific behavior is appropriate and permissable, or is improper and forbidden. Crime and criminality lie in the area of behavior that is considered improper and forbidden. There is, therefore, always a dual problem of explanation—that of accounting for the behavior, *as behavior,* and equally important, accounting *for the definitions* by which specific behavior comes to be considered as crime or non-crime.[24]

CONFLICT AND AUTHORITY

Austin T. Turk rejects Vold's contention that the study of crime involves a dual problem of explaining both behavior and definitions.[25] Turk argues that attempts to explain criminal behavior have always been fruitless and will continue to be so because *criminality is not behavior, but a status conferred upon that behavior.*

Turk presents a series of propositions in which he claims that there are no universal norms prohibiting any behavior. The behavior involved in acting illegally does not differ essentially from acting legally, and the application of law is inaccurate, subjective, and inconsistent. Thus, criminality is a state of being officially defined as punishable and it bears only a slender relationship to actual behavior.

After disposing of behavior as an issue, Turk presents a theory of *criminalization* (the process of being labeled as criminal) based upon the concept of *authority:*

> The study of criminality [is] the study of relations between the statuses and roles of legal *authorities*—creators, interpreters, and enforcers of right-wrong standards for individuals in the political collectivity—and those of *subjects*—acceptors or resisters but not makers of such law creating, interpreting, and enforcing decisions.[26]

However, Turk cannot completely avoid suggesting how behavior might be explained:

> *Lawbreaking* is taken to be an indicator of the failure or lack of authority; it is a measure of the extent to which rulers and ruled, decision-makers and decision-acceptors, are not bound together in a perfectly stable authority

relationship. Because an authority relationship can never be finally perfected, both accidental and deliberate resistance to legal norms, and therefore challenges to authority, will occur in any political-legal structure.[27]

Turk's theory specifies the factors contributing to the probabilities of conflict between authorities and subjects, and the probabilities those conflicts will result in the assigning of criminal status or criminalization. Central to the theory is a distinction between *cultural norms* (announced or publicized norms) and *social norms* (actual behavior). The *congruence* of these (the degree to which what is said corresponds to what is done) is an important factor in determining the likelihood of conflict. When congruence is high for both authorities and subjects over an issue, conflict is most likely. For example, if authorities say that extra-marital sex is wrong and do abstain themselves, conflict would probably result if a group of subjects proclaimed in both word and deed their favoring such activity. If congruence is low for both parties, the issue is primarily a symbolic one and unlikely to provoke conflict.

Other factors crucial to Turk's theory are the degree of *organization* of the subjects—the extent to which there is a system of group support for behavior; and the subjects' *sophistication*—their capacity to assess their own strengths and weaknesses relative to those of the authorities. Turk argues that conflict between authorities and subjects is most probable when there is a high congruence between cultural and social norms, and the subjects involved in the behavior are highly organized but relatively unsophisticated. The likelihood that conflict will result in criminalization depends upon the *power differences* between subjects and authorities, and the *realism of moves* by both sides (realism of moves refers to the tactical skills at gaining favorable positions of strength against the opposition).

The number and character of the factors in Turk's theory attest to its complexity. Its complexity and the difficulty in satisfactorily measuring the factors leave unresolved the obvious question. To what degree does Turk's theory explain conflict and criminalization? But the theory does alert us to the political nature of legal authority and to the interrelationships existing between decision-makers and those whom authorities expect to accept such decisions.

In contrast to the relationships suggested by Turk's theory are those more Marxian in their assumption that American society is divided into two classes, the rulers and the dominated. Crime and the legal system itself are seen as manifestations of the ruling class's attempt to protect its interests and to prevent the dominated class from becoming more powerful. The Marxian approach in American criminology is generally referred to as radical criminology.

A RADICAL THEORY OF CRIME

A radical theory or perspective toward crime not only attempts to explain crime's existence, but also proposes drastic social, political, and economic changes in order to eliminate crime. Radical theorists express little concern over criminal behavior. They see the cause of crime as lying within society and its legal system and feel that until both are changed the crime problem will persist.

Representative of the radical approach is Richard Quinney, who provides a contemporary Marxist explanation of crime.[28] Quinney's central concept is power, the ability to control others. Because power is unevenly distributed in society there is constant conflict between groups competing for the scarce resources that are more easily obtained by the more powerful. An important aspect of power is the ability to formulate public policy consistent with one's interests. By allowing the formulation of such policy, power becomes an instrument for creating the social meanings or "reality" of crime. Quinney's discussion of this matter is in the form of six propositions:

1. Official Definition of Crime: Crime is a legal definition of human conduct that is created by agents of the dominant class in a capitalist society. [Crime is not inherent in behavior but is a matter of judgment and definition.]

2. Formulation of Definitions of Crime: Definitions of crime are composed of behaviors that conflict with the class interests of the dominant economic class. [It follows that the greater the conflict between class interests, the greater the likelihood that the dominant economic class will *formulate* laws to control others.]

3. Application of Definitions of Crime: Definitions of crime are applied by the class that has the power to shape the enforcement and administration of criminal law. [The greater the conflict between class interests, the greater the likelihood that the dominant economic class will influence legal agents to *apply* the criminal law.]

4. Development of Behavior Patterns in Relation to Definitions of Crime: Behavior patterns are structured in relation to definitions of crime, and within this context persons engage in actions that have relative probabilities of being defined as criminal. [The behavior of the less powerful is more likely to be defined as criminal; the expectations and experiences of being labeled criminal in turn influence future behavior.]

5. Construction of Conceptions of Crime: Conceptions of crime are constructed and diffused in the course of communication. [What and who are criminal are constructed and disseminated by the powerful; the more the powerful are concerned over crime, the greater the likelihood that both the definitions of behavior and the behavior itself will increase.]

6. Construction of the Social Reality of Crime: The social reality of crime is constructed by the formulation and application of definitions of crime, the development of behavior patterns in relation to these definitions,

and the construction of conceptions of crime. [This is a composite of the previous five propositions.] [29]

Quinney also deals directly with the question of who possesses power to manipulate the criminal justice system in America. He argues that interest groups are grossly unequal in their influence. Public policy is actually determined by a very few, very powerful economic interests. There is, according to Quinney, an American ruling class consisting of the owners and controllers of the means of production, plus those who benefit directly from the system.

Quinney claims that the "official reality" that presents the legal system as beneficial for all is a myth. That system serves only the ruling class by furnishing it protection and by maintaining the existing social and economic conditions. Agencies and programs set up in recent years for the purposes of the "war on crime" and of legal "reform" are in fact devices to repress "class antagonisms" or potential rebellions that threaten established economic arrangements. "Crime control" under capitalism is actually "class control," according to Quinney.

The police, courts, prisons, and even criminologists are part of this system of repression. Whenever criminologists have sought the sources of crime within the individual, including how the individual was criminally socialized, they have ignored the political nature of the authority defining behavior as criminal. Research grants, training programs in law enforcement by universities, and government-supported scholarships are all means by which the ruling class secures both the allegiance of criminologists and strategic information from what Quinney calls "counterinsurgency research." The end product of current research on criminals and crime is the control and manipulation of humans by those who rule.

The thrust of Quinney's argument is presented in another six propositions:

1. American society is based on an advanced capitalist economy.
2. The state is organized to serve the interests of the dominant economic class, the capitalist ruling class.
3. Criminal law is an instrument of the state and ruling class to maintain and perpetuate the existing social and economic order.
4. Crime control in capitalist society is accomplished through a variety of institutions and agencies established and administered by a governmental elite, representing ruling class interests, for the purpose of establishing domestic order.
5. The contradictions of advanced capitalism—the disjunction between existence and essence—require that the subordinate classes remain oppressed by whatever means necessary, especially through the coercion and violence of the legal system.
6. Only with the collapse of capitalist society and the creation of a new so-

ciety, based on socialist principles, will there be a solution to the crime problem.[30]

Quinney's description of the relationship between power and criminal justice can be best termed a class conflict theory. On one hand there is the ruling class holding practically all the power and using that power, through the justice system, to maintain control over everyone else. On the other hand is everyone else—the powerless masses—who are either benumbed by complacency or too divided to resist effectively. Quinney's use of the phrase "solution to the crime problem" is misleading in its inclusiveness. The theory's application is actually limited to explaining legal reaction against behaviors threatening established economic interests. Thus there is no pretense at explaining such facets of the crime problem as a school janitor sexually molesting a ten-year-old student, parents brutally beating a baby because "it won't stop crying," or two friends trying to stab each other in a dispute over a fifty cent gambling debt.

But even when restricted to economic interests, the monolithic ruling class suggested by Quinney's propositions may not be so all-powerful according to other writers sympathetic with the notion of class conflict. Robert Lefcourt, for example, admits that pluralism in America is characterized to some degree by a system of checks and balances, a variety of diverse organized pressure groups, and by legislative and judicial compromise.[31] He concedes that interest groups have been responsible for civil rights legislation, strengthening of labor unions, and other laws challenging the power structure: regulations concerning industrial safety, product purity, air and water pollution and so on. But Lefcourt also contends that corporate power over the legal system is so great that the laws are rendered essentially impotent—at least the power distribution remains unaltered.

It cannot be denied that important changes occur when pressures are exerted. . . . What can be denied is that property relations can be changed by the pluralist process. Economic guidelines and laws give the major corporations in this free enterprise system ownership of the means of production, while the populations underlying the upper class are divided (into income, religious, ethnic, and racial groups) so that they are prevented from determining the material conditions of their lives or the policies of their government. It is now a well-established (though not so well-known) fact that economic inequality within the United States has remained generally constant throughout this century, showing that the "potential for unity" of the upper class is much greater than that of the middle or lower classes. Sociologists have shown that a cohesive white upper class, consisting of approximately one-half of one percent of the people in this country, controls every major bank and corporation and personally owns over one-quarter of the country's wealth, while eighty percent of all stock value is owned by less than two percent.[32]

Of course, there is a distinction between having power and abusing it. It is impossible to argue that power is not often misused in America. The criminal law, police, courts, and penal institutions have all been used to still voices of dissent and to ensure an order in the best interests of the powerful.[33] But whether the abuse of power should be curtailed by the development of more powerful competing interest groups or by the dissolution of capitalist society is a matter of ideology and assumptions not amenable to simple answers.[34]

The conflict perspective, radical or not, is *not* a statement of facts or of empirically verified relationships. Like the labeling perspective it directs attention toward a possible interpretation of facts. For our purposes the conflict perspective points out that groups have both varying interests and power, and that the law can be instrumental in promoting or defeating those interests. Beyond that, the extent to which certain groups influence the making and enforcement of law remains a matter for research.

What Is Deviant? (Continued)

It should be apparent by now that constructing a single theory of deviance would be a very intricate procedure. Minimally it would have to explain the existence of both the rules and the behavior. This would involve many questions. Why do particular norms exist? Are they supported generally in society or only by select power groups? Under what conditions do behaviors and individuals become subject to being labeled and reacted against as deviant? Why do particular behaviors defined as deviant arise and persist in society? Why do rates of behavior defined as deviant vary from one group to another, from one time to another, and so on? What is the process by which persons first engage in deviant behavior? Why do they continue in the behavior? Why do they quit?

All of this is much more than any current single theory can deliver. Because the existence of deviance is the result of both rules and behavior it is unlikely that an explanation of one will explain the other. But even reducing our expectations of any one perspective is not sufficient. Consider the following stories—all true.

The board chairman of the American Medical Association is charged with bank fraud in a conspiracy involving nearly $1.8 million.

An eleven-year-old boy is absent because of illness when a coal slag avalanche kills all thirty-three of his classmates in a school in Wales. He is shunned and his life is threatened by others in town who resent his survival.

A high school teacher with outstanding references and academic credentials is dismissed from her job for refusing to join her classes in reciting the Pledge of Allegiance.

An eight-year-old girl in Scotland stabs a playmate and is sentenced to eighteen months in a detention home.

A forty-year-old male persists in publicly picking his nose despite the anguish and admonitions of his wife and friends.

Judging by reactions alone, each of the above individuals is deviant by someone's standards. At first these do not seem to be particularly complex examples. Our problem is, of the perspectives considered so far, which would be applicable to these cases? The example of the dismissed teacher can be discussed in terms of group conflict because her behavior and the reaction to it appear politically motivated. And the case of the board chairman may be understandable in terms of learning experiences and situational variables.

The remaining cases, however, present serious difficulties. No perspective adequately deals with accidents, behavior of the very young, or the breach of social niceties as forms of deviance. Even the reactions to those behaviors cannot be satisfactorily handled by the labeling and conflict perspectives without stretching them far beyond their intended purposes. Thus, to be realistic, we must exclude from our consideration those forms of rule-breaking which are relatively unique or trivial.[35]

Now we must confront the problem of what is neither unique nor trivial. The extent of a behavior is presumably an empirical question—that is, it should be provable by evidence. But because statistics on deviance are obtained in an arbitrary and biased fashion, the actual incidence of a given behavior may not be even approximate. Furthermore, statistics are gathered by agencies with vested interests in compiling them; if there is no interested agency, there will be no statistics. In short, statistics on deviance are compiled by nonscientists in nonscientific ways for nonscientific reasons. But like it or not, we usually have to depend upon such statistics as a gauge of a behavior's assumed prevalence.

Whether a behavior is serious or not is also a sticky matter. Many textbooks on deviance are oriented toward behaviors that are presumed to violate societal norms.[36] Exactly how these norms are discovered is rarely made clear except with reference to official definition of the norms. With the possible exception of some acts (homicide of loved ones, rape of friends, and so on), there is no unofficial evidence of consensus within society concerning what should be treated as deviant—particularly if it involves people we really don't care about—or how it should be treated. This is assuming that by society one means all its members. But in the final analysis one cannot view society that way, particularly a highly pluralistic society such as the United States.

As we have learned from the labeling and conflict perspectives, that which becomes officially deviant can be regarded as a matter of who holds the power to make such decisions. In this context, the societal norms are really the norms of the powerful. Robert R. Bell admits, "Basically the ultimate measurement of whether or not an act is deviant depends on how others who are socially significant in power and influence define the act." [37] Ronald L. Akers concentrates on those behaviors "considered serious enough to warrant major societal effort to control them through the application of strong negative sanctions." The norms being violated are those "held by large or socially, economically, and politically powerful or significant segments of American society." [38] Gibbons and Jones sum up the usual position of sociologists toward the study of deviance:

> We can still have a substantive field of deviance study if we take as our goal the study of violation of criminal statutes, civil regulations, other codified conduct rules, and other identifiable behavioral standards that apply to persons throughout American society, whether these rules happen to be applauded by citizens or not. Indeed, this appears to be what many students of deviant behavior currently pay attention to, such that they focus attention on various transgressions of major rules, particularly of criminal statutes, many of which involve standards that run counter to widely shared attitudes of citizen groups. Major rules in this context refer to norms which are enforced by formal social control agencies. [39]

According to this interpretation, the sociological study of deviance is guided neither by costs in lives, dollars, human misery, and human integrity, nor by the sentiments of the citizenry. Instead it follows the signposts of law and the administration of that law; the study of deviance goes where the politically influential lead it. This search logically and ultimately ends with the populations of society's prisons and asylums. And who occupies these institutions?—the poor, the socially disadvantaged, the powerless.

Although sociologists recognize that the powerful are largely responsible for determining the character and application of the legal structure, they often ignore the implications for their work. The result is an overemphasis upon rule-breaking by the lower class and an avoidance of the significance of rule-breaking among the upper classes. Except for references to marihuana use among college youths, the occurrence of homosexuality among all classes, and the occasions of corporate price-fixing, criminological research has overwhelmingly concentrated on lower class individuals. The sociology of deviance has definitely been guilty of class bias. [40]

The powerful are not exempt from deviance. Indeed, by virtue of their position they are capable of causing considerably more harm than others:

The powerful have access to a greater number of and more varied *opportunities for deviance* when compared with the powerless, precisely because the former enjoy a greater number of and more varied *legitimate opportunities* in life. . . . Since the powerful do not conceive themselves to be potentially deviant in the same way as the powerless would (i.e., as a potential murderer, robber, or burglar), they are unlikely to commit these deviant acts. Instead, their self-concept is likely to encourage them to take advantage of the illegitimate opportunities open to them, because it enables them to consider the resulting acts of deviance, say, indirectly and impersonally killing and maiming thousands of motorists every year through the manufacturing of defective cars, as *non*deviant.[41]

The law and its application are not neutral toward the various conflicting interests existing within a morally pluralistic society. Failure to recognize this perpetuates an emphasis upon the common criminal and the notion that deviants are a distinct class of individuals driven by yet unknown biological, psychological, or social causes.

But merely recognizing that the law is influenced by the powerful does not relieve us of the problem of how to define deviance. Without guidelines we can easily become prey to our personal prejudices as to what is serious. In the above quotation the author, Alex Thio, is concerned over highway deaths resulting from defective cars. I might be more worried about sexual behavior solely for pleasure resulting from "defective" moral standards.

It is tempting to regard the law as merely a tool of the powerful. But it is more than that. It reflects norms that transcend those of a few influential interest groups. Some laws enjoy a high degree of consensus—neither the rich nor poor want to be murdered in their beds. Still others are specifically directed toward controlling the actions of the powerful—police, courts, corporations, and so on. This is not to say that such laws, including those having wide public support, are enforced consistently and without bias. Nor is this to claim that sanctions leveled against violators are always dispensed in relationship to the public's loss in lives and dollars. The law is nevertheless an indicator, however distorted, of both the societal norms and the norms of powerful interest groups. Often these overlap and it is a matter of some conjecture as to which belongs to which, but legal norms do provide us with a means of defining deviance without resorting to definitions based solely upon feelings of moral outrage.

For purposes of this book, *deviant behavior is that behavior which in the United States traditionally or currently may be subject to legal procedures aimed at curtailing the behavior. Such procedures may involve punishment, restoration of losses to victims, or involuntary hospitalization.*

Certain aspects of this definition require clarification and elaboration. Part of it involves the potential for legal action to stop the behavior. This means that although authorities have the legal capacity to act, they may do anything, from ignoring the behavior to actively suppressing it. In addition, the reader will note that whereas the definition is based upon legal codes, it is not limited to crime.[42] Crime is conduct in violation of the criminal law.

> Criminal law is a body of specialized rules of a politically organized society which contain provisions for punishment to be administered in the name of society upon substantiation of their violation.[43]

You will note that punishment is part of criminal law, and usually involves a sentence of a specific time in jail and/or a fine. But crime, with its potential for punishment, is only part of the definition of deviant behavior. Authorities have other means of controlling behavior. Some behaviors may be treated as *torts* or *civil wrongs* whereby the offenders are ordered to pay victims for their loss. This process of *restitution* is, as we shall later see, most likely to be used against respectable offenders such as corporations. The respectable may be deviant, but they are not criminals.

In still other cases, the behavior may bring about the offender's commitment to a hospital or some treatment setting for help. The instances that will concern us are those in which the offenders have little or nothing to say about this procedure: those defined as mentally ill, potential suicides, and sexual psychopaths.

Given the state of the field, to arrive at a definition of deviant behavior satisfactory to everyone is an impossible task. The reader may well complain that the legal emphasis of our definition is especially misplaced because it excludes the behavior of persons who experience social rejection without legality even at issue. For example, homosexual behavior and prostitution are not illegal in some states. The same is true of nudism and stripteasing, and being an alcoholic is legal anywhere. It can be argued, however, that traditionally people involved in such behaviors have directly confronted the law, and currently their legal status remains precarious at best. There is more than one way to deal legally with deviants—if they don't violate one law they can be charged with another. If all else fails they can be hospitalized for "treatment."

But the reader's complaint is legitimate. Deviance and violation of law are not necessarily the same thing. However, our definition will be used in this book for one compelling reason: the existence of legal means to cope with individuals' behavior is tangible evidence of a collective reaction defining the behavior as deviant.

Interest Group Conflict and Deviance

We have already indicated that no single perspective adequately explains the existence of both rule-making and rule-breaking behavior. The interest group conflict approach to be employed in the remainder of this book is no exception. Following chapters contain discussions of a wide variety of behaviors, many of which may be more convincingly explained by other perspectives. A conflict approach, however, has two important virtues: 1. it acknowledges that a relationship exists between deviant behavior and the processes of making and enforcing rules; 2. it recognizes that many acts of rule breaking are committed in the name of a group or cause, and for purposes other than immediate personal gain or satisfaction. By blending the conflict perspective with other assumptions about the nature of American society many of the more personal, individual behaviors and authorities' reactions to them become understandable, even if they are not satisfactorily explained.

The following propositions summarize the perspective of this book:

1. *Life in American society is characterized by conflicts of interests.* Our society contains many diverse groups whose interests are antagonistic to one another. Conflicts of interest are especially evident where access to unequally distributed scarce resources (wealth, status, and power) is concerned. Conflict arises and continues over these resources—which include the power to define what is "moral." The conflict situation in many instances is a one-sided battle since many groups lack organization, sophistication, and power to enhance or even protect their interests.

2. *Interest groups exert varying degrees of influence upon legislation and enforcement of law.* Law and its administration are not the works of gods but of humans; they are responsive to the wishes of those who can provide campaign funds, votes, prestige and other favors. Consequently, the law is not neutral in monitoring and controlling the activities of various interest groups.

3. *The application of law is a method by which more powerful interest groups can exert control over the less powerful.* Once power and its benefits have been attained they are not readily relinquished. The powerful resist any change that might undermine their position, and the law is a powerful weapon that can be used to thwart groups with competing interests. As Austin T. Turk has indicated, the likelihood of conflicts resulting in the application of law is dependent upon several factors. Nevertheless, existing laws and their enforcement generally favor either (a) both the more and the less powerful, or (b) the more powerful alone. Occasionally laws favor less powerful groups at the expense of the more powerful, but the application of such laws is far less systematic.

4. *Deviant behavior is, with few exceptions, a rational, learned response to social, economic, and political conditions.* The less powerful do not have legitimate access to scarce resources available to the more powerful. Thus the structure of society contributes to the oc-

currence of deviance because some groups cannot easily enhance or protect their interests without breaking the legal code. On the other hand, the powerful as well respond to social, economic, political conditions. In their efforts to maintain the dominance of their interests against incursions by the less powerful *and* by those within their own group, the powerful often violate their own rules. Thus it is not only the public that cheats corporations, but corporations cheat the public and each other.

5. *Deviant responses are supported by the learning of traditions, rewards, and motives.* In most instances the law prohibiting a behavior exists prior to the behavior itself; furthermore, most people who violate a law do not do so out of ignorance. Most law breakers are aware of the law, but break it anyway. The assumption of this book is that people are rarely compelled or driven into a specific behavior, but make decisions among various alternative behaviors. The selection of one behavior over another involves a calculation of risk and a justification based upon learning experiences.

These learning experiences are based upon broadly defined traditions of American society: independence, freedom of the individual, progress, and so on. One tradition that plays a predominant role in deviance is our heritage of violence.[44] Although some acts of violence are deplored, the nation has a long history of favoring violence for the purposes of protest, resisting change, and righting wrongs. The man of the frontier with his six-shooter influences contemporary society more than many would care to believe.

Other learning experiences involve rewards for breaking the law. Despite the admonition, "Crime doesn't pay," some crimes pay exceedingly well. The high profits from organized crime and corporate law-breaking are cases in point. Economic or material gain is but one potential reward. Others might be (a) status and esteem in the eyes of one's friends and family; (b) political advantage by reducing opponents' capacity or desire to resist; (c) escape from the pressures of one's personal misfortunes or from the demands made by family, friends, job, or society; and (d) the sheer joy of fun and adventure—a facet of being "immoral and illegal" often overlooked by serious-minded social scientists.[45]

Of course there are risks in any law-breaking behavior and the potential rewards must be perceived as compensating for those risks. In reality the risks for minor acts of deviance may be greater than for major ones; the misuse of millions of dollars may incur a lesser punishment than a filling station robbery of $75. Only the powerful have the opportunity to engage in large-scale deviance with minimal risks. Even among the powerless, however, the risks of deviance are relatively minor in comparison to the possible rewards from illegitimate behavior:

The "legitimate" jobs open to many ghetto residents, especially to young black males, typically pay low wages, offer relatively demeaning assignments, and carry the constant risk of layoff. In contrast, many kinds of crime "available" in the ghetto often bring higher monetary return, offer even higher social status, and—at least in some cases like numbers running—sometimes carry relatively low risk of arrest and punishment. Given those alternative opportunities, the choice between "legitimate" and "illegitimate" activities is often quite simple.[46]

Finally, learning experiences supporting deviant behavior involve verbalized motives explaining why a law may or should be violated in certain instances. From our discussion in Chapter 2 you may recall that such motives are especially relevant in relation to laws about which offenders agree in principle. Traditional statements and folklore enable the individual to defend her or his actions to others: "Meet force with force," "If somebody's too drunk . . ." and so on. Such verbalizations allow one to maintain a favorable self-image while attempting to persuade others that there is a reasonable explanation for rule-breaking behavior.

Conclusion

The above perspective points to society itself as a primary cause of deviant behavior. Much of that behavior emerges from conflicts of interests between parties struggling over scarce resources. Rules are necessary to control the conflict if a society is to survive, but rules favoring the powerful magnify the differences between the powerful and the powerless. In the process the powerful place the blame for deviance upon those without similar influence over the administration of law. The purpose of the remaining chapters is to review deviance as a phenomenon that is present at all levels of society. You will see that the forms of behavior vary, but that the differences are the result of available opportunities and experiences, not of inherent differences between classes or groups of persons.

NOTES

1. Some writers have a strong preference for one term over others, e.g., John I. Kitsuse, "Deviance, Deviant Behavior, and Deviants: Some Conceptual Problems," in *An Introduction to Deviance: Readings in the Process of Making Deviants,* ed. by William J. Filstead (Chicago: Markham, 1972), pp. 233, 235. A sampling of articles reveals *labeling* to be the term most often used.

2. Howard S. Becker, *Outsiders: Studies in the Sociology of Deviance* (New York: Free Press, 1963), p. 14.

3. Ibid., p. 9.

4. Kai T. Erikson, "Notes on the Sociology of Deviance," in *The Other Side: Perspectives on Deviance,* ed. Howard S. Becker (New York: Free Press, 1964), p. 11.

5. John I. Kitsuse and Aaron V. Cicourel, "A Note on the Uses of Official Statistics," *Social Problems,* **11** (Fall 1963), p. 135.

6. Kai T. Erikson, *Wayward Puritans: A Study in the Sociology of Deviance* (New York: John Wiley & Sons, 1966), pp. 25–26. This claim of constant rates of deviance has been challenged by Walter D. Connor, "The Manufacture of Deviance: The Case of the Soviet Purge, 1936–1938," *American Sociological Review,* **37** (August 1972), pp. 403–413; and Daniel Glaser, *Social Deviance* (Chicago: Markham, 1971), pp. 97–100.

7. The critics of the labeling approach are many, and often their arguments are too complex for adequate development in an introductory text. The following critiques are among the best: Ronald L. Akers, "Problems in the Sociology of Deviance: Social Definitions and Behavior," *Social Forces,* **46** (June 1968), pp. 455–465; Robert S. Broadhead, "A Theoretical Critique of the Societal Reaction Approach to Deviance," *Pacific Sociological Review,* **17** (July 1974), pp. 287–312; Nanette J. Davis, "Labeling Theory in Deviance Research: A Critique and Reconsideration," *Sociological Quarterly,* **13** (Autumn 1972), pp. 447–474; Jack P. Gibbs, "Conceptions of Deviant Behavior: The Old and the New," *Pacific Sociological Review,* **9** (Spring 1966), pp. 9–14; and "Issues in Defining Deviant Behavior," in *Theoretical Perspectives on Deviance,* eds. Robert A. Scott and Jack D. Douglas (New York: Basic Books, 1972), pp. 39–68; Edwin M. Lemert, "Beyond Mead: The Societal Reaction to Deviance," *Social Problems,* **21** (April, 1974), pp. 457–468; Edward Sagarin, *Deviants and Deviance: An Introduction to the Study of Disvalued People and Behavior* (New York: Praeger Publishers, 1975), pp. 121–144; Paul G. Schervish, "The Labeling Perspective: Its Bias and Potential in the Study of Political Deviance," *American Sociologist,* **8** (May 1973), pp. 47–57; Ian Taylor, Paul Walton, and Jock Young, *The New Criminology: For a Social Theory of Deviance* (London: Routledge & Kegan Paul, 1973), pp. 144–150; Edwin M. Schur, *Labeling Deviant Behavior: Its Sociological Implications* (New York: Harper & Row, 1971); and Alex Thio, "Class Bias in the Sociology of Deviance," *American Sociologist,* **8** (February 1973), pp. 1–12.

8. Emile Durkheim, *The Rules of Sociological Method,* 8th ed., trans. Sarah A. Solovay and John H. Mueller (Glencoe, Ill.: Free Press, 1938), p. 70.

9. Edwin M. Lemert, *Human Deviance, Social Problems, and Social Control,* 2nd ed., (Englewood Cliffs, N.J.: Prentice-Hall, 1972), p. 22.

10. Edwin M. Lemert, *Social Pathology: A Systematic Approach to the Theory of Sociopathic Behavior* (New York: McGraw-Hill, 1951), pp. 75–76. The discussion also incorporates a more recent work, Lemert, *Human Deviance,* pp. 62–92.

11. Lemert, *Social Pathology,* p. 76.

12. Ibid., p. 77.

13. The discussion is based upon Becker, *Outsiders,* pp. 25–39.

14. Milton Mankoff, "Societal Reaction and Career Deviance: A Critical Analysis," *Sociological Quarterly,* **12** (Spring 1971), p. 204.

15. Davis, "Labeling Theory," p. 460.

16. For detailed discussions of this issue see Mankoff, "Societal Reaction," pp. 204–218; Davis, "Labeling Theory," pp. 453–462; and Taylor, et al., *The New Criminology,* pp. 150–165. See also John Hagan, "Labeling and Deviance: A Case Study in the 'Sociology of the Interesting'," *Social Problems,* **20** (Spring 1973), pp. 447–458.

17. Bernard A. Thorsell and Lloyd W. Klemke, "The Labeling Process: Reinforcement and Deterrent?" *Law and Society Review,* **6** (February 1972), pp. 393–403.

18. Schervish, "The Labeling Perspective," p. 52. Quotation is from Elliot Freidson, "Disability As Social Deviance," in *Sociology and Rehabilitation,* ed. Marvin B. Sussman (Washington, D.C.: American Sociological Association, 1965), p. 98.

19. Thorsten Sellin, *Culture Conflict and Crime,* Report of the Subcommittee on Delinquency of the Committee on Personality and Culture, Bulletin 41 (New York: Social Science Research Council, 1938). For a discussion of this report see Donald R. Cressey, "Culture Conflict, Differential Association, and Normative Conflict," in *Crime and Culture: Essays in Honor of Thorsten Sellin,* ed. Marvin E. Wolfgang (New York: John Wiley, 1968), pp. 43–54.

20. Sellin, *Culture Conflict,* p. 29.

21. George B. Vold, *Theoretical Criminology* (New York: Oxford University Press, 1958), pp. 203–219.

22. Ibid., p. 214.

23. Ibid., p. 219.

24. Ibid., pp. v–vi.

25. The following discussion is drawn from Austin T. Turk, *Criminality and Legal Order* (Chicago: Rand McNally, 1969), pp. 1–78.

26. Ibid., p. 35.

27. Ibid., p. 49.

28. The following discussion is based upon Richard Quinney, *The Social Reality of Crime* (Boston: Little, Brown, 1970); *Critique of Legal Order: Crime Control in Capitalist Society* (Boston: Little, Brown, 1974); and "The Social Reality of Crime," in *Current Perspectives on Criminal Behavior,* ed. Abraham S. Blumberg (New York: Alfred A. Knopf, 1974), pp. 35–46.

29. Quinney, "Social Reality of Crime," pp. 38–43. In a more recent version of these propositions Quinney de-emphasizes the role of capitalism. The earlier version is presented here because it is more clearly Marxian in tone. Cf. Richard Quinney, *Criminology: Analysis and Critique of Crime in America* (Boston: Little, Brown, 1975), pp. 37–41. For a critique of the way in which Quinney uses Marxist theory see R. Serge Denisoff and Donald McQuarie, "Crime Control in Capitalist Society: A Reply to Quinney," *Issues in Criminology,* **10** (Spring 1975), pp. 109–119.

30. Quinney, *Critique of Legal Order,* p. 16.

31. Robert Lefcourt, "Law Against the People," in *Criminal Justice in America: A Critical Understanding,* ed. Richard Quinney (Boston: Little, Brown, 1974), pp. 261–263.

32. Ibid., pp. 261–262.

33. For discussions of the influence of the powerful upon the justice process, see Quinney's works, and William J. Chambliss and Robert B. Seidman, *Law, Order, and Power* (Reading, Mass.: Addison-Wesley, 1971).

34. For comparisons of ideologies regarding crime see William J. Chambliss, "Functional and Conflict Theories of Crime," MSS Modular Publications, New York, Module 17 (1974), pp. 1–23; and Walter B. Miller, "Ideology and Criminal Justice Policy: Some Current Issues," *Journal of Criminal Law and Criminology,* **64** (June 1973), pp. 141–162.

35. For a discussion of the boundaries of the field of deviance, see Don C. Gibbons and Joseph F. Jones, "Some Critical Notes on Current Definitions of Deviance," *Pacific Sociological Review,* **14** (January 1971), pp. 20–37.

36. Ibid., pp. 23–24.

37. Robert R. Bell, *Social Deviance: A Substantive Analysis* (Homewood, Ill.: Dorsey Press, 1971), p. 11.

38. Ronald L. Akers, *Deviant Behavior: A Social Learning Approach* (Belmont, Calif.: Wadsworth, 1973), pp. 7–8.

39. Gibbons and Jones, "Some Critical Notes," p. 32.

40. Thio, "Class Bias in the Sociology of Deviance"; and Alexander Liazos, "The Poverty of the Sociology of Deviance: Nuts, Sluts, and Preverts," *Social Problems,* **20** (Summer 1971), pp. 103–120.

41. Thio, "Class Bias in the Sociology of Deviance," pp. 6–7.

42. The subject matter of criminology and, by implication, the field of deviant behavior has been subject to perennial controversy since the early 1930s. For detailed discussions of the controversy see: Herman and Julia Schwendinger, "Defenders of Order or Guardians of Human Rights?" *Issues in Criminology,* **5** (Summer 1970), pp. 123–157; and "The Continuing Debate on The Legalistic Approach to the Definition of Crime," *Issues in Criminology,* **7** (Winter 1972), pp. 71–81. See also: Clayton A. Hartjen, "Legalism and Humanism: A Reply to the Schwendingers," *Issues in Criminology,* **7** (Winter 1972), pp. 59–69; and Gene Grabiner, "The Limits of Three Perspectives on Crime: 'Value-Free Science,' 'Objective Law' and State 'Morality,' " *Issues in Criminology,* **8** (Spring 1973), pp. 35–48.

43. Richard Quinney, *The Problem of Crime* (New York: Dodd, Mead & Co., 1970), p. 16.

44. Edwin M. Schur, *Our Criminal Society: The Social and Legal Sources of Crime in America* (Englewood Cliffs, N.J.: Prentice-Hall, 1969), pp. 125–131.

45. Some of these and other rewards for juvenile delinquency are discussed by John DeLamater, "On the Nature of Deviance," *Social Forces,* **46** (June 1968), pp. 452–454.

46. David M. Gordon, "Capitalism, Class, and Crime in America," *Crime and Delinquency,* **19** (April 1973), p. 175.

CRIME IN THE STREETS— AGAINST THE PERSON

One unhappy fact about the urban condition in the United States is the citizens' fear of crime. In high crime areas of large cities the sound of footsteps behind you on a deserted street, the sudden meeting with a stranger in a darkened hallway, and the unexpected knock at your apartment door are occasions of anxiety. Forty per cent of Americans are afraid to walk alone at night in their own neighborhoods.[1] Whether the basis for such fear is real or exaggerated, there are serious consequences for the people concerned. Many remain at home rather than risk going out for shopping or entertainment; their apartments become fortresses with barred windows, extra locks, and watch dogs; they take taxis, which many can ill afford, rather than traveling by bus or subway; and many carry weapons.

The subject of this and the following chapter will be those actions strongly condemned by public consensus: acts directly threatening one's person and property.[2] Because such acts are seen as threatening by both the legal authorities and most citizens, they are specifically prohibited by the criminal code, and the general public expects the code to be enforced. These are *crimes in the streets*—a term designating deeds committed by those "out there" who injure us and who force their way into our homes to seize our valuables.

The desire for guarantees of personal

safety and protection of property lies behind most people's conception of what crime is like. Crime is seen as something that happens *to* good citizens. It is perpetrated by unscrupulous strangers representing the "dangerous classes," which have so concerned criminologists for over a hundred years. All that stands between the good and the dangerous is a thin blue line of police. The everyday skirmishes between police and those apparently jeopardizing our security are of far more public concern than either the multi-billion-dollar activities of organized crime or the corruption and cheating that taint every layer of society. This concern with street crime is reflected officially in a kind of annual "battle report" on the "war" with crime, entitled *Crime in the United States.*

Uniform Crime Reports

In the fall of each year newspapers carry articles concerning the rise, fall, or leveling off of crime as compared to previous years. The articles point out such information as: eleven serious crimes occur each minute; the New York City area had nearly 125,000 violent crimes last year; and in one year nine million arrests are made nationally for all criminal acts except traffic offenses. The source of this information is an F.B.I. publication, *Crime in the United States,* usually referred to as *Uniform Crime Reports* in the more technical literature on crime statistics.[3] This publication presents crime statistics collected from approximately 11,000 law enforcement agencies representing 93 per cent of the national population.

The heart of the statistics are crimes known to the police. These are based primarily upon police department counts of citizen complaints about criminal activity and, to a lesser extent, upon the number of crimes witnessed by police themselves. Although it is tempting to regard these figures as measures of criminal activity, to do so is to ignore some glaring shortcomings. First, not all criminal acts will be reported to the police. There are several reasons for not reporting, but one of the most obvious is the case in which there is no victim—no one complains because no one feels he or she has been coerced or harmed by the illegal act. Examples here are illegal homosexual acts between consenting individuals, illegal drug sales and use, prostitution, and illegal gambling. These are matters of voluntary choice among participants, and only an uninvolved third party is likely to object.

Second, even in circumstances where victims exist no complaint may reach the police. It has long been suspected that some witnesses and victims do not report criminal activity even when it involves overt acts against persons and property. The extent of nonreporting was strictly a matter of conjecture until a president's crime commission conducted surveys on criminal victimization in the mid-1960s. From national surveys it can be concluded that the actual amount of crime involving victims is several times that reported in the *Uniform Crime Reports*.[4] For example, there may be three times as many robberies and burglaries as are recorded in the U.C.R.; and there may be three and a half times as many rapes. The most frequent reasons given by victims for not reporting are that the offense was a private matter or victim did not want to harm the offender, and police could not be effective or would not want to be bothered. In short, Americans often think it is not worthwhile to report that they have been victims of criminal acts, and the validity of the U.C.R. as a measure of criminal activity suffers accordingly.

To further complicate matters, the U.C.R. are of questionable use even for measuring reported crime. Despite the F.B.I.'s provision of consistent formulas and instructions for recording offenses, a crime complaint might be recorded in several ways among the multitude of law enforcement agencies. There is no assurance that what is recorded as a particular crime in one jurisdiction will be similarly recorded in another. Added to this are the problems of honest error, laziness, and deliberate manipulation of data by some agencies to make themselves look good. The statistics ending up in the *Uniform Crime Reports* have been influenced by so many different factors it is impossible to say what they really measure.

What, then, do the *Uniform Crime Reports* tell us? At best, they do indicate the crimes considered most serious by officials and provide some gauge of the activities that occupy law enforcement agencies. We mentioned earlier in this section that one of the annual revelations from the U.C.R. concerns whether crime is rising or not. This does not refer to all crime, but to seven offenses comprising the *Crime Index*. These crimes were selected for the index because they are regarded as among the most serious violations against one's person and property. They include: murder, forcible rape, robbery, aggravated assault, burglary, larceny-theft, and auto theft.

However, only a minor proportion of police activity is spent on the index crimes. In fact, *less than one fifth of all recorded arrests involve such crimes.* For example, practically as many arrests are made for drunkenness as for all the index crimes combined. Police make at least half as many arrests for victimless crimes such as prostitution, narcotics use, gambling, and drunkenness as for all index crimes. Although arrest figures provide no clue as to time spent in investigation, it is inescapable that a great deal of law enforcement time is spent controlling behavior that is unlikely to have elicited complaints. Despite the discrepancy between seriousness of crime and expenditure of police resources, there is little argument that index crimes are felt to be serious matters by most citizens. The remainder of this chapter will be spent on an examination of three such crimes.

Homicide and Aggravated Assault

These two crimes will be discussed together since the difference between them is frequently only a matter of degree. In the U.C.R. homicide is simply defined as the "willful killing of another" and does not include deaths caused by negligence, suicide, accident or justifiable homicide. Aggravated assault is defined as "an unlawful attack by one person upon another for the purpose of inflicting severe bodily injury usually accompanied by the use of a weapon or other means likely to produce death or serious bodily harm." Attempts to murder are included in this category. Understandably the distinction between homicide and aggravated assault may be simply a matter of circumstance: the potency of the weapon used, the ability of the victim to defend him or herself, the effectiveness of medical care, and luck. This writer recalls the not-too-bright youth who was bewildered by his act of murder, claiming, "I stabbed him in the stomach because I had heard it wasn't so dangerous to do that."

Insofar as crime statistics are concerned, those on homicide are considered the most accurate for the obvious reason that corpses are evidence not easily disposed of. On the other hand, statistics on aggravated assault are among the least reliable. Data from a nationwide survey indicate that close to half of all assaults are unreported.[5] Forty-five per cent of the victims who did not report claimed as a reason that the incident was a "private matter." The likelihood that an assault will be reported appears greatest when the offender is a stranger, the victim is not guilty of aggravating the situation, and the resulting injury is serious. But even statistics on reported assaults are heavily influenced by police department policies concerning the recording of fights resulting in minor injuries or between persons who wish to drop the matter after tempers have cooled.[6] Despite the messiness of the statistics on aggravated assault the parallels between the behavior and homicide give us confidence that the offense patterns should be roughly similar.[7] Thus the following discussion, although concentrating on homicide, is relevant to assault as well.

DIMENSIONS OF HOMICIDE

There is no surer way to fill an American courtroom or the front pages of newspapers than to conduct a murder trial. A blend of revulsion and fascination draws us toward murderers, like twenty-six-year-old Samuel M. De Nicola who in 1973 killed a college co-ed by stabbing her twenty-one times. His reason? He liked to kill—he got "satisfaction" out of it.[8]

The attraction toward homicide is often abetted by the "respectable" multiple murderers whose unconcern for human life seems so out of character. In this decade we have already had two outstanding examples. The first was Hubert Mullin, a one-time honor student, who killed ten people in response to telepathic messages. The most dramatic case is Dean Corll, candy store owner and electrician, who was described by neighbors as a "nice, polite man." Corll and his teenaged confederates would pick up young male hitchhikers and runaways, sexually assault them, torture them, and finally put them to death. The known count is twenty-seven, probably the second largest multiple murder case in United States history.[9]

The great majority of homicides, however, are motivated neither by mysterious messages nor by sadism. They usually occur, as we shall see, under far less complex circumstances than many would believe. Our task here is to present those facts about ordinary murder that can be ascertained from available data.

Fact One. The homicide rate is rising in the United States. This may come as no great surprise to most readers, but it is a trend that has developed only within the past fifteen years. The first nationwide data for the *Uniform Crime Reports* go back to 1933; for that year there was a homicide rate of 7.6 persons among every 100,000 persons in the national population.[10] After 1933 rates generally declined, with some fluctuations, until the lowest rate of 4.5 occurred in 1962 and 1963. Thereafter the rate began to climb steadily. The 1933 rate was surpassed by that of 1970—7.8. The rate had risen to 9.3 by 1973, the latest statistic available at this writing.

The rising rate of homicide has resulted in some interesting, if not disturbing, doomsday predictions. Dr. Arnold Barnett and his colleagues at the Massachusetts Institute of Technology have calculated the likelihood that persons born in a specific year will die by murder.[11] By optimistically assuming that current homicide rates *will be maintained at current levels,* Barnett projects that of those persons born in 1974 the following will be murdered: one in eighty-two in Los Angeles, one in sixty-seven in New York, one in sixty in Chicago, one in fifty-one in Miami, and one in thirty-five in Detroit (which has the dubious distinction of being called "Murder Capital, U.S.A."). By pessimistically assuming that rates will *grow* as they have over the past ten years, the figures become: one in thirty-three in Los Angeles, one in seventeen in New York, one in twenty-four in Chicago, one in twenty-one in Miami, and one in fourteen in Detroit.

The reader will note that these projections refer to the largest of American cities. This recognizes that the homicide rate is generally a function of city size: the larger the city the greater the number of persons per 100,000 population who are murdered.[12] What the projections fail to recognize is that the probabilities of being murdered are not evenly distributed throughout any city's population—some groups have a greater exposure to the risk of homicide than do other groups. This leads us to the second fact about homicide.

Fact Two. Murder occurs primarily within the lower economic levels and among males and blacks. The most thorough national analysis of homicide in the United States is a 1967 survey of data from seventeen large cities.[13] One basic conclusion is:

> In spite of reporting problems, the true rates of major violence appear to be much greater for those of lower socioeconomic status than for those of higher status. The poor, uneducated individual with minimal or no employment skills is more likely to commit serious violence than the person higher up on the socioeconomic ladder.[14]

In addition to being concentrated in the lower socioeconomic class, homicide is clearly related to sexual and racial characteristics. Table 4-1 presents the data from the seventeen-city study. As you can see, murder is first of all a male offense: 80 per cent of the offenders and 80 per cent of the victims were men. Furthermore, 73 per cent of the offenders and 70 per cent of the victims were black. You will also notice that there is very little crossover within these two characteristics: 63 per cent of the homicides involve males killing other males, and 66 per cent involve blacks killing blacks. In short, most murders are intrasexual and intraracial. The minor exception is that females, when they do kill, tend to kill males.

TABLE 4-1
SEX AND RACE OF HOMICIDE OFFENDERS AND VICTIMS,
17 CITIES, 1967 * (In per cent of total)

Victims	Offenders				
	Black Males	White Males	Black Females	White Females	Total
Black Males	40	2	13	1	56
White Males	5	16	1	2	24
Black Females	10	1	3	<1	14
White Females	1	5	<1	<1	6
Total	56	24	17	3	100%

* Derived from Donald J. Mulvihill and Melvin M. Tumin, *Crimes of Violence,* Staff Report Submitted to the National Commission on the Causes and Prevention of Violence, vol. 11 (Washington, D.C.: Government Printing Office, 1969), pp. 268–269.

Fact Three. Most murders are committed by persons acquainted with their victims. One of the great fears over crime in the streets concerns the possibility that one will be assaulted by a stranger. As it turns out, however, you are safer from strangers than from your family and friends. The proportion of murders occurring between acquaintances varies according to the city investigated,[15] but all studies are in agreement that if you are murdered, chances are that it will be by someone you recognize—whatever consolation that is. In the seventeen-city study, the 1967 data revealed the following relationships among homicide participants (regardless of who was the victim or the offender): husband-wife killings accounted for 16 per cent of all homicides; other family members, 9 per cent; close friends, lovers, neighbors, 13 per cent; and miscellaneous acquaintances (sex rivals, business colleagues, and so on), 25 per cent. The remaining 37 per cent involved strangers and an unknown category that undoubtedly contained mostly strangers.[16]

Because so many murders involve acquaintances, it is not surprising that slightly over one third of all murders occur in the home; the street that we all fear accounts for about one quarter, and the remainder occur inside other buildings such as bars.[17] Obviously under these circumstances police forces will remain relatively helpless to do anything about the murder rate. Until more murder moves into the street there is little any law enforcement agency can do to protect any of us.

Fact Four. Most murders occur over trivial matters. It makes interesting literature to plumb the inner depths of a Macbeth who murders because he is driven by the urgings of his wife and a lust for power. But the average murderer is no Macbeth. The non-Shakespearian dialogue ending in a death is more likely to go something like this:

"You got a cigarette?"
"Naw, I ain't got any."

Or:

"Hey, you're lookin' at me."
"No I ain't."
"Yes you are. Why you lookin' at me?" [18]

People die because they refuse to lend someone a dollar, they renege on five-dollar bets, or they are seen with someone else's girl friend. This writer recalls the boy who, being refused more white meat from the Thanksgiving turkey, left the dining room, came back with his rifle, and shot his father through the head.

Police data on immediate events leading up to a homicide are imprecise for obvious reasons, but they do indicate that *most murders are spontaneous events occurring over minor disagreements,* not the result of a long-considered determination to kill. The seventeen-city study found that quarrels, usually trivial, account for 43 per cent of all homicides.[19] Jealousy, revenge, and sexual reasons account for another 9 per cent. Nine per cent occurred during robberies, 21 per cent could not be ascertained from the data, and the remaining 18 per cent were thinly scattered among other categories.

Fact Five. A significant proportion of murder victims contribute substantially to their own deaths. The usual assumption about murder victims is that they are individuals caught up in circumstances over which they have no control. In truth a great number of homicides are *victim precipitated,* that is, the victim was the first to use force in the homicide incident. Data from the seventeen-city survey indicate that in at least 22 per cent of the homicides, the victims themselves precipitated the behavior leading to death. Some examples are:

> During a lover's quarrel, the male hit his mistress and threw a can of kerosene at her. She retaliated by throwing the liquid on him, and then tossed a lighted match in his direction.

> A drunken husband, beating his wife in their kitchen, gave her a butcher knife and dared her to use it on him. She said if he struck her again she would use it. He did and so did she.[20]

Fact Six. Alcohol is associated with a large proportion of homicides. It is important to point out at the onset that no drug, whether alcohol or any known narcotic, is capable of compelling someone to engage in homicide, rape, petunia pruning, or any complex form of behavior. In short, alcohol does not cause an act of homicide. But alcohol can modify behavior: it may cause a person to become more readily excited to impatience or anger; it may hamper a person's ability to evaluate a situation leading to physical aggression and danger; or it may reduce inhibitions that would otherwise restrict the expression of insulting and provoking remarks. Several old jokes are based on the theme of a crowded barroom in which a drunk shouts, "I can lick any man in the place!" Like so much humor, it has basis in reality. A little whiskey goes a long way toward spilling much blood.

(In Chapter 8 we shall see that there is a debate over the extent to which alcohol reduces inhibitions or affects social behavior. For now it is sufficient to say that alcohol is associated in some way with aggression in the United States.)

There are no national data on the extent to which alcohol is related to acts of aggression. However, city surveys provide evidence that the relationship is not a minor one; alcohol has been found in the murderers in as many as 83 per cent of the cases.[21] In a recent Boston study the blood alcohol concentration was measured on a sample of adult males admitted to a hospital emergency ward. Among those admitted for treatment of injuries resulting from fights and assaults, 56 per cent had alcohol present.[22]

A related issue is the extent to which other drugs such as heroin contribute to crimes of violence. The evidence here is particularly skimpy because medical examiners generally confine their checks for the presence of narcotics to a search for needle tracks rather than testing blood and tissue samples. However, researchers in Detroit and Philadelphia estimate that between one quarter and one third of the homicides in those cities—thus not indicative of the national picture—involve drug-using victims, and that the proportions have been increasing since 1969.[23]

The relationship between drug use and homicide can be partly explained by the presence of high rates for both within the same population: young, poor, urban, black males. But the overlap of drugs and homicide has been found to stem directly from risks associated with the world of drug use. Margaret A. Zahn and her associates discovered that the contexts of homicide differ considerably depending upon whether the victims were users or not. Whereas most nonusers die during domestic quarrels and arguments in bars, the majority of users are killed while engaged in illegal behaviors such as holdups and while in arguments concerning drugs. In short, the drug users' attempts to obtain illegal drugs or money for drugs heightens the risks of death by homicide.

VIOLENCE: AN AMERICAN VALUE

Attempts to explain homicide are hardly rare—they range from Lombroso's specifications of the murderer's atavistic characteristics to studies of abnormal brain functioning to a recent study linking rates of homicide with phases of the moon (the researchers found that a full moon over Miami is not only romantic but also lethal).[24] Any theory, in order to have wide application, must at least deal with the aspects of homicide discussed above. It must explain why the major proportion of murders are spontaneous affairs between acquaintances who are lower class males. It is tempting to limit an explanation to frustration and social-economic deprivation as causes. But social class alone does not account for differences in rates. Sizeable segments of any large industrial society occupy disadvantaged positions without invariably producing high homicide rates.

In order to understand homicide in America we must first recognize the traditional role violence has played here. Contrary to what many would prefer to believe, American history is filled with violence of great variety. For example:

> The United States has had the bloodiest and most violent labor history of any industrial nation in the world. Labor violence was not confined to certain industries, geographic areas, or specific groups in the labor force, al-

though it has been more frequent in some industries than in others. There have been few sections and scarcely any industries in which violence has not erupted at some time, and even more serious confrontations have on occasion followed.[25]

Labor violence is but a single example of the many types of violence characterizing American history. We also have a long tradition of racial conflict; the first slave uprising, which was brutally crushed, dates back to 1712. The modern era of racial conflict produced thirty-three major urban riots between 1900 and 1949. The bloodiest of these was in East St. Louis (1917) during which nine whites and at least thirty-nine blacks lost their lives. In the period from 1964 to 1968 over 200 riots occurred, producing little loss of life, but very high property damage.

Yet another example in our history of violence is the lynch mob, an American invention. It emerged in the back country of South Carolina in 1767 and was later named after Colonel Charles Lynch of Virginia. *The lynch mob is a spontaneously formed group for the purpose of punishing individuals, usually by hanging, for their alleged crimes.* All of this is without legal authority, although historically the authorities often chose to look the other way. Such mobs are thought by most people to be phenomena of the western frontier—where they were known as necktie parties. But they were common in the South as a post-Civil War method of maintaining white supremacy. It is estimated that from 1882 to 1903 lynch mobs in the South killed a total of 1,985 blacks, often without proof that an offense had even occurred.[26]

Our violence-drenched history is further exemplified by: 1. great blood feuds occurring between families in the mountains of Kentucky, West Virginia, Virginia, and central Texas during the final half of the last century; 2. the war between whites and American Indians that raged almost continuously from 1607 to 1890—a year that saw the massacre of 300 Sioux men, women, and children by U.S. troops at Wounded Knee, South Dakota; and 3. the activities of organized crime, which between 1919 and 1967 resulted in nearly a thousand gang murders in Chicago alone.[27]

Whether we refer to the violence surrounding the birth of our nation (for examples, the illegal Boston Tea Party and the frequent tarring-and-feathering of those loyal to England) or to organized crime's forceful elimination of informers and competitors ("cement overshoes" and a deep river, strangulation, or simply a few bullets), we are referring to a time-honored way of dealing with conflict situations. The American government itself has often used deadly force to control parts of its population. Examples range from the armed skirmishes in Ludlow, Colorado between strikers and the National Guard in 1914—resulting in over fifty deaths including a dozen strikers' children—to the National Guard killing of unarmed student war protesters at Kent State University in 1970.

But the ready resort to force is not restricted to government alone. Our history also includes many protests and crusades that turned into violent confrontations because at least one group perceived the government as being in error, indifferent, ineffectual, or as having no business in the dispute. It is a widespread value to regard violence, whether by the government or others, as a logical and legitimate means toward solving problems and accomplishing group goals.

What is known as the *frontier tradition* exemplifies to a great extent the American approval of violence.[28] Life on the American frontier required that individuals rely on their own initiative and resources for nearly everything necessary to exploit what the land had to offer. The same was true of justice. Decisions about lawbreaking often had to be made on the spot. The lack of official jails or courts for miles or the lack of funds to hire law enforcement officers often left little choice in handling suspected offenders—either do them in immediately or release them, possibly to return another day. Taking the law into one's own hands was practically the only alternative in many cases.

To establish order and to maintain a sense of personal security in the absence of official law enforcement, men frequently formed *vigilante* groups whose purpose was to implement the law as they felt the occasion demanded. The difference between the lynch mob and the vigilante group was a matter of degree; vigilantes were more organized and lasted longer—in some cases years. Up to 1910, at least 326 such groups had existed in the United States, about two-thirds of them west of the Mississippi.[29] In many areas vigilantes represented the only form of law; like lynch mobs they depended upon rapid judgment and execution by hanging. Their targets generally included murderers, robbers, horse thieves, and counterfeiters of money and bank notes. But frequently politics, color of skin, or religion were reasons enough for being judged by them. Some groups persisted despite the eventual presence of legal authorities, and in administering their own brand of justice these groups became outlaws themselves.

On-the-spot justice by individuals and by vigilantes was often necessary on the frontier. But the end of the frontier and the arrival of official justice did not erase completely the values to which the frontier had given birth. These values are legacies contributing to contemporary violence. First, there exists an *idealized version of manhood*. Manhood means confidence in physical prowess in man-to-man confrontations; it means being rough and ready with one's fists; and it means standing tall against affronts and danger. Neither the heroes nor villains of the frontier were sissies—like John Wayne they stood, firm of jaw and purpose, against adversity. Second, there exists a *tradition of gun ownership* in American society. Guns were once an absolute necessity for food and defense; today they are symbols of the independent spirit and masculinity associated with the man with the six-shooter, ready for a shoot-out at high noon. (More about guns will be discussed later.) Third, there exists a feeling of *independence from authority*. Vigilantes were conceived of as democratic organizations—products of the people, the ordinary folk. Americans still believe they have the right to avenge wrongs, to be armed, and to enforce the law themselves if appropriate authorities do not perform satisfactorily. The following passage expresses the purpose of one vigilante group formed in 1858; except for the quaint language the message is definitely applicable to contemporary America:

> Whereas, We are believers in the *doctrine of popular sovereignty;* that the people of this country are the real sovereigns, and that whenever the laws, made by those to whom they have delegated their authority, are found inadequate to their protection, it is the right of the people to take the protection of their property into their own hands, and deal with these villains according to their just desserts [sic].[30]

Fourth, there exists a belief in *violence as a successful solution to problems*. Obviously, violence is a direct way of dealing with the disagreeable. Be it a punch in the nose or a bullet to the brain, violence properly applied avoids the necessity of being accommodating; it can be a successful technique in eliminating sources of fear, competition, or anger, and it can be persuasive to others who may contemplate doing you wrong. The point is that violence can succeed in altering circumstances in one's favor, whether in group or individual conflict. Unquestionably, violence has done much to make America what it is. Its frontier lands were opened to whites by the near elimination of the Indians. In addition, its independence was achieved by revolution, its agricultural accomplishments in the South were realized through the subjugation of blacks, and its labor movement emerged in a crucible of violent conflict with management and government. To some degree civil rights accomplishments and the end of the Vietnam War were the results of violence.

The frontier with its environment of independence and brutality and the continued history of violence form a large part of the background of contemporary murder and mayhem in America. This is not to say that violence as a value is solely the result of tradition. Problems of gross inequality, both economic and social, also play a part in producing violence, but historical precedents undoubtedly continue to shape contemporary attitudes.

What are those attitudes? A 1969 survey of American males clearly indicates that a large proportion approve of extreme violence in situations not involving significant danger to life or property. In their conclusions the researchers voiced their concern:

> The fact that almost 50 percent of American men felt that shooting was a good way of handling campus disturbances "almost always" or at least "sometimes" is particularly disturbing. Most campus disturbances have not involved violence to persons or major damage to property. That 20 percent of American men considered it appropriate to kill in these circumstances indicates the ease with which many people will accept violence to maintain order even when force so used is entirely out of proportion to the precipitating incidents. The data imply that willingness to reach for a gun is easily evoked.[31]

The same researchers also found that 24 per cent of the respondents agreed with the statement, " 'An eye for an eye and a tooth for a tooth' is a good rule for living." Forty-four per cent felt that "Violence deserves violence." [32]

The researchers then asked some important questions:

> Where do Americans learn such values? Are we teaching such values in the early school years when we urge our boys to "hit back?" Do we teach such values in the typical courses in American history, with their uncritical justification of the slaughter of the Indians, the fight for independence, the frontier wars and all the other domestic and international conflict in which this country has engaged? Or is the endless violent retribution served daily by television and the movies as damaging as some critics allege? [33]

Such questions are still unanswerable. But one fact is inescapable—values justifying violence, whatever their source, are prevalent in American society.

A SUBCULTURE OF INTERPERSONAL VIOLENCE

Recognizing the existence of violence-justifying values in American society brings us only part way toward understanding why homicide occurs the way it does. The problem is that there are different types of violence designed to solve different kinds of problems. For example, there is the citizen who supports the police who shoot protesting students, or the plant manager who advocates hiring thugs to "bust some heads" to break up union activities. But these persons may not be at all inclined to the use of violence to solve interpersonal problems. They may never slap their girl friends for infidelity or exchange blows with those who insult them. The theme of violence has many variations, but the one of interest to us is that involving the great proportion of criminal homicides—those between lower class acquaintances over personal matters.

There is a segment of the American population that has been described as a *subculture of violence*. This term, suggested by Marvin E.

Wolfgang and Franco Ferracuti, refers to groups in which overt physical violence is the acceptable, if not expected, response to certain interpersonal situations.[34] Wolfgang points out some characteristics of this subculture in his study of homicide in Philadelphia:

> [T]he significance of a jostle, a slightly derogatory remark, or the appearance of a weapon in the hands of an adversary are stimuli differentially perceived and interpreted by Negroes and whites, males and females. . . . A male is usually expected to defend the name and honor of his mother, the virtue of womanhood (even though his female companion for the evening may be an entirely new acquaintance and/or a prostitute), and to accept no derogation about his race (even from a member of his own race), his age, or his masculinity. Quick resort to physical combat as a measure of daring, courage, or defense of status appears to be a cultural expectation, especially for lower socioeconomic class males of both races. When such a culture norm response is elicited from an individual engaged in social interplay with others who harbor the same response mechanism, physical assaults, altercations, and violent domestic quarrels that result in homicide are likely to be relatively common. The upper-middle and upper social class value system defines and codifies behavior norms into legal rules that often transcend subcultural [norms], and considers many of the social and personal stimuli that evoke a combative reaction in the lower classes as "trivial." Thus, there exists a cultural antipathy between many folk rationalizations of the lower class, and of males of both races, on the one hand, and the middle-class norms under which they live, on the other.[35]

Thus an argument can be made that many, if not most, assaults and homicides are not so widely condemned as often believed. The interests of some groups clearly define the situations under which physical violence will arise and death becomes a distinct possibility. If you were a male and were to enter a faculty club and confront a professor by calling his mother a practicing whore, about all you might get is a puzzled look and a turned back. The results probably would be quite different in a dockside tavern where you confronted a longshoreman with a similar comment. Although the consequences are not similar, the observers in either case would agree you got what you deserved. But in this instance the legal system is much more sympathetic to the norms of the professor than to those of the longshoreman; the professor did the "right" thing, the longshoreman would be arrested.

Threats to one's masculinity, reputation, and independence appear to be trivial in one context, but in others they may be anything but trivial. The longshoreman would have to respond aggressively or face ridicule and disdain from his friends. So, to him and to his friends the matter was not trivial. Thus a general value condoning violence to solve problems is adapted to fit specific personal situations without any feeling of guilt. As Wolfgang comments:

It is not farfetched to suggest that a whole culture may accept the violence value, demand or encourage adherence to it, and penalize deviation. During periods of war the whole nation accepts the principle of violence against the enemy. The non-violent citizen turned soldier adopts the value as an intimately internalized re-enforcement for his rationalization to kill. This is, of course, selective killing of an enemy, and in this respect is different from most homicide. But criminal homicide is also "selective," not [in]discriminate slaying. . . . And as in combat on the front lines where the "it-was-either-him-or-me" situation arises, there are similar attitudes and reactions among participants in homicide.[36]

But the existence of a subculture of interpersonal violence does not explain how assaults and homicides arise, because values alone do not create the situations and opportunities in which violence emerges.[37] For example, the longshoreman we mentioned above might have serenely passed his time in the bar had you not come in and made a nuisance of yourself. There must be situational factors that correspond to the justifications of violence. The following figure generally illustrates what we mean.

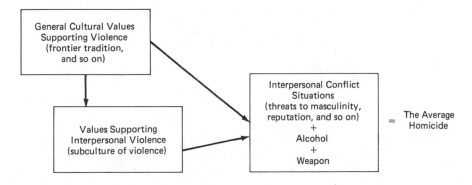

In short, homicides are comprised of several components, even though the results appear to be simple, spontaneous acts of passion. The culture not only provides values supporting violence—by implication values disregarding the importance of human life—but also generates situations that spark tempers to the point of overt aggression. Those situations usually include alcohol and a weapon, a combination that can turn a minor disagreement into a lethal conflict. But the dynamics of how values become translated into situations leading to homicide remain a matter of conjecture.

The reader will note that the preceding discussion and figure were limited to the components of average homicides—those between acquaintances over personal matters. Not included are certain other murders that are more fearsome despite their being in the distinct minority:

People are often killed by robbers even though they have meekly surrendered their valuables. Women are killed after giving their bodies to rapists. Elderly people are murdered as casually as if it were a matter of routine—like smoking a cigarette after dinner. Not so long ago, a luncheonette owner was killed, and his wife wounded, for not having apple pie on the premises. Here is the real reason murder is so horrifying: it is so often committed without adequate reason, or for no reason.[38]

For these kinds of murders no satisfactory explanation exists. We can conjecture that such callous indifference to human life when seeking money or sexual satisfaction stems from many of the same historical sources discussed above. But it is questionable whether such killings are supported by the expectations of any group or subculture. One might suggest that these so-called murders without reason represent a form of political terrorism, but to date that assumption is purely speculative and without any hard evidence. Until we know more about the circumstances and persons involved in apparently senseless murders, the dynamics of such acts remain a mystery.

The reader should not assume from this discussion that interpersonal violence is monopolized by the lower class while the other classes docilely go about their lives. A 1968 national survey of adults revealed the following:

The poor and less educated are not more likely than the middle class to resort to physical forms of aggression. We have assumed that middle-class persons vent their hostilities through more sedate channels; i.e., they are supposed to be more verbally violent. Actually physical violence is reported as equally common among all income groups and education levels. This finding is also true for *frequency* of physical violence. The middle class is not only as likely as others ever to have engaged in physical aggression, but have done so as often. If anything, the middle class is more prone toward physical assault (punching, beating, slapping) than the poor.[39]

Violence is pervasive in the United States. Lower class homicide rates only indicate a greater degree of violence.

"GUNS DON'T KILL PEOPLE"

The government of any society has an intense interest in controlling violence. Any government wants to maintain a monopoly on violence, if only to prevent the possibility of the government's violent overthrow. Whenever unauthorized violence occurs, the power of the state to manage its members is called into question. In extreme situations the people themselves may completely usurp the state's power, as they obviously did in the cases of vigilante and lynch groups. One way a government might exert control over illegal violence is to use the law to disarm the population, thus restricting the most potent means of violence to the police and armed forces. In America the citizens' right to bear arms is the focus of vehement interest group conflict, which is directly relevant to homicide.

Before discussing the character of this conflict, it will be helpful to briefly examine what guns mean to murder in America. The reader will recall that in our previous discussion the presence of a weapon was considered an important component in homicide incidents. The weapon's importance is clear from the statistics: 91 per cent of all murders in 1973 involved some weapon other than someone's hands or feet. The specific statistics on murder weapons are shown in Table 4-2.

TABLE 4–2
MURDER BY TYPE OF WEAPON USED, 1973

Handguns	53%
Knives and cutting instruments	18%
Hands and feet	9%
Shotguns	8%
Blunt objects, poisons, explosives, etc.	7%
Rifles	6%

Source: *Crime in the United States, 1973, Uniform Crime Reports* (Washington, D.C.: Government Printing Office, 1974), p. 9.

Clearly, guns play a crucial role in homicide: 67 per cent of all homicide victims were shot to death. Handguns alone account for over half. It is no coincidence that the geographic area with the highest proportion of guns also has the highest murder rate: 59 per cent of all households own weapons in the South (South Central and South Atlantic states).[40] By comparison, households of the East (New England and Middle Atlantic states) have a 33 per cent ownership rate. In 1973, the South's murder rate was 12.9 per 100,000; the East's was 7.6.[41]

Guns and violence have been partners in the tradition of American life:

> For many years the armed citizen-soldier was the country's first line of defense; the "Kentucky" long rifle opened the frontier; the Winchester repeater "won the West"; and the Colt revolver "made men equal." [42]

The frontier that required guns has long disappeared, but the American's love for guns surely remains. It is estimated that there are nearly 100,000,000 guns in civilian hands.[43] More than two-thirds of these are shotguns and rifles, mostly sporting weapons. But some 30,000,000 weapons are handguns and they are concentrated in urban areas. Chances are good that the highest proportion of handguns will be found in Detroit. In 1974 the Detroit Police Commissioner estimated that there was a handgun for every three persons in his city, or one gun for every household.[44]

Handguns are seldom intended for sport. Their purpose is starkly simple—to maim or kill a human being. This is particularly the case for the so-called Saturday Night Special. This type of weapon received its name from Detroit police in the late 1950s.[45] Detroiters who found it difficult to purchase a gun in their city drove to Toledo where cheap guns were sold in grocery stores, gas stations, flower shops, candy stores—anywhere. Because these sales usually were made on the weekends, the Saturday Night Special was born. Today, the term generally refers to any cheap ($3.50 and up) handgun with a short barrel; these weapons have no safety features, no engineering quality, and little accuracy. Because they are useless as hunting or target-shooting weapons, their only purpose is to shoot a human being at short range.

The widespread existence among civilians of guns designed specifically to kill humans reflects the easy availability of lethal weapons in America. The legal restrictions concerning handguns are mixed:

> Laws relating to the buying and keeping of handguns are mishmash, and except in a dozen states (notably the Northeastern bloc—New York, New Jersey, Connecticut, Massachusetts, Rhode Island, Pennsylvania) where the standards are high, they are mostly mish. In those areas of the country where handguns equate with *machismo* [masculinity, virility]—places like Louisiana, Arizona, Nevada, Texas, Mississippi—control laws are nonexistent or scarce or largely ignored. In Texas, for instance, there is no required waiting period before purchasing a gun, no required permit or registration of guns, no license needed for carrying weapons either openly or concealed, no license needed for carrying a gun in a vehicle.[46]

Thus in many places guns are not only available, but can be purchased with a minimum of difficulty; in 42 states no license is needed to buy a handgun. Even the federal laws are limited in their coverage. There are federal laws against the possession of automatic weapons, restrictions on mail order business, and the importation of foreign firearms. Does this mean that citizens do not want stricter gun controls? The evidence is that they do, but the lack of such legislation is a classic example of interest group conflict in which the majority does not necessarily prevail. As early as 1959 public opinion polls showed that a majority of citizens wanted strict federal regulation of firearms; a 1972 poll indicated that 71 per cent of adults feel that no one should own a gun without a police permit.[47] The history of attempts to legislate gun control is filled with controversy. Perhaps only drug and abortion issues cause so much emotion.

The primary resistance to any gun control legislation comes from the National Rifle Association, which through its monthly magazine, *American Rifleman,* can call to action approximately 1 million members. In 1968 the N. R. A. boasted that within seventy-two hours it could produce more than a half million pieces of mail to members of Congress on any gun legislation. One senator remarked:

I'd rather be a deer in hunting season than a politician who has run afoul of the N. R. A. crowd. Most of us are scared to death of them. They range from bus drivers to bank presidents, from Minutemen [a rightwing organization for conducting guerrilla warfare in the event of a communist invasion] to four-star generals, and from morons to geniuses, but they have one thing in common: they don't want *any*one to tell them *any*thing about what to do with their guns, and they *mean* it.[48]

N.R.A. arguments opposing gun control bills generally take three forms:

1. *Gun control is unconstitutional.* The Second Amendment to the American Constitution reads: "A well regulated Militia, being necessary to the security of a free State, the right of the people to keep and bear Arms shall not be infringed." From this, the N.R.A. claims, derives a constitutional right of Americans to own and legally use firearms. Opponents to this stand argue that no such guarantee is made for individual citizens; all that the second amendment ensures is the right of states to maintain armed citizen militias.

2. *"Guns don't kill people—people do."* The logic here is that the people, not the guns, need regulation. The analogy is often carried to its logical extreme by N.R.A. supporters: the automobile kills thousands every year, therefore it should be impossible to buy one. Rope, butcher knives, hammers, poisons, and so on also kill and should be banned. Consistent with this argument the N.R.A. prefers harsh penalties for persons committing crimes with guns rather than restricting the sales of guns themselves. A favorite N.R.A. legislator is Representative Bob Casey, a Texas Democrat, who submitted a bill in the U.S. House of Representatives to make any serious crime committed with a gun a federal offense with a mandatory twenty-five year prison sentence.

Opponents of the "guns don't kill people" position argue that the gun has but one purpose—to destroy something. Therefore its control, not its elimination, is desirable. The trouble with guns, these opponents stress, is that they are likely to be more lethal than any other weapon:

Homicide is seldom the result of a single-minded intent to kill. Most often it is an attack growing out of an altercation and committed in a rage that leads to fatal injuries. . . . . When a gun is used, the chances of death are about five times as great as when a knife is used.[49]

Furthermore, harsh penalties can be a double-edged sword. They might deter persons from using a gun in a crime, or they might encourage the avoidance of consequences by eliminating witnesses. In effect, a simple armed robbery could turn into a blood bath.

3. *"When guns are outlawed only outlaws will have guns."* There are actually two issues embodied in this claim. One concerns the likelihood that criminals will still have guns even if gun control legislation is passed. Gun control proponents are likely to concede this is true because so many guns are already in the hands of persons using them for illegal purposes. However, argue the proponents, laws can limit the transfer of guns from manufacturers, dealers, and so on to persons who might use them in crimes; and the law could drastically reduce the output of handguns that are so predominant in crime.[50]

The second issue in this argument against gun control focuses on the word *disarm*. A substantial proportion of gun control opponents argue that gun control will force law-abiding citizens to relinquish their weapons. A smaller but still substantial number contend that an armed population is necessary should a last ditch stand against communist invaders become necessary. Witnesses testifying at legislative hearings have suggested darkly that framers of gun control bills are working with foreign governments interested in taking over the United States.[51]

This aspect of the gun control debate creates a good deal more heat than light, especially since no major gun control bill has even remotely suggested disarming sportsmen or target shooters. But it does illustrate the emotion that the proposal of gun control generates.

There is, as you probably have guessed, more behind the drives to prevent gun control laws than constitutional and sociological issues. Gun manufacturers and gun-related industries, which advertise heavily in *American Rifleman,* constitute big business for whom gun control can only mean trouble. As one student of the industries puts it:

> Gun owners spend an estimated $2 billion a year, at the minimum, on this business—quite enough money to keep Congress and all state legislatures apprised of the desires of the gun and ammunition manufacturers, retail gun dealers, sports clothes manufacturers, gun magazine publishers, antique-gun dealers, hunting resort owners, and "conservation" groups which get a kickback from ammunition sales. At the bottom, it isn't tradition but trade that controls this issue.[52]

The N.R.A., a grass-roots organization of the common people, is ably assisted in its anti-gun control campaigns by another lobbying group: the National Shooting Sports Foundation. The N.S.S.F. membership is made up of major gun manufacturers, gun dealers, gun and sports magazines, and assorted gun-related firms; in short, it is a business interest group. Its primary means of influence are thousands of bulletins to various individuals and groups: sporting goods dealers, outdoor and sports writers, radio stations, and whatever media might provide a forum for criticizing proposed legislation.

To date, the combined efforts of the N.R.A. and the N.S.S.F., coupled with the public's apathy toward organizing counter-efforts, have proven effective in forestalling strict gun control legislation. Whatever you may think of the arguments either favoring or opposing such legislation, one lesson emerges. Attempts to control even those acts strongly condemned by public consensus and the criminal code (in this case, homicide) involve interest group conflict.[53]

Forcible Rape

The *Uniform Crime Reports* define forcible rape as "carnal knowledge of a female through the use of force or the threat of force." Included within the definition is assault to commit rape; not included is "statutory rape," which is the legal term applied to intercourse, with consent, with an underaged female. In most states an underaged female is one less than sixteen or eighteen years old. Also excluded from the definition are rapes in which males are the victims. Very few rape statutes in criminal codes provide for the possibility of males being sexually assaulted—the rape of males is thus legally impossible. In reality, despite the daydreams of many men, females rarely force sexual intercourse on males, but the rape of males *by* males is not so unusual. This aspect of sexual violence will be considered shortly, but first we will concentrate on the offenses of males against females.

Despite the shock and injury that are likely to result from rape, only a fraction of female rape victims ever report the incident to police. In a 1972 study of the five largest American cities (Chicago, Detroit, Los Angeles, New York, and Philadelphia) respondents were asked about being victimized by certain criminal acts. Of those females who claimed to have been sexually assaulted, only from 46 per cent (Los Angeles) to 61 per cent (New York) reported it.[54] But even reporting a rape does not insure its being recorded as an offense, especially if police feel things are complicated by a previous relationship. In the words of the *Uniform Crime Reports:*

> As a national average, 15 per cent of all forcible rapes reported to police were determined by investigation to be unfounded. In other words, the police established that no forcible rape offense or attempt occurred. This is caused primarily due to the question of the use or threat of force frequently complicated by a prior relationship between victim and offender.[55]

Much of the problem of obtaining accurate information on the occurrence and characteristics of rape stems from the nature of the act

itself. Unlike homicide cases where the victim can be obviously identified, in a supposed rape case the existence of a victim cannot always
be taken for granted. If, for example, the victim shows no signs of
being forced into the act—torn clothes, bruises, and so on—a question arises. Was the woman too frightened to put up any resistance,
or was the claim of rape simply an afterthought to ease pangs of conscience or to provide an alibi to a husband or parents?

The available data on the nature of force used in rape cases is
meager and to some extent inconsistent. A Philadelphia study by
Menachem Amir indicates that no overt force was applied in 15 per
cent of the rapes; in 28 per cent there was roughness; in 11 per cent
the victims were choked; and in 46 per cent of the cases the victims
were beaten to some degree.[56] In the seventeen-city survey discussed
earlier the researchers found that there were no physical injuries in 76
per cent of the rape cases. Incorporating the findings of both studies,
it appears that the use of force to counteract the woman's resistance
is common but additional physical harm is not.[57] This means that in a
substantial minority of cases there will be no obvious evidence of
force.

Police become especially skeptical that a rape has occurred if the
male is an acquaintance of the woman and if they suspect her of
being freer with sexual favors than she admits. Thus under some circumstances, even if a victim reports an actual offense, she faces the
problem of convincing the police that she was forced, not seduced,
and that it was a humiliating, not a joyful, experience. If a woman
does not choose to risk serious injury by resisting, she becomes suspect and may be further humiliated by legal authorities.[58] Add to
these problems those a woman must face as a rape victim, and there
is little incentive to report any but the most flagrant cases:

> Public exposure of rape will subject the victim to the risk of stigmatization
> on three levels: negative status is conferred because she is known as a vic-
> tim and loser, because an actual act of intercourse with an illegal partner
> has become common knowledge, and because a most intimate experience
> can be discussed openly. Sexual behavior of women is especially cloaked
> in secrecy. Public knowledge and open discussion is tantamount to leaving
> her naked in a crowd of curious observers. Public identification as a rape
> victim contributes to the self-conception and social identity of being "the
> kind of woman who gets raped." Trauma may in part derive from the fact
> that she may no longer be able to command the male companionship that
> was congruent with her higher pre-rape status.[59]

DIMENSIONS OF RAPE

Anyone attempting to discuss the "facts" of rape in the United States
does so in the face of some knotty problems. As we mentioned ear-

lier there is reason to believe that in at least one city, Los Angeles, fewer than half the rapes are even reported. We also know that some unknown proportion of reported cases will not be found in the statistics because police choose to disbelieve the women involved. So the following "facts" scarcely deserve the name if the intent is to portray more than what the official statistics tell us. Because research on rape using other than police records is rare, we are left with rather slim evidence about what the real picture of sexual assault is like.

Fact One. According to the Uniform Crime Reports rates of rape are rising. The *Uniform Crime Reports* record a steady, but not dramatic, increase in rape rates from a low in 1933 of 3.7 per 100,000 national population to 24.3 in 1973 (this amounts to 47 out of every 100,000 females).[60] Unfortunately we know even less about the willingness of women to report sexual assaults in the period from 1933 to 1972 than we do now. Over the years women's reporting practices and the police response to them may not have changed; on the other hand, maybe they have. In short, no one can convincingly argue that American males have become more sexually aggressive during the past forty-five years, without proving that women are either as willing or less willing to report than in the past.

Fact Two. According to official statistics, sexual assault occurs primarily within the lower economic levels and among males and blacks within those levels. Amir's Philadelphia study and the 1967 seventeen-city survey, both of which used official police records, clearly point to the lower social classes as the source of the greatest proportion of rapes.[61] They also show that race is an important factor. Table 4-3 presents data from the seventeen-city study. Seventy per cent of the offenders and 60 per cent of the victims were black. As with homicide, rape is primarily an intraracial offense. Practically all of the reported rapes of black females were by black males; 75 per cent of the rapes of white females were by white males.[62]

TABLE 4-3
RACE OF RAPE OFFENDERS AND VICTIMS,
17 CITIES, 1967 * (In per cent of total)

Victims	Offenders		
	Black	White	Total
Black	60	<1	60
White	10	30	40
Total	70	30	100%

* Derived from: Donald J. Mulvihill and Melvin M. Tumin, *Crimes of Violence*, Staff Report Submitted to the National Commission on the Causes and Prevention of Violence, vol. 11 (Washington, D.C.: Government Printing Office, 1969), p. 212.

Fact Three. According to official statistics, sexual assaults are committed by acquaintances and strangers in about equal proportions. As we mentioned earlier, the definition of what constitutes rape excludes some unknown proportion of serious sexual assaults: males attacking males. Yet another omission becomes obvious when we examine the relationship between the offender and his victim, namely, forcible sexual conduct when the offender is the victim's husband. The state's decision that two people are married automatically excludes the legal possibility of rape. This is not to say that husbands may not be charged with other offenses, simple assault for example, but there is a definite lack of official concern over conduct that could be as brutal and humiliating as any between strangers. Unquestionably good arguments can be made for the state staying as far out of the activities of the home as possible. Nevertheless, the neglect of rapes in marriage (assuming they would even be reported) further substantiates our point—statistics on rape provide no indication of the real extent of sexual assaults in our society.

Returning to the point of our third fact, it appears that fear of the stranger is somewhat more realistic for rape than for homicide. In the seventeen-city survey 53 per cent of the reported rapes were between complete strangers; close friends and relatives (other than husbands, of course) accounted for another 10 per cent; and the remainder were other acquaintances.[63] More than half (52 per cent) of the reported rapes occurred in the home. Most of these offenses were committed by relatives and acquaintances, not by the persons most feared—the marauding stranger who sneaks into the house to rape unsuspecting females. Most other rapes (34 per cent) occur in automobiles and other outside locations such as streets and alleys.

> Regardless of where and how a man or group of males may first approach a woman who is subsequently raped, the discernible pattern is toward finding a more intimate, nonpublic place, even if it is only the back seat of an automobile.
>
> .   .   .
>
> In the course of their daily activities, women often come in contact with relatives, good friends, paramours, and the like, in private indoor places. Without undue hesitation, women often accompany these same people to such places for social functions. In each case, the eventual offender is more able and the eventual victim more willing to interact in a private indoor location before the sequence leading to rape. On the other hand, while acquaintances, neighbors, co-workers, strangers, and the like, may seek and often gain an intimate indoor location for rape, the general reluctance of women to interact with less well-known men in this setting increases the likelihood of attack in automobiles or on the street.[64]

Thus it appears that females are often unwitting collaborators in setting up conditions favorable to sexual assault. Researchers and the offenders themselves also argue that women often contribute more to the rape than a private setting. However, the "fact" of female participation in rape is controversial and will be considered in some detail shortly.

Fact Four. A large proportion of reported rapes involve more than one offender. Our information about group rapes—one female and two or more males—is especially meager. Yet one study indicates that nearly half of the reported offenses involve more than one male. Specifically, Amir found in Philadelphia that 57 per cent of the victims were raped by one male; 16 per cent by two males; and the remaining 27 per cent by three or more.[65] How closely the Philadelphia data represent the national situation is unknown, but they lead us to suspect that group rapes may be more likely to be reported because of the greater humiliation and shock they may produce.

Fact Five. Alcohol is associated with a large proportion of reported rapes. When it comes to sexual activity alcohol can provide mixed results. On the one hand, alcohol lowers inhibitions and enables some persons to say and do things that they might not do while sober; on the other hand, too much drink reduces the male's sexual capacity—enough alcohol can render him impotent. Nevertheless, evidence from assorted studies indicates that drinking is a factor in one third to one half of reported rape cases.[66] The contribution that alcohol makes to the rape situation has not been established. We can only conjecture that alcohol provides a catalyst to violence by stimulating feelings of masculine self-confidence and misinterpretations of a woman's behavior.

VIOLENCE AND SEX

A quick review of the aspects of forcible rape indicates parallels with homicide and aggravated assault. According to official statistics the incidence of rape is disproportionately high among lower class black acquaintances. Thus it is tempting simply to classify sexual assault as another instance of a subculture of interpersonal violence.[67] But it is important to remember that the values supporting interpersonal violence have their roots in more general cultural values supporting violence as a means of solving problems. Despite the statistics, the case for assigning responsibility for sexual violence primarily to lower class, black males is not that convincing. Aggressiveness, if not open violence, by males toward females is pervasive in American society. Indeed, it may be argued that male sexual aggression in the United States has been the norm, not the exception.

It is traditional that men, whatever their social class, initiate sexual activity and continue to press for greater intimacy until prevented by the female. The problem is that the give-and-take situation between males and females is not at all clearly defined. When she wears abbreviated shorts is she just trying to keep cool (as she says) or trying to get him hot (as he says). When she says "No!" does she really mean yes? As song lyrics of early vintage go—"Your Lips Tell Me No! No! But There's Yes! Yes! in Your Eyes." Consequently, the male aggressor expects resistance to his advances, but he expects eventual surrender too. What remains undetermined is the degree of resistance to be overcome.

Studies of sexual aggressiveness by middle-class males are scarce, but their conclusions show that serious assaults against dates are not limited to the lower class as the official statistics would lead us to believe. One study of college co-eds in the 1950s found that one fifth of the sample had experienced forceful attempts at intercourse while on dates; six per cent had even undergone physical pain inflicted to gain their compliance.[68] A 1968 study of social science undergraduates in two universities revealed that nearly a quarter of the co-eds who had premarital intercourse did so the first time because they were forced or felt an obligation to the male.[69] Although this proportion was less than indicated by a similar study ten years before, it still represents a substantial number of co-eds who engage in their first act of intercourse because of pressures other than personal desire.

A third study of interest is a survey of male students at a large Midwestern university in the mid-1960s.[70] One fourth of these students reported that they had made forceful attempts at intercourse to the point where the girl had responded by fighting, crying, screaming, or pleading. Without stretching the data too far, it can be claimed that one fourth of the males at that university were technically guilty of at least attempted rape. Doubtlessly, very few if any such attempts (or successes) at that or any other university reach the *Uniform Crime Reports*. Contrary to the impression given by such official sources, the role of the male as a sexual aggressor cuts across social class lines.[71]

This role is tied to two social factors in American society: an *image of maleness* and the *dating game*.[72] The image of maleness is one of strength, activity, and independence compared with the weakness, passivity, and dependence of the female. Man is to be the initiator of sexual activity and he must be successful to be a "man." In its most extreme form this image of maleness embodies an actual contempt for women:

> There is the . . . principle, widely shared by most males, that women are to be exploited if possible. Part of the code of *Machismo*, the intense glorification of specifically male characteristics, such as courage in battle, recklessness, independence of family ties, etc., is a contempt for female characteristics, and a philosophy that urges the use of women as a mere instrument of pleasure. To be dependent on a woman and especially to

show her tenderness and consideration because she deserves it as a human being rather than because it is a useful device for overcoming her resistance, is thought to be foolish.[73]

Included in this image of maleness is the notion of a masculine sexual force, which once put into motion is beyond mere rationality. Being confronted by someone men believe to be a "teaser"—who suggests or promises but does not deliver—is a serious matter. Not only does it offend the masculine sense of "fairness," but may also initiate a process leading to violence, which is imagined to be irreversible. It appears that even social researchers are influenced by this notion. The responsibility or fault, if you will, for rape is rather muddled when "victim precipitation" is defined as:

> Rape situations in which the victim actually, or so it was deemed, agreed to sexual relations but retracted before the actual act or did not react strongly enough when the suggestion was made by the offender(s).[74]

It is as though a woman's provocation puts a man out of control. There is an ideology that no woman has a right to change her mind once she has even hinted she is contemplating sex.

The second factor contributing to the role of the male as a sexual aggressor is the nature of the dating game. Dating is an integral part of American society and leads eventually to courtship and marriage. However, it can also lead to rape because expectations are often unclear and unmet.[75] The expectations of the male stem from the attention, time, and money he expends. But it is more than pleasant and witty conversation that is to be his reward. He anticipates a progression of sexual intimacies with each date with the ultimate goal of "going all the way." But somewhere in this progression a point of contention can arise over how much he is "buying" and how much she is "selling." This is particularly likely to occur when there is no emotional commitment to the relationship by either party. For many such couples confrontations over rewards end dramatically, one way or another, with the demand: "Put out or get out!"

To complement the role of the male as a sexual aggressor it is necessary to introduce another notion—the female as a legitimate victim.[76] As we discussed in Chapter 2, part of learning deviant behavior involves the learning of *reasons for behavior*. In rape, such justifications rely heavily on stereotyped conceptions of women that make some of them seem legitimate targets of violence. Some common male justifications for applying force to obtain sex are:

1. Some women need to be raped. These verbalized motives concern the necessity of keeping women in their place:

> These dumb broads don't know what they want. They get you worked up and then they chicken out. You let 'em get away with stuff like that and the next thing you know they'll be walking all over you.

Or:

Women like a strong man who will knock them around once in a while—
that way they know the man is in charge.[77]

2. Some women deserve to be raped. These motives concern the
reputation of the woman. In the study of middle-class college males
the researcher found that:

The definition of a female as being sexually experienced is sufficient in
some male groups . . . to render her a legitimate target for any type of
sexual approach. Her prior experience qualifies her as public property for
all interested males and cancels her prerogative to accept or reject sexual
partners.[78]

3. Some women want to be raped. As we indicated earlier, the
woman is supposed to say no, but it is a male notion that she really
wants sexual intimacies. She may angrily resist, but the male may
presume she will be angrier if he quits than if he persists. After all, he
may reason, rape allows the woman to enjoy sex without feeling
guilty about it. In one study of eighty-five rape victims, the researcher
found two women who received marriage proposals from their rapists. In other cases:

After being raped by two men, another informant . . . was asked by her
rapists which of the two she enjoyed the most. And yet another informant
reported that her rapist was "furious because I wasn't getting turned
on." [79]

Whatever the verbalized motives, in many instances the components contributing to rape appear to align themselves as follows:

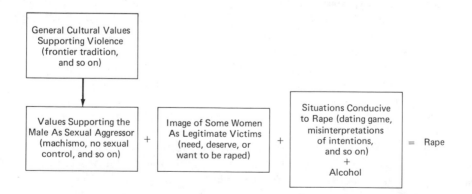

VIOLENT SEX AND CONFLICT

As we indicated previously, forcible sexual intercourse is not restricted to males violating females. Attacks also occur between

members of the same sex—both men and women. Practically nothing is known of attacks by females upon other females, but we have some evidence about males attacking males. That evidence comes from a two-year study (June 1966–July 1968) of sexual assaults in the prison system of Philadelphia.[80] The author, Alan J. Davis, concluded that the City of Brotherly Love had an epidemic of homosexual attacks in its institutions. Practically every slightly-built young man was sexually approached within a couple of days of his admission. Many were either repeatedly raped by gangs or had to enter into homosexual relationships with an individual for protection. Only the strong or the very lucky escaped rape.

In the three institutions studied, Davis estimates that 2,000 assaults occurred in the twenty-six-month period. Aside from indicating the obvious failure and lack of concern of the system in protecting its inmates, the nature of these assaults informs us of an often overlooked facet of rape—namely, that sexual conquest and degradation of another may represent more than a desire for sexual release. In the case of the Philadelphia study, the evidence indicates that sexual release is a minor factor in homosexual rape despite what is usually claimed about sexual deprivation suffered in the prison setting. One of the striking findings is indicated in Table 4-4.

TABLE 4–4
OFFENDERS AND VICTIMS OF
HOMOSEXUAL ASSAULTS, BY RACE *
(In per cent of total)

Victims	Offenders		Total
	Black	White	
Black	29	0	29
White	56	15	71
Total	85	15	100%

* Derived from Alan J. Davis, "Sexual Assaults in the Philadelphia Prison System," in *The Sexual Scene*, eds. John H. Gagnon and William Simon (Chicago: Aldine, 1970), p. 122.

The fact that the greatest proportion of assaults involved blacks against whites suggests that rape may be an expression of contempt, rebellion, and revenge. In short, it is a symptom of conflict:

A primary goal of the sexual aggressor, it is clear, is the conquest and degradation of his victim. We repeatedly found that aggressors used such language as "Fight or fuck," "We're going to take your manhood," "You'll have to give up some face," and "We're gonna make a girl out of you." Some of the assaults were reminiscent of the custom in some ancient

societies of castrating or buggering a defeated enemy. . . . Sexual assaults
. . . are not primarily caused by sexual deprivation. They are expressions
of anger and aggression prompted by the same basic frustrations . . .
[which] can be summarized as an inability to achieve masculine identification and pride through avenues other than sex. When these frustrations
are intensified by imprisonment, and superimposed upon hostility between the races and a simplistic view of all sex as an act of aggression and
subjugation, then the result is assaults on members of the same sex.[81]

Thus rape represents conflict—it is a supreme act of domination by
one human being over another; it is an expression of hatred. Perhaps
the best description of rape as conflict is expressed by the black revolutionary, Eldridge Cleaver:

I became a rapist. To refine my technique and *modus operandi,* I started
out by practicing on black girls in the ghetto—in the black ghetto where
dark and vicious deeds appear not as aberrations or deviations from the
norm, but as part of the sufficiency of the Evil of a day—and when I considered myself smooth enough, I crossed the tracks and sought out white
prey. I did this consciously, deliberately, willfully, methodically—though
looking back I see that I was in a frantic, wild, and completely abandoned
frame of mind.

Rape was an insurrectionary act. It delighted me that I was defying and
trampling upon the white man's law, upon his system of values, and that I
was defiling his women—and this point, I believe, was the most satisfying
to me because I was very resentful over the historical fact of how the white
man has used the black woman. I felt I was getting revenge.[82]

The conflict theme of rape extends well beyond interracial sexual
violence. Rape is symbolic of masculine power, not just physical
power but economic and political power as well. This is not to say
that a significant number of rapes have overt political overtones (although they may), but that rape is the outcome of conflict situations
encouraged by social expectations. Males are expected to express
their dominance—the notion that females and males interact as equal
parties is an exception.

Rape as both a symbol of and a means of sexual domination is a
theme recently elaborated upon by feminists. Susan Griffin calls rape
"The All-American Crime" and makes these observations:

Erotic pleasure cannot be separated from culture, and in our culture male
eroticism is wedded to power. Not only should a man be taller and
stronger than a female in the perfect love-match, but he must also demon-
strate his superior strength in gestures of dominance which are perceived
as amorous. . . .

The scenario is even further complicated by the expectation that, not
only does a woman mean "yes" when she says "no," but that a really
decent woman ought to begin by saying "no," and then be led down the
primrose path to acquiescence. . . .

To regard the rapist as the victim, a man driven by his inherent sexual needs to take what will not be given him, reveals a basic ignorance of sexual politics. For in our culture heterosexual love finds an erotic expression through male dominance and female submission. A man who derives pleasure from raping a woman clearly must enjoy force and dominance as much or more than the simple pleasures of the flesh.[83]

Griffin concludes her argument by insisting that rape is a form of terrorism designed to restrict the freedom of women and to make them dependent upon men for protection. The oppression of women by threat of rape is perpetuated by those who shift the blame for the offense to women themselves.

Rape is a form of mass terrorism, for the victims of rape are chosen indiscriminately, but the propagandists for male supremacy broadcast that it is women who cause rape by being unchaste or in the wrong place at the wrong time—in essence, by behaving as though they were free.[84]

Griffin's point is illustrated well by one of the better known jokes about rape. "There is no such thing as rape; woman can run faster with skirts up than man with pants down."

Clearly the increase in sexual freedom and the growth of the women's liberation movement have changed and will continue to change the expectations of the female's role and rights.[85] But this does not mean that the male image of manhood will necessarily change, or that justifications for sexual aggression will simply disappear. Until they do, rape will remain a fact of American life.

Conclusion

We end this discussion of violent crimes against the person with two brief observations. First, it is evident that we have a national heritage of violence and a widespread fondness for weapons that make interpersonal conflicts so much deadlier. Second, so much of our violence is directed not against outsiders but against those we know—those who frustrate, provoke, and anger us—but who, because we are not strangers, trust us. It is ironic that the specter of violence "out there" is so much within us.

NOTES

1. American Institute of Public Opinion, Study No. 861 (1972), cited in Michael J. Hindelang, Christopher S. Dunn, L. Paul Sutton, and Alison L. Aumick, *Sourcebook of Criminal Justice Statistics 1973* (Washington, D.C.: U.S. Department of Justice, 1973), p. 141.

2. John E. Conklin, "Criminal Environment and Support for the Law," *Law and Society Review,* **6** (November 1971), pp. 256–259; Peter H. Rossi, Emily Waite, Christine E. Bose, and Richard E. Berk, "The Seriousness of Crimes: Normative Structure and Individual Differences," *American Sociological Review,* **39** (April 1974), pp. 224–237.

3. In addition to this annual report the F.B.I. also issues more current quarterly reports on the incidence of the seven index crimes (discussed below) in the 154 largest cities during three-month periods.

4. The President's Commission on Law Enforcement and Administration of Justice, *Task Force Report: Crime and Its Impact—An Assessment* (Washington, D.C.: Government Printing Office, 1967), pp. 17–18. The most recent national survey indicating proportions of offenses reported was conducted in the first half of 1973. See *LEAA Newsletter,* December 1974, pp. 1, 5.

5. Richard Block, "Why Notify the Police: The Victim's Decision to Notify the Police of an Assault," *Criminology,* **11** (February 1974), pp. 555–569; and *LEAA Newsletter,* p. 5.

6. David Burnham, "How Safe is the City? Statistics Can Mislead," *New York Times,* October 16, 1973, p. 51.

7. David J. Pittman and William Handy, "Patterns in Criminal Aggravated Assault," *Journal of Criminal Law, Criminology and Police Science,* **55** (December 1964), pp. 462–470.

8. *New York Times,* January 19, 1974, p. 35.

9. *New York Times,* August 14, 1973, pp. 1, 18. There is reason to suspect that Herman W. Mudgett holds the record for the most murders. He may have killed at least 200 persons during the last decades of the nineteenth century. See Jay Robert Nash, *Bloodletters and Badmen : A Narrative Encyclopedia of American Criminals from the Pilgrims to the Present* (New York: M. Evans and Co., 1973), pp. 382–387.

10. Donald J. Mulvihill and Melvin M. Tumin, *Crimes of Violence,* Staff Report Submitted to the National Commission on the Causes and Prevention of Violence, vol. 11 (Washington, D.C.: Government Printing Office, 1969), p. 54.

11. Arnold Barnett and Daniel J. Kleitman, "Urban Violence and Risk to the Individual," *Journal of Research in Crime and Delinquency,* **10** (July 1973), pp. 111–116; and *Toledo Times,* April 9, 1974, p. 3.

12. This needs some qualification. What the F.B.I. calls "suburban areas" and "rural areas" do not fit the relationship—the rural areas tend to have higher rates than cities under 50,000. Among cities, however, there is a direct but not invariant relationship between size and rate. See *Crime in the United States, 1973, Uniform Crime Reports* (Washington, D.C.: Government Printing Office, 1974), pp. 104–105.

13. Mulvihill and Tumin, *Crimes of Violence,* pp. 207–391. The classic American work on homicide dealt with Philadelphia: Marvin E. Wolfgang, *Patterns in Criminal Homicide* (Philadelphia: University of Pennsylvania Press, 1958). Also see Harwin L. Voss and John R. Hepburn, "Patterns in Criminal Homicide in Chicago," *Journal of Criminal Law, Criminology and Police Science,* **59** (December 1968), pp. 499–508; and John R. Hepburn and Harwin L. Voss, "Patterns of Criminal Homicide: A Comparison of Chicago and Philadelphia," *Criminology,* **8** (May 1970), pp. 21–45.

14. Mulvihill and Tumin, *Crimes of Violence*, p. 95.

15. See Wolfgang, *Patterns in Criminal Homicide*, p. 207; Hepburn and Voss, "Patterns of Criminal Homicide," p. 32; and James Boudouris, "A Classification of Homicides," *Criminology*, **11** (February 1974), pp. 525–540.

16. Mulvihill and Tumin, *Crimes of Violence*, p. 217.

17. Ibid., p. 221.

18. Ibid., p. 231.

19. Ibid., pp. 230–233.

20. Victim-precipitated homicide was first investigated by Marvin E. Wolfgang, *Patterns in Criminal Homicide*, pp. 252–265. The illustrations used here are from Mulvihill and Tumin, *Crimes of Violence*, pp. 225–226.

21. Donald J. Mulvihill and Melvin M. Tumin, *Crimes of Violence*, Staff Report Submitted to the National Commission on the Causes and Prevention of Violence," vol. 12 (Washington, D.C.: Government Printing Office, 1969), pp. 642–647.

22. Denise Thum, Henry Wechsler, and Harold W. Demone, Jr., "Alcohol Levels of Emergency Service Patients Injured in Fights and Assaults," *Criminology*, **10** (February 1973), pp. 487–497. For a study that argues alcohol use may actually diminish the likelihood of assaultive behavior see Morton Bard and Joseph Zacker, "Assaultiveness and Alcohol Use in Family Disputes: Police Perceptions," *Criminology*, **12** (November 1974), pp. 281–292.

23. "Drugs, Murder Victims Linked," *Toledo Blade*, September 4, 1973, p. 20; Werner U. Spitz, "Much More on Why Detroit is Murder City," *New York Times*, June 16, 1974, Section 4, p. 12; and Margaret Z. Zahn and Mark Bencivengo, "Violent Death: A Comparison Between Drug Users and Non-drug Users," *Addictive Disease: An International Journal*, **3** (September 1974), pp. 282–295. The discussion is based on Zahn's work. See also Zahn and J. Glenn Snodgrass, "The Structure of Homicide in Two American Cities: The Homicide Victim," (paper presented at the meeting of the American Society of Criminology, Chicago, November, 1974).

24. Arnold L. Lieber and Carolyn R. Sherin, "Homicides and the Lunar Cycle: Toward a Theory of Lunar Influence on Human Emotional Disturbance," *American Journal of Psychiatry*, **129** (July 1972), pp. 69–74.

25. Philip Taft and Philip Ross, "American Labor Violence: Its Causes, Character, and Outcome,'" in *Violence in America: Historical and Comparative Perspectives*, A Report to the National Commission on the Causes and Prevention of Violence, eds. Hugh Davis Graham and Ted Robert Gurr, vol. 1 (Washington, D.C.: Government Printing Office, 1969), p. 221.

26. The discussion draws upon Richard Maxwell Brown, "Historical Patterns of Violence in America," in Graham and Gurr, *Violence in America*, pp. 35–64.

27. Mulvihill and Tumin, *Crimes of Violence*, vol. 11, p. 201.

28. The following discussion draws heavily upon Joe E. Frantz, "The Frontier Tradition: An Invitation to Violence," in Graham and Gurr, *Violence in America*, pp. 101–119.

29. Richard Maxwell Brown, "The American Vigilante Tradition," in Graham and Gurr, *Violence in America*, pp. 121–169.

30. M. H. Mott, *History of the Regulators of Northern Indiana* (Indianapolis: Journal Company, 1859), pp. 15–18, cited in Brown, "American Vigilante Tradition," p. 142. Italics added.

31. Monica D. Blumenthal, Robert L. Kahn, Frank M. Andrews, and Kendra B. Head, *Justifying Violence: Attitudes of American Men* (Ann Arbor, Michigan: Institute for Social Research, 1972), p. 243.

32. Ibid., p. 101.

33. Ibid., p. 250.

34. Marvin E. Wolfgang and Franco Ferracuti, *The Subculture of Violence: Towards an Integrated Theory in Criminology* (London: Tavistock Publications, 1967), pp. 150–163.

35. Wolfgang, *Patterns in Criminal Homicide*, pp. 188–189. Consistent with Wolfgang's comments are the findings of a survey concerning the perceived seriousness of various crimes. The researchers found that less educated black males view violence against acquaintances as much less serious than do other population groups. See Rossi et al., "The Seriousness of Crimes,"p. 231.

36. Marvin E. Wolfgang and Franco Ferracuti, "Subculture of Violence—A Socio-Psychological Theory," in *Studies in Homicide*, ed. Marvin E. Wolfgang (New York: Harper & Row, 1967), pp. 277–278. Cf. Wolfgang and Ferracuti, *The Subculture of Violence*, p. 156.

37. Sandra J. Ball-Rokeach, "Values and Violence: A Test of the Subculture of Violence Thesis," *American Sociological Review*, **38** (December 1973), pp. 736–749. For a social psychological explanation of how violence between intimates develops see William Goode, "Violence Among Intimates," in Mulvihill and Tumin, *Crimes of Violence*, vol. 13, pp. 941–977.

38. Saul Heller, "Anatomy of Murder," *Village Voice*, May 9, 1974, p. 104.

39. Rodney Stark and James McEvoy III, "Middle-Class Violence," *Psychology Today*, **4** (November 1970), p. 53.

40. George D. Newton, Jr., and Franklin E. Zimring, *Firearms and Violence in American Life*, Report Submitted to the National Commission on the Causes and Prevention of Violence (Washington, D.C.: Government Printing Office, 1969), pp. 9–10. For a theory of homicide based on "southernness" see Raymond D. Gastil, "Homicide and a Regional Culture of Violence," *American Sociological Review*, **36** (June 1971), pp. 412–427. Also see: Sheldon Hackney, "Southern Violence," in Graham and Gurr, *Violence in America*, pp. 387–404; and Colin Loftin and Robert H. Hill, "Regional Subculture and Homicide: An Examination of the Gastil-Hackney Thesis," *American Sociological Review*, **39** (October 1974), pp. 714–724.

41. *Crime in the United States, 1973*, pp. 60–62.

42. Newton and Zimring, *Firearms and Violence*, p. 1.

43. Franklin Zimring, "Eight Myths About Gun Control," *Toledo Blade*, July 30, 1972, Section B, p. 5.

44. NBC News: Special Edition, May 26, 1974.

45. Robert Sherrill, *The Saturday Night Special* (New York: Charterhouse, 1973), p. 98.

46. Robert Sherrill, "The Saturday Night Special and Other Hardware," *New York Times Magazine*, October 10, 1971, p. 60.

47. Richard Harris, "Annals of Legislation: If You Love Your Guns," *New Yorker*, April 20, 1968, p. 56; and American Institure of Public Opinion, Study No. 852 (1972) cited in Hindelang, *Sourcebook*, p. 143.

48. Harris, "Annals of Legislation," p. 57.

49. Newton and Zimring, *Firearms and Violence,* p. 48.

50. Zimring, "Eight Myths," p. 5.

51. Harris, "Annals of Legislation," pp. 74–80.

52. Sherrill, *The Saturday Night Special,* p. 99.

53. This discussion was based on Sherrill, *The Saturday Night Special;* Harris, "Annals of Legislation"; and Robert J. Riley, "Shooting to Kill the Handgun: Time to Martyr Another American 'Hero,' " *Journal of Urban Law,* 51 (February 1974), pp. 505–524.

54. U.S. Department of Justice, *Crime in the Nation's Five Largest Cities: National Crime Panel Surveys of Chicago, Detroit, Los Angeles, New York, and Philadelphia,* Advance Report, April 1974 (Washington, D.C.: U.S. Department of Justice, 1974), p. 28.

55. *Crime in the United States, 1973,* p. 15.

56. Menachem Amir, *Patterns in Forcible Rape* (Chicago: University of Chicago Press, 1971), p. 155.

57. Mulvihill and Tumin, *Crimes of Violence,* pp. 235, 237, 256.

58. Kurt Weis and Sandra S. Borges, "Victimology and Rape: The Case of the Legitimate Victim," *Issues in Criminology,* 8 (Fall 1973), pp. 101–107.

59. Ibid., pp. 103–104.

60. Mulvihill and Tumin, *Crimes of Violence,* p. 54; *Crime in the United States, 1973,* pp. 13, 59.

61. Mulvihill and Tumin, *Crimes of Violence,* pp. 96, 278; Amir, *Patterns in Forcible Rape,* pp. 70–71.

62. Cf. Amir, *Patterns in Forcible Rape,* p. 44.

63. Mulvihill and Tumin, *Crimes of Violence,* p. 217; cf. Amir, *Patterns in Forcible Rape,* pp. 233–234.

64. Mulvihill and Tumin, *Crimes of Violence,* pp. 223–224.

65. Amir, *Patterns in Forcible Rape,* pp. 185–200.

66. Ibid., pp. 98–100; Mulvihill and Tumin, *Crimes of Violence,* pp. 642–649; and Paul H. Gebhard, John H. Gagnon, Wardell B. Pomeroy, and Cornelia V. Christenson, *Sex Offenders: An Analysis of Types* (New York: Harper & Row, 1965), p. 194.

67. This is the thesis of Amir in *Patterns of Forcible Rape,* pp. 319–326.

68. Clifford Kirkpatrick and Eugene Kanin, "Male Sex Aggression on a University Campus," *American Sociological Review,* 22 (February 1957), p. 53.

69. Harold T. Christensen and Christina F. Gregg, "Changing Sex Norms in America and Scandinavia," *Journal of Marriage and the Family,* 32 (November 1970), pp. 625–626.

70. Eugene J. Kanin, "Reference Groups and Sex Conduct Norm Violations," *Sociological Quarterly,* 8 (Autumn 1967), pp. 495–504.

71. The basis for the discussion is F. Ivan Nye and Felix M. Berardo, *The Family: Its Structure and Interaction* (New York: Macmillan, 1973), pp. 198–202.

72. Weis and Borges, "Victimology and Rape," pp. 85–89.

73. William Goode, "Violence Among Intimates," in *Crimes of Violence,* eds. Mulvihill and Tumin, p. 971.

74. Amir, *Patterns in Forcible Rape,* p. 266. Data on victim-precipitated rape are understandably weak; Amir found 19 per cent in his Philadelphia sample, but the seventeen-city survey found only 4 per cent. See Mulvihill and Tumin, *Crimes of Violence*, pp. 226 and 228.

75. Weis and Borges, "Victimology and Rape," pp. 87–89; Goode, "Violence Among Intimates," p. 971.

76. Weis and Borges, "Victimology and Rape," pp. 79–80.

77. Gebhard et al., *Sex Offenders*, pp. 177–178, 205.

78. Kanin, "Reference Groups," p. 502. See also Amir, *Patterns in Forcible Rape*, pp. 249–252.

79. Diana E. H. Russell, "Rape and the Masculine Mystique," (paper delivered at the American Sociological Association meetings, 1973), p. 3.

80. Alan J. Davis, "Sexual Assaults in the Philadelphia Prison System," in *The Sexual Scene*, eds. John H. Gagnon and William Simon (Chicago: Aldine, 1970), pp. 107–124.

81. Ibid., pp. 123–124.

82. Eldridge Cleaver, *Soul on Ice* (New York: McGraw-Hill, 1968), p. 14.

83. Susan Griffin, "Rape: the All-American Crime," *Ramparts*, September, 1971, p. 28.

84. Ibid., p. 35. For a feminist perspective on the rape laws see Camille E. LeGrand, "Rape and Rape Laws: Sexism in Society and Law," *California Law Review*, **6**:3 (1973), pp. 919–941.

85. Weis and Borges, "Victimology and Rape," pp. 108–110.

5 CRIME IN THE STREETS— AGAINST PROPERTY

Despite the emphasis that murder, rape, and aggravated assault receive, they represent a small proportion of the estimated number of serious crimes as defined by the *Uniform Crime Reports*. In 1973, the foregoing crimes against the person constituted only 6 per cent of the index crimes. Robbery, burglary, larceny-theft, and auto theft made up the remaining 94 per cent.[1] Thus the crime picture, insofar as the police and F.B.I. are concerned, is dominated by property offenses. In this chapter we will briefly consider the dimensions of these crimes and some of the cultural factors contributing to them.

Robbery

The *Uniform Crime Reports* defines robbery as a crime "which takes place in the presence of the victim to obtain property or a thing of value from a person by use of force or threat of force." [2] *Uniform Crime Reports* statistics include robbery attempts as well as completed robberies. Furthermore, there is a breakdown according to whether a weapon was used (armed robbery) or not (strong-arm robbery—mugging, and so on). In our discussion we will not make a distinction between armed and strong-arm robbery except in specified instances. As a point of information: two thirds of all reported robberies involve a weapon.

DIMENSIONS OF ROBBERY

Information about robberies and robbers is even more scarce than it is for rape. Thus the reader is again cautioned to approach the following facts with care. Because one would assume that most robberies involve strangers and evoke some degree of fear in the victims, one would also assume there would be a high probability that the offenses would be reported. The latter assumption is apparently unfounded, however. According to a five-city survey (Chicago, Detroit, Los Angeles, New York, and Philadelphia) there is great variation in reporting:

1. Robbery of commercial firms is more likely to be reported than if the victim is a private citizen. Firms reported 83 to 91 per cent of their robberies compared to 47 to 52 per cent for individuals. This is not surprising considering that more money is probably involved in a robbery from a firm and, of course, the firm must report if it expects to be repaid by insurance companies.
2. Whether an individual reports a robbery depends on the characteristics of the offense. Only 27 to 39 per cent of individuals reported robbery attempts in which no injury occurred, but 50 to 75 per cent reported when an injury resulted. In short, large proportions of citizens do not report, even when they are physically harmed during the offense.[3]

Keep in mind these reporting inconsistencies as we now turn to the facts about robbery as represented by official statistics.

Fact One. According to official statistics, the robbery rate has leveled off since 1971. This represents a switch from the usual claims of climbing crime rates. Historically, the robbery rate has been relatively constant. Between 1935 and 1962 it fluctuated around 50 robberies per 100,000 national population. In 1963, the rate began a slow but steady rise to a high of 187 in 1971; it now shows signs of leveling off around 180. This leveling off is evident for robberies against both individuals and firms, and lacks any explanation at the present time.[4]

Fact Two. According to official statistics, the great majority of robbers are lower class black males. The pattern established in homicide and rape persists for robbery—offenders are predominantly black, involved in low skill occupations or unemployed, and male. One difference is that the intraracial offense pattern is not present. Whites usually victimize other whites, but the victims of blacks are somewhat more likely to be white (see Table 5–1). Females play a minor role in robbery as either victims or offenders; they make up only 20 per cent of the victims and 5 per cent of the offenders.[5] Robbery is predominantly an encounter between males.

TABLE 5–1
RACE OF ROBBERY OFFENDERS AND VICTIMS,
17 CITIES, 1967 * (In per cent of total)

		Offenders		
		Black	White	Total
Victims	Black	38	1	39
	White	45	16	61
Total		83	17	100%

* Derived from Donald J. Mulvihill and Melvin M. Tumin, *Crimes of Violence,* A Staff Report Submitted to the National Commission on the Causes and Prevention of Violence, vol. 11 (Washington, D.C.: Government Printing Office, 1969), pp. 214–215.

Fact Three. According to official statistics, the majority of robberies occur between strangers. According to the seventeen-city survey, the 1967 statistics indicate that 82 per cent of the robberies were committed by strangers; acquaintances and neighbors accounted for another 10 per cent.[6] This finding and the table above concerning the interracial nature of the offense are indications that property offenses, at least those that are reported, are not tied to interpersonal relations as are rape, aggravated assault, and homicide. In this respect robbery fits more precisely the notion of what crime in the streets means to the general public. And that brings us directly to the next fact.

Fact Four. According to official statistics, approximately half of all robberies occur in the streets. The seventeen-city survey found that 55 per cent of all robberies occur in outside areas such as streets, parks, lots, and alleys.[7] The home accounted for another 11 per cent and other inside locations such as service stations and other commercial establishments accounted for 21 per cent.

Fact Five. The roles of alcohol and drugs in robbery are unclear. This is, of course, a most unenlightening fact. But the evidence from the few available studies of the effect of alcohol on robbery is contradictory, and data concerning the relationship between drugs and robbery are too sketchy even to allow generalization.[8] Regarding the influence of either drugs or alcohol the most plausible hypothesis seems to be that they play an important role in unplanned offenses, but influence to a much lesser degree planned robberies.[9]

One of the more controversial issues in criminology is the particular association between heroin addiction and criminal activity. Because addicts support expensive habits but often work in low paying jobs or are unemployed, they must turn to one or more of a very limited number of alternative sources of funds: selling drugs, prostitution, or some form of theft. It appears that addicts prefer forms of theft such as shoplifting that do not involve any confrontation with the victim. But robbery does have the virtue of being a fast and direct means to money, and the addict's preference may mean little when the addict faces a shortage of drugs. Some researchers argue that the stereotype of the passive heroin user avoiding crimes of personal confrontation, such as robbery, is a myth. Instead the addict is often willing to take the risk of any crime so long as financial gain is likely.[10] Unfortunately, we have no evidence as to the proportion of robberies motivated by the desire for drugs.

Fact Six. The majority of robberies do not involve injury to the victims. The F.B.I. in its *Uniform Crime Reports* divides the index crimes into "crimes of violence" and "crimes against property." Robbery is included in the first along with murder, forcible rape, and aggravated assault. Although it is true that a weapon is usually present and the threat of harm is, by definition, always a part of robbery, its classification as a violent crime is misleading. Despite the potential for violence, the great majority of reported offenses appear motivated only by financial gain; the desire to inflict harm is, at most, a secondary consideration.

In the seventeen-city survey (1967) the researchers found that among reported robberies only 21 per cent involved injury to the victims. In fact, there were twice as many injuries to victims of unarmed as of armed robbery.[11] This does not mean that force is absent—people get shoved, knocked to the ground, and poked hard with a weapon—but the force is a deliberate means toward a goal. Violence in most robberies is simply a necessary tool for accomplishing important phases of the job: frightening victims into giving up valuables with minimal argument, and reducing chances of pursuit by enraged citizens.[12] Thus, it is doubtful that the traditions and subcultures of violence in the United States contribute to our understanding of robbery as a property crime. As André Normandeau points out:

> Robbers . . . are primarily thieves who occasionally, though rather rarely, use force to achieve their objects. The display of violence in this context is on the whole an isolated episode. It is general persistence in crime, not a widespread specialization in crimes of violence, which is the main characteristic of robbers. The term "violent offender class" could not be applied to robbers without distorting the factual data to fit preconceived ideas. Violence is only an occupational risk of a career of non-violent crime.[13]

TYPES OF ROBBERS

Classifying offenders into neat pigeonholes or types is a dangerous game. As with any individuals who have been officially tagged as robbers, rapists, or parking ticket violators, there are no assurances that they represent the great numbers of persons outside the legal system who are doing the same thing. Furthermore, typologies can easily oversimplify the complexity of motives and situations contributing to deviant behavior and to the continuation or cessation of such behavior.[14] Nevertheless, we present a suggested typology of robbers because it will clarify the dimensions of robbery just discussed, and because its application may be extended to other property offenders such as burglars, auto thieves, and shoplifters.

The author of this typology is John E. Conklin who drew his information from interviews with sixty-seven inmates committed to Massachusetts prisons for robbery offenses.[15] The four types are listed in decreasing order according to the amount of planning involved in their offenses.

1. *Professional Robbers.* As the term implies, these persons make their livings by robbery. They exhibit more skill than other robbers and focus on the big scores—at least $500. Before the offense they carefully plan how to overcome security measures (as would be found in banks, for instance) and how to make a sure escape. According to Conklin, not all these professionals engage exclusively in robbery; some get involved in other property crimes such as burglary. In general, the professionals can be distinguished from others by a high degree of commitment to a career of stealing in one form or another.

Researchers investigating professional property criminals find that their lives are supported by verbalized motives that make the crimes reasonable to them. Werner J. Einstadter, who studied armed robbers, found that professionals often avoid robbing individuals or small businesses. Instead their targets are establishments that are insured and can recover the losses—nobody is out anything.[16] The professionals' more general philosophy concerns the essential dishonesty of society and the interest group conflicts behind that dishonesty. One professional expresses his motives this way:

> The way I see it a guy has several ways to go in this world. If he's not rich in front, he can stay honest and be a donkey. Only this way he works for someone else and gets fucked the rest of his life. They cheat him and break his back. But this guy is honest.
>
> Now another way is he can start cheating and lying to people and maybe he can make himself a lot of money in business, legally I mean. But this guy isn't honest. If he's honest and tries to make it this way he won't get nowhere.
>
> Another way he can make it and live a halfway decent life and still be honest is to steal. Now I don't mean sneaking around and taking money or personal property from assholes who don't have nothing. I mean going

after big companies. To me this is perfectly honest, because these companies are cheating people anyway. When you go and just take it from them, you are actually more honest than they are. Most of the time, anyway, they are insured and make more money from the caper than you do.

Really, I think it is too bad it is this way. I mean it. I wish a guy could make a decent living working, which he can't do because those people who have it made got that way fucking the worker. And they are going to keep it that way. And all the crap about having to have laws protecting property. These are just laws set up by those people who got all the property and are going to make sure they keep it.[17]

2. Addict Robbers. As this term implies, these offenders rob as a result of drug habits that require funds to be maintained. Unlike the professionals, they do not think in terms of big scores—they worry only about getting enough for the next fix. Because they know they must have money by a certain time, some planning takes place but it is not nearly as involved as the planning done by professionals. Addicts, as we mentioned earlier, may attempt to lessen risk through planning; however, their desperation can result in carelessness and lead to arrest.

3. Opportunist Robbers. According to Conklin, these are probably the most common types of robbers. For them the situation plays an important role in the offense—little prior planning takes place and the robbery's occurrence depends very much upon the availability of vulnerable victims: drunks, old ladies, potential victims in isolated places. The take is often less than twenty dollars and goes for extras to elevate the robber's lifestyle a bit. Robbery for the opportunists is not a frequent activity, although they may occasionally be involved in other forms of property crime. Robbery is primarily a matter of convenience, not a long-term commitment.

4. Alcoholic Robbers. For these persons the situation is the paramount factor precipitating the offense. These robbers have no commitment to theft as a way of life nor do they plan at all in advance for the robberies, even to the extent of seeking out a vulnerable victim. For them the robberies "just happen" while they are under the influence of alcohol. Often they occur as afterthoughts to assaults or other contacts with victims. One example is provided by Conklin:

> [The] offender had just asked a clerk in a liquor store for a bottle of whiskey, and when he handed the clerk money to pay for the bottle, the clerk asked if there was anything else he wanted. The alcoholic at that moment decided that there was, and told the clerk to give him all his money. After a fight the alcoholic took some money and fled.[18]

Burglary

The *Uniform Crime Reports* defines burglary as "the unlawful entry of a structure to commit a felony or theft." [19] The use of force is not required to classify an act as burglary. The distinctions between robbery, burglary, and a third category, larcency-theft (to be discussed later), are confusing at times. As a rule of thumb, the reader can distinguish between them as follows: *robbery* involves *force* or threat of force against a *person; burglary* involves a *place* where the offender is illegally present; and *larceny-theft* is a general grab-bag category for most other forms of theft. Perhaps an example will help.

If the offender rings your apartment doorbell, you answer, and he demands your money or else, that is *robbery*. But if he rings the bell and you are not home, and he enters (forcefully or otherwise) and takes your valuables, that is *burglary*. If you invite him into the apartment and he pockets something of value while you are out of the room, that is *larceny*.

DIMENSIONS OF BURGLARY

The format followed to this point must be altered for burglary. This is partly because of the nature of the offense itself. Obviously there will be few cases of physical harm to the victim; the offenses will occur inside buildings, and most likely strangers will be involved. Furthermore, the kinds of national studies conducted on homicide, aggravated assault, rape, and robbery have not been done for burglary, auto theft, and larceny. This is not to say that studies of these topics are unavailable. We shall refer to some excellent ones shortly, but their scope is limited and their findings do not lend themselves to drawing a national portrait of facts on these offenses.

The five-city survey cited earlier indicates that household burglaries are reported to police in slightly over half of the cases. Burglaries of commercial establishments are reported in about three quarters of the cases.[20] Turning briefly to the *Uniform Crime Reports*, two interesting facts emerge.

Fact One. According to official statistics, the burglary rate has been rising. Burglary has historically displayed the most dramatic increase of any of the index crimes. Between 1935 and 1954 the rates indicate a relatively moderate, though erratic, increase from 242 to 342 per 100,000 national population. In 1955 the rates began to accelerate sharply, reaching 1,152 in 1971; in 1972 they dipped to 1,130 only to rise in 1973 to 1,211.[21] Exactly what the brief leveling reflected—actual burglaries, reporting rates, or recording procedures—is a matter of conjecture.

Fact Two. According to official statistics, the majority of persons ar-

rested for burglary are white males. This is a 180-degree switch from the statistics on robbers. Table 5–2 shows the contrast as reflected in the *Uniform Crime Reports.* Blacks are still overrepresented in burglary when one compares their 30 per cent of arrests with the proportion of blacks in the total population—13 per cent. Although it is understandable that a socially and economically depressed minority will be overrepresented in criminal statistics, why there is variation by type of offense is unclear. One might conjecture—although it is no more than conjecture—that opportunities for burglary are greater in white neighborhoods where there is a greater concentration of profitable targets, but where blacks would be conspicuous and at a disadvantage compared with white burglars. Thus blacks interested in theft of property are limited to robbery, but whites can more readily engage in safe crimes involving stealth.

TABLE 5–2
RACE OF PERSONS ARRESTED FOR ROBBERY AND
BURGLARY, 1973 *

		Offense (Per cent)	
		Robbery	Burglary
	Black	63	30
Race	White	35	68
	Other	2	2
	Total	100%	100%

* Derived from *Crime in the United States, 1973, Uniform Crime Reports* (Washington, D.C.: Government Printing Office, 1974), p. 133. Rounding of "Other" category has been adjusted to make totals equal 100%.

THE WORLD OF BURGLARY

Probably no other crime has the romantic aura often attached to burglary. Movies and television portray the cat burglar as dashing, clever, brave and rich from his theft of gems—everything that the common criminal is not supposed to be. But then some burglars are not common, and the mass media image does have a basis in reality. Probably the king of American burglars is Armand, who in 1968 made around $200,000 a year, owned a Ferarri and a Jaguar, and lived in a high-rent, five-room apartment in Manhattan.[22] He acquired all this as a result of six or seven carefully planned jobs a year. Scarcely one to argue that crime does not pay, Armand does have definite opinions about crime:

> You might laugh, but I'm for law and order. What I do is my business. I don't hurt anyone, and anyway most of the people who lose stuff are insured, and I could tell you about the way they inflate their losses. But this

mugging on the streets and the rapes and the way they have to coddle these creeps makes me sick.[23]

Armand is, of course, an exceptional burglar. But we know practically as much about the exceptions as we do about the commonplace. The more detailed studies of burglary concentrate on various aspects of offenses, victims, and the legal system's response.[24] Other studies deal primarily with the professionals—those offenders characterized by relatively high skills, by a commitment to a career in burglary, and by their making a livelihood of crime.[25] This emphasis on the professional is understandable when you realize that they at least exhibit a consistent pattern of behavior compared with other offenders whose previous criminal activity, if it existed, might have been extremely varied. Nevertheless, there exists a great gap in our knowledge about the motivations and characteristics of most burglars.

There does appear to be agreement among researchers that burglary is a very rational crime. That is, it is rarely a purely situational offense. To execute a burglary some degree of planning is undertaken by even the most inexperienced and amateur of burglars. Furthermore, it is rational because the potential payoff is high in comparison to what many could make in more legitimate pursuits. Economists have concluded that on the basis of economic considerations alone, and ignoring the risks of being caught and confined, burglary does pay. This is particularly true for youths who would be especially poorly reimbursed in the conventional labor marketplace.[26]

Ignoring the risk of entanglement with the law may be something few of us would care to do. But for those with a commitment to burglary as a career the risk is simply part of the job. The means of dealing with that risk points up an important characteristic of the world of burglary: successful burglary depends upon social support from a variety of individuals who contribute to the offense. Neal Shover has provided a description of three types of such individuals.[27]

1. Bondsmen and Attorneys. These persons are part of the legitimate world and openly assist the burglar in minimizing the risk of involvement with the law. Such persons are accepted within the legal establishment, and the established burglar relies upon good relationships with them to avoid confinement. He needs the trust of the bondsman to be released after arrest, and he needs the trust of the lawyer who will seek to delay trial, who will engage in backroom bargaining with prosecutors, and whose courtroom skills will gain the burglar the best possible outcome.

> When the good burglar [one with a reputation for being competent and trustworthy] is arrested—as he frequently is—he can count upon receiving the services of both a bondsman and an attorney, even if he has virtually

no ready cash. In lieu of a cash down payment the thief will be able to gain his release from confinement, and also preliminary legal representation, on the basis of his reputation and a promise to deliver the needed cash at a later date. He will then search for one or more suitable burglaries (or some other type of crime) which holds out the promise of a quick and substantial reward—so that he can pay his attorney and bondsman.[28]

In some cases, the attorney may be able to obtain a "fix"—an old American custom whereby police, witnesses, prosecutors, or judges conveniently ignore, forget, or withdraw evidence necessary for a conviction—for some price, of course.

2. *Tipsters*. A burglar does not become successful in selecting his targets by luck or accident. Without x-ray eyes, the burglar cannot know what valuables a residence contains, where they are located, and what security measures are active—that is, unless he or she has an information source. Persons willing to tip off burglars about potentially lucrative scores may have their occupations in the nonlegitimate world of gambling and prostitution, but they also come from all walks of legitimate life: watchmen, attorneys, jewelers, repairmen, beauticians, bartenders, detectives, and so on. Their motives remain unexplored—some are paid but many are not—but the tipsters' contributions to successful burglary are unquestionably substantial.

3. *Fences*. Once the burglar has made a score, if the loot is other than cash someone is needed to purchase the goods. Standing on a corner trying to sell television sets and snow tires is a risky business. Fortunately for the burglar there are people who deal in stolen goods with no questions asked. The fence is the middleperson in the world of property crime. Like a bona fide retailer in the legitimate world, a fence purchases goods for resale to the final users (provided, of course, a burglar does not again intervene to change the final users).

The purchase of stolen merchandise is but one function that the fence fulfills for the burglar. The fence can also be an instructor in how to recognize more marketable goods, how to improve thieving techniques, and how to locate out-of-work burglars who would be helpful for the next big score. But far and away the most important function of the fence is that of being a ready market for stolen goods; without this invaluable service burglary and other forms of property crime would be much more hazardous financial operations.[29]

Auto Theft

The sixth crime in the Crime Index is auto theft: the unlawful taking or stealing of a motor vehicle, including attempts. Completed auto thefts have the distinction of being reported from 92 to 96 per cent of the time according to the 1972 five-city survey of crime victims.[30] Although attempted auto theft fares much more poorly (26 to 35 per cent), auto theft statistics appear to be nearly as reliable as homicide statistics. The reasons seem rather obvious: an automobile represents a substantial investment for anyone, there should be little embarrassment connected with reporting its loss, and insurance reimbursement is dependent upon the car being officially listed as missing.

DIMENSIONS OF AUTO THEFT

This offense is not trivial in terms of its rate of occurrence. The F.B.I. claims that one of every 128 registered vehicles was reported stolen in 1973.[31] Despite this high occurrence researchers have spent relatively little time on the subject of auto theft. Consequently, we must derive the few facts about the offense from the *Uniform Crime Reports*.

Fact One. According to official statistics, the auto theft rate has leveled off since 1971. The rate declined in an erratic manner from a high of 245 per 100,000 national population in 1933 to a low of 108 in 1949. Thereafter it began a steady climb to a high of 457 in 1971; it dropped to 424 in 1972 and rose to 440 in 1973, but still lower than the 1971 high.[32] The leveling off may be attributed to technical reasons. In the beginning of 1970 the auto industry introduced a combination ignition, transmission, and steering column triple lock on all new cars. This was far superior to previous locks that could easily be defeated by hotwiring—either crossing ignition wires under the dashboard or making an electrical contact between the battery and ignition under the hood. In addition, new cars were equipped with buzzers that were activated whenever a driver attempted to leave without removing the key from the ignition.

These innovations do little to discourage the professional thief, who can get into a locked car and have the motor running in less than two minutes.[33] But the temptation of keys left in the ignition and the ease of starting a car without a key have diminished, so the more casual and opportunistic thefts have been cut down. More discussion of the professional car thief versus the joyrider will follow.

Fact Two. According to official statistics, the great majority of persons arrested for auto theft are white males. The pattern here is practically identical to that of burglary—about two thirds arrested are white and the remaining third are black.

Fact Three. According to official statistics, about three quarters of all autos stolen in a year are recovered.[34] Unfortunately, we have no information on the condition of these recovered autos—some, no doubt, are fit for a junk yard. Nevertheless, the statistic indicates that most are taken either for the purpose of short-term use (joyriding) or for removing parts (stripping) such as tape recorders, transmissions, and so on. We will discuss joyriders in more detail in the next section.

Fact Four. According to official statistics, the majority of persons arrested for auto theft are under eighteen years of age. In the 1973 *Uniform Crime Reports* 56 per cent of the auto thieves arrested were under eighteen. Burglary is, incidentally, also a young persons' crime: 53 per cent of those arrested for burglary in 1973 were under eighteen years of age.[35]

JOYRIDERS VERSUS PROFESSIONALS

One concludes from the meager literature that there are only two kinds of auto thieves. First, there are those reflected in dimensions three and four: teenagers who take a car in an impetuous moment, spend a few hours or a weekend with it, and finally abandon it. These are the joyriders who steal cars for recreation rather than for profit. Joyriders have been the topic of most of the limited research on auto thieves, probably because their characteristics run counter to those of most individuals who find their way into official crime statistics. Specifically, it has been found that persons arrested for joyriding tend to come from higher socioeconomic backgrounds and neighborhoods than do other types of offenders.[36]

Don C. Gibbons speculates on the dynamics of joyriding:

> Car thieves are relatively well-adjusted boys on good terms with most of their peers, particularly fellow joyriders with whom they steal cars. These boys are predominantly middle-class youths who have grown up in a relatively stable family setting but with problems of masculine identity for adolescent males. . . . The pimply lads who have communication difficulties with girls and other persons, the boys who are too small to engage in high school athletics, or the ones whose families move frequently within the city, so that the youngsters have difficulties in becoming socially integrated into school life, are the kinds of youths who are candidates for delinquent careers in joyriding.[37]

The second kind of auto thief is the professional. Although joyriding has become more difficult and probably less common because of technical innovations by the auto industry, the business of auto theft evidently has suffered little. The professional thief has the skills to quickly neutralize any mechanical protection an automobile has, including alarm systems. He also has the means by which to profitably dispose of his product. In 1971 a thief would be paid $150–$200 for each car he delivered in New York City. This could mean as much as $2,400 a week—a very comfortable living.

Once a car is delivered to dealers in stolen goods, it can be marketed in three ways. 1. It can be provided with new vehicle identification numbers, registration papers, and a paint job, and then sold. 2. It can be cut up into parts that are saleable. 3. It can be driven onto a ship and exported to a foreign country. This last method can be particularly lucrative; an efficient operation can arrange to have a car stolen and out to sea within five hours, bound for a customer willing to pay more than double the car's market price in the United States.[38]

The professional auto thief, like the professional robber or burglar, has appropriate verbalized motives to justify his business. One explains his work this way:

> What I do is good for everybody. First of all, I create work. I hire men to deliver the cars, work on the numbers, paint them, give them paper, maybe drive them out of state, find customers. That's good for the economy. Then I'm helping working people to get what they can never afford otherwise. A fellow wants a Cadillac but he can't afford it; his wife wants it but she knows he can't afford it. So I get this fellow a car at a price he can afford; maybe I save him as much as $2000. Now he's happy. But so is the guy who lost his car. He gets a nice new Cadillac from the insurance company—without the dents and scratches we had to take out of it. The Cadillac company—they're happy too because they sell another Cadillac.
>
> The only people who don't do so good is the insurance company. But they're so big that nobody cares *personally*. They got a budget for this sort of thing anyway. So here I am, a guy without an education, sending both my kids to college, giving my family a good home, making other people happy. Come on now—who am I really hurting? [39]

Larceny-Theft

This is the final category of crimes included among the index crimes of the *Uniform Crime Reports*. It provides a catchall for all unlawful taking of property without force or fraud. Because it does not include acts of fraud, the following crimes are not within the category: embezzlement, forgery, confidence games, or the writing of worthless checks. It must be recognized that any one of these acts might involve tremendous loss of money to someone, yet they are not considered serious enough for inclusion as major crimes. The larceny-theft category does include: shoplifting, pickpocketing, purse-snatching, thefts from autos (accessories or cargo), and bicycle thefts.

Statistics regarding this category are practically useless as any guide to trends or frequencies. First of all, between 1958 and 1972 the *Reports* restricted this category to thefts involving property valued at fifty dollars or over. Between those years the amount of larceny would appear to have risen on the basis of inflation alone—the thief who took fifty dollars' worth of goods in 1972 got far less for his or her effort than in 1958. In 1973 the F.B.I. began to include all larcenies regardless of value stolen, thus making comparisons with previous

years impractical. Second, evidence indicates that the reporting of larceny is especially unlikely. The survey of the nation's five largest cities
found that victims of "larceny with contact" (purse-snatching, pocket
picking) reported the incident only from 37 to 48 per cent of the time.
Incidents of larceny in the home were reported only 22 to 26 per cent
of the time.[40]

Since the larceny-theft category is a miscellaneous collection
plagued by serious statistical problems, nothing would be gained by
treating it as a single type of offense such as robbery or auto theft. Instead, we will concentrate on one form of behavior included in the
category—shoplifting. This particular offense is selected because it
has been researched sufficiently to allow for some elaboration.

EXTENT OF SHOPLIFTING

The retailing industry's accountants constantly deal with a concept
known as *inventory shrinkage,* or *shrink,* as it is called in the trade.
This refers to merchandise that cannot be accounted for by inventory,
sales receipts, damage, and so on—it has simply vanished. The extent
of shrinkage is not inconsequential; it can range from 1.2 per cent of
sales to a high of 8 per cent in major cities.[41]

Some shrinkage can be accounted for by bookkeeping errors, but
the remainder is attributed to two other sources: theft by employees and theft by customers. Naturally, the breakdown of how much
each of these sources contributes to shrinkage is uncertain, but it is
generally agreed that bookkeeping errors constitute less than half—
perhaps as low as one fifth.[42] Furthermore, there is debate as to how
the remaining proportion of shrinkage is divided. Some claim that internal theft by employees is four times as great as customer shoplifting, but others claim the proportions are nearly equal.[43] Regardless of
which proportions are accurate, about $5 billion worth of goods a
year vanishes through shrinkage. Our interest here is the shoplifting
aspect. Employee theft will be considered in the next chapter.

How many customers shoplift? Conservative estimates say about
one in sixty-one.[44] But an observational study conducted in a Manhattan department store found that of 500 persons selected at random,
one out of ten took merchandise they did not pay for.[45] Obviously,
the number of shoplifters patronizing a store depends much upon
the type of store. Supermarkets and discount stores are easier targets
than stores that exercise more control over the availability of merchandise. In general, it appears that whatever a store does not nail
down will disappear. In 1968 the major supermarket chains in Cleveland lost nearly 3,500 shopping carts worth nearly $96,000; in 1974 Los
Angeles supermarkets reported that 10 to 15 per cent of the stores'
total cart inventory was stolen every two weeks.[46]

TYPES OF SHOPLIFTERS

Just as with the property offenders discussed in other sections of this chapter, shoplifters can be most easily categorized as either professional or amateur. The professionals or *boosters* steal for the purpose of resale; amateurs or *snitches* take goods intended for personal use. Boosters, like other professional property offenders, are characterized by high degrees of skill, a commitment to earning a livelihood through criminal behavior, and connections with attorneys, bondsmen, and fences to make shoplifting as risk-free and profitable as possible.[47]

In 1972 there was a rumor of a traveling school for boosters in California. Tuition was between $1,500 and $2,000, but its graduates could make up to $1,000 a week.[48] Undoubtedly the school's curriculum included such tricks as learning how to steal as many as five women's suits while talking to the sales clerk, the use of the *booster box*—a package designed for concealing items inserted through hidden slots or hinged openings, and the art of *crotch-walking*. Hefty women can become especially adept at crotch-walking; they can hide items between their thighs without any change in their normal walk. The real experts can handle a small television set or a whole ham.

But the majority of shoplifters are amateurs. These are the legions of teenagers, housewives, office workers, and other "respectable" folk who steal for a wide variety of reasons: a budget sorely strained by inflation, irritation over lines at cash registers, anger at not finding a clerk when one needs one, and just for a thrill. If one can say that there is a typical shoplifter, it would be: "A white female, aged twenty-one to twenty-five, mother of one child, whose husband earns more than $10,000 a year."[49]

But this profile is misleading if it obscures the fact that amateur shoplifters come from virtually every segment of society: the rich, the poor, the very young, and the very old all shoplift. However, the profile of the typical shoplifter is important because it forces us to recognize that serious criminal behavior (as defined by the F.B.I.) is not monopolized by the socially and politically disadvantaged. The young housewife would not dream of sticking a gun in a clerk's face for a pair of fancy pantyhose. Yet, she can relieve the store of its merchandise just as surely as though she were carrying a Saturday night special.

Snitches vary greatly in the degree of skill and amount of planning that go into theft. Many amateur thefts are the result of situational factors such as deserted aisles and attractive displays of items that suddenly assume an importance unmatched by one's budget. But such impulse does not characterize all snitches. At the other extreme is a class of amateurs known as *shadow professionals* because they approach the methods of the professionals. Their techniques are innovative, their thievery is systematic and carefully preplanned. They differ from professionals primarily because they do not steal for a living, but for little luxuries and great thrills relieving the dullness of routine jobs and lives.[50]

To date the most thorough study of shoplifters is based on arrest data in Chicago in the late 1940s. Mary Owen Cameron describes one type of amateur who closely approximates the professional:

> Normally, he has no criminal association or connections; yet he (in department stores, most often she) comes into the store usually equipped with a large handbag, brief case, shopping bag, "bad bag" [paper bag with store's imprint which can be unfolded and used to conceal merchandise], or sometimes even booster bloomers [garments designed to hold merchandise, perhaps equipped with hooks or pockets] or a booster bag in which to carry off merchandise. She may have scissors or a razor blade to snip off price tags. She deliberately directs the sales clerk's attention elsewhere and slips various items into her bag when she believes herself unobserved. She may even bring with her a shopping list of items she wants to steal. . . . Having acquired a portion of her loot, she may go to a store rest room and flush price tags and other incriminating evidence down the toilet. She will wear as much as is possible of her recently stolen merchandise in order to lighten her load and then proceed to stash away the rest. Her loot at the end of the day may range from one to thirty pieces. . . . [Such shoplifters] are deliberate thieves who manifest intent to steal by preparation beforehand and who carry out their crimes with system and method. They are sufficiently practiced that only by considerable interrogation can they be differentiated [from] professional thieves. Although they are . . . almost always technically "first offenders" when apprehended by store police, their behavior indicates only that they have not been *caught* before; it does not indicate that they have not previously shoplifted—quite the contrary.[51]

One other type of shoplifter needs mentioning. Store security men place drug addicts into a category separate from boosters and snitches.[52] Addict-shoplifters are the easiest to spot: high school-aged males loping down department store aisles looking for enough unguarded merchandise to support their daily habit. They are in an obvious hurry and exercise little caution; they are likely to just grab and run. In large urban areas, addicts probably constitute over 5 per cent of all apprehended shoplifters.

REACTIONS TO SHOPLIFTING

The most recent sociological research on shoplifting does not concern either the extent of shoplifting or the types of shoplifters and their techniques. Rather the emphasis is upon the *reaction of audiences,* both customers and store employees, who witness shoplifting incidents. This research interest is consistent with the *labeling perspective* of deviance that we discussed in Chapter 3. The reader will recall that this perspective concerns the *production of deviance* whereby *rates of deviant behavior* are produced by persons and agencies who translate rule-breaking behavior into deviant behavior. One implication of this perspective is pointed out by Darrell J. Steffensmeier and Robert M. Terry:

> Much of the literature in the [labeling] perspective has argued that differential treatment is accorded persons with poor social backgrounds, less than perfect social identities, or "bad" reputations. Many analyses of deviant categories are founded on the assumption that particular classes of people are more likely to perform deviant acts and to be particular types of deviant persons. Such studies are highly consistent in arguing that respectability decreases the likelihood of deviant imputations, whereas "unrespectability" has the opposite effect.[53]

In looking at shoplifting from the labeling perspective, the question to be answered is, to what degree does respectability protect a person from being labeled as a shoplifter? To answer this question Steffensmeier and Terry staged incidents in which a "thief" openly shoplifted in front of a customer. The "thieves" were varied according to sex and appearance. Appearance was either hippie—soiled jeans, denim jacket, no socks, unruly hair, and so on—or straight—neatly dressed and groomed. Results indicated that customers were more likely to report the incident to a clerk if the hippie was involved. The sex of either the "thief" or the customer had little influence on the reporting rates.[54] The researchers concluded that clear support exists for the labeling perspective's contention that assigning a label of deviance depends not only upon the act but upon the identity of the actor as well.

This conclusion, however, is made doubtful by a similar study conducted by a team of psychologists headed by Donald P. Hartmann and Donna M. Gelfand.[55] These researchers used only a female "thief" who also varied her appearance between being hippie and straight. But they found that appearance had little effect on reporting rates. Although the two studies are not identical in form, there seems to be no reason to believe that design differences contributed substantially to the differing results.

In one respect both studies are in agreement: *fewer than 30 per cent of the customers reported the incident to store employees without prompting or encouragement.*[56] Hartmann and his associates conclude that there exists a widespread attitude that "it's the store's concern, not mine." Indeed, it is far more convenient to minimize the act of theft or to deny responsibility than to get involved in something that will be time-consuming, inconvenient, and possibly embarrassing or worse should there be a mistake. Apparently when it comes to shoplifting, the offender need not be overly concerned with his or her respectability in the eyes of others since thievery is protected by a shield of indifference. One might feel a twinge of moral indignation when some scruffy individual runs off with a bag of Kitty Litter but, after all, so what?

Still another study of audience reaction to shoplifting deals with the reaction of store personnel. The vast majority of apprehended shoplifters are caught by clerks or by private police employed by the store, not by public police who deal with the other index crimes. This introduces another level of decision-making. Assuming a shoplifting incident is reported to or seen by employees, they must decide the next course of action—release or referral to public police. From a study of this process by Michael J. Hindelang, we must again conclude that the respectabilility of offenders seems to have little influence on how they are treated.[57] Although Hindelang's data did not include the appearance of offenders in terms of dress, cleanliness, and so on, he did find that personal characteristics such as age, sex, and race were not related to the probability of being turned over to the public police for prosecution. Instead, the characteristics of the offense itself were important: the retail value of the items stolen, what is stolen (liquor is particularly likely to get one referred), and how the items are stolen (it is speculated that placing goods under one's clothes or into another bag seems more deliberate to store officials than does sticking them into a pocket, which could be mere absentmindedness).

One other conclusion from shoplifting studies is of interest here—less than half the apprehended shoplifters are referred to public police. Thus we must recognize that many known shoplifting offenses will not be recorded in the *Uniform Crime Reports*. This seems especially likely if the value of the goods is relatively low. In 1968, Hindelang found that the average value of goods stolen by apprehended offenders, regardless of whether or not they were referred to the police, was under $4.00.[58] By comparison, the *Uniform Crime Reports* for that year showed the mean average value of shoplifted goods to be $28.00.[59]

Although there is something to be said for the *Reports* being restricted to more serious offenses, it is obvious that the *Uniform Crime Reports* project an extremely distorted picture of the extent of larceny because of reporting failures at various levels. Scientific studies of theft indicate that it is widespread, involves all manner of people, and pays off—so long as concern over risk does not outweigh any advantages. Public indifference, a market for stolen goods, and a justice system that can be manipulated all contribute to the successful livelihoods of the professionals. But professionals evidently represent only a small proportion of the thieves; amateur theft is pervasive, so too are the values supporting it.

Larceny in the American Heart

Throughout our discussion of property crimes we have been confronted with a paradox. Many people fear crime and take all kinds of precautions to frustrate those who would rob, burgle and steal—yet those who become victims usually do not report the incidents. Why is there, on one hand, this fear of crime and, on the other hand, an indifference toward seeking official remedy? Surveys have attempted to answer this question and have concluded that victims who fail to report most often think that nothing can be done or that the offense is too unimportant to warrant being reported.[60]

Although it may seem lamentable that the public does not have more confidence in its law enforcement system, the lack unfortunately is not unreasonable. Police do have an adequate record of solving cases of murder, aggravated assault, and even rape, when they are reported. In 1973, police cleared by arrest over half of these offenses—that is, they identified some persons as offenders, presumably had sufficient evidence to charge them with an offense, and took them into custody.[61] Because these offenses often involve persons acquainted with one another, the police success is not too surprising. But crimes involving property are another matter.

In 1973 police cleared by arrest only 27 per cent of the reported robberies, 19 per cent of the larcenies, 18 per cent of the burglaries, and 16 per cent of the auto thefts. Thus there is no real incentive to report property crimes aside from officially going on record for insurance purposes, civic duty, and so on. But the efficiency of the criminal justice system is even more dismal if you are interested in seeing that those who are arrested face the wrath of justice. The fact that an offense is cleared by arrest tells you nothing about the final disposition of the offender. In 1973 from 14 to 25 per cent of the property offenders formally charged by police were either acquitted or dismissed.[62] The apparent ineffectiveness and indifference of the criminal justice system is illustrated by a Washington, D.C. study tracing the disposition of persons arrested during a three-month period for carrying concealed weapons: of 361 arrested, 162 were dismissed by the prosecutor, 17 were dismissed by a judge, and 25 were found not guilty.[63] Only 43 per cent of those arrested were convicted. Of these, 66 per cent were placed on probation and promptly back on the street—never to carry a gun again, of course.

Public apathy toward reporting crime is understandable in light of official inefficiency and lack of concern. But also underlying the reluctance to report property crimes may be a begrudging admission that such acts are an unavoidable part of everyday American life. Relieving persons of their property, like violence, is part of our heritage—ranging from American settlers seizing Indian lands to the confidence men who constantly bamboozle the public by selling cancer cures or get-rich-quick schemes. American heroes are those who have shown extraordinary courage, diligence, and initiative in science, industry, politics, entertainment, sports—and crime. Our heroes walk on the moon, hit a record number of home runs, and rob banks. Jessie James, Al Capone, and Bonnie and Clyde are easily as heroic to us as Thomas Edison or Hank Aaron. Despite the bluster over crime in the streets, theft is considered tolerable if violence is kept to a minimum and is done with class:

> Armed robbers are . . . irritating because they cannot be trusted to stay on their own side of the tracks; but even armed robbers have a place in the nation's heart because they touch, in a maverick sort of way, the theme of capitalism we love so much. Are they not, after all, simply nomadic low-overhead merchants with a kind of hard-sell? [Carl V. ("Boo Boo") Green described] the mechanics of pulling a grocery store holdup, a type of enterprise Boo Boo was very experienced at. "Everybody has a job to do and if he does it like he's supposed to, ain't no trouble at all," Boo Boo explained. "Got one man whose job is to watch the door. Got one man whose job is to hold a gun on the customers. Got one man whose job is to get the money out of the register. And *your* job (meaning Whitey, the store manager) is to shut up and hand over the money so nobody gets hurt." As forced mergers go, Boo Boo described one as nearly compatible with the business ideals of America as most of the mergers approved by the Justice Department. Some of the great family fortunes of this nation were developed out of the same strict attention to everyone's just doing his job.[64]

But theft is most tolerable to Americans if it is gentle and unassuming without the waving of guns and threats. Shoplifting nicely fits these requirements and can be thought of as an only slightly distorted miniature picture—a microcosm—of the streak of larceny running through American society. (If shoplifting involves as many as one in ten store customers, it is difficult to argue that it is not representative of American theft.) Shoplifting is a fraternity and sorority, a common meeting ground, of all religions, classes, and races. Shoplifters are stumbling junkies, secretaries, professional thieves, co-eds, house-wives, well-to-do, and radical hippies. In short, they are at once the respectable and the unrespectable, the bad and the beautiful.

Examples of "respectable" shoplifters appear especially prevalent among price tag switchers—those who substitute a lower price tag for a higher one and then purchase the product. According to a study by Stuart Hadden and John Steiner most of these are middle to upper class individuals; in short, your mainstream American "normals." [65] Their motivations are described by the researchers as cavalier. The switchers see themselves as acquiring goods for a fair price, as victimizing a company that deserves it, and as making a strike against the capitalist system. Because they are "normal" and can easily shift the blame for the mistagging onto the store, switchers are especially difficult to detect and to stop. In the meantime, they cost stores millions each year and are part of the crime problem.

It is ironic that good citizens should be part of the crime problem, but all that distinguishes them from criminals is the degree of violence used. Much of this distinction has to do with opportunity. The criminal must break into buildings or point a gun because he or she has few other alternatives. The good citizens, on the other hand, have many alternatives. Their respectability permits them violence-free theft unaccessible to the poor and the unemployed.

A good example of the larceny in the American heart concerns theft from hotels and motels. It is estimated that in 1974 *one of every three guests* stole something from his or her room. This includes sheets, bibles, ashtrays, towels, lamps, television sets, and, in one instance, the room's wallpaper. As in all forms of theft, there are the amateurs and the professionals. The professionals are few but thorough. They can get the contents of an entire room into a truck in a few minutes. But the amateurs' souvenir-collecting is costly. One first-class New York hotel must replace over 2,000 towels every month.[66] Of course, the amateurs have verbalized motives justifying theft:

> An advertising executive who stole a lamp: "I'll be damned if I'm going to throw out $36 just for a place to sleep, especially after I paid only $18 for the same sort of room in another town the night before."

> A woman who travels frequently and who has not had to purchase a sheet or towel for years: "I've paid for those things. The places I've stayed at haven't lost anything because they jack up their prices so."

> A woman with a closet full of hotel "souvenirs": "There's nothing wrong with taking little things from hotels. I think they expect you to take at least a towel. Anyway, if you have something marked with their crest it's good publicity for them. After all, I show off these things to my friends." [67]

THE RIP-OFF PHILOSOPHY

At the foundation of much of American theft is the notion that organizations are more legitimate targets than individuals are. The reader will recall that professionals in particular point out that what they steal is insured and that the individual victim does not suffer significantly, if at all. Although there is no scientific evidence to prove it, we are probably safe in assuming that most amateur thieves would agree that stealing from large chain stores is far more justifiable than from small, privately-owned, "mom and dad" operations. A classic study of how organization size affects attitudes toward stealing was conducted by Erwin O. Smigel in the early 1950s.[68] He found that most of his respondents disapproved of stealing, but felt that if one must steal it should be from large business or government rather than from small business. One can deduce that had "individuals" been a choice they would have been considered even less justifiable victims than small businesses.

Government and large businesses are seen as logical victims of theft because they can most readily afford it and can make adjustments in taxes or prices to accommodate losses. Smigel also found that the selection of preferred victims stemmed from resentment and distrust. Inefficiency, ruthlessness, and impersonality of large bureaucracies all were given as reasons for stealing from government and business. These reasons hint that a conflict exists between organizations and those who sense they are being exploited by those organizations. This is not to suggest that your everyday amateur shoplifter is making a political statement by lifting a jar of dry roasted cashews. But for some unknown minority an elaboration of similar themes produces a full-blown ideology not only justifying but compelling theft from organizations.

Ripping-off is a term for stealing that emerged with the youth culture of drugs and rock music in the late 1960s. The term then had intense political connotations—theft was to be a means by which wealth would be redistributed from capitalist institutions back to the people. The bible of the rip-off philosophy was written by Abbie Hoffman and appropriately entitled, *Steal This Book*. The book is a catalogue of means, both legal and illegal, of obtaining free food, lodging, education, and so on, and includes chapters on shoplifting techniques, street fighting, and how to collect welfare and unemployment payments. Hoffman briefly explains the book's ideology:

> [*Steal This Book*] implies that the reader already is "ideologically set," in that he understands corporate feudalism as the only robbery worthy of being called "crime," for it is committed against the people as a whole. Whether the ways it describes to rip-off shit are legal or illegal is irrelevant. The dictionary of law is written by the bosses of order. Our moral dictionary says no heisting from each other. To steal from a brother or sister is evil. To *not* steal from the institutions that are the pillars of the Pig Empire is equally immoral.[69]

The premise of the rip-off philosophy is that American society itself is a rip-off, that major corporations in particular and capitalism in general are guilty of far greater crimes than any individual. Thievery thus becomes political behavior that incidentally allows the individual to survive while working against instead of for the system. According to Hoffman:

All our rip-offs together don't equal one price-fixing scheme by General Electric. What we have to create is a nation of revolutionary outlaws and do away with the concept of money entirely. We want a society where your birth certificate is your passport, and everything is free.[70]

Whether one views business as too evil, too big, or simply too inefficient, the result is the same. The rip-off philosophy provides a morality in which one can violate the law without any sense of guilt. Regardless of whom one might sympathize with—business or citizens who steal from business—a great deal of time, effort, and imagination is expended in devising means of theft, means of counteracting theft, and means of counteracting the counteractions. A favorite target of the rip-off philosophy is the phone company. American Telephone and Telegraph estimated that nearly $22 million worth of free calls were made in 1970.[71] But as A.T.& T. makes approximately $10 billion a year in profit, it may be difficult for all but the most hardened capitalist or stockholder to generate much indignation.

Hoffman claims that "ripping-off the phone company is an act of revolutionary love." [72] Whether revolutionaries or not, American citizens have for years challenged the ingenuity of the phone company by various slugs, phony credit cards, and electronic tampering. One of the most resourceful devices for giving the phone company a headache is known as the *blue box*—a device emitting signals that allows one to tap into long-distance systems without the necessity of an operator. The owner of such a box can make calls to anywhere in the world for nothing. The more sophisticated users, known as *phone phreaks*, hold extended conference calls with each other, tap into the lines of unsuspecting callers, and talk to acquaintances in many foreign countries, all at no cost.[73] Phreaks are generally not revolutionaries; they have no interest in destroying the phone company but only want to meet its challenges:

Did you ever steal anything?
Well yes, I—
Then you know! You know the rush you get. It's not just knowledge, like physical chemistry. It's forbidden knowledge. You know. You can learn about anything under the sun and be bored to death with it. But the idea that it's illegal. Look: you can be small and mobile and smart and you're ripping off somebody large and powerful and very dangerous.[74]

Conclusion

If you rely solely on the *Uniform Crime Reports* you will have these impressions. First, crimes against property in the United States are fundamentally violent matters—your property disappears because you are forced to give it up or because someone snatches it away

while you are not looking. At least they are all acts that can be de-
terred by greater wariness, stronger locks, meaner dogs, and more
sophisticated alarm systems. Second, since lower class, urban blacks
are overrepresented among the index crimes, it becomes easy to pin-
point who the criminal element in our society is.

But when looking closely at just a couple of forms of theft, it becomes evident that many respectable people are involved. Apparently
there is an element of larceny in the American public. A spirit of
thievery, ripping-off, or whatever you want to call it is present in practically every segment of society, particularly when the target is seen as
big, bungling, and bureaucratic. Furthermore, this spirit is supported
by a variety of motives ranging from excessive prices to class warfare
to a purely unpolitical motive of adventure.

True, the lower class, urban, black male who steals is more likely to
rely on force, but then he has fewer alternatives. Others who steal are
more fortunate—they are blessed with opportunities that make unnecessary any unpleasantness of weapons or of sneaking around with
one eye open for the cops. These lucky individuals are involved in
many forms of property theft that are not reflected in the *Uniform
Crime Reports'* index crimes. These forms of deviance may be subtle,
some to the point of being barely noticeable. But ultimately they may
cost more in dollars, human suffering, and loss of public trust than all
the index property crimes combined.

NOTES

1. *Crime in the United States, 1973* (Washington, D.C.: Government Printing Office, 1974), p. 1.
2. Ibid., p. 15.
3. *Crime in the Nation's Five Largest Cities,* Advance Report, April 1974
(Washington, D.C.: U.S. Department of Justice, 1974), pp. 28–29.
4. Donald J. Mulvihill and Melvin M. Tumin, *Crimes of Violence,* A Staff
Report Submitted to the National Commission on the Causes and Prevention
of Violence, vol. 11 (Washington, D.C.: Government Printing Office, 1969),
p. 54; and *Crime in the United States, 1973,* pp. 17, 61. For a discussion claiming that the increase in reported robbery in the 1960s represented an actual
increase in rates see John E. Conklin, *Robbery and the Criminal Justice System* (Philadelphia: J. B. Lippincott, 1972), pp. 10–38.
5. Mulvihill and Tumin, *Crimes of Violence,* pp. 214–215.
6. Ibid., p. 217; cf. André Normandeau, "Patterns in Robbery," *Criminologica,* 6 (November 1968), p. 5.
7. Mulvihill and Tumin, *Crimes of Violence,* p. 221. The *Uniform Crime
Reports* use a very general term, "highway," to denote all outside locations.
In 1973 this category accounted for 48.6 per cent of all robberies: *Crime in the
United States, 1973,* p. 120.
8. Mulvihill and Tumin, *Crimes of Violence,* pp. 644–646; Arnold Sagalyn,

CRIME IN THE STREETS—AGAINST PROPERTY 169

The Crime of Robbery in the United States (Washington, D.C.: U.S. Department of Justice, January 1971), pp. 15–16; and Conklin, *Robbery*, pp. 50–57.

9. Gerald D. Wolcott, "A Typology of Armed Robbers" (unpublished M.A. thesis, Sacramento State College, 1968), as cited in Sagalyn, *Crime of Robbery*, p. 16.

10. Edward Preble and John J. Casey, Jr., "Taking Care of Business—the Heroin User's Life on the Street," *International Journal of the Addictions*, **4** (March 1969), pp. 1–14.

11. Mulvihill and Tumin, *Crimes of Violence*, p. 235.

12. Conklin, *Robbery*, pp. 102–122; and Sagalyn, *Crime of Robbery*, pp. 8–10. For a discussion of victim confrontation in bank robbery, see Peter Letkemann, *Crime As Work* (Englewood Cliffs, N.J.: Prentice-Hall, 1973), pp. 107–116.

13. Normandeau, "Patterns in Robbery," p. 12.

14. For a discussion of the pitfalls of typologies, see Clayton A. Hartjen and Don C. Gibbons, "An Empirical Investigation of a Criminal Typology," *Sociology and Social Research*, **54** (October 1969), pp. 56–62.

15. Conklin, *Robbery*, pp. 63–78.

16. Werner J. Einstadter, "The Social Organization of Armed Robbery," *Social Problems*, **17** (Summer 1969), pp. 80–81.

17. John Irwin, *The Felon* (Englewood Cliffs, N.J.: Prentice-Hall, 1970), p. 11.

18. Conklin, *Robbery*, p. 76.

19. *Crime in the United States, 1973*, p. 19.

20. *Crime in the Nation's Five Largest Cities*, pp. 28–29.

21. Mulvihill and Tumin, *Crimes of Violence*, pp. 54–55; and *Crime in the United States, 1973*, p. 59.

22. This discussion of Armand is based on Nicholas Pileggi, "1968 Has Been the Year of the Burglar," *New York Times Magazine*, November 17, 1968, pp. 54–80.

23. Ibid., pp. 54–55.

24. John E. Conklin and Egon Bittner, "Burglary in a Suburb," *Criminology*, **11** (August 1973), pp. 206–231; and Harry A. Scarr, *Patterns of Burglary*, 2nd ed. (Washington, D.C.: U.S. Department of Justice, 1973).

25. There is a continuing debate concerning exactly what the professional criminal is. For the best discussion of this issue, see Letkemann, *Crime As Work*, pp. 20–32. For a history of professional crime see James A. Inciardi, *Careers in Crime* (Chicago: Rand McNally, 1975), pp. 5–82 passim.

26. William E. Cobb, "Theft and the Two Hypotheses"; Gregory Krohm, "The Pecuniary Incentives of Property Crime"; and J. Patrick Gunning, Jr., "How Profitable Is Burglary?" in *The Economics of Crime and Punishment*, ed. Simon Rottenberg (Washington, D.C.: American Enterprise Institute for Public Policy Research), 1973, pp. 19–38.

27. Neal Shover, "Structures and Careers in Burglary," *Journal of Criminal Law, Criminology and Police Science*, **63** (December 1972), pp. 540–549; and "The Social Organization of Burglary," *Social Problems*, **20** (Spring 1973), pp. 499–514.

28. Shover, "Social Organization," p. 510.

29. For an analysis of the fence as a middleman and the application of marketing theory to fencing, see Ted Roselius and Douglas Benton, "Marketing

Theory and the Fencing of Stolen Goods," *Denver Law Journal,* **50**:2 (1973), pp. 177–205. For other discussions of fencing, see: Duncan Chappell and Marilyn Walsh, "Receiving Stolen Property: The Need for Systematic Inquiry into the Fencing Process," *Criminology,* **11** (February 1974), pp. 484–497; Chappell and Walsh, " 'No Questions Asked': A Consideration of the Crime of Criminal Receiving," *Crime and Delinquency,* **20** (April 1974), pp. 157–168; and Carl B. Klockars, *The Professional Fence* (New York: The Free Press, 1974).

30. *Crime in the Nation's Five Largest Cities,* p. 29.

31. *Crime in the United States, 1973,* p. 26.

32. Mulvihill and Tumin, *Crimes of Violence,* p. 54; and *Crime in the United States, 1973,* p. 59.

33. Peter Hellman, "Stealing Cars Is a Growth Industry," *New York Times Magazine,* June 20, 1971, p. 41.

34. *Crime in the United States, 1973,* p. 120.

35. Ibid., p. 128.

36. The best review of studies on auto theft will be found in Don C. Gibbons, *Society, Crime, and Criminal Careers,* 2nd ed. (Englewood Cliffs, N.J.: Prentice-Hall, 1973), pp. 314–320. The classic study in this area is William W. Wattenberg and James Balistrieri, "Automobile Theft: A 'Favored Group' Delinquency," *American Journal of Sociology,* **57** (May 1952), pp. 575–579.

37. Gibbons, *Society, Crime, and Criminal Careers,* p. 314.

38. The discussion is based on Hellman, "Stealing Cars," pp. 41–45.

39. Ibid., p. 45.

40. *Crime in the Nation's Five Largest Cities,* pp. 28–29.

41. Isadore Barmash, "Pilferage Abounds in the Nation's Stores," *New York Times,* October 28, 1973, Section 3, p. 9.

42. Ibid.; and Isadore Barmash, "In Retailing, 'Shrinkage' Is Outdistancing Profits," *New York Times,* April 12, 1970, Section 3, p. 1.

43. Isadore Barmash, "High Cost of Crime Adding to Retailers' Price Tags," *New York Times,* May 11, 1969, Section 3, p. 3; Barmash, "Pilferage Abounds"; and "The Case of the Missing Bucks," *Investors' Reader,* **56** (January 6, 1971), p. 24.

44. Barmash, "In Retailing," p. 1.

45. Ibid.; and Peter Hellman, "One in Ten Shoppers Is a Shoplifter," *New York Times Magazine,* March 15, 1970, p. 34.

46. Judie Bailey, "Cart Blanche," *Cleveland Plain Dealer,* November 15, 1969, Section B, p. 2; and *New York Times,* May 8, 1974, p. 34.

47. The discussion is based upon Hellman, "One in Ten," pp. 34–49; and Mary Owen Cameron, *The Booster and the Snitch: Department Store Shoplifting* (New York: Free Press of Glencoe, 1964), pp. 39–60.

48. Robert A. Wright, "Nation's Retail Merchants Mobilize Security Systems to Combat Fast-Growing Shoplifting Trend," *New York Times,* May 21, 1972, Section 3, p. 59.

49. Ibid.

50. Hellman, "One in Ten," p. 39.

51. Cameron, *Booster and the Snitch,* pp. 59–60.

52. Hellman, "One in Ten," pp. 34, 39; cf. Cameron, *Booster and the Snitch,* p. 49.

53. Darrell J. Steffensmeier and Robert M. Terry, "Deviance and Respectability: An Observational Study of Reactions to Shoplifting," *Social Forces,* **51** (June 1973), p. 418.

54. Ibid., pp. 422–424. For analysis of other variables from the same study, see Robert M. Terry and Darrell J. Steffensmeier, "The Influence of Organizational Factors of Victim Store on Willingness to Report a Shoplifting Incident: A Field Experiment," *Sociological Focus,* **6** (Fall 1973), pp. 27–45.

55. Donald P. Hartmann, Donna M. Gelfand, Brent Page, and Patrice Walder, "Rates of Bystander Observation and Reporting of Contrived Shoplifting Incidents," *Criminology,* **10** (November 1972), pp. 247–267.

56. Ibid., pp. 257, 261–264; and Steffensmeier and Terry, "Deviance and Respectability," pp. 420–421.

57. Michael J. Hindelang, "Decisions of Shoplifting Victims to Invoke the Criminal Justice Process," *Social Problems,* **21** (April 1974), pp. 580–593. Practically identical findings are noted in another study, Lawrence Cohen and Rodney Stark, "Discriminatory Labeling and the Five-Finger Discount: An Empirical Analysis of Differential Shoplifting Dispositions," *Journal of Research in Crime and Delinquency,* **11** (January 1974), pp. 25–39.

58. Hindelang, "Decisions of Shoplifting Victims," p. 582.

59. *Crime in the United States, 1968,* p. 24.

60. *Crime in the Nation's Five Largest Cities,* pp. 4–5; and The President's Commission on Law Enforcement and Administration of Justice, *Task Force Report: Crime and Its Impact—An Assessment* (Washington, D.C.: Government Printing Office, 1967), pp. 17–18.

61. *Crime in the United States, 1973,* pp. 28–30.

62. Ibid., p. 116.

63. Robert Sherrill, *The Saturday Night Special* (New York: Charter House, 1973), p. 233.

64. Ibid., p. 323.

65. Personal correspondence with Stuart Hadden. Study will appear in a forthcoming issue of *International Journal of Criminology and Penology.*

66. The discussion is based on Michael S. Lasky, "One in 3 Hotel Guests Is a Towel Thief, Bible Pincher, or Worse," *New York Times,* January 27, 1974, Section 10, pp. 1, 18–19.

67. Ibid., pp. 18–19.

68. Erwin O. Smigel, "Public Attitudes Toward Stealing as Related to the Size of the Victim Organization," *American Sociological Review,* **21** (June 1956), pp. 320–327. For a related study, see Terry and Steffensmeier, "Influence of Organizational Factors," pp. 27–45.

69. Abbie Hoffman, *Steal This Book* (New York: Pirate Editions, 1971), p. iv.

70. Michael Drosnin, "Ripping Off, The New Life-Style," *New York Times Magazine,* August 8, 1971, p. 52.

71. Ibid., p. 13.

72. Hoffman, *Steal This Book,* p. 75.

73. Ron Rosenbaum, "Secrets of the Little Blue Box," *Esquire,* **75** (October 1971), pp. 117–125, 222–226.

74. Ibid., p. 223.

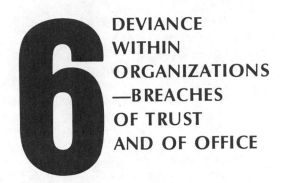

6

DEVIANCE WITHIN ORGANIZATIONS —BREACHES OF TRUST AND OF OFFICE

White-Collar and Occupational Crime

In 1939 Edwin H. Sutherland directed sociologists' attention toward what he called "white-collar crime." [1] In his presidential address to the American Sociological Society, Sutherland declared that the single-minded concern over persons officially designated as criminal—who are, of course, primarily from the lower class—resulted in misleading theories about the causes of crime, theories focusing on feeblemindedness, slums, unstable families, and so on. These theories ignored the criminality of business, professional, and political persons—those who are respected and looked up to. Upper-class persons may not commit armed robbery, but they do bribe public officials, misrepresent products in advertising, embezzle, defraud the Internal Revenue Service, and generally cost society incredible sums of money. Respectable people are involved in what Al Capone called the "legitimate rackets."

Because white-collar crimes were clearly not the result of poverty or of any known individual malady, Sutherland concluded that such crime existed because of *differential association*, a process whereby behavior is learned in association with those defining

173

the behavior favorably and in isolation from those defining it unfavorably. As examples, Sutherland provided cases in which acquiring the art of "practical business" often involved the learning of unethical or illegal procedures from those who were successful:

> He [the beginner in business] learns specific techniques of violating the law, together with definitions of situations in which those techniques may be used. Also, he develops a general ideology. This ideology grows in part out of the specific practices and is in the nature of generalization from concrete experiences, but in part it is transmitted as a generalization by phrases such as "we are not in business for our health," "business is business," or "no business was ever built on the beatitudes." These generalizations, whether transmitted as such or abstracted from concrete experiences, assist the neophyte in business to accept the illegal practices and provide rationalizations for them.[2]

Sutherland goes further to point out that businessmen are not only exposed to definitions favorable to white-collar crime, but are also isolated from contrary definitions because business is generally shielded from any criticism. At the extreme, to be critical of industry is to be un-American, if not downright communistic. But for the most part to criticize business is complicated because business interests are economically and politically powerful and are interwoven with the only element of society that could successfully challenge them—government.[3]

The concept of white-collar crime formulated by Sutherland was limited to "crime committed by a person of respectability and high social status in the course of his occupation."[4] This definition failed to recognize that many respectable people besides highly esteemed corporate executives are involved in deviant behavior in connection with their job or profession. Service station owners make unnecessary repairs on cars, salespersons sell ill-fitting shoes and clothes to gullible customers, and dentists yank perfectly sound teeth out of unsuspecting heads. Because the collar of the offender may be white, blue, tan, or pink the status of the individual or the occupation seems irrelevant.

Furthermore, the term crime is misleading since many acts of deviation in an occupation may not be in violation of the traditional criminal code.[5] This is particularly the case when an organization or corporation rather than an individual is considered to be the violator. When a corporation engages in unfair labor practices, unfair competition, false advertising, or patent infringement, specific government agencies are empowered to impose restrictions upon such practices. If, for example, a furniture manufacturer advertises a pine bureau as being constructed of "Indonesian mahogany," the Federal Trade Commission is responsible for investigating any complaints and instituting prosecutions. As we shall see later, the penalties imposed against corporations for violations are usually minor at best. In the advertising case a promise by the corporation that it will desist from further publication of its fraudulant claim is usually sufficient insofar as the F.T.C. is concerned. Imagine the time when you are arrested for speeding or for possession of illegal drugs—just tell the police that prosecution is unnecessary since you are hereby desisting from further criminal activity. Good luck.

The reader should recognize, however, that much of what is included in white-collar crime *may* be treated as crime in the traditional sense. For example, the F.T.C. can recommend that certain kinds of illegal acts by corporations be prosecuted in criminal courts where the perpetrators presumably would be treated just as burglars, muggers, and so on. As we shall elaborate in Chapter 7 criminal prosecution is rare. When it does occur the penalties are minor in terms of both the damage to the public by the companies, and the companies' abilities to easily absorb the cost of the penalties.

Despite the problems with Sutherland's particular definition, his central point is inescapable; upper-class persons commit many acts of deviance that are related to their occupational positions. These positions provide them with opportunities to engage in behavior unavailable to the unemployed or those employed in lower status occupations. By extending the context of such behavior, however, it is evident that the concept of white-collar crime can be expanded to include all violations of law that occur in occupational activities. It has been suggested by Richard Quinney that because blue-collar as well as white-collar individuals can violate the law in the course of their occupations, the concept of *occupational crime* would be more appropriate than that of white-collar crime.[6]

Another important contribution of Sutherland's work is the focus upon *organizations,* both business and governmental, as important elements in the study of deviance. Sociologists have long been interested in *organized crime*—businesses set up specifically for the purpose of obtaining profit from illegal enterprises—but only recently have they recognized that legitimate organizations and individuals can also be involved in a network of deviance.[7] The organization may be victimized by individuals, employees, clients, or both; and employees or clients may be victimized by organizations.

One of the more comprehensive classifications of deviance involving organizations and individuals is suggested by Herbert Edelhertz, part of which is presented here.

A. Crimes in the course of their occupations by those operating inside business, Government, or other establishments in violation of their duty of loyalty and fidelity to employer or client.

1. Commercial bribery and kickbacks, i.e., by and to buyers, insurance adjusters, contracting officers, quality inspectors, government inspectors and auditors, etc.
2. Bank violations by bank officers, employees, and directors.
3. Embezzlement or self-dealing by business or union officers and employees.
4. Securities fraud by insiders trading to their advantage by the use of special knowledge, or causing their firms to take positions in the market to benefit themselves.
5. Employee petty larceny and expense account frauds.
6. Frauds by computer, causing unauthorized payouts.
7. "Sweetheart contracts" entered into by union officers.
8. Embezzlement or self-dealing by attorneys, trustees, and fiduciaries.
9. Fraud against the Government.
   (a) Padding of payrolls.
   (b) Conflicts of interest.
   (c) False travel, expense, or per diem claims.
B. Crimes incidental to and in furtherance of business operations, but not the central purpose of the business.
   1. Tax violations.
   2. Antitrust violations.
   3. Commercial bribery of another's employee, officer or fiduciary (including union officials).
   4. Food and drug violations.
   5. False weights and measures by retailers.
   6. Violations of Truth-In-Lending Act by misrepresentation of credit terms and prices.
   7. Submission or publication of false financial statements to obtain credit.
   8. Use of fictitious or over-valued collateral.
   9. Securities Act violations, i.e., sale of nonregistered securities to obtain operating capital, false proxy statements, manipulation of market to support corporate credit or access to capital markets, and so on.
   10. Collusion between physicians and pharmacists to cause the writing of unnecessary prescriptions.
   11. Dispensing by pharmacists in violation of law, excluding narcotics traffic.
   12. Deceptive advertising.
   13. Commercial espionage.
C. White-collar crime as a business, or as the central activity.
   1. Medical or health frauds.
   2. Advance fee swindles.
   3. Phony contests.
   4. Bankruptcy fraud, including schemes devised as salvage operations after insolvency of otherwise legitimate businesses.
   5. Securities fraud and commodities fraud.
   6. Chain referral schemes.

7. Home improvement schemes.
8. Land frauds.
9. Charity and religious frauds.
10. Personal improvement schemes:
    (a) Diploma mills
    (b) Correspondence schools
    (c) Modeling schools
11. Insurance frauds
    (a) Phony accident rings.
    (b) Looting of companies by purchase of over-valued assets, phony management contracts, self-dealing with agents, inter-company transfers, and so on.
    (c) Frauds by agents writing false policies to obtain advance commissions.
12. Ponzi schemes.
13. False security frauds, i.e., Billy Sol Estes or De Angelis type schemes.
14. Purchase of banks, or control thereof, with deliberate intention to loot them.[8]

This chapter and the next discuss examples of deviance roughly corresponding to Edelhertz's three general categories. This chapter concerns individuals who violate the trust of the organization employing them. This includes persons in government, either elected or appointed, who violate the public trust. Specifically, we will discuss two forms of employee theft—pilfering and embezzlement—police corruption, and political corruption. The following chapter will first examine acts of deviance against individuals and other organizations by organizations that are otherwise legitimate enterprises. This corresponds to Edelhertz's category B and is closest to what Sutherland had in mind when he defined white-collar crime. The latter part of the next chapter concerns deviance by organizations specifically designed to engage in illegal activities. Thus the discussion will correspond to category C and, for convenience, organized crime will be considered as well.

Employee Theft

As you are already aware, statistics on theft are at least 90 per cent guesswork. Nevertheless, they hold a fascination for us if only because numbers at least represent one kind of reality. Although it is pure conjecture as to the accuracy of the representation, at least the numbers give us something to argue about. The F.B.I. estimates that in 1973 robbery cost American citizens $100 million, burglary $856 million, and larceny-theft $603 million.[9] Total losses from these index property crimes amounted to about $1.6 billion that year.

Estimated loss from inventory shrinkage alone in retail establish-ments in 1973 was $4.8 billion.[10] Obviously, any estimates must be viewed with considerable skepticism. The index crime statistics are probably low because of nonreporting of offenses, and inventory shrinkage figures can only be apportioned to bookkeeping errors, shoplifting, and employee theft by the wildest of guesswork. Experts estimate that 30 to 75 per cent of all shrinkage is a result of internal theft.[11] Nevertheless, even from a conservative standpoint, it is obvi-ous that employee theft is one of the most costly, if not the most costly, offenses perpetrated by individuals in the United States. In-deed, nearly 1,000 businesses go bankrupt annually because of em-ployee theft.[12]

Furthermore, employee theft is scarcely limited to those retail es-tablishments on which the $4.8 billion figure is based. For example, the construction industry estimates that a half billion dollars worth of material and equipment vanishes yearly from construction sites, and most of the theft is attributed to construction workers.[13] Add to this the theft from the armed forces, governmental agencies, and other businesses and you probably would be justified in estimating that at least $10 billion worth of goods are stolen each year.

For purposes of our discussion we have divided employee theft into two types: *pilferage* refers to theft of goods, whereas *em-bezzlement* refers to misappropriation or misuse of funds entrusted to one's care. The distinction is necessary because studies of em-ployee theft have concentrated on one or the other rather than both, and because embezzlement generally is a lone offense whereas pil-ferage can involve several persons working in concert. In addition, nearly all employees regardless of position can pilfer, but employees who embezzle must be in special positions of trust allowing them access to funds.

EMPLOYEE PILFERAGE

Who is the pilferer? Mark Lipman, who heads an investigatory agency specializing in department stores and factories, provides this profile:

> Some are punks and some are executives, but the average company thief is a married man, has two or three children, lives in a fairly good commu-nity, plays bridge with his neighbors, goes to church regularly, is well thought of by his boss. He is highly trusted and a good worker, one of the best in the plant. That's why he can steal so much over such long periods and why it's so hard to discover his identity.[14]

By American middle class standards one could not imagine a more "respectable" individual. Furthermore, Lipman is not referring to someone involved in nickel and dime stuff, but in systematic thievery that can amount to thousands of dollars in a few years. For example, eleven workers in a trucking firm and a department store receiving department stole a quarter of a million dollars worth of merchandise by a simple device. When the truckers delivered 100 cases of merchandise they kept 20, but the receiving staff signed for 100. The twenty cases were sold to a fence and the booty divided among the conspirators.[15]

Techniques of employee theft vary greatly and depend, of course, upon the position of the employee and his or her access to goods. The innovation that often goes into thievery is illustrated by the case of a certain pants factory. Some employees simply zipped up completed trousers into the clothes they were wearing. But many women had what they called a buddy system. They carried out pieces they had been working on at quitting time, met outside to exchange pieces, and completed the trousers on their home sewing machines.[16]

Other more common techniques are

1. Cashiers who ring up a lower price on single item purchases and pocket the difference, or who ring up lower prices for "needy" friends going through the checkout.
2. Clerks who do not tag some sale merchandise, sell it at the original price, and pocket the difference.
3. Receiving clerks who have duplicate keys to storage facilities and who return to the store after hours.
4. Truck drivers who make fictitious purchases of fuel and repairs, and who split the gains with truck stops.
5. Finally, employees who simply hide items in garbage pails, incinerators, or under trash heaps until they can be retrieved later.[17]

In some instances theft from employers involves more than materials. In New York City, for example, construction contractors estimate that they lose more than six million dollars a year in excess overtime wages. An electrician puts it this way:

> Guys like me . . . make their real money working overtime. Say there's 60 feet of pipe sitting on the floor, all you need to finish a job. You shove it under a tarp, then tell the foreman he didn't order enough. So he orders some more pipe, which takes a couple of hours at least, so you get your overtime and, if you want it, some pipe, too.[18]

Why do employees pilfer? Undoubtedly no single answer can be given if only because there is wide variety of pilferers. Although there is no research on types of pilferers, it seems safe to assume that they, like shoplifters, range from the systematic professional types to the sporadic amateurs. At one extreme, there are those like the three electricians who steal over $150,000 worth of materials and sell them to fences associated with organized crime.[19] At the other extreme are the employees who occasionally run off with a ballpoint pen and a box of paper clips for their own use.

A study of pilfering was conducted by Donald N. M. Horning, who interviewed employees of an electronics assembly plant. Horning found that the workers divided property into three categories: company property (power tools, machinery, testing equipment); personal property (items owned by other workers, items marked as personal); and property of uncertain ownership. The pilfering of items in this last category was considered legitimate by the workers: unmarked clothing, small tools, and most items that are small, plentiful, and inexpensive—nails, screws, scrap metal, electrical tape, wipe rags.[20] As one respondent claimed:

> Most of it belongs to the Company—but there are some things that are furnished by the Company which ya might say we own—for instance, I got me a little electric fan that I made from junk I found out there—I've got my name painted on it . . . it's mine.[21]

Consistent with our discussion of shoplifters in the last chapter, pilferers express verbalized motives that make organizations more legitimate targets of theft than individuals. One of Horning's respondents reacted this way:

> It's a corporation. . . . It's not like taking from one person . . . the people justify it that the corporation wouldn't be hurt by it . . . they just jack the price up and screw the customer. They're not losing anything. The Company told us that last year they lost $30,000 . . . but that was for losses of all types. It gives them a nice big tax write-off. I'll bet you a goddamn day's pay that they jack that son-of-a-bitchin' write-off way up too.[22]

Horning found no widespread justification for large scale theft even from the company, but he did find that a large majority of his respondents had pilfered and that stealing was not regarded as immoral as long as it was confined to property of uncertain ownership, and the goods were not sold but taken for personal use. Besides, as some respondents claimed, "The Company expects it."

That an organization expects its employees to steal may not be a far-fetched excuse at all. A study of black males in a Washington, D.C. slum revealed that opportunities and expectations of employee theft served to depress wage levels.

> Owners of small retail establishments and other employers frequently anticipate employee stealing and adjust the wage rate accordingly. Tonk's employer explained why he was paying Tonk $35 for a 55–60 hour work-week. These men will all steal, he said. Although he keeps close watch on Tonk, he estimates that Tonk steals from $35 to $40 a week. What he steals, when added to his regular earnings, brings his take-home pay to $70 to $75 per week. The employer said he did not mind this because Tonk is worth

that much to the business. But if he were to pay Tonk outright the full value of his labor, Tonk would still be stealing $35 to $40 per week and this, he said, the business simply would not support.[23]

Elliot Liebow, the author of the study, argues that the employer's and employee's mutual expectation about theft is not as equitable as it seems. The system actually forces the employee to steal—the one who does not is penalized. But the employee who does steal runs the constant risk of being caught and punished by the employer for whatever reason he or she may have. Furthermore, the employee gains little in terms of self respect in a situation where someone condescendingly allows the employee to steal.[24] Thus the ultimate loser is the employee.

The degree to which the live-and-let-steal philosophy of employers in slum businesses extends to other organizations is impossible to say, but one industrial psychologist recommends—with a straight face—that companies set up a system of "controlled larceny" for their employees.[25] Lawrence R. Zeitlin claims that most pilfering is due to the nature of most retail jobs, which offer limited chances for advancement, no decision-making powers, and boredom—in short, *job dissatisfaction*. Pilfering is both a way of getting back at the system and a means of introducing intellectual and physical challenges into everyday tedium. Theft thus serves as a "safety valve for employee frustration." If management can control theft, that is, keep it within bounds of around $1.50 per employee per day, it can actually avoid the higher cost involved in reorganizing jobs and increasing wages and benefits. Zeitlin adds the warning:

> I should emphasize that a man who enriches his job by stealing does not suddenly become a "good" employee; rather he gives the *appearance* of a good employee so as not to attract attention to his illicit activities. But in many cases this is all that is necessary. Simply *being there* is sufficient for many jobs. It is common knowledge in financial circles that the man with his hand in the till is never absent.[26]

The likelihood that employee theft boosts morale is not farfetched. On one hand theft can serve as an unofficial reward system.[27] Work that is unsatisfactory in its own right can be made palatable when one feels appropriately compensated. If compensation is not forthcoming in the paycheck, an organization can provide unofficial rewards by extending pilferage "rights" to valued employees, e.g., by ignoring so-called government jobs—work done for employees by maintenance crews using company materials and time. But there is often a thin line between what a company allows for inducement and reward, and what it regards as outright theft. From the employee's standpoint this line is easy to cross if the company does not recognize the employee's contributions.

> Some executives ambiguously feel a "right" to use materials and services whether granted or not, and if questioned would defend their practice as a due reward. These are the managers who put in much overtime (emergencies, meetings, etc.) without extra compensation, and who resent the time-and-a-half overtime pay of hourly-paid workers. . . . Frequently these are also the officers who angrily agree that the organization owns them and in turn, quite within the range of normal madness, protest a counter ownership of its resources. These managers would say, sociologically, that unofficial demands call for unofficial rewards. Where people have been "oversold" by higher management's attempt to win their identification, they may of course expect greater reward then they receive and resort to supplementation.[28]

On the other hand, theft can arise more directly from frustration and boredom: the reward is in the act of theft itself—in the doing. John Lofland has referred to the "adventurous deviant act," the act undertaken because of the excitement and thrill of being bad.

> Account must be taken . . . of the likelihood that deviance can be fun, or, in the current vernacular, it can be kicks. . . . If many kinds of deviant acts are simply more fun than considerable portions of conventionality, the widespread popularity of them would appear no more mysterious than the popularity of conventional adventures. If deviance could not be fun, it would hardly be necessary to preach against the joys of sin. (And, if crime did not pay, it would hardly be necessary so adamantly to argue otherwise and so strenuously to attempt its control.) [29]

The poet Matthew Prior wrote in the seventeenth century that "Virtue is its own reward." He was obviously too early to be acquainted with the virtues of working in American business. Job dissatisfaction evidently has a way of neutralizing any reservations about being good to one's employers.

EMBEZZLEMENT

Pilferers come from many stations within organizations, from janitors to executives. They steal everything from pencils to twenty-ton cranes; and although sometimes they sell their loot, most of the time they use it themselves. But the real stars among employee thieves are the embezzlers. In most cases they occupy positions in the middle or upper echelons of the organization, they are trusted beyond question, and they are stealing the organization blind. *Embezzlers are persons who use their positions of trust to acquire the employers' money for their own use.* The following are examples of embezzlers. Although the money involved is usually great, the cases are representative of the range of persons who embezzle.

Orville E. Hodge, a highly respected politician, was elected state auditor of Illinois in 1953. Almost immediately he began looting the treasury by writing state checks to fictitious persons for alleged services and cashing them himself. By 1956, when a Chicago Daily News reporter blew the lid off, Hodge had embezzled $2.6 million. Once considered a potential candidate for governor in 1960, he merely said, "I don't know why I did it. I must have been temporarily insane." [30]

Charles Einstein, a $120-a-week accounts-payable clerk at G.A.F. Corporation, was driven to work in a chauffeured limousine with a bar and stereo system. He lent the driver $20,000, and took his wife and four friends on several trips from New York City to Las Vegas, Puerto Rico, and Honolulu—all expenses paid by Einstein. Is this a man who knows how to stretch a dollar? No. In a span of two and a half years he had written about $380,000 worth of checks, which he cashed, to a mythical William Harman. [31]

The very best of people become embezzlers but it is impossible to say just how many there are or how much they steal. These two cases made newspaper headlines because of the amount of money involved. Obviously, such news is embarrassing to the agencies and companies that have been so badly duped for so long. It seems likely that the fear of bad publicity keeps most of the less costly but no less disconcerting incidents out of both the newspapers and the criminal records. It has been estimated that fear of publicity, loyalty to the straying employee, and other reasons result in only about 1 per cent of all trust violations being prosecuted. [32]

Why do people embezzle? Is it a matter of fast women and slow horses, or keeping up with the neighbors? The closest answer to these questions comes from Donald R. Cressey, who sought to determine the sequence of events present whenever persons violate their positions of financial trust. After eliminating from his sample those who had not taken the position of trust in good faith—that is, those who formulated their intent to embezzle before taking the job, Cressey's conclusion was:

> Trusted persons become trust violators when they conceive of themselves as having a financial problem which is non-shareable, are aware that this problem can be secretly resolved by violation of the position of financial trust, and are able to apply to their own conduct in that situation verbalizations which enable them to adjust their conceptions of themselves as trusted persons with their conceptions of themselves as users of the entrusted funds. [33]

As you can see, the process of trust violation involves three steps. The first, the non-shareable financial problem, refers to money difficulties that the individual feels must be kept secret because he or she feels ashamed. These difficulties are extremely varied, according to Cressey, but they all have a basis of being status-related. But seeking to maintain or increase one's standard of living and respectability will not cause embezzlement unless it creates a non-shareable problem for the individual. It matters not if a person fears debt because of gambling, a new swimming pool, or business setbacks; it is the failure to reveal the problem to anyone that can lead to embezzlement. Cressey cites one case of a banker who feared financial difficulty because his salary did not meet the ordinary expenses of his family:

> No, [my wife] didn't know about it. I never told her. I took care of all the finances in the family. It wasn't her job. When it was all over she said I should have told her, that she could have cut down on a lot of things. She never knew how much I made. That's one thing, if I had it all to do over again I'd tell her all about everything.[34]

Failure to reveal financial problems to others does not alone cause embezzlement, however. The individual must also *perceive that funds entrusted to her or his care can be used to relieve the financial problem*. Many times this is learned as part of acquiring the skills of the job. As one auditor put it:

> By the time an accountant has done some auditing work he learns what an auditor is for—it becomes common knowledge to him. Naturally, I knew I shouldn't take it, but still the fact that I was the only one making the reports, I knew I shouldn't be found out.[35]

Once the individual has defined a financial problem as non-shareable and realizes the possibility of resolving it by embezzlement, a third and last step remains: the individual must *adjust the concept of her or himself as a trusted employee with the concept of a person violating that trust*. This adjustment involves *verbalized motives*—or what Cressey calls "vocabularies of adjustment." The particular motives found among embezzlers center especially around the idea that they simply were "borrowing," not stealing the money—the funds would be used to clear up some difficulties and then returned with no one harmed.[36] Other motives define the embezzlement as justified since the employer paid too little salary or was crooked, or both. In other instances, a kind of to-hell-with-it attitude emerges in which a combination of financial troubles, drink, and so on get to be too much.

Cressey is careful to point out that these motives are not dreamed up to account for long past behavior. Instead, trusted persons acquire the motives in advance from the culture and apply them to their own specific situations. They are reasons for violating trust that are available to all respectable individuals.

> [Verbalized motives] are not something invented by embezzlers (or anyone else) on the spur of the moment. Before they can be taken over by an individual, these verbalizations exist as group definitions in which the behavior in question, even crime, is in a sense *appropriate*. There are any number of popular ideologies that sanction crime in our culture: "Honesty is the best policy, but business is business"; "It is all right to steal a loaf of

bread when you are starving"; "All people steal when they get in a tight spot." Once these verbalizations have been assimilated and internalized by individuals, they take a form such as: "I'm only going to use the money temporarily, so I am borrowing, not stealing," or "I have tried to live an honest life, but I've had nothing but troubles, so to hell with it." [37]

ORGANIZATIONS AS VICTIMS

So far in this chapter we have concentrated upon two forms of deviance in which persons within organizations victimize those organizations by violating a trust. This deviance represents a borderline between the crimes in the streets of earlier chapters and the deviance by organizations in the next chapter. With a few exceptions pilfering and embezzling are actions by little, though "respectable," people. Their respectability generally shields them from both detection and the embarrassment of being regarded as common criminals if detected.

The people's littleness is also reflected in the magnitude of their offenses. Again, with a few exceptions, the acts of individual pilferers and embezzlers amount to very little—Zeitlin thinks perhaps $1.50 per day is a reasonable figure for pilferers. Collectively, however, the impact of the little people is considerable—not because they individually steal so much but because so many steal.

There is an undercurrent of public indifference, if not actual resentment, toward organizations and their property. The public is thus more accepting of theft from organizations, and verbalized motives justifying such theft are prevalent. It is felt that organizations, for various reasons, can afford and deserve losses. The commonly accepted ethics applying to relations between individuals simply are not extended to corporations and governments.

The lack of employee responsibility toward organizations is perhaps understandable in light of at least two factors. First, the impersonality of large organizations in particular makes it difficult for employees to form strong allegiances to the company. Employees' work days are spent with co-workers; the company provides only the context in which work occurs. True, the company pays one's salary. But that can stop any time. The company exists to make a profit. When you cease to be profitable, the company will do whatever it can to dismiss you. Your co-workers may miss you and regret your leaving— the company will do neither. If you have allegiances to anyone it will be to your work group, not the organization, because the company has no allegiance to you.[38] Second, relationships between individuals and organizations have traditionally been based upon conflict. As we mentioned in an earlier chapter, the American labor movement was especially bloody. Attempts to unionize workers and to obtain shorter hours, higher pay, and better working conditions frequently met with violent resistance from companies. Thus there remains the legacy of an antagonistic relationship between unions and companies. On the one hand the union attempts to protect the workers' interests against the whims of the company; on the other hand the company attempts to extract from the workers as much as possible for as little as possible.

This is, of course, an oversimplified version of a very complex situation. Nevertheless the conflict between workers and employers is re-enacted continuously in strikes. More frequently the strikes are primarily symbolic affairs where the sides suspend contact with one another while brief negotiations take place between officials of both sides. In more extreme cases the strikes are prolonged—they become nasty as threats and incriminations fly. Property may be damaged, a few people shot at, and opposing factions vow to bring each other to their knees. Workers have ample precedent on which to view their employer as an enemy or at least someone (or thing) who provides a particular salary, pension plan, vacation plan, or whatever only because forced to. Consequently, there is little reason to treat the organization's property with much more than indifference.

The conflict between individuals and organizations extends beyond union-management quarrels. A long-standing principle of American business is caveat emptor. Literally translated "Let the buyer beware," this means that sellers of products or services have no responsibility for quality, unless something is specifcally guaranteed by a warranty. In short, what you buy is what you get. The fine print of contracts and insurance policies with their restrictions, plus many cases of outright fraud against customers have led to misunderstanding, resentment, and cynicism toward business by the American public. Although offenses *by* organizations will be discussed in detail in the next chapter, suffice it to say here that persons, as citizens and employees, know that companies are guilty of their own particular brand of immorality. The ethical standards expected of employees are often not met by employers. Thus the property of corporations is less than sanctified and its theft more easily justified.

Police Corruption

I like policemen. It gives me a very secure feeling,
knowing that it's that blue uniform that is all that
stands between me and him robbing and killing me.
Woody Allen

There was a time, when life seemed far simpler, that the policeman radiated an image akin to sainthood. Calendars given away by lumber stores in small towns carried pictures of a ruddy-cheeked officer stopping traffic to allow a duck and her brood to cross the road—at an appropriate crosswalk, of course. Nothing illegal about this officer. Times have changed. In the sixties the image for many Americans was the bullnecked policeman clubbing a bloody, helpless figure—a white student or any black, take your pick. The seventies have brought still another image. For Americans in several major cities the appropriate calendar picture would be of two officers stealing television sets through a store's rear door, while out front a policeman stands lookout as he casually takes a bribe from a heroin pusher.

None of these images are entirely accurate or fair for most police officers, but unquestionably the image of the police as a bulwark against crime has been severely shaken. The thin blue line is definitely crooked in many places.

Before beginning our discussion of police corruption, some limits must be imposed on the subject. Policemen's oath of office includes a promise to "enforce and uphold" all laws within their jurisdiction, whether state, county, or municipal. Because of their position as law enforcers, police are involved with many laws of which the average citizen has little knowledge or concern. Police must know not only what behaviors or conditions are illegal, but also how to legally deal with offenders. Consequently, they may violate their office and public trust in many ways: they may ignore flagrant violations, they may act illegally when making arrests or controlling individuals, and, of course, they may themselves break laws, just as any other citizen.

The following discussion will not consider acts of brutality by police or illegal means used to apprehend offenders or to obtain evidence. Our omission of these topics is not meant to minimize their importance. But, however distasteful these behaviors may be, they are at least consistent with the general goals of police work—to control criminal activity.[39] Our concern is with *acts contrary to public expectations involving deliberate support of or involvement in illegal activity, and the deliberate neglect of duty.* In short, we will consider those violations of public trust concerning what a policeman or policewoman is doing while on duty.

MEAT- AND GRASS-EATERS

The contemporary wave of police corruption scandals began in 1970 on both coasts. In Seattle it was discovered that policemen were receiving at least $144,000 a year from a vice ring; in New York City the *New York Times* printed a story charging police with receiving systematic payoffs from gamblers, narcotics peddlers, and other law violators, and reporting that officials in both the police and city administrations had been informed of the corruption but failed to take action. There followed a procession of similar scandals in Chicago,

Atlantic City, Albany, Philadelphia, and Indianapolis. The major cities were not unique. During the same period much smaller cities such as Bowling Green, Ohio and Newburgh, New York dismissed sizeable proportions of their police forces because of various forms of corruption.

The type of offenses involved in these scandals ranged from the mildly amusing to the grotesque:

> In Albany, police broke into parked cars if they saw something inside they wanted. On occasion they jacked cars up and stole the tires.
>
> Also in Albany, Trixie's house of prostitution paid police $600 a week to remain open. On Fridays, payoff day, the traffic of detectives and uniformed officers coming in to get their protection money was so heavy that the brothel was closed to customers from 5:30 to 9:00 p.m.
>
> Still in Albany, officers collecting money from parking meters "nickel-and-dimed" the city out of over $36,000 a year.
>
> In Atlantic City a hotel operator paid $10,000 annually to more than 60 city policemen to assure that his hotels would not be closed for violations of health and fire regulations. One patrolman asked that he be notified immediately of any death in the hotels so he could get whatever money was in the dead person's pockets.[40]

The scandal receiving the greatest national attention was New York City's. Events leading up to the scandal began in 1966 and 1967 when two officers, David Druk and Frank Serpico (whose activities were described in a best selling book and a movie), took information of serious police corruption to a number of highly placed officials.[41] The resulting action was minimal. In 1970, after the New York Times published the charges, Mayor John V. Lindsay authorized a Commission to Investigate Allegations of Police Corruption and the City's Anti-Corruption Procedures with Judge Whitman Knapp as chairman. This commission came to be known as the Knapp Commission.

The commission found that corruption was widespread in the New York City police force and that it was not confined to the lower ranks but reached up to the hierarchy.[42] Like all forms of thievery discussed in previous chapters, police corruption can be roughly divided into amateur and professional categories, depending upon the degree of commitment. Corrupt police are informally described as being either grass-eaters or meat-eaters.[43] The great majority are grass-eaters who simply accept whatever payoff police work happens to throw their way. They take under-the-table payments and gifts, but do not aggressively pursue them. Meat-eaters, on the other hand, spend many of their working hours seeking out situations that they can exploit for large financial gain. A single payoff may range from $5,000 to $50,000.

A model meat-eater testified before the Knapp Commission.

William Phillips—owner of five private airplanes on a $12,000 annual patrolman's salary—described himself as a "super thief." [44] Money came to Phillips from all kinds of sources: gamblers, pimps, loan sharks, illegal liquor dealers, bowling alleys, garages, and so on. An unusual source was an undertaker who paid 10 per cent of the price of a funeral for any new body that Phillips informed the undertaker about. After a phone call from Phillips the undertaker would rush to the relatives of the recently deceased to say, "I understand there's been a tragedy in the family. . . ."

Perhaps one of the best indications of Phillips' professionalism was his ability to find out, merely by a phone call, whether any specific officer on the force could safely be approached with a corrupt proposal. That he could do this also indicates the extent to which corruption had permeated the police department—Phillips had innumerable friends scattered throughout the department who were corrupt and who knew whoever else was corrupt. After his testimony, Phillips ran out of friends in a hurry. In 1974 he was convicted of the 1968 murders of a pimp and a prostitute. Phillips' lawyer claimed it was a frame-up by angry police and the prosecutor's office. [45]

The Knapp Commission found that the principal opportunities for police corruption came from the following sources:

1. Gambling. In order to avoid police intervention with their operations, gamblers pay a form of insurance:

> The heart of the gambling payoff system was found to be the plainclothes "pad." In a highly systemized pattern . . . plainclothesmen collected regular bi-weekly or monthly payoffs from gamblers. . . . The pad money was picked up at designated locations by one or more bagmen who were most often police officers but who occasionally were ex-policemen or civilians. The proceeds were then pooled and divided up among all or virtually all of the divisions's plainclothesmen. . . . Division plainclothesmen generally met once a month to divide up the money and to discuss matters concerning the pad—i.e., inviting plainclothesmen newly assigned to the division to join, raising or lowering the amounts paid by various gamblers, and so forth. [46]

The average monthly share per man in these operations ranged from $400 to $1,500, depending upon the area of the city.

2. Narcotics. Patterns of corruption involving drugs were many. Below are listed just a few in addition to the usual bribe-taking:

(a) Keeping money and/or narcotics confiscated at the time of an arrest or raid.
(b) Selling narcotics to addict-informants in exchange for stolen goods.

(c) Passing on confiscated drugs to police informants for sale to addicts.

(d) Flaking, or planting narcotics on an arrested person in order to have evidence for a law violation.

(e) Padding, or adding to the quality of narcotics found on an arrested person in order to upgrade an arrest.

(f) Introducing potential customers to narcotics pushers.

(g) Revealing the identity of a government informant to narcotics criminals.

(h) Providing armed protection for narcotics dealers.

(i) Offering to obtain hit men to kill potential witnesses.

3. *Prostitution.* It is an unwritten rule among police that taking money from prostitutes is a risky business because prostitutes are considered unreliable and likely to become informants. Nevertheless, brothels, prostitution bars, and streetwalkers often had to make payoffs to New York police.

4. *Construction.* Ordinances in connection with construction work are described by the commission as a "dizzying array." To put up a building in New York requires a minimum of forty different permits and licenses. In addition there are obvious problems with noise, dust, double-parking, obstruction of sidewalks, and so on that are also covered by ordinances. The inspection of certain permits and the enforcement of construction ordinances are the responsibility of the police. Thus construction work provides another opportunity for police corruption—it is easier for contractors to make payoffs than to comply with all the ordinances. Such practices as paying fifty to one hundred dollars per week for double-parking concrete trucks are costly. According to testimony received by the commission the price of city building may be increased as much as 5 per cent because of bribes paid police.[47]

5. *Bars.* The commission estimated that payoffs from construction and from liquor bars were the most common source of illegal outside income for uniformed police. Bars are especially likely targets if they cater to prostitutes, drug users, gamblers, or homosexuals soliciting partners. Also vulnerable are places operating at hours forbidden by law or operating without a license. But even bars that seemingly would have no worries from police in fact did. For example, police would threaten to flush soap down the toilet and then write the bar a summons for having no soap in the men's room.

The Knapp Commission found other ways police make money, but the above list suffices to show the wide range of forms that corruption may take.[48] But policemen may violate the public trust in subtler ways. A typical grass-eater tactic would be to withhold recovered property that had been stolen or lost. The New York City department, understandably concerned over the honesty of its officers, conducted an interesting experiment in 1973.[49] Fifty-one patrolmen were handed "lost" wallets containing twenty dollars or more by strangers who asked the police to turn the wallets in. Fifteen or 30 per cent of the patrolmen kept the money without making a report. What this test of the department's integrity proves is impossible to say. It would seem safe to conclude, however, that the blue uniform so trusted by Woody Allen does not confer anything approaching sainthood.

ROTTEN APPLES OR ROTTEN BARRELS?

Traditional explanations of police corruption begin with the assumption that the great majority of police are good cops, and the police system is generally flawless. It follows then that not only are bad cops in a small minority, but also that their very presence is inconsistent with anything in the system itself. The usual metaphor employed is apples. Briefly, the logic is that the barrel and most of the apples are sound; all that is needed is a means of screening out rotten apples, either before they get into the barrel or before they contaminate the good apples.[50]

Add to the barrel of apples a dash of public apathy and hostility. Police receive little support from the public they serve—police are poorly paid, they work long hours, the public is indifferent to the standards required for police, and the public shows police little respect. The recipe for corruption is now complete. The remedy for excessive apple rot is likewise clear: better screening of police applicants, higher standards for recruits, better pay, and more effective police-public relations.

It is impossible to argue with any of these claims about the characteristics of the policeman's job and the public's reaction toward police. It would be unrealistic to argue that the above-mentioned proposals would not improve police. But as an explanation of police corruption the rotten apple theory fails to confront a crucial reality: namely, that while some corruption may be attributed to individuals and to inadequate recruiting, it is also true that *tendencies toward corruption are built into the law enforcement system.* The Knapp Commission was especially concerned about laying to rest the rotten apple theory when it pointed out that corruption was not only widespread and included upper-level officers, but also had been ignored by administrators and good police for years. The corrupt policemen is not isolated; rather he is "only one part of an apparatus of corruption." [51] Thus the barrel itself must be suspect.

Three factors contribute to corruption within the law enforcement system:

1. Public Encouragement of Corruption. The Knapp Commission found that the offering of gratuities to police by businesses was widely accepted by both the police and the community as part of the police job.[52] The gratuities were in the form of free meals, free hotel rooms, free drinks, Christmas payments, free merchandise, and miscellaneous tips for services rendered.

> The fact is that the public by and large does not regard gratuities as a serious matter. While some may be offended by the occasionally arrogant way in which some police officers demand what they consider to be their due, most people are willing to allow a police officer who spends long hours providing protection for an area to stop in for a quick free meal or cup of coffee at an eating establishment which enjoys the benefit of his protection.[53]

Of course, the public does not approve of police robbing or blackmailing citizens, but its approval of gratuities does, in its own way, encourage graft, however petty and grass-eating it may be. The free cup of coffee, the bottle of whiskey at Christmas, and the discount on purchased goods—the public offers these only with the best of intentions. In some cases gifts are offered out of respect and appreciation for the job policemen do. But in most cases they are small incentives and thanks for paying a little more attention at night to places of business. In still other cases, they are in gratitude for overlooking minor infractions such as overparking or double parking by customers. Then there are those citizens who, when stopped for speeding, will hand over driving licenses with a ten dollar bill inducement not to write a summons.

In a three-city survey (Boston, Chicago, and Washington, D.C.) conducted in 1966 by Albert J. Reiss, Jr., one third of all businesses in high-crime areas openly admitted giving favors to police in the form of free merchandise or services; at the very least they gave discounts.[54] Observers riding in squad cars found that one third of all officers on duty did not pay for their meals.

> Many officers reported large discounts on purchases of durable goods. On most occasions, free goods or discounts are not solicited, largely because officers know well which businesses offer them and which do not. The informal police networks carry such information, obviating in most cases open solicitation. Presentation of self in uniform is all that is necessary to secure many benefits. These transactions are viewed as "favors" by the line and tacitly approved by their superiors.[55]

Buying favors—that is what most police corruption is about. While a distinction can be made between taking favors for legitimate reasons as opposed to the illegitimate ones connected with narcotics and prostitution, the difference is fundamentally a matter of degree. The end result is that all parties—the good citizens, the organized gangsters, and the police—know the police can be bought. Only two questions remain. For what purpose can they be bought? And how much will it cost?

2. Police Solidarity. Out of all the police scandals one fact seems inescapable: of the many honest police who were apparently aware of the widespread corruption in their departments, extremely few were willing to do anything about it. Although heavy, meat-eating corruption may meet resistance among officers, the milder grass-eating variety can go on for years, not because it is carried on with great stealth, but because even those who are uninvolved choose to look the other way.

This apparent indifference of police toward corruption in their ranks is not simply a result of misplaced loyalty. Instead it is indicative of the solidarity of police that emerges as a necessary element of the job.[56] Few occupations are so close-knit as police work. In large part this is a result of the policemen's isolation from the rest of society. Although the public may appreciate whatever protection police offer, there is also an underlying resentment of their authority. The police are obliged to regulate other people's lives—they ticket speeders, pick up drunks, investigate suspicious behavior, and impose themselves in many ways. Because of their authority police are not readily accepted into the social world of others, particularly of blacks. To combat this rejection police rely upon whatever support they find within their own occupational group. At the same time police view the rest of society as not only unsympathetic but also uncomprehending about the nature of police work.

In addition to authority, there is another element of law enforcement that contributes to police solidarity. Although the typical police day is filled with routine and a certain amount of boredom, the threat of danger is always there. The ordinary citizen is unlikely to help a policeman in trouble—the citizen simply feels unresponsible for becoming involved. Thus when it comes down to the dirty work of anticipating fighting or shooting, the policeman relies only on his buddies.

> The ordinary citizen does not assume the responsibility to implicate himself in the policeman's required response to danger. The element of danger in the policeman's role alienates him not only from populations with a potential for crime but also from the conventionally respectable (white) citizenry, in short, from the segment of the population from which friends would ordinarily be drawn.[57]

It is not inaccurate to describe police as consisting of tight, informal groups who see themselves as alone against an uninformed and indifferent, if not hostile, world. Any illegal practices emerging within police groups can develop into secret standards for those groups. These standards are perpetuated by passing them on to recruits coming into the ranks. If any recruit resists participating, his acceptance by the group is withheld. He then finds himself isolated from his colleagues, and he may face risks by himself—all because he lacks group "loyalty." To remain completely honest in such situations is difficult enough. As a compromise to creating a storm within the ranks, the honest policeman may simply overlook corruption in order to protect the cohesiveness of the department and to avoid interference from outsiders who do not understand police work.

3. *Laws That Encourage Corruption.* The reader will recall from our discussion of the Knapp Commission that the principal opportunities for police corruption came from gambling, narcotics, prostitution, construction, and bars. The laws concerning these activities have one thing in common—they are difficult to enforce since *there are no victims who will complain.* Participants in gambling, narcotics dealing, and in prostitution generally are voluntary, whether sellers or buyers. Construction contractors are merely trying to cut through a maze of red tape in order to build more efficiently and profitably. Bar owners who violate the law are convenient for their customers—as soon as the public quits drinking late (early?) and stops using bars for various illegal purposes, bars can close at a legal hour and cater to a better clientele.

Whether gambling, prostitution, and after-hours drinking cause harm or not is essentially irrelevant insofar as the police are concerned. Laws prohibit the behavior, and police are responsible for enforcing these laws.[58] But the nature of the acts outlawed encourages police corruption. The combination of large demand—which means large money—and the lack of persons to complain means that large bribes are available and that the continuation of illegal activities, which are supposed to be suppressed, will attract little attention.

The Knapp Commission felt that the dangers of corruption from these laws often outweighed the dangers from the behaviors themselves.[59] They recommended that criminal laws against gambling be repealed and that other means be undertaken for handling prostitution and narcotics. Regarding other opportunities for corruption, the commission categorically stated:

> As a simple matter of efficiency there is no justification for using the police—with all their powers and prerogatives—in the enforcement of many miscellaneous regulations. It is ridiculous to have an armed officer wasting

his time (and that of his partner and supervising sergeant) checking restaurant washrooms to find out whether they are properly supplied with soap. We believe that the police should be taken out of bars and restaurants and away from building sites and returned to their principal job of protecting lives and property.[60]

Police corruption involves more than the rotten apple theory suggests. There are aspects of the entire law enforcement barrel that lead us to wonder less why some police become corrupt and more about why so many resist the corrupting influences surrounding them.

Political Corruption

Aside from some examples of embezzlement, so far we have limited our discussion of breaches of trust and of office to individuals employed in the lower and middle levels of business and government. But the highest ranking officials are scarcely free of temptation or fault when it comes to misusing their positions. The political arena is especially fertile for corruption because powerholders are capable of bestowing extraordinary favors and are, of course, desirous of retaining that capability. Thus corruption in government emerges in two different forms: that for *personal economic gain* and that oriented toward the *perpetuation of power*. Unquestionably, the two are often interrelated, but the distinction is necessary as we shall see.

The most noted historical precedent for political corruption in America was Tammany Hall. Tammany, almost a synonym for corruption, is a popular term for the New York County (Manhattan Island) Democratic committee. Formed as a society of American patriots in 1789, it had become an efficient and corrupt political organization by 1830.[61] Throughout its history Tammany underwent innumerable scandals, but the biggest involved William "Boss" Tweed (1823–1878).

Tweed and his cronies on the Board of Supervisors systematically sacked New York City's finances in many ways. For example, Tweed bought 300 church benches for $5 apiece and resold them to the city for $600 each; and as part owner of a printing company he sold supplies to the city—six reams of paper, two dozen penholders, four ink bottles, a dozen sponges, and three dozen boxes of rubber bands for $10,000.[62] But his most spectacular means of making money was through the construction of the County Court House. It cost the city at least $13 million in the 1860s—about four times the cost of the British Houses of Parliament. According to the financial records the costs of the court house included such items as: $40,000 for a yearly supply of brooms (at a time when brooms cost a dime), and over $7.25 million for furnishings estimated to be worth $625,000.

How much did Tweed corruption cost New York City? The best estimate appears to be that from 1865 to 1871 the total stealing amounted to $200 million.[63] Despite Tweed's downfall and the disrepute of Tammany Hall, a large proportion of Democratic voters in New York was willing to follow Tammany's lead. In a matter of years Tammany Hall was as powerful a political force as ever. Approximately every two decades between 1870 and 1940 Tammany politicians created some scandal involving rackets, graft, or police payoffs. All that distinguished most of its leaders from Tweed himself was the magnitude of their corruption; evidently none were capable of stealing as much as he.

Obviously, systematic data on contemporary corruption in public office are not available. The extent is impossible to gauge since we can only rely on periodic scandals and exposés that may never reveal the full stories. We do know that since 1969 there has been a series of revelations about corruption in the government. First, there have been those involving *personal economic gain*.

Both Maryland and New Jersey have especially been hit by scandals revealing corruption that can only be described as systematic. In Maryland there has been a long-time practice of politicians receiving kickbacks from engineers and architects doing state business. One figure of national prominence was Spiro T. Agnew who was accused of accepting such payments while he was the Baltimore county executive, the governor of Maryland, and the vice president of the United States. As a result of these charges Agnew resigned as vice president and pleaded no contest to an income tax charge.

The New Jersey scandal involved eight mayors, two secretaries of state, three judges, a state treasurer, a chief of police, a former speaker of the state assembly, and several individuals of lesser office, including a city council president and a Democratic county chairman.[64] The charges included tax evasion, extortion, and bribery.

Shifting from the local and state level to the national level, we find that in the past few years many persons in positions of public trust have lost their offices because of dishonesty. For instance:

> An associate justice of the Supreme Court of the United States resigns after disclosures of improper relationship for personal gain with a convicted stock swindler.
>
> The administrative assistant to the speaker of the House of Representatives is convicted for committing perjury before a grand jury on behalf of a notorious influence peddler.
>
> The administrative assistant to a senator is convicted in connection with a bribe attempt to fix a Securities and Exchange Commission investigation.
>
> A judge of the United States Court of Appeals and former governor of Illinois is convicted in connection with financial gains from favored treatment given to a racetrack owner.[65]

As we mentioned earlier, skulduggery on the American political scene is not restricted to goals of personal economic gain. In their attempts to retain power politicians and their subordinates have often bent the democratic electoral process. In its simplest, most traditional form this type of political corruption was embodied in ballot switching. In one long past New York election, an official dropped marked ballots on the floor when they were handed to him; he then inserted previously marked ballots into the box he kept beside him. If voters protested too vehemently, they were arrested.[66] More often balloting is manipulated by the padding of voter registration lists with phony voters: persons in prisons and cemeteries, dogs, and children. People are then hired to vote early and often.

In the nineteenth century

> gangs of barroom gladiators [were] hired to intimidate and terrorize the legitimate voter. Thus a respectable citizen who seemed likely to vote the "wrong" ticket might find himself slugged and thrown into the street, where, as one observer reported, "He would meditate on the beauties of our free institutions for a few moments, and depart, a sadder if not wiser man." [67]

It is hoped that blatant ballot switching and intimidation of voters are things of the past, but this decade has seen the greatest national political scandal, Watergate. The scandal first broke in June 1972 with the discovery of illegal electronic eavesdropping and a break-in of the Democratic National Committee headquarters in the Watergate Hotel in Washington, D.C. Those arrested in the break-in offense were discovered to be associated with a fund-raising organization for President Nixon, the Committee for the Re-election of the President. During the next two years the scandal grew as evidence emerged concerning illegal actions by presidential aides and Cabinet officers.

Eventually, the investigations revealed that high-level individuals in the administration had obstructed justice by such means as paying hush money to the Watergate burglars, wiretapped many telephones on the slimmest of national security pretexts, pressured the Internal Revenue Service to harass political "enemies" with income tax audits, instigated other burglaries to obtain evidence against American radicals, and used "dirty tricks" to disrupt and discredit Democratic candidates. One trick involved sending letters on a candidate's stationery to voters at primary election time. The letters alleged that the opposing Democratic candidates were guilty of an assortment of misbehaviors—having an illegitimate child, being arrested for homosexual offenses, being arrested for drunken driving, and consorting with call girls.

Still other charges emerged out of the Watergate affair: presidential misuse of public funds, the president's support of a lobby's interest in exchange for a $2 million campaign contribution, and fraudulent preparation of the president's income tax returns. It was also found that the president had at least tacitly approved of the cover-up of the Watergate case. In an unprecedented move, President Richard M. Nixon resigned from office as the evidence against him and his confidants mounted in 1974. The new president, Gerald Ford, pardoned ex-President Nixon. Thus the precise nature of his offenses may never be known.

Perhaps even the other dimensions of the Nixon administration corruption will never be fully revealed, but the breadth of corruption is at least signified by the kinds of persons who either admitted illegal activity or were convicted of such activity: the acting director of the F.B.I., secretary of the treasury, two attorney generals, commerce secretary, White House chief of staff, chief domestic advisor to the president, plus numerous special counsels and aides to the president. Never in the history of the United States have so many of the most politically powerful been implicated in such a wide web of abuse of power to keep power.

Conclusion

Deviance by highly respected, highly educated, and highly paid individuals is a very real fact of American life. Add to the political corruption the vast numbers of "good" citizens who habitually steal from their employers, and the substantial proportions of our police forces who exploit their positions for personal gain. Against this background we must alter our conventional viewpoints regarding such problems as crime in the streets. An awareness of deviance by the respectable, particularly the respectable involved in an interest group conflict such as politics, alerts us to be cautious about explanations based on either individual characteristics or upon disadvantaged backgrounds. Nicholas von Hoffman, a syndicated columnist, puts the problem into a humorous but valid perspective:

> [Those involved in Watergate] are not to blame. Society is the real culprit. . . .
>
> From youngest boyhood these men were doomed, turned into CPAs or locked up in law schools where tender young minds learn the most vicious habits.
>
> Without any therapy or counseling they were released into the community at large—without parole supervision or halfway houses.
>
> Who can blame them if they associated with board members, corporate officers, and presidential candidates?
>
> What they needed was guidance and an older man to be a fatherly pal, but what they got was admission to the country club and high-paying jobs.

What else can society expect from boys who've never been given a chance to hang out on street corners? . . .

So the next time you hear somebody say [the attorney general] should go to jail, say, "No. Give him a chance. Give him a social worker, let him live in a slum and eat off food stamps." [68]

NOTES

1. Edwin H. Sutherland, "White-Collar Criminality," *American Sociological Review,* 5 (February 1940), pp. 1–12.

2. Edwin H. Sutherland, *White Collar Crime* (New York: Holt, Rinehart and Winston, 1949), p. 240.

3. Ibid., pp. 247–249.

4. Ibid., p. 9.

5. The controversy over the proper definition of white-collar crime is best exhibited in a series of articles found in Gilbert Geis, *White-Collar Criminal: The Offenders in Business and the Professions* (New York: Atherton Press, 1968), pp. 347–431.

6. Earl R. Quinney, "The Study of White Collar Crime: Toward a Reorientation in Theory and Research," *Journal of Criminal Law, Criminology and Police Science,* 22 (June 1964), pp. 209–210.

7. For an introductory statement concerning the study of deviance in the organizational context see Albert J. Reiss, Jr., "The Study of Deviant Behavior: Where the Action Is," *Ohio Valley Sociologist,* 32 (Autumn 1966), pp. 1–12.

8. Herbert Edelhertz, *The Nature, Impact and Prosecution of White-Collar Crime* (Washington, D.C.: U.S. Department of Justice, Law Enforcement Assistance Administration, May 1970), pp. 73–75. Edelhertz has a fourth major category not given here: crimes by persons operating on an individual, ad hoc basis. This includes credit card frauds, bankruptcy frauds, individual income tax violations, and others.

9. *Crime in the United States, 1973* (Washington, D.C.: Government Printing Office, 1974), pp. 15–24.

10. "To Catch a Thief," *Newsweek,* September 23, 1974, p. 79.

11. Ibid.; Monty Hoyt, "The Artful Dodgers," *Toledo Blade Sunday Magazine,* June 24, 1973, p. 4; and Isadore Barmash, "Pilferage Abounds in the Nation's Stores," *New York Times,* October 28, 1973, Section 3, p. 9.

12. Barmash, "Pilferage Abounds," p. 9.

13. Allan J. Mayer, "Builders Seek to End the Ancient Tradition of On-the-Job Stealing," *Wall Street Journal,* June 19, 1972, p. 1.

14. Mark Lipman, *Stealing: How America's Employees Are Stealing Their Companies Blind* (New York: Harper's Magazine Press, 1973), p. 160.

15. Isadore Barmash, "In Retailing, 'Shrinkage' is Outdistancing Profits," *New York Times,* April 12, 1970, Section 3, p. 5.

16. Lipman, *Stealing,* pp. 48–49.

17. Derived from Hoyt, "Artful Dodgers," pp. 4–7; and "The Case of the Missing Bucks," *Investor's Reader,* 56 (January 6, 1971), pp. 24–25.

18. Mayer, "Builders Seek to End the Ancient Tradition," p. 13.

19. Ibid.

20. Donald N. M. Horning, "Blue-Collar Theft: Conceptions of Property, Attitudes Toward Pilfering, and Work Group Norms in a Modern Industrial Plant," in *Crimes Against Bureaucracy,* eds. Erwin O. Smigel and H. Laurence Ross (New York: Van Nostrand Reinhold, 1970), pp. 46–64. For a descriptive study of apprehended pilferers see Gerald D. Robin, "Employees As Offenders," *Journal of Research in Crime and Delinquency,* **6** (January 1969), pp. 17–33.

21. Horning, "Blue-Collar Theft," p. 50.

22. Ibid., p. 55.

23. Elliot Liebow, *Tally's Corner: A Study of Negro Streetcorner Men* (Boston: Little, Brown, 1967), pp. 37–38.

24. Ibid., pp. 38–40.

25. Lawrence R. Zeitlin, "A Little Larceny Can Do a Lot for Employee Morale," *Psychology Today,* **5** (June 1971), pp. 22–26, 64.

26. Ibid., p. 26.

27. This discussion is derived from Melville Dalton, *Men Who Manage: Fusions of Feeling and Theory in Administration* (New York: John Wiley & Sons, 1959), pp. 194–217.

28. Ibid., pp. 202–203.

29. John Lofland, *Deviance and Identity* (Englewood Cliffs, New Jersey: Prentice-Hall, 1969), p. 110.

30. Gerald Kloss, "Exposing the Hodge Scandal," *Milwaukee Journal,* January 31, 1963, p. 36.

31. " 'Good Time Charlie' Spends $380,000 Beyond Income," *Toledo Blade,* March 7, 1971, p. 1.

32. Jerome Hall, *Theft, Law and Society,* 2nd ed. (Indianapolis: Bobbs-Merrill, 1952), pp. 304–312.

33. Donald R. Cressey, *Other People's Money: A Study in the Social Psychology of Embezzlement* (Belmont, Calif.: Wadsworth Publishing, 1953), p. 30.

34. Ibid., p. 43.

35. Ibid., p. 83.

36. Ibid., pp. 114–138.

37. Donald R. Cressey, "The Respectable Criminal," *Transaction,* **3** (March–April 1965), p. 14. For a study applying Cressey's model to pilferers, see Gerald D. Robin, "The Nonshareable Problem Theory of Trust Violation," *Criminologica,* **7** (February 1970), pp. 48–57.

38. For a classical study of the influence of the group upon production levels, see Donald Roy, "Quota Restriction and Goldbricking in a Machine Shop," *American Journal of Sociology,* **57** (March 1952), pp. 427–442.

39. A different rationale for distinguishing between police brutality and corruption is found in Barbara Raffel Price, "Police Corruption: An Analysis," *Criminology,* **10** (August 1972), pp. 161–162.

40. The examples are from Ronald Sullivan, "25 Atlantic City Policemen Are Indicted," *New York Times,* August 31, 1973, p. 29; Ralph Blumenthal, "Officer in Albany Says Fellow Police Joined in Thievery," *New York*

Times, September 21, 1973, p. 54; Blumenthal, "Ex-Patrolman Testifies He Committed 16 Break-Ins With Other Albany Police," *New York Times,* September 20, 1973, p. 47; and Blumenthal, "A Policeman's Plot: The Wolves Patrol the Sheepfold," *New York Times,* September 30, 1973, Section 4, p. 8.

41. Peter Maas, *Serpico: The Story of an Honest Cop* (New York: Viking Press, 1973).

42. *The Knapp Commission Report on Police Corruption* (New York: George Braziller, 1973), pp. 1–3.

43. Ibid., pp. 65–66.

44. Ibid., pp. 51–56; and Michael Blaine, "Please Don't Eat the Slips," *Village Voice,* December 13, 1973, p. 103.

45. Alfred E. Clark, "Jury Convicts Phillips of 2 Brothel Murders in 1968," *New York Times,* November 22, 1974, p. 22.

46. *Knapp Commission,* p. 74.

47. "Police: Cops as Pushers," *Time,* November 8, 1971, p. 17.

48. For a more general typology analyzed on several dimensions, see Julian B. Roebuck and Thomas Barker, "A Typology of Police Corruption," *Social Problems,* **21** (1974), pp. 423–437.

49. Paul L. Montgomery, "15 Policemen Keep Money 'Lost' in Test," *New York Times,* November 17, 1973, p. 1.

50. This metaphor was especially favored by the New York City Police Department. See *Knapp Commission,* pp. 6–11.

51. Ibid., p. 7. For a theory of police corruption encompassing characteristics of police work, the community, police organization, and other variables see Lawrence W. Sherman, "Introduction: Toward a Sociological Theory of Police Corruption," in *Police Corruption: A Sociological Perspective,* ed. Lawrence W. Sherman (Garden City, N.Y.: Anchor Books, 1974), pp. 1–39.

52. *Knapp Commission,* pp. 170–182.

53. Ibid., p. 181.

54. Albert J. Reiss, Jr., *The Police and the Public* (New Haven, Conn.: Yale University Press, 1971), pp. 161–162.

55. Ibid., p. 162.

56. This discussion is based upon Jerome H. Skolnick, *Justice Without Trial: Law Enforcement in Democratic Society* (New York: John Wiley, 1966), pp. 49–62; and Ellwyn R. Stoddard, "The Informal 'Code' of Police Deviancy: A Group Approach to 'Blue-Coat Crime,' " *Journal of Criminal Law, Criminology and Police Science,* **59** (June 1968), pp. 202–204.

57. Skolnick, *Justice Without Trial,* p. 54.

58. For a discussion of various forms of victimless crimes, see Gilbert Geis, *Not the Law's Business? An Examination of Homosexuality, Abortion, Prostitution, Narcotics and Gambling in the United Sates* (Washington, D.C.: National Institute of Mental Health, 1972).

59. *Knapp Commission,* pp. 18–19, 89–90, 112–115, 122.

60. Ibid., p. 20.

61. This discussion is drawn from Gustavus Myers, *The History of Tammany Hall,* 2nd ed. (New York: Burt Franklin, 1917).

62. Gerald Kloss, "The Biggest Grafter of Them All," *Milwaukee Journal,* February 22, 1963, p. 42.

63. Myers, *History of Tammany Hall,* pp. 248–249.

64. "More Corruption in N.J.—and Elswehere," *Crime and Delinquency,* **19** (April 1973), pp. 282–283.

65. Examples are drawn from Whitney North Seymour, Jr., *Why Justice Fails* (New York: William Morrow, 1973), pp. 99–100.

66. Alexander B. Callow, Jr., "Fraud! Fraud!," *New York Times Magazine,* September 27, 1964, p. 66.

67. Ibid., pp. 62, 64.

68. Nicholas von Hoffman, "We Want Our Pandas," *BG News* (Bowling Green State University student newspaper), May 3, 1973, p. 2.

7

DEVIANCE BY ORGANIZATIONS —CRIME IN THE SUITES

The reader will recall from the previous chapter that Sutherland defined white-collar crime as violations of the law by persons of respectability and high social status in the course of their occupations. His specific examples concentrated on actions by corporations that illegally attempted to increase profits and gain competitive advantage. Of course, a corporation is not a person. Those acting as a corporation Sutherland referred to as businessmen.[1] The corporation itself is:

> An organization formed under a state statute for the purpose of carrying on an enterprise distinct and separate from the persons who are interested in it and who control it; ". . . an artificial being, invisible, intangible, and existing only in contemplation of law." *The Trustees of Dartmouth College* v. *Woodward* (1819) 17 U.S. 518, 636. . . .
>
> In a corporation—particularly a large corporation with many stockholders—those who have contributed to the capital of the business do not ordinarily conduct its affairs. Management is concentrated in the hands of a Board of Directors, elected by the stockholders, who may own only a small portion of the stock. Stockholders cannot bind the corporation by their acts merely because they are stockholders.[2]

The businessmen to whom Sutherland referred were not the owners or stockholders, but could be any number of individuals within a corporation who make and implement decisions concerning planning, manufacturing, distribution, pricing, and advertising. They can range from members of the board of directors to the heads of departments, and down to the great array of lesser-ranked managers *who act for and in the name of the corporation* when dealing with other employees, other companies, and the public. These individuals may cause the corporation to engage in such illegal behavior as: 1. undermining the effectiveness of collective bargaining efforts by unions, 2. conspiring with competitors to keep prices on a uniform level with theirs, or not to cut prices on certain products, 3. drastically cutting prices in only one product area for the purpose of eliminating competition, and 4. misrepresenting products in advertising or in sales practices.

Since Sutherland's introduction of the concept of white-collar crime, it has been recognized that patterns of deviance exist in many forms and at many levels within organizations and occupations. As a consequence there have been several attempts to delineate specifically the forms of such deviance and to distinguish them from other forms of deviance.[3] For our purposes we have simplified the matter by considering behavior in terms of its relationship to the organization in which it occurs. In the last chapter we provided examples of deviance in violation of trust within business and government—the individuals' behaviors were inconsistent with or detrimental to the goals of the organizations. In this chapter we review acts by organizations in which the individuals' behaviors are consistent with organizational goals. In the cases of industry and government, the discussion parallels Sutherland's concept of white-collar crime. The deviance is used to further the operations of organizations whose purposes are otherwise legitimate, but the pursuit of illegitimate practices is not central to the organization. In the cases of organized crime and business frauds, however, deviance is central to the very existence of the organizations.

Deviance By Industry

Now as through this world I ramble,
I see lots of funny men,
Some will rob you with a sixgun
And some with a fountain pen.

Woody Guthrie *

One of the nice things about being robbed "with a fountain pen" is that you rarely notice it. Should a mugger forcibly relieve you of thirty dollars in a dark street your indignation knows no bounds. But television manufacturers who have fixed their prices will pocket your thirty dollars "bonus" much more easily and with no complaint from you. Of course, the manufacturer needs the money less than the mugger, but the manufacturer's methods at least seem painless—you don't even know it happened.

The cost to the public of price-fixing and related practices by American industry is naturally impossible to estimate with any certainty. But Senator Philip A. Hart, Chairman of the Senate Judiciary Subcommittee on Antitrust and Monopoly, took some guesses in 1971.[4] He claimed that at least 30 per cent of the public's spending bought "no product value." This means that 174 to 231 billion dollars' worth of consumer annual spending purchased worthless products or services. Some of this figure stems from simple inefficiency in industry, but a substantial proportion can be attributed to deliberate practices. As examples, Hart claimed that about $9 billion a year is wasted on auto repairs that are either poorly done or not done at all; monopolistic price-fixing costs $45 billion; and another $14 billion is the result of deceptive grocery labeling.

It is time to get down to basics. Despite any claims to the contrary, the foremost goal of any business in a capitalist society is to make a profit. Without profit no business can long survive (unless it is lucky enough to be supported by government subsidy). The roads to profit are many. Ideally, the best way is to make a better product or service that the public needs and at a price consistent with the quality. But we depart from ideals when we recognize that some products are difficult to make better than those of one's competitors. One can build a better quality automobile like the Rolls-Royce, but what can one do to improve golf tees? Furthermore, not everyone can produce the better product. Managers must face up to the realization that their product is only equal to, or perhaps a good deal worse than, their competition's.

To further complicate matters, what the public needs is strictly a matter of interpretation. Beyond food, water, air, and shelter the public actually *needs* nothing. If it feels it needs television, should not a portable, black-and-white set do? Somehow, by independent discovery or persuasion, the public must discover it needs a "home entertainment center"—color television, tape deck, radio, and phonograph complete in a laminated cabinet with a Spanish provincial design. Persuasion, of course, is the job of advertising, which tries to convince the public of the need for a product and of the superiority of a particular brand.

Finally, there is the matter of price. An item's price must cover the cost of production plus some profit. But to the bargain-hunting public a lower price may be a stronger selling point than high quality. Obviously, maintaining a given quality while reducing price to undercut competition can be a risky business, particularly if production costs are uniform among competitors. Reduced prices must result in higher sales to make up for lost profits. Things can become sticky should competitors decide to fight by reducing their prices as well. Thus there is compelling reason to maintain a harmony on prices among competitors.

In the pursuit of profit companies most often transgress the law in these three areas: quality of product or service, advertising, and pricing. However, the range of ways in which business cheats the public, as well as its competitors and employees, is great. In many cases, the actions are not technically illegal although the ethics are clearly questionable. For example, in the dressmaking trade there is a practice known as *knocking-off a style*. Briefly, this means copying another manufacturer's design at a lower price.[5] This most frequently occurs among smaller manufacturers whose own designers have run out of inspiration. In order to meet deadlines for shows or production, managers shop in better dress stores for likely candidates that can be easily copied.

Knocking-off styles is relatively innocuous compared to most schemes that work to the consumer's disadvantage. An example of blatant fraud against the public is the case of Foolproof Protection, Inc., a company that sold burglar alarms door-to-door to lower income families in New York City.[6] Appealing to the fear of persons who are likely to be targets of burglary, salesmen pushed an alarm system that supposedly rang in both the apartment and the police station. This cost about $500 over three years; for an additional $770 another alarm was included that would automatically call the fire department in the event of fire. The material and installation probably cost the company a total of seventy-five dollars for the entire system. The system was of inferior quality and was in no way connected to either the police or fire department.

Although Foolproof Protection sounds like a fly-by-night door-to-door operation, it was more than that. It was the only active subsidiary of a holding company, Detective Systems, Inc., whose stock was traded over-the-counter; it had an agreement with a leading department store to sell the alarms under the store's name; and Detective Systems received loans of over a million dollars from five banks. One investigator pointed out:

> The Foolproof case illustrates [a] way in which major corporations help gyp the American public—not directly, not visibly, but from behind the scenes, by extending mutually profitable lifelines to companies whose business practices they do not wish to know very much about. . . .
>
> Any of [the institutions which aided Foolproof] could have done some simple investigation of the company before doing business with it. . . . A few hours' statistical analysis would have demonstrated that of all the

retailers in the city, Foolproof sued most often [to force customers to continue payments]. Telephone calls or visits to the company's customers, particularly those customers who had refused to pay, would have revealed that the salesmen were routinely lying. . . . No company made these checks before doing business with Foolproof; they were interested only in making money and then getting out fast when cracks appeared in the ceiling. Each time a major company made a deal with Detective or Foolproof, the prestige of the burglar alarm company increased, so that other large corporations felt "safe" in doing business with it.[7]

But major companies are guilty of far more than simply supporting small frauds. Many are directly involved in illegal behavior detrimental to other companies, their own employees, and the public.[8] The following examples are presented with two purposes in mind: first, to illustrate that the very largest corporations engage in deviant behavior; and second, to illustrate the wide range that such behavior takes.

PRICE-FIXING AND THE ELECTRICAL INDUSTRY

In the late 1800s the American economy was moving toward what Marx termed "monopolistic capitalism." Great trusts arose in which vast and diverse industries were concentrated in the hands of a few combinations such as John D. Rockefeller's Standard Oil. One result of these monopolies was the virtual elimination of competition based upon prices—prices were fixed by agreement of the companies under control of the same trust. But price-fixing was only part of the problem:

> Producers of raw materials were compelled to accept whatever the trust chose to pay, for there was no other buyer; labor was forced into line by the closing of troublesome plants, and by the circulation of blacklists that prevented agitators from obtaining employment; politicians were influenced by free railroad passes, by campaign contributions, and by outright bribes. Powerful lobbies became the "third house" of Congress.[9]

The public, particularly labor organizations, farmers, and small businesses, demanded something be done about a situation in which wealth and power were increasingly concentrated in the hands of a very few. The result was the Sherman Act of 1890, which made illegal the monopolizing of trade and any contract, combination, or conspiracy attempting to eliminate competition.[10] Although the Sherman Act and subsequent antitrust laws were instrumental in breaking up some monopolies—Standard Oil was broken into thirty-eight units in 1911—the concentration of power into the hands of a few corporations has recently accelerated. In 1941, 1,000 of the largest corporations held two thirds of all corporate assets; today, only 200 corporations do. Between 1948 and 1968 these 200 firms acquired over 3,900 companies with assets of over $50 billion.[11]

The American corporations' thirst for growth is probably best exemplified by International Telephone and Telegraph Corporation (ITT).[12] It climbed from a position of being the fifty-second largest American corporation in 1959 to ninth at present. It has over 300 subsidiaries and over another 700 subsidiaries of subsidiaries. The government focused attention on the company in 1969 when ITT attempted to acquire the Hartford Fire Insurance Company with the intention of drawing upon its cash reserves to support other operations. A suit was filed by an assistant attorney general in the Nixon administration on the grounds that the acquisition gave ITT too much power. Just how much power ITT already possessed became evident during the Watergate scandal. It was discovered that top ITT officials met repeatedly with top administration officials, including the vice president and the attorney general, seeking a way to sidetrack the government action. While these negotiations were going on the company pledged $400,000 to the Republican national convention. Nine days later, ITT was permitted to keep the Hartford company. Coincidence? Perhaps.

In addition to providing access to the highest officials in government, the monopoly situation makes it easier for competitors to engage in price-fixing. The most dramatic recent example began in the mid-1940s when various heavy electrical equipment manufacturers decided to fix prices among themselves. What has come to be known as the Electrical Conspiracy involved twenty-nine companies controlling 95 per cent of the industry.[13] Most prominent were General Electric and Westinghouse, but there were also companies such as Allen-Bradley, Allis-Chalmers, and McGraw-Edison involved.

The conspirators—all executives—met in the best tradition of gangsters scheming to knock off a series of large banks. They met in obscure places; they did not eat together while at the same hotel; their communications were sent in plain envelopes to home addresses; they used only public telephones; and they even devised a code for telephoning about aspects of their conspiracy. Essentially, their task was to fix prices on equipment and to agree upon what company should submit the lowest bid on contracts about to be let. By the time the ax fell on the operation in 1960, it is estimated that in the previous seven-year period alone the conspiracy had fixed prices and rigged bids on the sale of $7 billion worth of equipment. The loss to the public is estimated at $1.7 billion.

The genuinely outraged judge sentenced seven of the conspirators to thirty days in jail; twenty-one others were given suspended thirty-day sentences. Someone who broke into a parking meter might spend more time in jail, but you must recognize that locking up executives for antitrust violations was an unprecedented move. The lawyer for a General Electric vice president begged that his client not be put "behind bars with common criminals who have been convicted of embezzlement and other serious crimes." Still another attorney argued, "Why punish these men? It is a way of life—everybody's doing it." [14]

No top executives were implicated, and one General Electric attorney stressed that the case really involved only certain individuals, not the company—a kind of rotten apple theory transplanted from police corruption explanations. But the judge was not convinced.

> In a broader sense, [the companies] bear a grave responsibility for the present situation, for one would be most naive indeed to believe that these violations of the law, so long persisted in, affecting so large a segment of industry and, finally, involving so many millions upon millions of dollars, were facts unknown to those responsible for the conduct of the organization. [15]

The companies themselves were fined a total of $1.8 million. But never underestimate the power of American business. Top executives of the companies persuaded the Internal Revenue Service that all legal expenses, fines, and damages could be written off as "ordinary and necessary" expenses of doing business. Senator Philip A. Hart questioned whether a bank robber could likewise deduct his legal expenses. [16]

How widespread is price-fixing? This is impossible to answer accurately, of course, but a sizeable proportion of the business community at least believes it is common. A 1970 survey of the presidents of the thousand largest manufacturing corporations asked whether many engage in price-fixing. Of the top 500, 47 per cent stated that such was the case; of the next 500, 70 per cent felt the same. [17]

We mentioned earlier that the concentration of a few companies controlling the major proportion of an industry was a contributing factor to deviance; it facilitates getting together and eventually reaching agreements. [18] But the basic motivations of the participants remain unexplored. Gilbert Geis suggests that persons and the corporations they represent are drawn into trust activities simply because of the attractiveness of a secure market.

> The elimination of competition meant the avoidance of uncertainty, the formalization and predictability of outcome, the minimization of risks. It is, of course, this incentive which accounts for much of human activity, be it deviant or "normal." [19]

Geis also points out that for individual conspirators, three conditions appeared to be crucial to their participation:

1. *A perception of gains* stemming from the behavior, such as advancement within the corporation or as a means to more efficiently carry out duties.
2. *Verbalized motives* that allowed them to violate the law and still maintain an image of themselves as law-abiding and respectable persons. These motives assumed a theme that no one was injured: "I do not know that it is against public welfare because I am not certain that the consumer was actually injured by this operation," and "We did not fix prices . . . all we did was recover costs."
3. *Market conditions* in which competition was particularly strong, enforcement of antitrust statutes was weak, and company demand for profits was high.[20]

It would appear then that the concentration of industry provides a situation conducive to deviance by corporations who are beset by profitmaking pressures. But there is more to corporate deviance than that, as an examination of the automobile industry shows.

"WOULD YOU BUY A USED CAR FROM THIS MAN?"

Not too long ago this question was a humorous way of indicating that the person in question had the scruples of a used car dealer—in a word, none. But the entire auto industry, ranging from manufacturers to new car dealers to repairmen, has also been found wanting in both reputation and ethics. A survey conducted in the mid-1960s indicated that while 74 per cent of the public rated bankers as honest and trustworthy, only 3 per cent thought the same about new car dealers.[21] Some of the practices which have earned this reputation include:

1. *Forcing accessories.* New cars arrive with unordered accessories that the buyers must pay for to get the cars.
2. *Used car markups.* Since dealers make only around $200 on a new car, they try to compensate by large markups on used cars—they may make $400 on a $2000 used car, compared with $200 on a $4000 new car.
3. *Service gouging.* This simply refers to overcharging for service. For example, dealers may charge for more labor time than actually used, charge for repairs not made, and replace parts unnecessarily.
4. *High finance.* Dealers may finance cars themselves, borrowing money from a bank and lending it to a buyer at higher interest rates. Occasionally a dealer will recommend a poor credit risk to a loan shark and receive a commission in return.
5. *Parts pushing.* This involves overcharging for parts, or using rebuilt parts while charging for new ones. Sometimes mechanics will use a new part when the old one could be repaired more cheaply.[22]

Why do such practices arise? It is argued by William N. Leonard and Marvin Glenn Weber that they grow out of the excessive power that automobile manufacturers possess, both in a general sense and more specifically in their relationship to dealers.[23]

In 1921 there were eighty-eight automobile manufacturing firms in the United States. Today there are four, three of which account for 97 per cent of all domestic model sales. The keystone company is General Motors, which accounts for over half the sales. General Motors has withstood several attempts to break it up. There is slight likelihood it will be dissolved in the near future, or that any new strong competitors will emerge because of the tremendous costs involved. The auto industry is thus one of the securest of any, despite occasional annoyances such as imports and gas shortages. Prior to the 1974–75 slump in car sales, the industry earned higher profits than practically any other in America. It is estimated that the noncompetitive state of the industry costs consumers $1.6 billion annually.[24]

Leonard and Weber claim that the concentrated market power of auto manufacturers adversely affects other aspects of the industry. Specifically, they state that unethical or illegal behavior on the part of dealers stems directly from manufacturer pressures over which the dealers have no control. In short, Leonard and Weber argue that dealers are coerced into deviant behavior. The heart of the problem is the intense pressure put upon dealer franchises to be sales-oriented—bonuses and other rewards come only with increasing sales; service is simply a necessary evil.

In recent years manufacturers have stepped up the sales pressure by setting up factory stores, which sell at a discount in competition with other dealers. This compels dealers to shave prices. If they cannot make up the losses by increased sales an alternative is to make them up by giving less than fair value in service.

Dealers have had other problems in addition to the intense emphasis on sales exerted by manufacturers. These problems involve the warranties issued by manufacturers to increase sales. Warranties supposedly protect the motorist by guaranteeing that certain auto defects will be repaired at no cost should they be detected within a certain period of time, for example, within two years or before 24,000 miles. According to Leonard and Weber, warranties turned out to be sales gimmicks and the burden of honoring them fell upon the dealers.

> Manufacturers used the warranty to limit their liability under the law and further limited the effectiveness of the warranty by establishing cumbersome paperwork and procedures for dealers and by compensating the dealers in labor and parts below the levels charged for regular repairs. As a result, dealers tended to avoid warranty work, or provided poor service to new car owners. Dealers made motorists wait for service, often

failed to work on cars brought into the shop or told owners they could not fix them, sometimes "discovered" additional repairs which could be charged, and padded bills. The improper behavior of dealers . . . reflects the market power of manufacturers, who unilaterally drafted the warranties . . . but then undermined warranty service by creating conditions which induced dealers to operate unethically in providing repairs.[25]

KILLING COMPETITION

Not all deviance by businesses takes place within the context of apparent harmony found in the electrical and auto industries. Organizations cheat on each other as well as on their customers. This most commonly takes the form of stealing secrets, such as the knocking-off of dress styles, which we discussed earlier. Thefts of customer mailing lists, manufacturing techniques, and product ideas are means of competition that have deep historical roots in America. It is claimed that the Industrial Revolution here was given its impetus by the theft of an invention.[26] In 1769 Richard Arkwright developed a cotton thread spinning machine that helped put Britain into the forefront of textile technology. America's textile technology at the time was abysmal and the government offered large rewards for improvements. An apprentice of Arkwright, Samuel Slater, memorized the equipment and journeyed to the United States in 1790, where he built a copy of the invention and thus launched the country into the Industrial Revolution.

Few industries in the contemporary United States are quite as cutthroat as the computer industry. In 1973, for example, Telex Corporation was ordered to pay International Business Machines (IBM) $21.9 million for copying IBM manuals and for hiring IBM employees to obtain trade secrets from them. In general, however, the computer arena shows few evenly-matched battles—IBM is far and away the champion, and can be a ruthless one at that. At present it probably commands over 75 per cent of the computer business in the United States. Furthermore, it could undoubtedly destroy all competition if it dared.

One of the tricks IBM has used to kill, or at least maim, competition was played on Control Data Corporation (CDC). In 1965 CDC entered the market with the world's largest computer. This announcement sent CDC stock from 32 to 161 in a few months. But the stock was sent tumbling and potential customers backed off when IBM announced it was coming out with an improved version of the CDC equipment. After the damage had been done, the IBM machine never saw the light of day.

In 1971 and 1972, IBM engaged in a price campaign designed to convert competitors into dying companies. William Rodgers described the plan as a complex one, costing IBM $75 million, in which the company intentionally changed product designs in order to make competitors' inventories obsolete and in which it increased prices on noncompetitive products in order to recoup losses—all to bring wandering customers back to the fold.[27]

> The business that had ebbed away from IBM to small companies drifted back with the tide. With two to three billion dollars in cash reserves on hand, IBM adapted the old gasoline price war technique, in which the chain with the most money could sell at a low price until competing stations were wiped out, then restore or rearrange prices to a nicely profitable level and go on as a growth company.

> By the end of 1971, pretty much as projected, the Commercial Analysis Section, a kind of special intelligence and think tank unit of IBM's, cheerfully informed the management that independent companies were under control. Competing sales in two major lines of tape and disk equipment, for example, which had sustained Telex, Memorex, and a couple of others, had fallen off by 48 to 62 percent.[28]

Again, it is an instance in which the biggest strives to become even bigger without regard to legality or ethics.

YOU ARE WHAT YOU EAT

So far we have discussed only those acts of organizational deviance that affect the public's pocketbook—acts of robbery in which the weapon used is a fountain pen, in Woody Guthrie's words. Some acts by business are even less savory, however, since they directly jeopardize our health and our lives. The range of such activities is great. For example, there are instances of deliberately endangering safety as in the case of B. F. Goodrich and the brake assemblies for the A7D, an Air Force light attack fighter. When their brake models constantly failed during laboratory tests, engineers at Goodrich deliberately altered test procedures and falsified technical data to convince the Air Force and the airplane contractor that the brake met all required specifications. When the brake was eventually tested on the plane itself, several near crashes occurred during landings, including one in which a wheel locked and the plane skidded nearly 1,500 feet before stopping. The Air Force demanded to see the raw test data and officials at Goodrich panicked.[29] A conversation during a subsequent conference of the engineers is enlightening.

> The meeting was called, Sink began, "to see where we stand on the A7D." What we were going to do, he said, was to "level" with [the aircraft contractor] and tell them the "whole truth" about the A7D. "After all," he said, "they're in this thing with us, and they have the right to know how matters stand."
> "In other words," I asked, "we're going to tell them the truth?"

"That's right," he replied. "We're going to level with them and let them handle the ball from there."

"There's one thing I don't quite understand," I interjected. "Isn't it going to be pretty hard for us to admit to them that we've lied?"

"Now, wait a minute," he said angrily. "Let's don't go off half-cocked on this thing. It's not a matter of lying. We've just interpreted the information the way we felt it should be."

"I don't know what you call it," I replied, "but to me it's lying, and it's going to be damned hard to confess to them that we've been lying all along."

He became very agitated at this and repeated, "We're not lying," adding, "I don't like this sort of talk." [30]

Another example of deliberate deception and manipulation of test results occurred in the ethical drug industry. (It should be noted that the term "ethical" here does not refer to morality but to drugs sold only by physicians' prescription.) The company in question, the William S. Merrell Company, marketed a drug called MER/29 designed to lower cholesterol levels. [31] The Federal Drug Administration requested further testing before marketing, but Merrell assured the F.D.A. that animal tests had been satisfactory. In 1960 Merrell began a large-scale sales campaign praising the drug to physicians. Almost immediately physicians began to notice side effects from the drug: inflammation of the skin, falling hair, color change of hair, and loss of sex drive. Merrell instructed its salesmen to shift the blame toward other drugs the patients might be taking.

It was not until 1962 that the F.D.A. discovered that Merrell had falsified test results. In Merrell's laboratory tests using monkeys and dogs, several had become ill using the drug. The relationship between the illness and MER/29 was deliberately masked either by replacing the sick animals with healthy ones, or by claiming that the control animals—those not receiving the drug—also became ill. In rat studies in which whole samples had died, the results simply were not reported to the F.D.A.

Our examples so far have involved falsification of test results concerning new products. But the handling and treatment of old products also can pose dangers to the public. One industry that affects everyone except vegetarians is the meat packing industry, which has the dubious distinction of being the target of some of the earliest government investigations into unsanitary food. In 1899, a general from the Spanish-American War charged that "embalmed meat" sold to the army by Armour, Swift, Wilson, and others had killed more troops than enemy bullets. Theodore Roosevelt is quoted as saying he would have preferred to eat his hat than canned meat during that war. [32]

This industry also inspired a sensational novel, *The Jungle*, written by Upton Sinclair at the turn of the century as a criticism of capitalism in general and the Chicago stockyards in particular. He described in lurid detail how rats overran piles of meat stored under leaking roofs. In an attempt to be rid of the pests, packinghouse workers put out poisoned bread. Little attempt was made to separate the components that eventually went into the sausage hamper: poisoned bread, dead rats, dung, and of course, meat.

Then President Theodore Roosevelt secretly commissioned a study of Chicago meat packers that found Sinclair had not exaggerated the case.[33] An outraged public overcame opposition of the House Agriculture Committee, and in 1906 Roosevelt signed into law the Meat Inspection Act. But this law covered only meat sold in interstate commerce. As late as 1967 nearly 15 per cent of the meat slaughtered and 25 per cent of the meat processed in the United States were not inspected according to federal standards. Surveys of packing houses in Delaware, Virginia, and North Carolina found the following tidbits in the meat: animal hair, sawdust, flies, abscessed pork livers, and snuff spit out by the meat workers. To add even further flavoring, packing houses whose meat did not cross state lines could use 4-D meat (dead, dying, diseased, and disabled) and chemical additives that would not pass federal inspection. Such plants were not all minor operations; some were run by the giants—Armour, Swift, and Wilson.

In 1967 consumer groups began agitating for legislation making federal inspection mandatory even for plants not engaging in interstate commerce.[34] The argument was that since the states had refused to take responsibility, the federal government must. Opponents of the legislation included the Secretary of Agriculture and the meat packers who were working to "preserve our free enterprise system." But in the end The Wholesome Meat Act was signed into law on December 15, 1967; the law specified that state inspection standards must at least match federal standards within two years or the state industries would fall under federal inspection. In practice, however, the United States Department of Agriculture (U.S.D.A.) had taken over no state inspections by December of 1970, although two-thirds of the states had not been certified and the deadline was a year past. It was not until May of 1971 that the U.S.D.A. finally took over four states, all the others having been certified under often questionable circumstances.[35]

But the existence of law does not ensure compliance. The meat industry still has its share of violations that are especially frightening because they can mean disease and death to consumers. For example, a perennial problem is Number 2 meat. If meat is returned by a retailer to a packer, it can be resold as Number 2 meat to a different customer if it meets standards of wholesomeness. One 1969 case involved a Hormel plant located in the Los Angeles area that sold a great deal of Number 2 meat to San Diego schools.

> When the original customers returned the meat to Hormel, they used the following terms to describe it: "moldy liverloaf, sour party hams, leaking bologna, discolored bacon, off-condition hams, and slick and slimy spareribs." Hormel renewed these products with cosmetic measures (reconditioning, trimming, and washing). Spareribs returned for sliminess, discoloration, and stickiness were rejuvenated through curing and smoking, renamed Windsor Loins, and sold in ghetto stores for more than fresh pork chops.[36]

The Hormel situation persisted because the U.S.D.A. inspector chose to look the other way. The fact that Hormel paid him $6,000 annually for "overtime" no doubt helped. Lack of sufficient inspectors, however, probably contributes to offenses more often than bribery does.

> Inspectors in North Carolina report that companies repackage unsold meat without having it rechecked by the inspector. An Associated Press reporter, visiting three meat packaging plants in August, 1971, saw bacon, hams, wieners, and cold cuts which were rotten a solid green with mildew stacked on return tables. Since federal inspectors only spot check the packaging plants, the meat can be cleaned up and sold as new stock with no one the wiser.[37]

More food for thought: Even though meat packers may rigorously comply with federal standards for their products, consumers may be surprised at what goes into the meat they eat. Take the time occasionally to look at the contents label of a meat product and see the chemical additives that are present. These additives may perform many tasks, such as preservation and making the product's appearance more attractive, but their impact upon the human system is frequently unexplored. It should be noted that even when federally inspected, prepared foods may contain some "extras." According to regulations food need not be completely free of animal hairs and other tidbits, they simply may not exceed specified levels. And the labels do not always tell the whole story about the edible contents. As Robert Sherrill points out:

> The consumer is . . . confronted by such *pièces de résistance* as the hot dog, which by law can contain 69 per cent water, salt, spices, corn syrup and cereal, and 15 per cent chicken; that still leaves a little room for goat meat, pigs' ears, eyes, stomachs, snouts, udders, bladders and esophagus—all legally okay. There is no more all-American way to take a break at the old ball game than to have water and pigs' snouts on bun, but you might prefer to go heavier on the mustard from now on.[38]

The above examples of deviance by industry by no means encompass the entire variety of ways "respectable" businesses extract extra dollars at public expense. For instance, it is much less costly for industries to discharge raw wastes into rivers or the air than to use other means of disposal, which do not pollute. The magnitude of industry's contribution to the spoiling of the environment is overwhelming when you consider that it accounts for one third of all solid waste, one half of all air pollution, and more than one half of all water pollution.[39] Pollution by industry is not merely an assault to the senses, it is in violation of the law.[40] Yet many firms persist in disregarding the law.

Nor have we considered one of the oldest (now illegal) sales gimmicks in retailing—bait and switch. This tactic assumes many forms but it basically involves luring customers into the store with advertisements of low priced items, only to have salespersons "switch" the customers to higher priced goods by pointing out certain defects of the advertised product, claiming delivery delays, and so on. The company promotes this practice by a system of rewards that encourages sales personnel to sell higher priced models but deters them from selling the advertised ones. In July of 1974 the Federal Trade Commission charged Sears, Roebuck & Co. with baiting and switching in selling major home appliances, so the practice is scarcely limited to small-time operators.

Nor have we discussed the various ways in which both industries and unions often take advantage of their workers and members. Examples here include the disregard for workers' safety as in the case of the Pittsburgh Corning Corporation, which delayed time and again the installation of equipment that would have protected asbestos workers from contracting lung cancer and other diseases.[41] Organizations have also jeopardized the financial well-being of their members; in numerous cases industrial and union pension plans failed to benefit those contributing to them. Up until September of 1974, when a federal law guaranteeing private pension plans was enacted, employers often cancelled plans; they laid off persons approaching retirement, thus making them ineligible for a pension; and they often mismanaged funds so that there was not enough money to pay the retired.

According to Ralph Nader and Kate Blackwell:

> Approximately 34 million wage and salary workers are relying on the private pension's promise of retirement income. It is an important promise. For most people it means the difference between poverty and a modestly adequate standard of living after they retire. But implicit in the fine print of the private pension system is the probability that *one-half of the people covered by pensions will never collect a penny.*[42]

The list could go on. But it should be evident that deviance originating in the executive suites is at least as costly as that in the streets. The victims faced with the alternatives of rotten meat, early death by lung cancer, or poverty in old age as a result of the inability to collect a pension might even prefer an occasional mugging.

THE BADNESS OF GOOD BUSINESS

It is tempting to lay all the faults of business at the doorstep of profit. Without the profit incentive, it can be argued, business need not involve itself in most of the practices we have just discussed. But this argument considerably oversimplifies a very complex matter and it ignores the great number of businesses and their executives who operate within the bounds of legality. Nevertheless, *pressure for profit* remains the single most compelling factor behind deviance by industry whether it be price-fixing, the destruction of competition, or the misrepresentation of a product.

As we pointed out in connection with the electrical conspiracy and the auto industry, competition in the marketplace can make survival difficult if a corporation does not resort to illegal practices. The influence of competition upon deviance is best suggested by Richard Quinney's study of pharmacists. Quinney found that the orientation of pharmacists toward their occupation varied according to whether they viewed themselves as being in a *business* role (being a good salesman and successful businessman) or in a *professional* role (being active in pharmaceutical rather than business matters). The business-oriented pharmacists were much more likely to engage in illegal prescription practices because the professional norms represented by the prescription laws had little relevance for business behavior.[43]

In addition to the general pressure for profit that characterizes the business world, within particular industries and companies there can be more specific pressures that generate deviance. In a survey of executives who read the *Harvard Business Review*, it was found that pressure from superiors was a matter of deep concern:

> The sales manager of a very large corporation phrases his views most bluntly: "The constant everyday pressure from top management to obtain profitable business; unwritten, but well understood, is the phrase 'at any cost.' To do this requires every conceivable dirty trick. . . ." Another executive says, "As controller, I prepared a P&L statement which showed a loss. An executive vice president tried to force me to falsify the statement to show a profit in order to present it to a bank for a line of credit. I refused and was fired on the spot."
>
> A young engineer testifies that he was "asked to present 'edited' results of a reliability study; I refused and nearly got fired. I refused to defraud the customer, so they had others do it." [44]

Perhaps these quotations overemphasize the degree to which individuals are forced rather than coaxed or otherwise influenced into deviance on behalf of the organization. In any case, the executives surveyed appeared to believe that:

> If an executive acts *ethically*, . . . this is attributable to his own set of values and his ability to resist pressure and temptation, with some credit due to his superiors and company policy.
> If an executive acts *unethically*, . . . it is largely because of his superiors and the climate of industry ethics.[45]

The goal of business is to provide a product or a service that will produce a profit for the owners or stockholders. Any businessman or woman who ignores that goal is obviously derelict in his or her role. The problem is, at what point does the pursuit of profit by a company, or even a total industry, translate into illegal and unethical practices? And, at the individual level, when does one's identity as part of an organization dictate involvement in illegal behavior on behalf of the organization? These are difficult questions that have no ready answers, but it does appear that monopolization of an industry by just a few companies aggravates the situation.

One factor that clearly promotes deviance by industry is the *indifference of society toward offenders*. The criminal justice system in the United States has two tracks. One is for the poor who are accused of crime in the streets, and it is based on a philosophy similar to one in the game of Monopoly: "Go directly to jail. Do not pass Go and do not collect $200." The other track is for those others we have been talking about. Although their actions may have cost the public millions of dollars and jeopardized public health and safety, these individuals rarely see the inside of a jail cell.

In Russia persons found guilty of bribery, blackmarketing, and embezzlement of public property can be put to death. In the United States we are treated to the following spectacle related by Whitney North Seymour, Jr.:

> On January 15, 1973, two cases were called for sentencing before a United States District Judge in Manhattan's Federal Court. The first was *United States v. Velasquez*. A twenty-two-year-old Puerto Rican woman with two children, five and four years old, pleaded guilty to aiding in the theft of part of a group of welfare checks amounting to a total of $2,086. The woman had come to New York only a few years before, could not speak English and was on welfare herself. She was living with her husband in Brownsville, a poverty-stricken section of Brooklyn. Her husband was a diabetic and she provided insulin for him. She had no prior criminal record. The judgment of the court: imprisonment for eighteen months.
> The next case was *United States v. Delatorre*. An educated white-collar defendant pleaded guilty to commercial bribery and extortion in the amount of $23,000, as well as perjury and [inducing another to commit]

perjury. The judge went out of his way to point out, along with other considerations, that the defendant had two young children and no prior criminal record. The judgment of the court: a suspended sentence.[46]

Seymour provides still other instances of the contrasting treatment meted out to rich and poor in federal court. For example, three unskilled laborers who managed to steal a shipment worth $63,000 were sentenced an average of four years in prison. The mastermind of a stock manipulation scheme, which cost the public four million dollars, however, was chairman of the board of directors of a national bank; his sentence was one year.[47]

But if rich individuals fare well in court, rich companies fare even better. We have already mentioned how General Electric and Westinghouse received preferential treatment from the I.R.S. in spite of their "indiscretions." An additional example is an auto parts factory that dumped its wastes, including oil and sewage, into a stream. An Ohio municipal court judge ordered the company to pay twenty-five cents.[48]

In another case, thirteen companies, including Gulf Oil, 3M, and American Airlines, made illegal contributions to political campaigns. The average fine was $4,000, but because the companies' average annual gross income was $20,000 a minute, it took each about twelve seconds to pay.[49]

But these are extreme examples because the companies were directed by the courts to pay fines. More typical is the case of Sunoco, which ran false advertising about the power and uniqueness of its gasoline from 1969 to the beginning of 1972. In 1974 the Federal Trade Commission ruled that the company had used misleading advertising. The judge issued a *cease and desist order*—in other words, he told Sunoco to stop doing what it had not been doing for over two years. Furthermore Sunoco did not even have to go through the inconvenience of running new advertising confessing to its deception. The judge felt the public had had a change in attitude about buying gasoline on the basis of claims for power.[50]

The indifference of society toward corporate offenders is embodied in the structure of the law, which is designed to control such offenders. Although imprisonment for the offenses is possible, the likelihood of an executive going to jail is practically nil. Once an action is started against a company the worst that can happen is that someone who can prove damages from illegal conspiracy can recover three times those damages. Although this appears to be a substantial penalty, in reality it is seldom levied.[51]

More likely the corporate violations will draw either a straight fine or will be resolved through a *consent decree*—a voluntary settlement negotiated between the defendant and the government. The consent decree has been variously defined as a "Don't Do It Again Decree" and as an "instrument whereby a firm, in effect, says it has done nothing wrong and promises never to do it again." [52] If the decree is subsequently violated by the company the criminal actions that can be taken by the government are severe, but in the meantime the consent decree is a particularly easy way to get off the hook for deliberate illegal behavior. Furthermore, the decree effectively cuts off the likelihood of being forced to pay triple damages.

Thus corporate deviance does pay. Companies may reap whatever profits they can from illegal behavior until the government catches them. Then they can simply agree not to do it again. If they are fined, the impact is usually unnoticeable—the maximum fine under the Sherman Act, for example, is $50,000, a trivial amount for most corporations. Because fines are so small it may be argued that they are merely license fees for committing illegal acts. Mark Kennedy questions how the basic notion of a fine should be conceptualized:

> Is it actually a penal sanction? Is it, to the contrary, a tax levied for the privilege of violating criminal law? Or, is it a price charged by the State for the right or license to violate laws for which only the poor would be imprisoned? In any case, the State either becomes an entrepreneurship which exchanges the right to violate criminal law for a price called a fine—or else it becomes an agency in which the fine is standard fiscal policy very like a tax on the rich and less rich to pay for punishing the poor for having violated criminal laws the State itself created! [53]

This brings us to the crux of an important issue; there is little in the social reaction to deviance by industry that indicates condemnation of the behavior. Corporations and their executives are considered respectable, regardless of their behavior. Small wonder, then, that executives feel they can do little wrong in the name of profit. Since the system of justice treats them with deference there is ample support for their verbalized motives that they have done nothing wrong or that their behavior is best for all concerned.

We are not suggesting that businessmen who fix prices or who falsely claim their deodorant overpowers the opposite sex should be lined up and shot. But it must be recognized that deviance by industry not only imposes an incredible financial burden on society, but also kills and maims. There is an obvious conflict of interest between businesses that pursue profits at the expense of consumers and the consumers who bear the consequences of that pursuit. A public awakening to this conflict began in the mid-1960s with the emergence of the *consumerism movement*. Sparked by the work of Ralph Nader, one of the first results of the movement was the National Traffic and Motor Vehicle Safety Act of 1966, which required auto manufacturers to recall and repair cars that exhibited engineering defects jeopardizing safety. There followed several other laws and actions reflecting the public's new concern with product safety (e.g., the restriction on cigarette advertising, and the labelling of cigarettes as dangerous to health) and with environmental preservation (e.g., the failure to support development of a supersonic transport plane having high noise and pollution potential).

Despite recent legal protection for consumers against the mistakes or deliberate deceptions of industry, the American public still does not express the same moral outrage toward illegal and unethical businessmen as it does toward drug addicts and muggers. As Gilbert Geis points out:

> Corporate offenses . . . do not have biblical proscription—they lack, as an early writer noted, the "brimstone smell." But the havoc such offenses produce, the malevolence with which they are undertaken, and the disdain with which they are continued, are all antithetical to principles we as citizens are expected to observe. It is a long step, assuredly, and sometimes an uncertain one, from lip service to cries of outrage; but at least principled antagonism is latent, needing only to be improved in decibels and fidelity. It should not prove impossible to convince citizens of the extreme danger entailed by such violations of our social compact.[54]

Business Frauds

So far in this chapter we have discussed acts of deviance that further the goals of an organization but are not central to that organization. The remaining two sections will examine organizations that are specifically designed to engage in illegal activities. The first section will cover businesses that carry out their activities under the guise of respectability. Although these businesses' services or products are presumably legitimate, the organizations, which produce them are systematically defrauding their customers. The second section will discuss organized crime, which makes no pretenses at all of legitimacy.

Business frauds vary tremendously and involve practically any service or product imaginable: weight reducing machines, life insurance, potions giving bridegroom strength to those with waning sexual powers, land, medicines, and burial plots. The businesses themselves vary greatly in their size and stability. They may contain only a single swindler who deceives both the customers and fellow employees, or the entire organizational staff may be involved in the conspiracy. Some organizations, such as the mail order frauds, may have a long-term permanent office; home improvement frauds, however, are likely to be quite transient. A good example of the latter is a traveling "company" that seals asphalt driveways at bargain prices.

The price becomes understandable during the first rain when the sealer (used crankcase oil, actually) rushes down the nearest sewer.

Most of the greatest business frauds have centered around an individual offender who uses a business to further his goals. The undisputed king of the frauds is *Ivar Kreuger* who looted 500 million dollars between 1917 and 1932. Kreuger became a millionaire as a legitimate businessman; by 1917 he controlled match production in Sweden. But when he turned toward gaining monopolies in other countries he resorted to illegal practices, including bribery. He also lent money to shaky governments such as France, Spain, and Poland in exchange for a monopoly on match production in those countries. He became a truly international businessman by having financial interests in thirty-seven countries including the United States, where he established the International Match Company. On the surface the enterprises seemed honest, but Kreuger was pocketing huge sums of money and then covering his thefts by switching assets among his companies or by creating nonexisting assets. He also established a labyrinth of holding companies and subsidiaries, many of which were dummy firms which served as his personal bank accounts. Meanwhile he continued to attract investor funds on the basis of the large dividends that he paid.

His undoing came with the arrival of the depression. When stock prices dropped Kreuger had to produce funds to cover his looting. He invested wildly in the stock market and lost $50 million. As a desperation move he turned to forgery, producing $142 million in bogus Italian government bonds to use as collateral for loans. But the loans were turned down, and in 1932 Kreuger shot himself to death.[55]

FALSE SECURITY FRAUDS

The largest American business swindles involve the taking of money on the basis of nonexistent collateral. The greatest such frauds became known in the 1960s, and the largest individual swindler was *Anthony ("Tino") De Angelis*. By the time the De Angelis affair was over twenty-seven firms and two respected Wall Street brokerage houses were in ruins, and a wide variety of companies and individuals were trying to recover $219 million. Like Kreuger, De Angelis first came by business success honestly. He was the son of poor immigrants and by 1962 he accounted for three quarters of America's exports of soybean and cotton seed oils. To finance his continued rapid growth De Angelis needed to borrow huge sums of money. Such sums require huge collateral as security for the loan. De Angelis' collateral was certificates attesting to his ownership of oil—much of which was nonexistent.

An unsuspecting collaborator was American Express Warehousing, which stored, inspected, and vouched for the oil's existence. Amexco was easily taken in by De Angelis' men. They would pump oil from one tank to another to fool the inspectors, fill tanks with water except for a thin slick of oil on top, climb to the top of empty tanks and shout down to the accepting inspectors on the ground that the tank was full. By other manipulations, such as forging his own receipts for nonexistent oil, De Angelis at one time had loans out on three times as much oil as the tanks could possibly hold. By 1964 De Angelis' creditors really began looking into those tanks. Instead of finding 1.8 billion pounds for which receipts were held, they found only 100 million pounds.[56]

Ironically, in 1962 when De Angelis was gearing up to swindle millions, another famous scandal involving false security was breaking. This involved Billie Sol Estes, who swindled $22 million out of some of the top finance companies in the nation. Estes' operations were extremely complicated and varied, but essentially they involved the following.[57] He persuaded farmers in west Texas to buy storage tanks for anhydrous ammonia, a liquid fertilizer, on installment terms. He then leased the tanks back at prices equaling the installment payments. Many farmers never saw the tanks, but did not care because they were not out any money. Estes' profit came when the company that supposedly built the tanks—which was controlled by three Estes associates—sold the farmers' installment notes to several finance companies. The companies thought the notes were secured by mortgages on tanks but only 1,800 of the 30,000 tanks ever existed.

The finance companies, of course, did attempt to check on the collateral. Estes, however, worked out a scheme by which serial numbers could be changed on the tanks in a couple of hours. In one case an inspector saw the same tank three times with three different sets of numbers.

Estes was a deeply religious man—he could quote Scripture endlessly and was an elder and frequent preacher at local Churches of Christ. But he also had a sense of humor. He kept a monkey in his home and when asked about it, he would reply, "You know why I have that monkey there? I want to keep reminding myself how goddamn dumb those finance companies are."[58]

Probably the largest of all business swindles is still being unraveled at the time of this writing. The scandal concerns the *Equity Funding Corporation of America,* a company that suddenly collapsed in 1973. As with all such scandals the details are complex, but one of the more fascinating aspects is the way space age technology has arrived in the world of deviance. One of Equity Funding's subsidiaries, a life insurance company, claimed to have about 90,000 policy holders, but more than 60,000 existed only in the tapes of a computer. Within the computer "people" lived and died; meanwhile, Equity sold the policies of these nonexistent clients for cash to other insurance companies, and its executives pocketed the money. However, the insurance scandal is but a portion of an enormous securities fraud whose cost to the public may reach over a billion dollars.

PONZI SCHEMES

One of the great American business swindlers has the distinction of having his name permanently attached to a particular form of fraud: Charles "Get Rich Quick" Ponzi. Very simply the Ponzi scheme involves paying high dividends to early investors with money taken from later investors, who are lured by the original high dividends paid.[59] Ponzi's idea was hatched in June 1919, when he discovered that postal reply coupons purchased in Spain for one cent were redeemable in the United States for five cents. He borrowed money from his friends and repaid them double their money in ninety days. News like that travels fast. By the spring of 1920 Ponzi's outfit, Financial Exchange Company, was taking in nearly $200,000 per day from investors, mostly little people who were dumping their life savings on him. He convinced most of them not to draw out their money but to keep it in for even greater profits. He was thus able to pay off those who did pull out—he had stopped dealing in postal coupons because the limited number printed did not begin to approach what he needed. After he had taken in over $15 million and lived like a king, the roof fell in. A newspaper revealed the fraud, and investors demanding their money back found none. Ponzi spent nine years in prison and died in a charity ward in 1949.

The most recent large-scale Ponzi scandal broke in 1974 and may turn out to be the largest in history, with investors' losses reaching over $100 million. The company involved is the *Home-Stake Production Co.*, an oil-drilling company in Tulsa, Oklahoma. Unlike the original Ponzi victims, the victims in this case were generally well-heeled and often prominent individuals from the arts, sports, politics, and business: e.g., Jack Benny, Bobbie Gentry, Diahann Carroll, Bob Dylan, Senator Jacob K. Javits, the president of Bethlehem Steel, the chairman of National Cash Register, and numerous executives from General Electric.

Home-Stake was particularly attractive to well-to-do investors because it appealed as a tax shelter and it was known to pay high dividends besides. In reality, however, the company used little of the investors' money for drilling oil. Instead, the funds were used to pay dividends to attract more money and for the personal use of Home-Stake executives. To fool the curious, the company had numerous ruses such as "wells" that were shallow holes drilled where it was known that no oil existed at those levels, and irrigation pipes painted orange and coded with oil-field markings in locations where no wells had even been drilled.[60]

HOME IMPROVEMENT SCHEMES

Ponzi schemes appeal primarily to people's greed. Their desire for profit through the quick buck or the great tax loophole seems no less compelling than the force that drives corporate executives to break the law on behalf of their companies. When their greed, with a sprinkling of gullibility, finally trips them up, the losses seem justified in light of the anticipated, though frustrated, gains. But other victims of other business frauds are more pathetic examples. When the cheated are already cheated by society because they are struggling against disadvantages of race, color, age, and poverty, and when their only sins appear to be gullibility, misunderstanding, and an inability to defend themselves, then the schemes assume a particularly vicious character.

This is particularly the case with some home improvement schemes. Instances of crankcase oil used as "sealer" on the driveway or inferior aluminum siding are annoying but seldom devastating. An example of a devastating scheme is the case of Monarch Construction Company in Washington, D.C., which between 1963 and 1966 robbed more than 1,000 people of at least $4.25 million. The victims were primarily poor, old, and black ghetto residents who were in the process of purchasing their homes. The Monarch Construction Co. sold "towne house fronts"—facades of aluminum siding, shutters, wrought-iron railings, and lantern-type lights reminiscent of the early part of this century. It seemed the kind of improvement that would tone up the old row houses so common in Washington, D.C. In reality, the materials and workmanship were usually shoddy, and the "improvements" were an expensive proposition—often expensive beyond belief.

The sales assault began with a visit from a slick black salesman who falsely associated himself with urban renewal. He made Monarch sound like a company that wanted to help poor blacks fix up their homes. With the promise of low monthly payments and increased value to the home, sales came easily. One example of the results is the case of Roy and Mary Turner, who had bought their house for $11,500 and had paid off $7,000 of it. They signed a contract with Monarch for a $3,000 facade with monthly payments of $76. On the promise of a cheaper contract the Turners destroyed the first contract and signed a blank paper to "make the loan official." They then discovered they owed $13,000 to loan companies that had paid Monarch and could legally collect from the Turners regardless of the quality of

Monarch's work. To Turner this meant monthly payments of $224—a healthy sum for a sixty-two-year-old earning less than $5,000 a year.

As the Turners fell behind in their payments they were harrassed by abusive telephone calls. When they had their phone removed, their neighbors were called at all hours of the night. The pressure finally got to the Turners, and they simply moved out. Their house, in which they had invested nearly $10,000, was sold at auction to a savings and loan company for $1,000. But the Turners' ordeal was not over. They still owed nearly $5,000 to the loan companies, and the phone calls began again. Today the Turners are officially bankrupt, swindled out of money and hope.

The Monarch operation finally ended and its three top executives were convicted in 1971. Their sentences? On their promise to make restitution—for a grand total of $20,000—each received a suspended sentence and probation for five years. One whose net worth was $1.6 million agreed to pay $12,000 over the probationary period. The savings and loan companies that so readily permitted loans at the request of the fraudulent company were not even prosecuted. Instead they continue to collect. Many of Monarch's victims will be paying on their loans into the 1980s.[61]

The Monarch case points out, as did the Foolproof Protection case discussed earlier in this chapter, that the fraudulent organization is often substantially assisted in its practices by "respectable" institutions. The District of Columbia casually issued Monarch a license to conduct its business, and savings and loan institutions bought the debts owed Monarch with no questions asked.

> If there is a single moral in Monarch, it is that [the owner of the company] could not have done it alone. He had to have the cooperation of the community's noncriminal elements, in fact, society's respected individuals and institutions, to make Monarch succeed. Without everyone doing his part— the bankers, the settlement officers, the brokers, the notaries public, the legal profession, the D.C. License Department, the Federal Housing Administration—Monarch could not have happened. Thus, it was not the work of one man or even a group of corrupt men; it was in a sense an unwitting community project.[62]

Home improvement swindles of the magnitude of the Monarch case seem less likely today. At least its lingering trail of tragedy can be averted since contracts such as the Turners signed are now unenforceable. Consumer credit laws and the courts have extended greater protection to buyers who are in inferior bargaining positions—the little people who if they wish to make deals with large companies (insurance companies, loan agencies, and so on) must sign contracts "as is." Such contracts may be judged unenforceable when the terms are not made sufficiently clear as a result either of deliberate withholding of information or deception, or of complex terminology inconsistent with the buyer's education. Should the terms be deemed too extreme or unfair by the court's standards, the contract is no longer binding.

Of course, it is one thing to say that the law will protect consumers from certain unsavory tactics by business, but another to assume the little consumer will seek out that protection or that similar frauds will not occur again. The real lesson from the Monarch case is the extent to which business can and will go in "mugging" its customers.

MEDICAL FRAUDS

The business frauds discussed so far have exploited people's greed, gullibility, defenselessness. But people are vulnerable in other ways, especially in the matter of physical well-being, perhaps even survival. There is in America a great emphasis upon youthful appearance. Sexual prowess is not simply a matter of preference but an absolute necessity, and death is not accepted gracefully. Life is to be prolonged regardless of the cost.

The reality is that many ills currently have no cures; in many cases what medical assistance can be given is extremely limited, expensive, and uncertain. But Americans are attuned to the wonders of science. Even before space age technology they became used to medical breakthroughs as a matter of routine. It is difficult not to believe that someone, somewhere has found a sure-fire answer to our physical complaints. This is fertile ground for the medical fraud.

There are many forms of medical fraud—usually called quackery. The range is suggested by a typology of quackery developed by Julian B. Roebuck and Robert Bruce Hunter:

1. Fraudulent Nostrums and Devices.
   a. Nostrums for incurable diseases. Persons suffering from incurable cancer, and, particularly, arthritis are especially susceptible to quack medicines promising cures or at least relief from pain. These range from magic salves, bath salts, alfalfa tea to a cancer nostrum known as Collodaurum—a solution of gold and water.
   b. General panacea or pep-you-up types of nostrums. These are the modern counterpart of the snake oils sold by traveling medicine men of the past. These tonics promise aid in preventing practically any illness you can imagine. They alleviate less serious problems such as sexual impotency and nervousness, and, in general, rid you of that run down feeling. Like the snake oils they often contain substantial amounts of alcohol but little else of value.
   c. Nutritional supplement and diet pills. Quacks are not the only

ones who appeal to the notion that Americans do not get enough nutrition from their foods. The legitimate drug firms sell countless multiple vitamin supplements by appealing to this erroneous assumption. Both vitamin and diet pills are of dubious value and can be dangerous to health. An example of a potentially dangerous diet plan is the Kelpidine Reducing Plan, which combines very low caloric intake with a product containing a seaweed (kelp) and iodine.

d. Bogus healing and diagnostic devices. These devices range from vibrators, whirlpool baths, and uranium mitts to the more exotic instruments with flashing lights and dials. An example of the latter was the Magnetron. Advertised as a cure for arthritis, prostate gland trouble, varicose veins, diabetes, failing heart, and tumors, it gave the user a slight, totally unbeneficial electric shock. Its cost to build: $20; its selling price: $197.50.

2. Illegal and unorthodox practices by licensed healers. This category refers to state licensed healers, other than medical doctors, who engage in illegal practices such as advertising fraudulent claims, selling useless curative devices and medicines, and any other behavior that exceeds the limits of their legally defined practices. The healers who usually fit in this category are osteopaths and chiropractors.

3. Unorthodox practices by medical doctors. This refers to physicians who engage in illegal practices. Roebuck and Hunter provide the example of one Dr. Abrams who developed a diagnostic machine. His fraud was discovered when another doctor sent Abrams a drop of chicken blood for analysis. Abrams returned a diagnosis of diabetes, malaria, cancer, and syphillis.[63]

Such medical frauds can obviously be very costly in terms of human suffering because the "cures" may be dangerous in themselves, and because the victims are lulled into a sense of false security and fail to seek out competent medical help. The frauds are financially expensive as well. As early as 1961 medical quackery was estimated to be at least a billion-dollar annual business, half of this going toward vitamin and health food quackery and a quarter toward arthritic quackery.[64] But as one senator pointed out:

It seems to me that there are losses that go far beyond the original purchase price for the phoney treatment, the useless gadget, the inappropriate drug or pill. How can we measure the cost in terms of suffering, disappointment, and final despair? Do we really know how many Americans are quietly using therapy or products that give them neither cure nor the hope of cure? Can we be sure that we know the full extent of operations by questionable clinics and neighborhood practitioners? [65]

The Great American Con Game

In closing our discussion of deviance by organizations we should point out the interesting parallels between these activities and certain forms of fraud known as *confidence games* or *bunkos*.[65] As their name suggests, these swindles involve a belief of trustworthiness among the participants. The swindlers are salespersons who must be convincing about their own reliability and about the importance of buying their scheme. Like any salesperson, they must prepare to exploit the weaknesses and to overcome the resistances of their victims.

As in the world of legitimate business, the thirst for profit often plays an important role in this persuasion process. A student of confidence games, David W. Maurer, describes one such operation reminiscent of the Ponzi scheme:

> [The confidence man] must first inspire a firm belief in his own integrity. Second, he brings into play powerful and well-nigh irresistible forces to excite the cupidity of the mark [victim]. Then he allows the victim to make large sums of money by means of dealings which are explained to him as being dishonest and hence a "sure thing." As the lust for large and easy profits is fanned into a hot flame, the mark puts all his scruples behind him. He closes his bank account, liquidates his property, borrows from his friends, embezzles from his employer or his clients. In the mad frenzy of cheating someone else, he is unaware of the fact that he is the real victim, carefully selected and fattened for the kill. Thus arises the trite but nonetheless sage maxim: "You can't cheat an honest man." [67]

The most common confidence game—the *pigeon drop*—exploits this combination of gullibility and greed. According to New York City police it accounts for 65 per cent of all confidence complaints.[68] Although it has several variations the basic theme is as follows.

A package, wallet, or pocketbook containing money is "found" by a con woman (in New York City, at least, this is almost exclusively a female crime). She solicits the advice of the potential victim about what to do because there is no identification in the wallet. Another "stranger" approaches and she too enters the conversation; neither the "finder" nor the "stranger" let on that they know each other. After a good deal of discussion and reassurances, it is decided to split the money among the three participants. But to ensure everything is "legal" one or both of the con women go off to "consult a lawyer." Upon returning they reveal that the lawyer says the money can be split but that each party should prove that she has the means of reimbursement should the loser of the money ever show up. The victim goes to her bank, withdraws the needed good-faith money, and gives it to one of the women to deliver to the lawyer. When the victim later goes to the lawyer's office to pick up her share of the loot and the good-faith money, she discovers that no such lawyer exists and that her newfound "friends" have vanished without a trace.

Not all con games involve the lure of the easy buck. Some exploit people's eagerness to help others. The commonest of this type is the *bank examiner swindle*. Although there are variations, this scheme essentially involves the "F.B.I." or "bank officials" soliciting the help of the eventual victim in catching an embezzler. To do so, the victim must draw out his or her savings and turn them over to the "officials" or "F.B.I." waiting outside for the purpose of recording the serial numbers or some similar ruse. Naturally, a receipt is given for the money, and the victim is cautioned that he or she should tell no one because secrecy is so important in such delicate police work.

The conditions facilitating successful confidence schemes bear a striking resemblance to the conditions enabling organizations to flim-flam the public. As in confidence games, the belief in easy money, instant youth, or simple cure-alls combined with gullibility and blind trust in organizations conditions the public for its own victimization. There is public faith in the adage, "What is good for General Motors is good for the country."

The American public thus seems to be pulled in two directions. As we discussed in Chapter 6 there is, on one hand, a cynicism about business. This prompts large portions of respectable people, both employees and customers, to loosen their ethics concerning property rights and theft. On the other hand, the public often takes at face value business's claim that profit is the very least of its concerns. To believe public relations firms is to believe that the sole goal of business is to make a better world for us all. It is the faith in this image of business's conscience that makes the public susceptible to being duped by price-fixing, deceptive advertising, and corporate lack of concern for safety and the condition of the manufacturing environment.

True, trust in American business has some justification. In the past forty years the real per capita income of Americans has tripled and technological advances have elaborated, if not enriched, our lives. It is also true that trust is part of the glue that holds society together. It at least seems easier to trust your fate to well-dressed executives than to a group of strangers lurking in the slums. And it does seem unfair to equate corporation executives with common criminals because your run-of-the-mill mugger is unlikely to market a deodorant to control underarm wetness.

The deviance of American business is much like a great con game, nevertheless. In their pursuit of profit American corporations exploit our search for health, wealth, and happiness. Because we trust them they can connive, lie, cheat, and steal, while clad in the garb of respectability. The pity is that public acceptance extends to the halls of justice. There, slight differentiation is made between honest and dishonest businesses. The image of respectability remains unshaken even in the face of the most blatant deceptions and gouging. The most outright business frauds are treated with the same deference and gentleness accorded those businesses that operate within a more legitimate framework.

Evidently legislation and even prosecution are not sufficient to control business fraud. The public will have to exhibit greater indignation and thereby prod the zeal that prosecutors and judges now reserve for crime-in-the-street offenders. In the meantime, the American public must also learn to spot a con game when it sees one.

Organized Crime

MAFIA STAFF CAR—Keepa You Hands Off!!
Bumper sticker

This bumper sticker sums up rather well what many Americans know about organized crime. It is run by Italians and they are not to be trifled with. The Mafia is familiar to most as an association of closely knit families who exert nearly total control over illegal gambling, who have a very strict code of honor, and who kill a lot of people. The most famous example of this last is the St. Valentine's Day Massacre of February 14, 1929 when five of Al "Scarface" Capone's boys lined up seven mobsters belonging to George "Bugs" Moran and machine-gunned them down.

It is difficult to separate fact from fiction about organized crime. Obviously it thrives best in secrecy, and even the experts continue to disagree over several of its characteristics. What is known about organized crime definitely places it into our category of deviance by organizations. Much of organized crime is a *business*, like business its goal is *profit*, and its means to that end is to establish a *monopoly* by destroying the competition. That is why some of Moran's business associates met their untimely end—they were victims of the free enterprise system in its most extreme form.

CHARACTERISTICS AND STRUCTURE OF ORGANIZED CRIME

Before proceeding to a detailed discussion of organized crime we should offer a definition of exactly what we will be talking about. This is not as simple as it sounds. Organization alone is not the key term since burglars, shoplifters, and even rapists might work together as teams, but their organization, no matter how formal, would not qualify them as organized crime.[69] The President's Commission described organized crime as follows:

The core of organized crime activity is the supplying of illegal goods and services—gambling, loan sharking, narcotics, and other forms of vice—to countless numbers of citizen customers. But organized crime is also extensively and deeply involved in legitimate business and in labor unions. Here it employs illegitimate methods—monopolization, terrorism, extortion, tax evasion—to drive out or control lawful ownership and leadership and to exact illegal profits from the public. And to carry on its many activities secure from governmental interference, organized crime corrupts public officials.

. . .

What organized crime wants is money and power. What makes it different from law-abiding organizations and individuals with those same objectives is that the ethical and moral standards the criminals adhere to, the laws and regulations they obey, the procedures they use are private and secret ones that they devise themselves, change when they see fit, and administer summarily and invisibly.[70]

There are several characteristics of organized crime alluded to in the above definition worth emphasizing. First, *organized crime provides illegal goods and services*. The exact nature of these goods and services will be discussed later, but for the purpose of describing the enterprise it is important to note that the customers are a blend of both the respectable and the not-so-respectable. Without a demand for commodities not legally available, organized crime would be a marginal operation at best. This points up a basic distinction between ordinary crime and organized crime—few would grieve over the sudden disappearance of rapists, robbers, burglars, and so on, but if organized crime were to vanish, a great number of unhappy people would result.[71] This is not to say that organized crime does not get involved in predatory behavior, as evidenced by the commission's reference to extortion and terrorism, but it owes its continued existence primarily to the public demands that it fills.

A second characteristic of organized crime is *corruption*. In order to carry on its business without interference it is necessary for organized crime to neutralize the threat of law enforcement.[72] The forms of corruption are varied, but most consist of outright bribery, campaign contributions, and promises to deliver (or not deliver) voters. The favors or threats of organized crime can taint the low and the high. Those beholden to the wishes of the gangster range from policemen on the beat to their supervisors, from city prosecutors to judges, from newspaper reporters to publishers, and from council members and mayors to members of state and federal legislatures. Should one doubt the extent of organized crime's influence on the entire political scene, one might consider this: an estimated 15 per cent of the costs of local and state political campaigns are financed by organized crime.[73]

So important is corruption to organized crime that each of the major crime families has at least one position actually titled, corrupter.

> The person occupying this position bribes, buys, intimidates, threatens, negotiates, and sweet-talks himself into a relationship with police, public officials, and anyone else who might help "family" members maintain immunity from arrest, prosecution, and punishment. . . . In one or, perhaps, two instances, a single corrupter does all the "fixing" for his "family," which means that he is responsible for the political dishonesty of a geographical territory. More commonly, one corrupter takes care of one subdivision of government, such as the police or city hall, while another will be assigned a different subdivision, such as the state alcoholic-beverage commission. A third corrupter might handle the court system by fixing a judge, a clerk of court, a prosecutor, an assistant prosecutor, a probation officer.[74]

Like the public demand for illegal goods and services, the corruption of members of legal and political organizations is not merely an incidental characteristic of, but rather a critical element for the survival of organized crime. Like other forms of deviance by organizations, organized crime does not exist in isolation from other segments of society; gangsters do not impose their wills upon society despite vigorous protestations and resistance. Families in organized crime have corrupters because there are persons who are corruptible. To understand organized crime, then, it is important to recognize that it is more than a collection of families. *It is an alliance between government and criminals.*[75]

Therein lies perhaps the greatest danger of organized crime—its alliance with government undermines the political process just as surely as having goons beating up voters outside polling places would. As Donald R. Cressey points out:

> [Organized crime] functions as an illegal invisible government. However, its political objective is not competition with the established agencies of legitimate government. Unlike the Communist Party, it is not interested in political and economic reform. Its political objective is a negative one: nullification of government.
> Nullification is sought at two different levels. At the lower level are the agencies for law enforcement and the administration of criminal justice. When a [gangster] bribes a policeman, a police chief, a prosecutor, a judge, or a license administrator, he does so in an attempt to nullify the law-enforcement process. At the upper level are legislative agencies, including federal and state legislatures as well as city councils and county boards of supervisors. When a "family" boss supports a candidate for political office, he does so in an attempt to deprive honest citizens of their democratic voice, thus nullifying the democratic process.[76]

The third and last characteristic of organized crime is the *use of violence for enforcement.* A business dealing in illegal goods and services is generally in no position to appeal to the legitimate government for a redress of grievances. Individuals who cheat the organization or otherwise fail to live up to the expectations must be disciplined from within organization. But the enforcement violence of organized crime should not be confused with violence used to eliminate competition as exhibited in the so-called gang wars. The St. Valentine's Day massacre was the result of a dispute over control of bootlegging operations. In more recent history the largest of such wars involved the Joseph Profaci gang and the Gallo mob, a faction which broke off from the dominant Profaci gang. Profaci monopolized vice in Brooklyn and the upstarts wanted some of the action. The result was a four-year (1961–1965) gang war resulting in eight deaths and three disappearances. Although the main actors in the feud have all gone to their eternal rewards, factions from both sides sporadically kill each other in the spirit of seemingly endless hostility. At least three killings in Brooklyn in 1974 have been connected with the aftereffects of the Gallo-Profaci clash.[77]

The gang war type of violence, however, does not distinguish organized crime from any number of individual entrepreneurs who get into squabbles over the marketing of prostitutes or drugs; organized crime just does it on a larger scale. What sets organized crime apart is the existence of *its own equivalent of the criminal law*. There are rules of conduct and means of enforcing those rules. According to Cressey, the structure of organized crime includes a position of "enforcer," who makes arrangements for the killing or injuring of individuals as directed by a judicial authority.[78] The enforcer does not personally confront the wrongdoer; he merely employs the executioners. Plainly, organized crime thus functions not only as a business but as a government as well.

The term *government* must be used cautiously here. Some students of organized crime conceive of its structure as a tightly knit bureaucracy with a ruling national commission—in short, a structure similar to what one would expect in any formal government. These students, as well as the press and law enforcement officials generally, refer to organized crime as the *Mafia* or *Cosa Nostra* (Our Thing)—this being a more complex, more bureaucratic form of the earlier Mafia.[79] A leading proponent of the Cosa Nostra theory is Donald R. Cressey who claims the following facts.

1. A nationwide alliance of at least twenty-four tightly knit "families" of criminals exists in the United States. (Because the "families" are fictive, in the sense that the members are not all relatives, it is necessary to refer to them in quotation marks.)
2. The members of these "families" are all Italians and Sicilians, or of Italian and Sicilian descent, and those on the Eastern Seaboard, especially, call the entire system "Cosa Nostra." Each participant thinks

of himself as a "member" of a specific "family" and of Cosa Nostra (or some equivalent term).

3. The names, criminal records, and principal criminal activities of about five thousand of the participants have been assembled.

4. The persons occupying key positions in the skeletal structure of each "family"—consisting of positions for boss, underboss, lieutenants (also called "captains"), counselor, and for low-ranking members called "soldiers" or "button men"—are well known to law-enforcement officials having access to informants. Names of persons who permanently or temporarily occupy other positions, such as "buffer," "money mover," "enforcer," and "executioner," also are well known.

5. The "families" are linked to each other, and to non-Cosa Nostra syndicates, by understandings, agreements, and "treaties," and by mutual deference to a "Commission" made up of the leaders of the most powerful of the "families."

6. The boss of each "family" directs the activities, especially the illegal activities, of the members of his "family."

7. The members of this organization control all but a tiny part of the illegal gambling in the United States. They are the principal loan sharks. They are the principal importers and wholesalers of narcotics. They have infiltrated certain labor unions, where they extort money from employers and, at the same time, cheat the members of the union. The members have a virtual monopoly on some legitimate enterprises, such as cigarette vending machines and juke boxes, and they own a wide variety of retail firms, restaurants and bars, hotels, trucking companies, food companies, linen-supply houses, garbage collection routes, and factories. Until recently, they owned a large proportion of Las Vegas. They own several state legislators and federal congressmen and other officials in the legislative, executive, and judicial branches of government at the local, state, and federal levels. Some government officials (including judges) are considered, and consider themselves, members.

8. The information about the Commission, the "families," and the activities of members has come from detailed reports made by a wide variety of police observers, informants, wire taps, and electronic bugs.[80]

Although there is agreement that there are twenty-four crime families, five of them in New York City, the extent to which there is a national organization or commission linking them together is hotly debated. Students of the role of Italians in organized crime claim that evidence for the existence of a highly organized, centrally operated criminal organization is simply not convincing. According to Joseph L. Albini, organized crime operates not as a formal organization but as a "system of power relationships." The leaders are those who can at any given time exert the most influence over legal agencies and who provide the most lucrative opportunities for making money.

Rather than being formally structured organizations, the syndicates in the United States are informally structured systems of patron-client relationships. The patron is the individual who has achieved a power position where he can grant favors to those beneath him in the underworld. He also serves as a client to those legal power sources who can offer him protection in return for his pay-off services. This system of patron-client relationships—a system which, by its very nature is one constantly immersed in conflict, cooperation, and accommodation—is, in our view, the nature of the structure and functioning of syndicated crime in the United States.[81]

A middle road between the positions of Cressey and Albini is that of John E. Conklin, who conceives of organized crime as consisting of highly organized families loosely linked to one another only by common interests:

Local crime families are highly organized, both on the basis of kinship and, increasingly, on the basis of rational bureaucratic structure. Nationally, links between families exist, especially in times of crisis and conflict. Indeed, it would be surprising if no bonds existed among those with common interests. However, the evidence of a monolithic national structure is less compelling. The basic unit of operation is the local gang, with conflicts between the families sometimes being referred to the most influential and well-respected bosses for resolution.[82]

Whether this compromise view represents the true nature of things will be open to conjecture until we have far better information than is now available. Nevertheless, the existence of organized crime—however organized—need not be debated. And like so many forms of deviance discussed in this book, it has its roots in rather early American history.

FROM MUSCLE TO RESPECTABILITY

On January 16, 1920 the Eighteenth Amendment of the United States Constitution went into effect. It prohibited "the manufacture, sale, or transportation of intoxicating liquors within, the importation thereof into, or the exportation thereof from the United States, and all territory subject to the jurisdiction thereof for beverage purposes. . . ." In short, alcoholic beverages were illegal. Thus began Prohibition, a period lasting nearly fourteen years, during which many people believe organized crime had its birth.

Unquestionably, without Prohibition organized crime would not have gained the power it has today, but its origins go back to the early nineteenth century. Gus Tyler describes the development of organized crime as an evolutionary process in which illegal violence moved from the streets of urban slums into the world of business and finance. The earliest gangs in New York City were Irish immigrants, who were dominant from 1820 to 1890. These gangs emerged in the slums during a time of conflict between ethnic, political, and economic groups. They made their own rules and enforced them with their fists.

Their principal activities were idling and fighting—"free-floating chunks of violence," in Tyler's phrase. With names like Bowery Boys, Dead Rabbits, and Shirt Tails, they were first guided primarily by prejudice and struck out at other ethnic groups and whoever was reckless enough to invade their territory. They provided the raw material for the beginnings of organized crime, for they soon discovered that money could be made with muscle.

Starting with extorting money from whorehouses, gambling houses, and opium dens, the gangs soon began selling their violence to whoever could afford it. They became mercenary armies whose skill and disdain for the law placed them in demand for such activities as breaking up picket lines, terrorizing voters, marching in protest demonstrations, kidnapping, stuffing ballot boxes, and so on. Jay Gould, a nineteenth-century robber baron, bragged, "I can hire one half the working class to kill the other half."

By 1850 the gangs of New York City had become an important force in politics. Not surprisingly, Tammany Hall was quick to see their value, especially at election time. With a gang in his pocket, a politician could be assured that the voting would go his way. If he chose to operate bars, gambling houses, or whorehouses in his district, as many ward leaders did, the gang guaranteed that no outside influences would disrupt their smooth operation.

At the turn of the century, the Irish began to lose their grip as the gang leaders in New York City. The East European Jews were taking over. At the same time gang operations began to shift from protection and extortion toward actual control of prostitution and gambling. The gangster-as-businessman arrived on the scene and moved with ease in all circles, among "politicians and statesmen, bankers and bums, high society and low hoods, beautiful women and spendthrift sports."

The dominance of Jews in organized crime was short-lived, however. By 1920 the recently immigrated Italians were replacing them and the newcomers could not have arrived at a better time. With the ratification of the Eighteenth Amendment they now had another illegal commodity to sell besides violence, sex, and gambling: alcohol. But alcohol was a commodity with a difference. First, it was a bulk product that had to be manufactured, transported, and distributed. This required giant breweries and distilleries, vast warehouses, tank cars, trucks, and retail outlets. There had to be interstate and international alliances, and a high degree of cooperation from police and politicians. In short, it meant a degree of *organization* that the gangs had never required before.

Second, in addition to providing an impetus for greater organization, Prohibition gave the gangsters *respectability*. In the Roaring Twenties America was a nation of outlaws enjoying bathtub gin, speakeasies, and hipflasks. The Prohibitionists had grossly miscalculated; America had a thirst that was not eliminated by the passage of a law. The bootleggers who satisfied that thirst were accepted as part of the public scene. There were few raised eyebrows as politicians, businessmen, and any manner of good citizens openly rubbed elbows with gangsters. The funerals of major bootleggers brought mourners from the highest echelons of government and finance. According to Tyler, "Prohibition did more to give organized crime respectability than any other single force in our national history." [83]

With the repeal of the Eighteenth Amendment in December 1933, organized crime lost its biggest money maker, but not its organization or its respectability. With the enormous sums made from bootlegging it expanded its gambling operations and moved into other areas such as real estate, industrial racketeering, and control of labor unions. Aside from occasional disruptions, the competitiveness and resulting ferocious gang wars became a thing of the past. Organized crime is no longer characterized by the gangster who has only his muscle to sell. Today, it is a full-scale business, and a monopoly besides. And like any other American business it pursues profits in as many ways as it can.[84]

ETHNIC SUCCESSION

In our discussion of the passage from muscle to respectability, we mentioned another transition undergone by organized crime: the changing ethnic backgrounds of its leaders. In New York, America's heartland of organized crime, the control shifted from Irish to East European Jews to Italians. Nationally, practically every ethnic group—including the Chinese and Australians on the West Coast—have at one time or another been involved in organized crime.

New migrants to urban America found that the streets were not paved with gold. The road to success was rocky indeed because of discrimination and a lack of economic power, and many legitimate avenues were already occupied by those who had come before. But politics and crime were immediate alternative means. As Stuart Hills points out:

> Historically, organized crime, along with the political machine, has represented an important means to obtain wealth, power, and fame. Each major immigrant group has taken its turn successively in the upper echelons of syndicated crime. With the rags-to-riches paths preempted by earlier arrivals, opportunities in organized crime have provided shortcuts to the

great American dream of individual success. When the members of each group found increasing opportunities in more conventional forms of enterprise as discriminatory barriers declined, the group itself became less prominent in the world of gangs and rackets.[85]

The survival and present dominance of Italians in organized crime is the result of an historical accident, not to any unique ethnic characteristics. Italians were among the last of large scale immigrations and they found even city politics already dominated by other groups. Although the Italians began arriving in the 1890s, no potent Italian political bloc rose in major northern cities until the late 1930s.[86] Because most Italian immigrants were from rural backgrounds and few possessed occupational skills, they found it especially difficult to break out of the slums and into positions of power. The Italians' first signs of strength came from within the ranks of organized crime. Prohibition brought the gangsters into contact with entrenched politicians who needed money, and who were needed for protection of bootlegging operations.

Once Italian organized crime got its foot in the political door it was simply a matter of time before strong Italian politicians began to emerge. Meanwhile the gangsters remain remarkably democratic in their support of politicians; many Irish and Jews, as well as Italians, owe their political life to organized crime.

If organized crime is a stepping stone to respectability for immigrant groups, who will be its next leaders? The logical successors would be the current inhabitants of the urban slums—blacks and Puerto Ricans. From our obviously limited knowledge it appears that some of the brightest blacks and Puerto Ricans are entering organized crime.[87] However, so far their operations are restricted both in type and geography: narcotics and gambling within the ghetto areas. Italians are still at the top and exercise control over the far-flung enterprises—both legal and illegal—outside as well as inside the urban slums. Whether the Italians will eventually be displaced by the emerging newcomers remains to be seen.

SOURCES OF PROFIT

As we have seen, organized crime's first product was muscle. Then it expanded into gambling, prostitution, and bootleg alcoholic beverages. Today, like General Motors, it involves many enterprises, some of which it dominates completely and others in which it maintains only minor interest. These enterprises can be grouped as follows: 1. illegal goods and services, 2. thievery, 3. racketeering, and 4. infiltration of business.[88]

1. Illegal goods and services. This category remains the principal source of income for organized crime. And within the category, *gam-*

bling is the greatest money maker. Just how much money is, of course, subject to the usual guessing game, but experts estimate that it involves $50 billion a year with $15 billion of that being clear profit for organized crime.[89] Although some of these gambling profits come from large bettors, the great bulk of it comes from small ones—most of whom are poor slum-dwellers. The most lucrative gambling operation is the *numbers* or *policy* racket. In 1968 it was estimated that 75 per cent of all adult and late-teen-aged slum residents in New York City spent an average of four dollars a week on numbers. This means that the populations of Harlem, South Bronx, and Bedford-Stuyvesant spend $150 million on numbers each year.[90]

Numbers or policy is a form of lottery usually based on horse-racing results. The name derives from the time when poor people bet with money they had saved to pay insurance policy premiums. A participant bets fifty cents or more to pick a winning number. There are some variations but the simplest involves selecting a three-digit number that corresponds to a set of figures taken from the win, place, and show totals of racetrack pari-mutuels. For example, if a track paid out $73.80 for the third and fourth races, $80.40 for the fourth and fifth races, and $108.00 for the fifth and sixth, the winning number would be 308—take the first figures immediately to the left of the decimal points in sequence. The odds of winning are 1 in a 1,000 and the payoff is 600 to 1.

An illegal service that may even replace gambling as the major source of income is *usury or loan-sharking.* For the individual who needs money in a hurry with no questions asked this is a valuable service, but the interest is high—ranging from 1 to 150 per cent a week. For most small borrowers it is 20 per cent a week or $600 in repayment for $500 loaned. It is quick money, but collection can obviously get a bit sticky because no legal action can be taken against tardy borrowers. But the mob has its ways of encouraging clients, ranging from thinly veiled threats against one's family to burly collectors like the one in Chicago known as "The Leg Breaker."

In many cases, the lenders may care little whether the loan is even collected because persons in debt to organized crime may prove beneficial in several ways. For example, when the spiraling interest engulfs a small businessman beyond hope, the gang may take over his business for even greater profit than the loan repayment would have provided.[91]

Loan-sharking can lead to ways of persuading otherwise honest individuals to aid organized crime. A longshoreman can provide information on the arrival and location of valuable cargo, a businessman may have to become a fence, and government officials may be in positions to award contracts.[92] In short, the debt becomes a lever that allows organized crime to further its interests and expand its influence into the legitimate world.

Narcotics are another illegal commodity that organized crime finds profitable. It deals only at the very top, however, importing and selling wholesale bulk lots. The armies of smaller dealers and street pushers are necessary to the operation, but are not part of the organization. At one time, the importation and distribution of narcotics were practically monopolized by organized crime, but some observers claim it is relinquishing much of its operation to Cubans and others willing to take the greater risks involved.[93] Today, organized crime makes its narcotics money by handling overseas arrangements for shipping and by providing capital for purchases. For these services it receives a percentage of the profits.

Organized crime is still involved in *bootlegging*. For example, it legally purchases tens of thousands of cartons of cigarettes in South Carolina, Kentucky, and Virginia, and illegally resells them in states like New York, Pennsylvania, and Florida.[94] The source of profit is the disparity in state taxes imposed on cigarettes. In North Carolina the tax is two cents a pack, while in New York and Florida it is twelve and fifteen cents, respectively. Bargain-hunting smokers ask no questions, and bootlegged cigarettes can be sold considerably cheaper—and at a profit—than can legitimate ones. A cigarette wholesaler group estimates that over a five-year period, state tax divisions lost nearly a half billion dollars because of bootleg sales.

2. Thievery. As you might guess, theft by organized crime does not involve the ordinary housebreaking activities. Rather it ranges from the stealing and marketing of automobiles to the hijacking of cargo from trucks, warehouses, and docksides. Thefts of this sort require inside information on cargo movements and means of rapidly disposing of large quantities of valuable materials. Such capabilities are well beyond the resources of most would-be thieves, except those associated with organized crime.

Like everything else it does, organized crime steals big. For example, organized crime is believed to be behind 90 per cent of the truck hijackings that occur in major cities, and in 1973 it is estimated that thefts from trucks amounted to $4.2 million in New York City alone.[95] One truck alone contained $750,000 worth of tin ingots. Practically anything of value is considered fair game: optical lenses, precision valves, sweaters, furs, and so on.

A recently developed form of theft by organized crime involves *securities,* including corporate stocks and bonds and various kinds of government notes and bonds. It is estimated that the total losses for brokerage houses alone was more than $2 billion in 1974. Add the losses of banks, transfer agents, and other securities handlers, and the total may be as high as $20 billion.[96] The following excerpt from Senate hearings on stolen securities describes the operation:

The four main targets or sources of stolen securities are as follows: (1) brokerage houses, and in this category stock exchanges should also be included, (2) banks, (3) the U.S. mails and, (4) thefts from individuals. This category would include thefts from private homes, corporate offices, and the like.

Our investigation reveals that thefts of securities from brokerage houses, stock exchanges, and banks are almost always the product of an inside job. In some cases the thieves are individuals who act on their own to steal the securities, but who must depend on a contact or connection with an organized criminal group to move or fence the securities they steal.

In some cases, employees of these financial institutions are put under pressure to steal securities because of gambling debts, debts to loan sharks, narcotic addiction, strong-arm pressure, and other forms of extortion.

Registered mail has been a major target at the principal airports in this country and the theft of mail has resulted in very substantial losses. Testimony will show conclusively that these thefts were connected with organized crime.

. . . There are four major ways that stolen securities are converted to cash: (1) they can be resold through brokers, (2) they can be placed in banks as collateral for loans, (3) they can be placed in the portfolios of insurance companies or any other entity which has a need to present a more favorable financial posture, (4) they can be transported outside the United States where they can be resold, placed in banks as collateral or used to create devices such as trust accounts or escrow accounts which, in turn, can be used to establish other devices such as letters of credit, certificates of deposit, or payment guarantee bonds which can be redeemed in banks in this country.[97]

3. *Racketeering.* As we mentioned in our discussion of the history of organized crime, one of its earliest operations was extortion of funds from illegal businesses such as prostitution and drugs. Today, the "protection" of these enterprises is undertaken by the police, while organized crime turns its attention to legitimate businesses. In its simplest form, racketeering involves the sale of "insurance" to proprietors to provide that their companies remain free of unusual "accidents" such as delivery people being beaten up, store windows being broken, merchandise being vandalized, and so on.

In its more elaborate form racketeering involves the manipulation of labor. By infiltrating the upper levels of a union hierarchy, gangsters are in a position to negotiate contracts with companies. From this position organized crime can keep the companies in line by threats of strikes or walkouts and, at the same time, keep the companies relatively happy by allowing contracts that hold labor costs at a minimum. In return for these "sweetheart contracts" organized crime, of course, receives some consideration from the companies such as under-the-table payoffs or increased company input into the union pension fund, which the gangsters are systematically looting. Tyler provides still other examples of labor racketeering:

> In industries that farm out work, the underworld can make a labor supply available and generally does it at bargain rates. The operators of the underworld know where cheap labor plants have been set up (in come cases criminal money is in control of such plants), and they know how to evade unions and union standards. When a firm is having difficulty with a legitimate union, the underworld can be called in to maintain labor "peace," either by a bribe or by a beating or killing. On a more sophisticated level, the underworld acts as mediator: getting a little more out of the employer than the union might have by itself and checking the union better than the employer might have himself, while collecting the difference, sometimes from both sides. Where an employer sees trouble ahead with a legitimate union, the underworld can provide an illegitimate union, a "racket" union with "sweetheart" agreement and a bar, both legal and criminal, against outside interference.[98]

In a manner of speaking, racketeering by organized crime is another form of providing an illegal product. Employers wishing to obtain competitive advantage by obtaining the cheapest available labor or by short-circuiting the union's bargaining power can do so with the assistance of gangsters—for a fee. The loser in the conflict is likely to be the weakest, the workers whose interests are undermined by the coalition of management and gangsters.

Ultimately, even management will perhaps lose. Any relationship between legitimate business and organized crime, whether established by seduction, coercion, or trickery, is a fragile arrangement. It continues on a cooperative basis only at the pleasure of the gangsters, and, as we shall see, business often finds itself being devoured by its partner.

4. Infiltration of business. One of the greatest concerns of those studying organized crime is its acquisition of legitimate businesses. Already, its holdings are said to be worth tens of billions of dollars.[99] The reasons for organized crime's infiltration of the legitimate business sector appear to be threefold. First, a legitimate business can be used as simply another way to make a profit either legitimately or illegitimately, depending on how the business is run. Second, the enormous sums of money made from illegal dealings have to be put someplace where they will not appear too conspicuous and will not cause embarrassing problems with the Internal Revenue Service should it inquire about the source of funds. Legitimate business thus not only serves as an outlet for money, but can also provide a facade of respectability and a front for additional illegal operations if necessary. Third, the acquisition of legitimate business by organized crime may represent an attempt to gradually phase into respectability the younger, as yet innocent, generations of the families.

The last reason is of consequence only if one gets concerned over bad money doing good. But the other reasons make being an honest businessperson even more difficult than it would be under the normal competitive (or not-so-competitive) system. Imagine the problems presented by having to compete against another company that has the support of organized crime. The President's Crime Commission cites one example of a city in which organized crime gained a monopoly on garbage collection by using cash reserves to offset temporary losses when it lowered prices to drive competitors out of business.[100]

One tactic of organized crime that has come to recent attention is *planned bankruptcy* or *scam*. The most frequently used variation of this scheme is the one-step scam.[101] In this operation a successful business is either purchased or obtained in exchange for an unpaid loan. No notice of change in management is provided to Dun and Bradstreet or other credit agencies; thus, the new owners can trade on the previous owner's good credit reputation. Manufacturers and suppliers are approached by company representatives to arrange for the purchase of merchandise. On the basis of earlier dealings with the company or of the good credit rating, these manufacturers and suppliers accept orders. But once the ordered goods are received by the company, the merchandise is sold to either a fence or a surplus property operator with a large enough inventory to intermix the scam merchandise with the normal inventory. The gangsters continue to sell off the company's property and newly ordered goods, and finally they force the company into bankruptcy just as planned.

Conclusion

We have discussed several kinds of organizations that range across the entire spectrum of legality. The differences between these organizations are differences of degree, not of kind. All are designed to pursue profit by efficiently providing a product or a service in response to a demand. In order to maximize profits, they all endeavor to eliminate competition. True, the respectable industries have the approval of government, but without an alliance with government created by corruption, organized crime could not exist, either.

Furthermore, the government inadvertently creates a monopoly for organized crime by means of the criminal law. The suppression of trade in forbidden but demanded commodities primarily affects the small, less organized and less efficient operators, whereas the powerful ones become even stronger. This is analogous to the government looking the other way whenever a legitimate business systematically destroys its competition by illegal means.

The parallels between legitimate and illegitimate business are not meant to obscure or diminish the dangers of organized crime to the functioning of society. But it should be recognized that both forms of business develop within a competitive economy in response to real demands, and their deviance derives from the same context. Deviance by organizations is often a rational response to conflicts of interest, whether between legitimate business competitors or between the government that sets standards of conduct and the people who refuse to comply with those standards.

NOTES

1. Edwin H. Sutherland, *White Collar Crime* (New York: Holt, Rinehart and Winston, 1949), pp. 83–88.

2. *Prentice-Hall Encyclopedic Dictionary of Business Finance* (Englewood Cliffs, N.J.: Prentice-Hall, 1960), pp. 174–175.

3. For various typologies and discussions of this issue see: Herbert A. Bloch and Gilbert Geis, *Man, Crime, and Society,* 2nd ed. (New York: Random House, 1970), p. 307; Marshall B. Clinard and Richard Quinney, *Criminal Behavior Systems: A Typology,* 2nd ed. (New York: Holt, Rinehart and Winston, 1973), pp. 187–222; Herbert Edelhertz, *The Nature, Impact and Prosecution of White-Collar Crime* (Washington, D.C.: U.S. Department of Justice, 1970), pp. 73–75; and Gilbert Geis, "Upperworld Crime," in *Current Perspectives on Criminal Behavior,* ed. Abraham S. Blumberg (New York: Alfred A. Knopf, 1974), pp. 114–125.

4. Philip A. Hart, "Congressional Consumer Investigations: What Do They Tell Us?" (Remarks to New York Consumer Assembly, March 7, 1970, New York, New York).

5. Leonard S. Bernstein, *"How's Business?" "Don't Ask!"* (*Tales From the Garment Center*) (New York: Saturday Review Press, 1974), pp. 51–65.

6. Phillip G. Schrag, *Counsel for the Deceived: Case Studies in Consumer Fraud* (New York: Pantheon Books, 1972), pp. 116–162.

7. Ibid., pp. 157–158.

8. The most thorough contemporary discussion of corporate wrongdoing is Ovid Demaris, *Dirty Business: The Corporate-Political Money-Power Game* (New York: Harper's Magazine Press, 1974).

9. Ibid., p. 13.

10. For a discussion of the history of antitrust legislation see Mark J. Green, *The Closed Enterprise System: Ralph Nader's Study Group Report on Antitrust Enforcement* (New York: Grossman, 1972), pp. 47–60.

11. Ibid., pp. 8–9; and Demaris, *Dirty Business,* p. 38.

12. For a complete history of ITT see Anthony Sampson, *The Sovereign State of ITT* (New York: Stein and Day, 1973).

13. This discussion is based on Richard Austin Smith, "The Incredible Electrical Conspiracy," *Fortune*, **63** (April 1961), pp. 132–180, and (May 1961), pp. 161–224; Green, *Closed Enterprise System*, pp. 153–157; and Demaris, *Dirty Business*, pp. 10–13.

14. Demaris, *Dirty Business*, p. 10.

15. Green, *Closed Enterprise System*, p. 157.

16. Demaris, *Dirty Business*, p. 12.

17. Green, *Closed Enterprise System*, pp. 149–150, 472.

18. William N. Leonard and Marvin Glenn Weber, "Automakers and Dealers: A Study of Criminogenic Market Forces," *Law and Society Review*, **4** (February 1970), pp. 408–410.

19. Gilbert Geis, "The Heavy Electrical Equipment Antitrust Cases of 1961," in *White-Collar Criminal: The Offender in Business and the Professions*, ed. Gilbert Geis (New York: Atherton Press, 1968), p. 116.

20. Ibid., pp. 108–112, 116–117.

21. David Ogilvy, "What's Wrong with Your Image—and What You Can Do About It" (Speech to Annual Convention of National Automobile Dealers Association in Las Vegas, Nev., February, 1965), cited in Leonard and Weber, "Automakers and Dealers," p. 423, note 3.

22. Leonard and Weber, "Automakers and Dealers," p. 415.

23. Ibid., pp. 407–424. For a brief history of the development of the auto industry see Green, *Closed Enterprise System*, pp. 241–243.

24. Green, *Closed Enterprise System*, p. 4.

25. Leonard and Weber, "Automakers and Dealers," p. 422.

26. Lawrence Stessin, "Trade Secrets and the Industrial Revolution," *New York Times*, September 30, 1973, Section 3, p. 5.

27. The discussion draws heavily on William Rodgers, "IBM on Trial," *Harper's Magazine*, **248** (May 1974), pp. 79–84.

28. Ibid., p. 83.

29. Kermit Vandivier, "The Aircraft Brake Scandal," *Harper's Magazine*, **244** (April 1972), pp. 45–52.

30. Ibid., p. 51.

31. This description of the Merrell case is based on John G. Fuller, *200,000,000 Guinea Pigs: New Dangers in Everyday Foods, Drugs, and Cosmetics* (New York: Putnam, 1972), pp. 82–91.

32. Demaris, *Dirty Business*, pp. 6–7.

33. Harrison Wellford, *Sowing the Wind: A Report from Ralph Nader's Center for Study of Responsive Law on Food Safety and the Chemical Harvest* (New York: Grossman Publishers, 1972), pp. 3–6.

34. Ibid., pp. 8–25.

35. Ibid., pp. 27–44.

36. Ibid., p. 69.

37. Ibid., pp. 70–71.

38. Robert Sherrill, *New York Times Book Review*, March 4, 1973, p. 3.

39. Mark J. Green, "Big Business As Everyman's Villain," *New York Times*, June 30, 1974, Section 4, p. 4.

40. For a history of pollution legislation see Michael K. Glenn, "The Crime of 'Pollution': The Role of Federal Water Pollution Criminal Sanctions," *American Criminal Law Review*, **11** (Summer 1973), pp. 835–882.

41. Paul Brodeur, *Expendable Americans* (New York: Viking Press, 1974). For a discussion of the wide spectrum of industrial hazards and occupational diseases see Rachel Scott, *Muscle and Blood* (New York: E. P. Dutton, 1974).

42. Ralph Nader and Kate Blackwell, *You and Your Pension*, rev. ed. (New York: Grossman Publishers, 1973), p. 5.

43. Richard Quinney, "Occupational Structure and Criminal Behavior: Prescription Violations by Retail Pharmacists," *Social Problems*, **11** (Fall 1963), pp. 179–185.

44. Raymond C. Baumhart, "How Ethical Are Businessmen?" *Harvard Business Review*, **39** (July–August 1961), pp. 6–19, 156–176, cited in Geis, *White-Collar Criminal*, pp. 132–133.

45. Ibid., p. 125.

46. Whitney North Seymour, Jr., *Why Justice Fails* (New York: William Morrow, 1973), p. 43.

47. Ibid., pp. 46–47.

48. Glenn, "The Crime of 'Pollution,' " p. 882.

49. Green, "Big Business as Everyman's Villain," p. 4.

50. *Federal Trade Commission News Summary*, July 12, 1974, pp. 1, 4. This biweekly publication provides brief descriptions of current cases being considered by the F.T.C.

51. The discussion is derived from Green, *Closed Enterprise System*, pp. 162–218.

52. Ibid., pp. 178–179; and Phillip A. Hart, "Swindling & Knavery, Inc.," *Playboy*, **19** (August 1972), p. 158.

53. Mark C. Kennedy, "Beyond Incrimination: Some Neglected Facets of the Theory of Punishment," *Catalyst*, **5** (Summer 1970), p. 18.

54. Gilbert Geis, "Deterring Corporate Crime," in *Corporate Power in America*, eds. Ralph Nader and Mark J. Green (New York: Grossman Publishers, 1973), p. 189.

55. The source for this discussion is Martin Abramson, "Kreuger, Swedish Match King, Struck It Rich, Investors Lost," *Milwaukee Journal*, June 18, 1962, Green Sheet, pp. 1–2.

56. The source of this discussion is "Crime: The Man Who Fooled Everybody," *Time*, June 4, 1965, pp. 20–21.

57. For a detailed discussion of the Estes operation see "Estes: Three-Sided Country Slicker," *Fortune*, **66** (July 1962), pp. 166–170, 269–281.

58. Ibid., p. 166.

59. For a discussion of Ponzi's career see Jay Robert Nash, *Bloodletters and Badmen: A Narrative Encyclopedia of American Criminals from the Pilgrims to the Present* (New York: M. Evans and Co., 1973), pp. 448–451.

60. The discussion is based on David McClintick, "The Big Write-Off: Rich Investors' Losses in New 'Ponzi Scheme' Could Hit $100 Million," *Wall Street Journal*, June 26, 1974, pp. 1, 23.

61. The discussion is based on Jean Carper, *Not with a Gun* (New York: Grossman Publishers, 1973).

62. Ibid., p. 205.

63. Julian B. Roebuck and Robert Bruce Hunter, "Medical Quackery As Deviant Behavior," *Criminology*, **8** (May 1970), pp. 46–62. The examples are from that article and from U.S. Congress, Senate, Special Committee on

Aging, *Frauds and Deceptions Affecting the Elderly; Investigations, Findings, and Recommendations: 1964,* A Report of the Subcommittee on Frauds and Misrepresentations Affecting the Elderly, 80th Cong., 1st sess., January 31, 1965, pp. 1–11.

64. U.S. Congress, *Frauds and Deceptions,* p. 8.

65. Ibid., p. 9.

66. A similar theme is developed in Edwin M. Schur, *Our Criminal Society: The Social and Legal Sources of Crime in America* (Englewood Cliffs, N.J.: Prentice-Hall, 1969), pp. 177–188.

67. David W. Maurer, *The Big Con: A Story of the Confidence Man and the Confidence Game* (New York: Signet Books, 1962), pp. 13–14.

68. Michael T. Kaufman, "Elderly Warned of Con Games As Complaints Rise," *New York Times,* March 28, 1973, p. 45. For the most thorough, though dated, compilation of types of confidence games see John C. R. MacDonald, *Crime Is a Business* (Stanford, Calif.: Stanford University Press, 1939).

69. The problem of distinguishing "crime that is organized" from "organized crime" is discussed in Thomas C. Schelling, "What Is the Business of Organized Crime?" *Journal of Public Law,* 20:1 (1971), pp. 71–84. See also Joseph L. Albini, *The American Mafia: Genesis of a Legend* (New York: Appleton-Century-Crofts, 1971), pp. 35–48.

70. The President's Commission on Law Enforcement and Administration of Justice, *Task Force Report: Organized Crime* (Washington, D.C.: Government Printing Office, 1967), p. 1.

71. Donald R. Cressey, *Theft of the Nation: The Structure and Operations of Organized Crime in America* (New York: Harper & Row, 1969), pp. 72–74.

72. Ibid., pp. 248–289; and Albini, *American Mafia,* pp. 67–77.

73. Cressey, *Theft of the Nation,* p. 253.

74. Ibid., pp. 250–251.

75. William J. Chambliss, "Vice, Corruption, Bureaucracy, and Power," *Wisconsin Law Review,* 4 (1971), pp. 1150–1173; see also John A. Gardiner, *The Politics of Corruption: Organized Crime in an American City* (New York: Russell Sage Foundation, 1970).

76. Cressey, *Theft of the Nation,* p. 248.

77. Mary Breasted, "Gallos vs. Colombos, Brooklyn's War Without End," *New York Times,* September 22, 1974, Section 4, p. 6.

78. Cressey, *Theft of the Nation,* pp. 165–166, 179–180.

79. Robert T. Anderson, "From Mafia to Cosa Nostra," *American Journal of Sociology,* 71 (November 1965), pp. 302–310.

80. Cressey, *Theft of the Nation,* pp. x–xi.

81. Albini, *American Mafia,* p. 258; cf. pp. 264–267, 300–302.

82. John E. Conklin, "Organized Crime and American Society," in *The Crime Establishment: Organized Crime and American Society,* ed. John E. Conklin (Englewood Cliffs, N.J.: Prentice-Hall, 1973), p. 13. See also Francis A. J. Ianni, *A Family Business: Kinship and Social Control in Organized Crime,* (New York: Russell Sage Foundation, 1972), pp. 87–106, 109–110.

83. Gus Tyler, ed. *Organized Crime in America: A Book of Readings* (Ann Arbor: University of Michigan Press, 1962), p. 150.

84. The discussion is based primarily on Tyler, *Organized Crime,* with emphasis on Tyler's editorial comments and his reprinted selection from Herbert

Asbury, *The Gangs of New York* (New York: Alfred A. Knopf, 1927), pp. 89–178 *passim*. See also Albini, *American Mafia*, pp. 177–211.

85. Stuart L. Hills, *Crime, Power, and Morality: The Criminal Law Process in the United States* (Scranton, Pa.: Chandler Publishing, 1971), p. 109.

86. For discussions of why Italians dominate contemporary organized crime see Daniel Bell, "Crime As an American Way of Life: A Queer Ladder of Social Mobility," in *The End of Ideology*, rev. ed., ed. Daniel Bell (New York: Free Press, 1962), pp. 127–150; and Ianni, *A Family Business, pp. 54–59.*

87. Francis A. J. Ianni, *Black Mafia: Ethnic Succession in Organized Crime* (New York: Simon and Schuster, 1974), pp. 313–330 *passim*.

88. These are suggested by Gus Tyler, "The Crime Corporation," in *Current Perspectives on Criminal Behavior: Original Essays on Criminology*, ed. Abraham S. Blumberg (New York: Alfred A. Knopf, 1974), pp. 198–205.

89. Ibid., p. 201; and Ianni, *A Family Business*, p. 6.

90. Nicholas Gage, "Organized Crime in City Bleeds Slums of Millions," *New York Times*, September 27, 1970, Section 1, p. 85.

91. The discussion is based on Cressey, *Theft of the Nation*, pp. 77–91.

92. Tyler, "The Crime Corporation," pp. 201–202.

93. Gage, "Organized Crime in the City," p. 85.

94. This discussion is based on Linda Charlton, "Crime Thrives on Bootlegged Cigarettes," *New York Times*, May 9, 1971, Section 1, pp. 1, 42.

95. "Truck Hijacking in City Is a $4.2-Million Business," *New York Times*, May 20, 1974, pp. 1, 15.

96. Jack Anderson, "Alarming Rise Noted in Securities Crimes," *Toledo Blade*, January 19, 1975, Section B, p. 5. For a sociological analysis of this operation see Matthew G. Yeager, "The Gangster as White Collar Criminal: Organized Crime and Stolen Securities," *Issues in Criminology*, **8** (Spring 1973), pp. 49–73.

97. Testimony of Philip R. Manuel in U.S. Congress, Senate, Subcommittee on Investigations, *Hearings Before the Permanent Subcommittee on Investigations of the Committee on Government Operations*, 92nd Cong., 1st sess., June 8, 9, 10, and 16, 1971, pp. 63–64.

98. Tyler, "The Crime Corporation," p. 203.

99. Ianni, *A Family Business*, p. 6. For a description of one "family's" legitimate business interests, see pp. 87–106.

100. The President's Commission, *Organized Crime*, p. 5.

101. Edward J. De Franco, *Anatomy of a Scam: A Case Study of a Planned Bankruptcy by Organized Crime* (Washington, D.C.: U.S. Department of Justice, November 1973), pp. 5–7.

8 DEVIANT DRUG USE

If someone were to confide in you that the teacher of this course is using drugs, what would your reaction be? Would you take a closer look at those cigarettes he or she relies on so much? Would you start looking for needle marks, glazed eyes, slurred speech, incomprehensibility? (Indeed, drug use may seem to be a likely explanation for several puzzling aspects of this course including the unintelligible questions on examinations). Or would you decide that the statement "using drugs" really conveys little information?

It would certainly be logical to adopt the last position. After all, there are many forms of drugs and people use them for many reasons. For example, they take antibiotics to cure sore throats, insulin to relieve the symptoms of diabetes, or plain aspirin for headaches. Furthermore, many people consume drugs every day without consciously thinking of them as drugs: those who smoke inhale an alkaloid known as nicotine that stimulates the nervous system; those who drink coffee, tea, and Coca-Cola are taking caffeine, another alkaloid and stimulant, which is also found in the student's final exam time friend, No-Doz. In short, your knowledge of your teacher would be enhanced very little by the hypothetical statement.

The term *drug* is a very broad and nebulous concept. *A drug is any substance other than food that by its chemical nature affects the structure or function of the living organism.*[1] This definition is so broad that about all we can say about people who use drugs is that they are taking something other than food that alters them in some manner. Only when we specify the intended effects of the drug use do we come any closer to understanding either the user or the reaction to the user. Our information about the teacher is increased somewhat if we find that he or she is doing any of the following: taking antihistamines to control a runny nose, taking barbiturates to calm shattered nerves, or taking arsenic to end it all.

But which of these is *deviant* drug use? The use of antihistamines to avoid symptoms of a cold or hay fever seems unlikely to be defined as deviant unless one professes allegiance to Christian Science, a religion advocating that disease should be treated only by spiritual means. Doing anything with the express intent of destroying yourself is definitely frowned upon in the United States—whether you use arsenic or a shotgun you will probably end up in a mental hospital should you fail. But the use of barbiturates is a mixed picture. Barbiturates are widely available through medical prescription, but taking them without a prescription makes one liable to imprisonment for using a dangerous drug. Clearly, the deviant aspect of drug use is a matter of ethical and political definition.

Drug Use As Deviance

From the legal standpoint most deviant drug use in the United States involves *psychoactive drugs—substances with the capacity to influence behavior by altering feeling, mood, perception, or other mental states.* There are two fundamental means of modifying one's relationship with the environment; either change the environment or change your insight into that environment. Generally, the former is more satisfying, but the latter is more convenient. There are several ways to change one's insights, including a change in religion, political beliefs, or general life philosophy. But a common means is through the use of psychoactive drugs. Distraught parents and teachers gulp barbiturates, and suddenly the unpredictable and ungrateful youth of the nation become much easier to bear. Truck drivers on the road and students cramming for examinations find that amphetamines keep them attentive to their monotonous tasks.

Barbiturates and amphetamines are psychoactive drugs, as are alcohol, caffeine, nicotine, tranquilizers, heroin, marihuana, and LSD. They all have the *capacity* to alter one's mental state. The term *capacity* is used advisedly here since the effect of any specific drug upon any specific person is impossible to gauge. As Erich Goode points out, the consequences of taking a particular drug are not based solely upon the properties of chemicals, but also upon an individual user's expectations and experiences with the drug:

> All drugs will have a range of physiological sequelae, will touch off a number of physiological responses in the organism. But it takes a human consciousness to react to these effects subjectively—that is, to internally *experience* and *reflect on* these "effects." Some of these effects may be ignored; others will be enjoyed and sought out under the influence. . . . Users learn that certain effects are "supposed" to happen and that others will not. These expectations and group definitions of drug effects have a powerful influence on what the user experiences under the influence.[2]

The variability of drug effects is easily exemplified by most persons' experiences with individuals under the influence of alcohol: some become lively and outgoing, others become morose and withdrawn, and still others become belligerent and aggressive. Furthermore, the social influences of drug effects make it difficult to automatically translate the results of tests on laboratory animals to humans. For example, Goode cites the case of mice and rats who, under the influence of the active chemical in marihuana, lose interest in food and sex, while many humans find that smoking marihuana increases their interest in both.[3]

SOME TERMINOLOGY

Keeping in mind the variations in effects on human behavior, we can divide the psychoactive drugs into the following categories: *depressants, stimulants, hallucinogens,* and *marihuana.*[4] We use this classification to sort out some common *physiological* responses among the great array of different drugs, but within each category the drugs vary both in their potential for affecting mental states and in their particular effects, depending upon individual users and the context of drug use. For example, caffeine and cocaine are both stimulants, but cocaine has a much greater capability of altering perception and behavior. Also, persons using morphine (a drug derived from opium) will vary in their perceptions of the physiological experience depending on whether they are using it to kill pain or to get high.

1. *Depressants* serve to depress the central nervous system; that is, they act as sedatives by lowering its activity. They can produce relaxation, drowsiness, deadening of pain, and easing of anxiety. At sufficient dosage levels they can cause death. For some users, depressants can also cause euphoria (a feeling of well-being), belligerence, or even depression.
2. *Stimulants,* on the other hand, perform the opposite function from depressants—they are primarily capable of producing increased ac-

tivity, alertness, and excitation. Depending on the circumstances of use, they may result in feelings of elation, a sense of intellectual brilliance, euphoria, irritability, or anxiety.

3. *Hallucinogens,* as the term suggests, produce sensory experiences which represent a "reality" not verifiable in the non-drug state. Generally, however, the user recognizes them as being connected with the drug. The effects can be quite dramatic: feeling that time is no longer measurable or relevant, reacting emotionally to objects that otherwise would be unnoticed and unimportant (fly specks on window, lint on rug, and so on), fusing of senses ("seeing" music, or "smelling" love), and losing one's identity in the universe, woodwork, or whatever.[5]

One user of a hallucinogen known as psilocybin describes his experience this way:

> Over the mantle there was a portrait of some great-grand relative who had frowned down on the living room for years and whom Mike and I had nicknamed Ugly Nell. Suddenly, Mike said gravely, "Quick, look at Ugly Nell—she just winked."
>
> I looked up at the old girl to find her smiling broadly. Mike had already gone into peals of laughter over this hallucination, and in a few moments I was also laughing hysterically. We kept pointing at the portrait, laughing so hard that we fell onto the floor. It took great will power to calm ourselves down and sit quietly listening to the rich sounds of the stylus swishing back and forth near the center of the record. When I rose to turn the player off, Mike commented, "Good, there's too much going on now anyway." . . .
>
> With the idea that we should eat in order to experience heightened sense of taste, I pointed toward the kitchen and mumbled something about food. Mike understood perfectly and accompanied me into the next room. When I opened the door of the freezer, I had a strong temptation to run my fingers over everything inside and feel different textures of the frozen foods. Instead, I took out two TV dinners and peeled the foil coverings back. We both had great fun feeling the fried chicken inside, for it was at once greasy, crisp, and frozen, and we could feel these qualities separately as well as all at once. I then bit into a pea with my front teeth, pressing the halves to the roof of my mouth. I could taste the ice and the pea as distinct properties and also noticed a great change in taste and texture as the pea thawed. Mike then tried one. "It tastes green," he said. I tested another. "Yes, green, too." . . .
>
>   *   *   *
>
> [Later when we] settled back to listen to Berlioz's *Symphonie Fantastique,* we were slowly "coming down," yet listening to music was still a unique experience. The sound surrounds you—you virtually drown in it. It becomes a physical sensation, almost as tactile as taking a bath, and different sounds seem to have different textures: you can feel the high notes just as you can normally feel the bass. Your listening mind seems to be

working so fast that you can fully comprehend each single sound before the next one comes along.[6]

4. *Marihuana* was once classified as a hallucinogen but today researchers often place it in a class by itself. When used at sufficient strength it can produce effects associated with hallucinogens: loss of time sense and a feeling of increased sensory perception. Goode describes the most common effects mentioned by users.

Euphoria; relaxation; a sense of one's mind wandering, a kind of stream of consciousness; a sensation that time is slowed down; . . . an impairment of one's short-term memory; a feeling of ravenous hunger; a strong increase in the enjoyment of one's senses—food tastes better, music sounds richer, more exciting, touch becomes more sensuous, one's sexual orgasm becomes more intense; one feels far more inclined to find more things amusing, silly, uproarious; moving about feels more sinuous, smoother, more graceful and sensuous; one feels a kind of "floating" sensation; there is a reduced and impaired ability to think logically, rationally, in a linear fashion; one finds it difficult or impossible to read well or at all; there is a kind of "eureka" feeling about ordinarily common and usually uninteresting experiences and insights.[7]

The basic types of common illegally used psychoactive drugs are presented in Table 8-1 with some of their more specific characteristics. There are many drugs not specifically listed there—for example, there are several kinds of barbiturates (Amytal, Nembutal, Seconal, and others), which can be divided into short-acting and long-acting substances. And, of course, there are several kinds of alcohol (beer, gin, wine, and so on)—but these are essentially variations within the basic types, and their differences are not important to this discussion.

Some of the terminology in the table requires explanation, particularly because it is relevant to why the use of some drugs is labeled as deviant. The first term is *tolerance*. This refers to the ability of the human system to adapt to and to build up resistance to the effects of some drugs. A person has built up a tolerance to a drug when he or she must increase the dosage in order to obtain the effects of earlier dosages. Heroin has an especially high potential for tolerance. Long-term users often take daily doses that would kill others not experienced with the drug.

A second term of importance is *physical dependence*. By this is meant that the human system adapts to prolonged use of the drug in such a manner that *withdrawal symptoms* occur when use is stopped. You will note in Table 8-1 that the depressants have the potential for physical dependence; however, the symptoms differ somewhat among alcohol, barbiturates, and heroin. The withdrawal symptoms of alcohol and heroin—drugs which we will consider in detail—are

TABLE 8-1
COMMON ILLEGALLY USED PSYCHOACTIVE DRUGS

Type-Name	Legal Status *	Tolerance	Physical Dependence	Comments
Depressants				
Alcohol (booze, liquid refreshment, hootch, suds, brew)	Restrictions on sale, but easily available. Persons under its influence subject to minor penalties.	Yes	Yes	Widely used.
Barbiturates (barbs, dolls, phennies, red devils, sopers, yellow jackets)	Legal only through prescription. Major to moderate penalties depending upon jurisdiction.	Yes	Yes	Widely used both legally and illegally.
Heroin (H, horse, junk, shit, smack)	Unavailable legally. Major penalties.	Yes	Yes	Not widely used relative to most other drugs.
Stimulants				
Amphetamines (bennies, pep pills, uppers)	Legal only through prescription. Major to moderate penalties.	Yes	No	Widely used both legally and illegally. Methedrine (speed) is a very potent form.
Cocaine (coke, snow)	Unavailable legally. Major penalties.	Yes	No	Possibly the drug with the fastest growing popularity.
Hallucinogens				
LSD (acid)	Unavailable legally. Major to moderate penalties.	Yes	No	Also called *psychedelics*.
Marihuana (grass, pot, tea)	Unavailable legally. Major to minor penalties depending upon jurisdiction.	No	No	Hashish (hash) is an imported, more potent form.

* The penalties refer to simple possession of the drug. Illegally selling or dealing and possession for sale nearly always carry more severe penalties. The distinction between simple possession and possession for sale is based on the quantity of the drug.

presented here. Alcohol withdrawal symptoms include tremors, sweating, nausea, rapid heart beat, rise in temperature, jerky reflexes; in cases where large amounts have been consumed over a long period, convulsions and delirium tremens may occur. Delirium tremens is characterized by confusion, delusions, and vivid visual hallucinations—often humorously referred to as "pink elephants," although the victim undoubtedly is not laughing. Heroin withdrawal can cause anxiety, restlessness, body aches, insomnia, yawning, tears, runny nose, perspiration, contraction of the pupils, gooseflesh, hot flushes, nausea, bowel movements, diarrhea, rise in body temperature and respiratory rates, abdominal cramps, ejaculations, and loss of body weight.[8] It should be noted, however, that withdrawal from heroin is not necessarily the wrenching agony portrayed by the mass media. In many respects it resembles the effects of the flu. But its intensity varies according to the individual and to the strength of the usual drug dosage. Some heavy users can kick their habit and experience minor irritations, but some light to moderate users act as though they were at death's door. In short, psychological as well as physiological influences operate in the withdrawal process.

In our discussion of drug terminology we must touch on some other concepts frequently associated with deviant drug use. One of these is the term, *addiction*. Although it is easy to assume that addiction is a widely accepted *scientific* term, in fact it is not. For one thing the term has strong moral and emotional overtones. Try shouting "There's an addict at the door!" and everybody within earshot will reach for weapons. For another, the term is highly imprecise. The confusion stems from the variety of patterns characterizing the use of drugs. The original intent of the term was to distinguish repetitive drug use resulting from a *compulsion* associated with a combination of *tolerance, physical dependence,* and a *psychic* (sometimes called psychological) *dependence.* Another term, *drug habituation,* was generally applied to repetitive drug use associated with only a psychic dependence.

Part of the problem with the addiction-habituation conceptualization stems from the very slippery notion of *compulsion.* The term suggests a loss of control—the person must have the drug, the effects of the drug completely dominate the user's life, and no alternative ways of behaving are open except as dictated by the drug. Some people do indeed seem to exhibit compulsive behavior but it is difficult, if not impossible, to specify the point at which it is present. Regardless of how often a drug is used by an individual, when can that person's behavior be described as a matter of *having* to take the drug rather than merely *wanting* to?

To complicate matters there is a tendency to link compulsion only with those drugs having a high potential for physical dependence.

Apparent compulsive use can also arise with drugs that do not cause physical dependence. Furthermore, the difference between individuals who must have that cup of coffee, a tranquilizer, or a shot of heroin, is only a matter of degree. Who is more addicted: the guy who bums cigarettes saying he "has to have another coffin nail," or the junkie cruising the department store for goods he can convert into his next fix?

As with so many facets of social life, there are no clear-cut distinctions that can be made between one type of individual and another. The world is not divided into addicts, habitual users, and everyone else. At best we can say that there are drug users and nonusers, and the drug users vary according to their *dependence* upon drugs. But such dependence cannot be automatically measured by anything we know about the drug itself. Regardless of the chemical qualities of a drug, the effects it produces, the ability to build tolerance, or the likelihood of withdrawal symptoms, the way the drug is used varies tremendously from one individual to another. In short, *patterns of drug use are more contingent upon personality and social factors than upon attributes of the drugs.*[9]

The National Commission on Marihuana and Drug Abuse (commonly known as the Shafer Commission after its chairman, Raymond P. Shafer) rejected the notions of habituation and addiction in favor of a *continuum of drug dependence* ranging from minimal preoccupation with drug-using to compulsive dependence as indicated by total preoccupation at the expense of other activities such as employment, family relations, health, and so on. In order to impose some structure upon the continuum, the commission suggested the drug use patterns shown in Table 8–2.

The reader will note that as one approaches the more dependent end of the continuum the possibility of the user's experiencing harm increases. But for many psychoactive drugs societal reaction against their use hinges not on the user's degree of dependence but upon mere use. It makes no difference whether you smoke a single marihuana cigarette a year, or one every four hours; if you are caught you are liable to legal sanctions. This leads us to still another term often used in the context of deviant drug use: *drug abuse.* The following quotation was selected from a federal government pamphlet entitled *Drugs of Abuse:*

> Man has used drugs since the beginning of time. He also abused these powerful drugs to escape from life and betrayed their medicinal value. Today, drug abuse remains a problem to society. To solve the problem, man must educate himself to the potent nature of the drugs of abuse. . . . Doctors prescribe morphine to relieve pain, but addicts rank it second to heroin. They may abuse morphine when heroin is scarce. . . . [Legal] narcotics [narcotics—a nonscientific term originally referring to pain-killers,

TABLE 8–2
A TYPOLOGY OF DRUG DEPENDENCE *

Type of Use	Frequency of Use	Dosage	Motivation	Consequences
Experimental	10 or fewer times (total)	Low	Curiosity	Generally none; occasional psychological or physiological damage
Social-Recreational	Highly variable, but greater than experimental	Low-moderate	Sharing a pleasurable experience with friends	Generally none; possible escalation to greater frequency and dosage
Circumstantial-Situational	Highly variable	Low-moderate	Adjusting to a situation—lowering stress, preparing for examinations, getting "up" for athletic contests, and so on	Possible reliance on drug for other situations leading to escalation of use
Intensified	At least daily	High	Achieving relief from persistent situation; to be "normal"	Possible decrease in efficiency for other functions
Compulsive	Continuous	Very high	Seeking continuous security or comfort either from situations leading to initial drug use or from later consequences of drug use—loss of job, breakup of family, withdrawal symptoms, and so on	Abandonment of other functions

* Derived from National Commission on Marihuana and Drug Abuse, *Drug Use in America: Problem in Perspective* (Washington, D.C.: Government Printing Office, 1973), pp. 94–98, 137.

now denoting more potent drugs such as opium, morphine, cocaine, and their derivatives] contain small amounts of narcotic drugs in combination with other drugs. They include codeine cough syrups and preparations of camphorated tincture of opium such as paregoric. When used as directed, they are reasonably safe and free of addiction potential. But young people frequently abuse exempt narcotics and addicts may substitute them when more potent drugs are not available.[10]

Can you guess from these statements what *abuse* really is? The word has no complex technical meaning; it is simply another way of saying something is wrong. It is a value term that certainly has histori- cal *precedent; self-abuse* is a time-honored term for masturbation. By extension, mothers could accuse children of abusing cookies be- tween meals, and teachers might be dismayed by students abusing examination questions. In reference to psychoactive drugs, law en- forcement officials have adopted an obvious code; physicians and re- spectable patients *use* drugs, all others *abuse* them. Drug abuse is clearly a value term, and the Shafer Commission recommended that it be dropped.

> The term has no functional utility and has become no more than an arbi- trary code word for drug use which is presently considered wrong. Con- tinued use of this term, with its emotional overtones, will serve only to perpetuate confused public attitudes about drug-using behavior.
>
> Drug abuse, or any similar term, creates an impression that all drug- using behavior falls in one of two clear-cut spheres: drug use which is good, safe, beneficial and without social consequence; and drug "abuse" which is bad, harmful, without benefit and carrying high social cost. From either a descriptive or an evaluative standpoint, the matter is much too complex to be handled in such a polarized fashion.[11]

It is apparent that the official American drug policy is to eliminate nonmedical drug use.[12] In actual practice the implementation of this policy is surrounded by many inconsistencies. For example, alco- holic beverages, coffee, and tobacco contain psychoactive drugs, and they are *used* as psychoactive substances, not as medicine, by the public. (The "medicinal" quality of alcohol has long been a source of American humor, as illustrated in a quip by W. C. Fields, "Always carry a flagon of whiskey in case of snakebite and further- more always carry a small snake.")

In addition, a sizeable proportion of the American public obtains drugs legally through prescription, but uses them as mind-altering substances. A survey conducted by the Shafer Commission found that 10 per cent of the adult population used ethical psychoactive drugs (sedatives, tranquilizers, and stimulants) for nonmedical purposes: to see how they work, to help accomplish something, to enjoy the feel- ing, and so on.[13] Furthermore, these drugs are typically prescribed for nonmedical reasons—to help relax, to relieve anxiety, to help cope with day-to-day experiences. They are not meant to cure, but to help deal with harsh non-drug realities.

Considering the numbers of people who drink alcoholic beverages, smoke, use ethical psychoactive drugs, and use over-the-counter drugs such as No-Doz, Compoz, and Sominex, one can only conclude that official objection to psychoactive drug use arises not solely on the basis of medical versus nonmedical usage. The majority of Americans use some form of drugs for other than medical reasons, but most who are caught in the net of illegal drug use—the "abusers"—are the relatively powerless: the poor, the black, and the uneducated. In this chapter the reader should bear in mind that there is a sizeable amount of psychoactive drug use by the more "respectable," and that such use is encouraged by a multimillion dollar industry that constantly advertises to Americans how pleasant drugs can be. Every home with a television set has a pusher right in the living room.

The remainder of this chapter will be devoted to discussions of three types of psychoactive drugs. They have been selected for the contrasts they offer. *Alcohol* is a widely used legal drug leading to many forms of deviant behavior; *heroin* is an illegal drug of limited use leading to some forms of deviant behavior; and *marihuana* is a widely used illegal drug leading to practically no form of deviant behavior.

Alcohol

"A woman drove me to drink, and I never even
wrote to thank her."
W. C. Fields

It is appropriate to open the section on alcohol with another quotation by W. C. Fields because he represented the ambivalence Americans feel toward drink. Drinking is seen as congenial, disgusting, escapist, or pitiful, depending upon your perspective. The cocktail party is an American institution where people find refuge from the trials of everyday drudgery; the conversation becomes increasingly witty as pleasant people sample hors d'oeuvres along with martinis and whiskey sours. But skid row is an American institution too. Here the company is less attractive; men in vomit-stained clothes stand about sampling bottles of Thunderbird wrapped in brown paper bags. The one thing that cocktail parties and skid row have in common is alcohol. No psychoactive drug is so frequently used, and none brings about so much joy and misery at the same time.

It was not until 1857 that the chemical origins of alcohol were discovered by Louis Pasteur, but the social origins reach far into history. Sometime in our dimmest past, someone discovered that fruit juices provided unusual effects after being exposed to the air in a warm place. It was probably about the same time or shortly thereafter that someone discovered that a broth made of cereals ferments into interesting liquids if malt is added—thus, the basis of beer and ale was found. The more potent beverages—whiskey, gin, brandy, and so on—had to await the discovery of the distillation process, but the wine and beer of early times were clearly capable of attracting an enthusiastic following. Egypt had a brewery flourishing in 3700 B.C., and taverns were so common in Babylonia that around 2300 B.C. King Hammurabi issued regulations concerning their management. The Bible is filled with references to wine, ranging from the Psalms ("Wine that maketh glad the heart of man": Psalms 104:15) to the miracle of Cana where Christ changed water into wine for a wedding party. It was St. Paul who counselled his young colleague Timothy, "Drink no longer water, but use a little wine for thy stomach's sake and thine own infirmities" (I Timothy 5:23).[14]

But the importance of alcohol in history is best exemplified by the Greeks and Romans.

> [The Greek god, Dionysus,] more than any other, epitomizes the story of alcohol—its derivation from plants, man's need of it, and even his occasional slavery to it. For most of his life Dionysus was carefully excluded from Olympus, a goal open only to the greatest. At first he seems to have been no more than god of vegetation in general, with no implication of special competence or knowledge. Later he became the specific custodian of the vine, from which he gradually became the god of what the vine produced. From being the god of wine, no Greek could deny him ultimately the right to become the god of what wine might do. As the god of intoxication Dionysus was finally admitted to Olympus. . . .
>
> The Romans, far less temperate than the lucid Greeks, imported the god Dionysus, but changed his name. For them, and ever since, he became Bacchus, and *bacchanalian* a symbol of indulgence, which if not invented by the Romans was certainly perfected by them. As Martial saw it, Rome seemed "one vast saloon," and years later a Roman house of any pretensions, and some quite poor ones, included a *vomitorium*. Rome then consumed twenty-five million gallons of wine a year—about two quarts per week per head, including children and slaves.[15]

ALCOHOL AS A DRUG

Despite its link to the gods, alcohol is inescapably a drug, and as its dosage is increased it begins to affect the performance of the human system. The terms we usually associate with the extreme results are *intoxicated, drunk, plastered, three sheets to the wind,* and any of a variety of words and phrases designating someone who has drunk too much. As we have pointed out above, alcohol acts as a depressant on the central nervous system. Alcohol is not digested, but rather is immediately absorbed into the blood stream through the walls of the stomach and small intestine. The blood then rapidly carries it to the brain. As the level of alcohol in the blood rises, coordination, reaction time, vision, and general skilled performance levels are affected. If enough alcohol reaches the brain one begins to stagger, weave, and speak with a slur. It is possible to drink so much as to affect even automatic functions such as breathing after which, of course, death can occur.

Thus, intoxication is a matter of degree. With the development of devices to quickly measure the amount of alcohol in the blood the definition of *intoxication* or *influence* (Ohio, for example, has a crime of driving under the *influence* of alcohol) became a matter of legislation. There is still uncertainty about what alcohol level inevitably results in detectable influences on reflexes, reaction time, and other skills; however, it is generally agreed that .03 to .05 per cent alcohol in the blood produces obvious changes.[16] In most states you are presumed too intoxicated to drive an automobile if your alcohol level is .10 per cent or above.

The alcohol content of the blood at any given moment depends upon several factors: speed of drinking, body weight, presence of food in the stomach, body chemistry, and type of beverage. Table 8-3 shows the general relationship between blood-alcohol levels and quantity of beverage of an average 155-pound individual who rapidly consumes 90-proof (45 per cent alcohol) whiskey on an empty stomach.

TABLE 8-3
BLOOD-ALCOHOL LEVELS AND SENSORIMOTOR BEHAVIOR

Quantity of 90-proof Whiskey	Percent Blood-Alcohol Level	Behavior
3 oz. (2 shots)	.05	Sedation; effects on sensorimotor skills become obvious
6 oz.	.10	Impairment to coordination and vision
12 oz.	.20	Would be called "drunk" by most observers; staggering, slurred speech, poor judgment
15 oz.	.30	Unconsciousness
30 oz.	.50 +	Heart beat and breath slow; death may result

Source: National Institute of Mental Health, *Alcohol and Alcoholism: Problems, Programs, and Progress,* rev. ed. (Rockville, Maryland: National Institute of Mental Health, 1972), p. 4. The "Behavior" column has been expanded by the author.

Increased blood-alcohol levels cause behaviors we usually associate with drunkenness, that is, behaviors other than reduced efficiency and performance. These behaviors concern the mood of drinkers and the way they behave socially under the influence of alcohol. This is a much more difficult issue than merely measuring reflex speed and visual acuity. People act in so many ways: they fight, they become easier to seduce, they become saddened, they laugh a lot, they get sullen, they become philosophical, they curse, they have no interest in sex, they sing, and so on. And "being drunk" is an important verbalized motive. People who "lose control" cannot really be blamed because they were "drunk." In 1974 a baseball game was forfeited by the Cleveland Indians because the home fans assaulted the visiting team. The reason: it was ten cent beer night, and anybody should know that a drunken crowd is likely to get out of hand. That particular gimmick to increase attendance will not be tried again for a while.

Such social behaviors are usually connected with the notion that alcohol impairs the higher brain functions by lowering inhibitions. Typical of this interpretation is the following:

> The apparent "stimulation" from alcohol is the result of the lower brain centers being released from higher brain controls. This reduces inhibitions, and behavior which is untoward when the individual is sober becomes acceptable. For example, ... an always proper, ladylike woman may become obscene and promiscuous when intoxicated.[17]

This is a particularly attractive notion. If it can be assumed that alcohol erodes an individual's reason and conscience, then all kinds of unwanted behavior by others and by ourselves become more acceptable, or at least more understandable. Although persons may be chided for getting drunk, *behavior while drunk* is not seen as an accurate reflection of who the persons really are. For example, one behavior particularly incomprehensible and disgusting to Americans is sexual contact between an adult and a child. Adult offenders in these cases are usually reluctant to claim that they were "normal" when the act or acts occurred; an especially popular excuse is that they had been drinking or were drunk at the time.[18] Armed with this excuse they specifically point out that if they have any problem at all, it is not a *sex* problem but a *drinking* problem.

However, the idea that alcohol incapacitates morals as well as sensorimotor skills is challenged by Craig MacAndrew and Robert B. Edgerton. In their study of drunken comportment they state that while differences between sober and drunken behavior are often great and quite obvious, the behavioral changes are inconsistent and vary from one time to another for a single individual, to say nothing of the differences between individuals.[19] In contrast to the diversity of drunken comportment in the United States, studies of other smaller, more homogeneous societies indicate that in some societies individuals get very drunk indeed, but exhibit no indication they have lost their inhibitions. In still other societies drunken behavior has changed over time, and in others the behavior varies according to the situation. The thesis that alcohol numbs the social control of persons simply cannot handle these differences among societies. MacAndrew and Edgerton conclude:

> Rather than viewing drunken comportment as a function of toxically disinhibited brains operating in impulse-driven bodies, we have recommended that what is fundamentally at issue are the learned relations that exist among men living together in a society. More specifically, we have contended that the way people comport themselves when they are drunk is determined not by alcohol's toxic assault upon the seat of moral judgment, conscience, or the like, but by what their society makes of and imparts to them concerning the state of drunkenness. . . .
>
> * * *
>
> Persons learn about drunkenness what their societies impart to them, and comporting themselves in consonance with these understandings they become living confirmations of their societies' teachings. We would propose that this formulation is similarly applicable to our own society, but with this difference: our society lacks a clear and consistent position regarding the scope of the excuse and is thus neither clear nor consistent in its teachings. Because our society's teachings are neither clear nor consistent, we lack unanimity of understanding; and where unanimity of understanding is lacking, we would argue that uniformity of practice is out of the question. Thus, although we all know that in our society the state of drunkenness carries with it an "increased freedom to be one's other self," the limits are vague and only sporadically enforced, and hence what (if anything) the plea of drunkenness will excuse in any specific case is similarly indeterminant. In such a situation, our formulation would lead us to expect that what people actually do when they are drunk will vary enormously; and this is precisely what we find when we look around us.[20]

ALCOHOL USE AND DEVIANCE

For Americans, alcohol is an unpredictable and dangerous drug. It can impair physical performance, persons under its influence often behave erratically and bring harm to themselves and others, and its continued use can lead to high degrees of dependence, physical deterioration, and great personal expense to self and to social relations.

As with practically all forms of deviance, statistics concerning the magnitude of alcohol-related problems must be handled with care. The following facts about alcohol in America have been derived from available data.

1. *The proportion of Americans drinking alcoholic beverages is increasing.* The evidence for this statement comes from Gallup surveys taken in 1939 and in 1974.[21] In 1939, 58 per cent of the adults eighteen years and older said they drank at least occasionally; by 1974 this figure had risen to 68 per cent—77 per cent of the males and 39 per cent of the females. The increase in drinkers has been nearly twice as great among females as among males.

Of course, by itself, the fact that more persons are drinking is of little consequence to anyone except breweries, vineyards, and distilleries. The problem is that for a certain proportion of the public, drinking will create grief for themselves and others. And it seems likely that an increase in the proportion of persons drinking occasionally will be accompanied by a similar increase in the proportion of those drinking more frequently and in greater quantity. The Gallup organization had no comparable figure for 1939, but in the 1974 sample 18 per cent of the drinkers claimed they "sometimes drink to excess," and 12 per cent admitted that their drinking "caused trouble in the family."

2. *A large proportion of interpersonal violence is related to alcohol use.* As we pointed out in Chapter 4, the majority of homicides and aggravated assaults, and nearly half of all forcible rapes may be alcohol-related. It is impossible to estimate even approximately the contribution that alcohol makes to violent situations, but because of the extent of its presence it cannot be ignored as a possible major factor in precipitating, or at least justifying, aggression.

3. *Alcohol offenses constitute the largest single arrest category.* In 1973, 18 per cent of all arrests made by police were for drunkenness. Another 9 per cent were for disorderly conduct and vagrancy—classifications often used by some police forces instead of a drunkenness charge. Yet another 10 per cent of the arrests were for driving under the influence. This means that 37 per cent of all arrests involve persons who legally, at least, had been drinking too much. Add still another 3 per cent of arrests for violation of liquor laws—selling to minors, violations of closing hours, and so on. The use of alcohol clearly emerges as *the* drug problem, especially when compared with the 7 per cent of arrests made for violation of the drug laws.[22]

One qualifying statement must be made about the above statistics: the percentage of arrests for alcohol-related offenses has been *decreasing* over the last few years, and will probably continue to do so. For example, in 1960 36 per cent of all arrests were for drunkenness alone. Adding disorderly conduct, vagrancy, and driving under the influence, the total comes to 56 per cent.[23] This does not mean that there are fewer persons today getting drunk; it simply reflects a change in legal policy. In many major cities police now utilize facilities specifically designed to provide medical and other services for those under the influence of alcohol. Referral to such detoxification or alcohol rehabilitation centers is used in lieu of arrest. Furthermore, some states such as Maine, Alaska, Iowa, Massachusetts, and Arizona have removed drunkenness as an offense from their legal codes.

These actions are consistent with recommendations made by the President's Commission on Law Enforcement and Administration of Justice in 1967. The commission observed that a small percentage of individuals accounted for a large percentage of arrests. (In 1972 the National Institute of Mental Health estimated that 40 per cent of all arrests for nontraffic, alcohol-related offenses were accounted for by 5 per cent of the persons arrested.) [24] An example of one such individual is Benson Begay of Phoenix, Arizona; between December 1948 and mid-1973 (with a gap of four years in the army), Benny was arrested 396 times for being drunk. As one officer put it, "Benny was doing a life sentence on the installment plan for liking beer." [25]

Recognizing that repeated incarceration does nothing to remedy the situation and that arresting drunks is very costly to the justice system, to say nothing of its impact on those arrested, the commission recommended:

> Drunkenness should not in itself be a criminal offense. Disorderly and other criminal conduct accompanied by drunkenness should remain punishable as separate crimes. . . . Communities should establish detoxification units as part of comprehensive treatment programs.[26]

4. *A large proportion of automobile fatalities and injuries are related to alcohol use.* A spokesman for the National Highway Traffic Safety Administration sums up that agency's research findings as follows:

> We believe that alcohol is the most pervasive single factor found in all fatal and serious highway crashes and that, in fact, alcohol plays a significant, if not controlling role in at least half of all highway fatalities and serious injury. Furthermore, we recognize that this half of highway fatalities is primarily the responsibility of a relatively small group of heavy or problem drinkers. Our data suggest that only one driver in four ever drinks heavily enough to become a significant threat on the highway due to alcohol, and that even among these individuals the majority of the problem lies in individuals whose alcohol consumption is so excessive that they give evidence of having a significant drinking problem.[27]

Specifically, the N.H.T.S.A. believes that 7 per cent of all drivers are problem drinkers and responsible for two thirds of all alcohol-related highway fatalities. Since over 55,000 lives are lost annually on our highways, the responsibility of these drinkers is very great indeed.

5. *Alcohol is dangerous to safety and health.* In addition to

automobile fatalities, alcohol provides other hazards to survival. Available data consistently indicate that persons under the influence of alcohol, particularly the excessive drinkers, are more vulnerable to higher injury and fatality rates than the general population. Various studies show that the following are all significantly higher among alcohol-dependent individuals: suicide, accidental poisoning, home accidents, occupational accidents, death by fire, and drowning.[28]

Besides making persons susceptible to accidental death, drinking is implicated in causing deterioration of the body's organs, particularly the heart, brain, and liver. Until recently alcohol dependence and physical impairment were assumed to be only indirectly related. The usual explanation was that as preoccupation with alcohol increased, concern over an adequate diet decreased, thus making the drinker more susceptible to disease. In short, it was believed that alcohol-associated diseases were the result of *malnutrition*. Current evidence, however, indicates that alcohol directly causes physical damage as well as reducing the consumption of nutrients.

The disease usually associated with alcohol dependency is *cirrhosis*—a disease of the liver. At least two out of three persons suffering from cirrhosis are dependent on alcohol. Recent research reveals that alcohol itself has a toxic effect on the liver that cannot be prevented by enriched diets; improper diets, in turn, aggravate the situation. The importance of this disease is evident from its position as the third leading killer—behind heart disease and cancer—of New Yorkers between the ages of twenty-five and sixty-four.[29]

Furthermore, it appears that the impact of alcohol on American society is increasing. According to statistics published by Metropolitan Life Insurance Company, deaths recorded as due to alcoholic disorders have risen considerably.[30] The most dramatic rise has been among nonwhite males—between 1958–59 and 1968–69 their mortality rate from such disorders jumped 132 per cent. For nonwhite females the increase was 103 per cent; white females, 55 per cent; and white males, 38 per cent. Metropolitan Life regards the statistics on alcohol-related mortality to be underreported because there is a reluctance to cite alcohol as a cause of death if it is possible to assign another cause or complication.

Despite inaccuracies in data, it is inescapable that more deaths, disease, and financial and emotional loss result from alcohol use than from all of the other psychoactive drugs combined. Not only is the drug lethal in itself, but it is a major factor in violent crime and accidents. An estimated $25 billion annually is lost through job absenteeism, lost production, medical expenses, and accidents resulting from alcohol. Then there are the intangible and unmeasurable expenses of disrupted families, desertions, and countless emotional problems arising from drinking. Alcohol truly constitutes America's greatest drug problem.[31]

ALCOHOLISM, DISEASE, AND PROBLEM DRINKING

The problems associated with alcohol have nothing to do with your silver-haired grandmother sipping a Christmas sherry, nor with the vast majority of drinkers whose use of alcohol never gets them into difficulty with their health, their employer, their family, or the law. As one might infer from the previous section there appears to be a hard core of users who constitute the principal source of arrests for intoxication and who end up in the alcohol mortality statistics.

In the unlikely event that a Martian landed in your backyard and said, "Take me to your alcoholics," where would you take her, him, or it? Assuming that the visitor would like to see them in their natural setting rather than in a hospital, you would probably include on your tour the skid row of any major city. Here the Martian would find a neighborhood of rundown buildings containing cheap hotels, employment agencies for unskilled labor, mission houses, and many bars. Its residents would be almost exclusively men at the very bottom rung of the social ladder, men homeless and without power or attachment to the rest of society.[32]

It is a popular notion that the alcoholic is likely to end up on skid row, and persons of evangelic fervor find it easy to draw parallels between drink and sin as well as between the physical-mental-social degradations and hell. Despite this moral lesson your Martian friend would leave earth with an inaccurate impression of excessive drinking in America, were skid row the only stop on the tour. In the first place he would be misinformed about the amount of drinking that occurs on skid row. Howard M. Bahr tells us:

> Although perhaps one man out of every three skid row men is a problem drinker for whom drinking is the dominant activity of life rather than an avocation, most skid row men are not problem drinkers, and they are not on skid row because of their drinking. Nevertheless, the proportion of problem drinkers in the skid row population is higher than in any other urban neighborhood. Merited or not, the stigma of alcoholism is apt to be imputed to the possessor of a skid row address.[33]

Second, the Martian would have no inkling of the extent of alcoholism in America generally. Not only are skid rows disappearing (the homeless men are being dispersed, they are not disappearing), but they contain merely a small fraction of all alcoholics. Most estimates claim that no more than 3 to 8 per cent of all alcoholics are found on skid row. Even if you had taken your friend to the various alcohol treatment facilities you would still be missing an estimated 70 to 85 per cent of the nation's alcoholics.

Well then, how many alcoholics are there? According to Earl Rubington the best estimate we have is derived from a formula involving the number of deaths as a result of cirrhosis. This method has been criticized, but it remains the best we have and it shows that there are

5.5 million alcoholics in America.[34] (For all its problems the cirrhosis formula for alcoholism is a model of precision when compared with the "guesstimates" concerning heroin or other illegitimate drugs. As a point of comparison, most experts would probably accept a half million as the approximate number of heroin addicts.)

This brings us to an issue that we have been purposely avoiding: exactly what or whom are we talking about? We have used the familiar term *alcoholics* so far, and the time has come to tackle the thorny problem of what this term is supposed to mean. Should you define alcoholism as "addiction to alcohol," you would satisfy the overwhelming majority of the American public, but many researchers in the field are decidedly uneasy over this use of the term.

You will recall that earlier in the chapter we rejected the notion of addiction in favor of a continuum of drug dependence. Obviously as one approaches the extreme end of dependence (compulsive type), the more likely it is that the person will conform to what is usually thought of as *alcoholism*. But the problem with the term *alcoholism* is its lack of preciseness. One of the pioneers in the study of alcoholism, E. M. Jellinek, defined alcoholism very loosely as "any use of alcoholic beverages that causes any damage to the individual or society or both." [35] Jellinek was purposely broad in his definition to impress upon his readers that there are many species of alcoholism. He specifically suggested at least five types (which he labeled alpha through epsilon, based on the Greek alphabet), the apparently most prominent type in America being *gamma alcoholism*, characterized by tolerance, withdrawal symptoms, craving, loss of control, and the progression from psychological to physical dependence.[36]

Although Jellinek provided an extremely broad definition of alcoholism, his notion of gamma alcoholism clearly dominates the contemporary view of what alcoholism is. Included in that view is the philosophy of Alcoholics Anonymous, a large organization of individuals who have experienced problems with their drinking. Much of the attractiveness of Jellinek's concept lies in its labeling of alcoholism as a *disease;* alcoholism is seen not as the result of personal weakness or lack of will power but as a matter of *involuntary behavior* stemming from *predisposing factors* within the individual.[37]

In abbreviated form, these are the phases of alcoholism outlined by Jellinek.

1. Prealcoholic symptomatic phase. The prospective alcoholic begins drinking socially and discovers drink gives relief from tensions. Within a period of six months to two years the individual's tolerance for tension decreases and he or she drinks more frequently to obtain relief. (Jellinek claims the phases are less clear cut and frequently more rapid for women than for men.)

2. Prodromal phase. Begins with the onset of blackouts—amnesia or loss of memory the next day about what occurred while drinking the evening before. The individual becomes more preoccupied with alcohol at social gatherings; drinks ahead of time to ensure he or she gets enough; tries to get more drinks without the knowledge of others; and begins to develop some guilt about drinking.

3. Crucial phase. The drinker loses control thus marking the beginning of the "disease process." This does *not* refer to why the individual starts to drink—that is attributed to the original psychological factors. Instead, it means that once drinking begins the individual has no ability to control the quantity of drinks until the supply is exhausted or the individual is too intoxicated to continue. Several other symptoms occur in this phase, roughly in this order: the drinker acquires alibis or rationalizations for drinking; gets remorseful; has periods of total abstinence (goes on the wagon); changes drinking patterns; loses friends and jobs; behavior becomes alcohol-centered (he begins to be concerned about how activities might interfere with his drinking instead of how his drinking may affect his activities); contemplates or actually tries to escape problem by moving; protects alcohol supply by hiding beverages; and neglects diet.

4. Chronic phase. Begins with the onset of benders—prolonged bouts of intoxication lasting days at a time. Other symptoms that follow include: ethical deterioration; impairment of thinking; drinking of non-beverages containing alcohol (e.g., rubbing alcohol); loss of alcohol tolerance; indefinable fears; tremors; and recognition that he or she is totally defeated by alcohol. It is at the end of this phase that the individual is most accessible to treatment if it is available.[38]

Despite the popularity of Jellinek's scheme and the widespread belief that alcoholism is a disease, in recent years there has been increasing skepticism of such descriptions. For example, unless alcoholism is unlike any other form of disease, its symptoms should be uniform and consistent among persons labeled as alcoholics. But research indicates that the symptoms are neither uniform nor consistent in sequence. One review of the existing research concludes, "There is no single ordered progression of symptoms, to which an overwhelming majority of those labeled as 'alcoholics' comply."[39]

The problem is that viewing alcoholism as a disease is of no value in either describing *what alcoholism is* or *what causes it*. Although it is generally agreed that the "disease" involves a loss of control—in the sense that a person cannot refrain either from starting to drink or from continuing to drink once started—it is also recognized that no physiological factor has been isolated that accounts for this. What does this leave us with?—psychological dependency. And how do we know a person is psychologically dependent? Well, he or she does not seem to be able to stop drinking. So we find ourselves going around in circles.

Compounding the problem of the disease concept of alcoholism is the fact that the best known cure for drinking problems is Alcoholics Anonymous—an organization that uses no medicines or surgery. Instead, it relies on group support and "a power greater than ourselves" to neutralize "loss of control." In this sense alcoholism is a disease that a Christian Scientist can appreciate far more than a physician can.

This is not to imply that the theme of alcoholism as disease is without consequences. After all, persons with a disease are sick and cannot be responsible for their behavior. If you come down with mononucleosis you get sympathy, excused from classes, and lots of presents. Even if you contract venereal disease, at worst you are accused of sleeping with some disreputable character, but you are still given some time and treatment in order to recover. In short, being labeled sick affects the *social response* toward the persons so labeled. But insofar as alcoholism is concerned, the labeling process brings us no closer to understanding why people drink too much too often. As one critic of the disease concept points out:

> The major advantage of defining alcoholism as an illness is social. It legitimates social support for rehabilitation of the alcoholic instead of punishment. To say that alcoholism is an illness should not be construed as a statement about the etiology [the cause or origin] or treatment of alcoholism.[40]

Because alcoholism as a disease defies meaningful definition, it seems logical to treat alcohol dependence in the manner suggested earlier for all drug dependence—it is a matter of degree, not an all-or-nothing situation. This means abandoning attempts to study alcoholics, and instead concentrating on all persons whose drinking creates problems whether they seem to have control over their drinking or not.[41] Thus a notion of *problem drinking* is preferable to one of alcoholism. One of the most uncomplicated definitions is that given by the Cooperative Commission on the Study of Alcoholism: "Problem drinking is a *repetitive use of beverage alcohol causing physical, psychological, or social harm to the drinker or to others.*"[42]

CORRELATES OF PROBLEM DRINKING

The literature on drinking habits is enormous, diverse, and inconclusive, but one finding is consistent: drinking problems vary from one social group to another. The differences between ethnic groups are especially striking. For example, the impact of drinking among primitive societies ranges from nil to highly disruptive.[43] Among modern-day cultures, the Irish and the French have many drinking problems, but Jews, Italians, and Chinese have few.[44]

One of the more sophisticated studies of different ethnic groups within the United States was conducted by Richard Jessor and his associates.[45] Known as the Tri-Ethnic Study, it involved a small Colorado community of Spanish-American, American Indian, and Anglo-American members. The interdisciplinary research team set as their task the identification of the interrelationships between problem drinking and both social and personality variables.[46] The social variables were based on the concept of *anomie* as suggested by Robert K. Merton and others. The researchers proposed that the probability of problem drinking increases in groups characterized by: 1. lack of opportunities for group members to obtain valued goals of American culture, 2. lack of group consensus on what appropriate norms are, and 3. opportunities to learn and engage in deviant behavior.

The personality variables were based on a social learning theory similar, but not identical to, the *differential association theory* of Edwin H. Sutherland. Here the researchers proposed that the probability of problem drinking increases in groups characterized by the following: 1. the perception that the opportunity structure will not fulfill personal goals through socially acceptable means, 2. alienation—feelings of isolation and powerlessness, and 3. personal toleration of deviant behavior and a tendency toward immediate gratification.

In their results Jessor and his associates found that ethnic differences in problem drinking (Anglos having the fewest problems, Indians the most, and the Spanish in between) were related to each of the variables listed above. When the variables were used in combination they appeared to explain even more of the ethnic differences in problem drinking then when used singly. The researchers concluded that both social and personality variables were necessary to an adequate understanding of problem drinking.

The findings of the Tri-Ethnic project are supported in part by a study that we shall simply refer to as the *national survey*. This survey, conducted by Don Cahalan among others, is based on intensive personal interviews with adults representing the total population of the United States. The first stage of the study covered a sample of over 2,700 and occurred in 1964–65; [47] in 1967 a subsample of over 1,300 of the same individuals were again interviewed to detect any emerging drinking problems. These problems could be any of the following: binges; behavior associated with Jellinek's gamma alcoholism; feelings of psychological dependence on alcohol; and problems with relatives, friends, employment, the law, health, and finances.[48]

The national survey found drinking problems to be associated with the following variables:

1. Favorable attitudes toward drinking measured by responses to items such as "drinking does more good than harm," "good things can be said about drinking," and "I enjoy getting drunk once in a while."

2. Environmental support for heavy drinking—measured by items on how many friends and relatives drink heavily, parents' attitudes toward drinking, parents' drinking habits, and so on. This resembles Jessor's measurement of opportunities to learn and engage in deviant drinking behavior.

3. Alienation and maladjustment—measured by several items concerning feelings of helplessness, unhappiness, and so on. One scale used was identical to the one used by Jessor to measure alienation.

4. Impulsivity and nonconformity—measured by items similar to Jessor's toleration of deviant behavior and a tendency toward immediate gratification.

5. Unfavorable expectations—measured by items similar to Jessor's perception of the opportunity structure.

6. Looseness of social controls—this referred to primary group ties to family, close friends, and so on. Jessor had no similar measure.[49]

The national survey data indicate that all of these variables are related to drinking problems; however, some are clearly more predictive than others. For both sexes, *attitude toward drinking* is especially important. For males, who are more likely to have drinking problems, *environmental support* is also crucial. For females, *alienation and maladjustment* comprise the second most important variable.

Don Cahalan sums up the conclusions of the national survey this way:

> In general, the findings bear out the conclusion that both sociological and psychological factors are important in the development of problem drinking. The sociological—that is to say, the external environmental—factors determine whether the individual is encouraged or permitted to drink heavily; and the psychological factors can operate to help to bring about or to maintain a level of drinking which may be above that normally encouraged or permitted for the person's environment. Thus if one sets aside the major factor of attitude toward drinking, it was found that for men the external environmental factors played a more conspicuous role among the correlates of problem drinking, . . . while for women the variable of alienation and maladjustment appeared to be more influential than the sociological factors. . . . It is speculated that it takes more psychological pressures for a woman than for a man to persist in problem drinking, in the face of general disapprobation of heavy drinking for women.[50]

The fact that both the Tri-Ethnic and national surveys focus on the interaction between sociological and psychological variables should not mislead the reader into believing that such an approach predominates in alcohol studies. The amount of research and writing in the area is, to put it mildly, vast. But if any single theme is paramount it is that excessive drinking is symptomatic of maladjustment in individuals.[51] Although some recognition is given to social factors, the major thrust is that the individual cannot cope with his or her situation and turns to alcohol as a way out. A popular example is the dependency approach to problem drinking, which, most simply put, ascribes great significance to oral-dependency needs; alcohol gratifies these needs while allowing the individual to maintain a facade of adult independence and assertiveness.[52] In recent years, another individual-centered approach has attracted growing attention. This is the *power need* hypothesis suggested by David C. McClelland and his associates, who suggest that males drink primarily to feel strong, and that those who drink excessively have excessive power concerns and low inhibitory tendencies to start with.[53]

What these and similar approaches fail to consider is that *the meaning that drinking has for individuals is a result of a learning process.* Drinking occurs in social contexts—one learns from others *how* to drink and *why* to drink, as well as *when* drinking is appropriate and when it is not. The exact links between the characteristics of a society, learning to drink, and problem drinking have yet to be determined—although the Tri-Ethnic and national survey projects are steps in the right direction. Eventually, the explanation of problem drinking may be found in such models as that suggested by Robert F. Bales nearly thirty years ago.[54]

Bales hypothesized that rates of problem drinking (he used the term *alcoholism*) in a culture—presumably a subculture as well—were related to a combination of three factors:

1. *The extent to which a culture produces inner tensions in its members.* Bales suggested such culturally induced tensions as guilt, conflict, anxiety, and sexual tensions. Obviously, however, Jessor's use of anomie as a social correlate of problem drinking is also consistent with this factor.

2. *The types of attitudes toward drinking that the culture produces.* Bales claimed that there were essentially four types of such attitudes.

(a) Complete abstinence—by definition this should prevent problem drinking; however, Bales recognized that prohibition sometimes "overshoots the mark and encourages the very thing it is designed to prevent." For whatever reason, when persons *do* drink in cultures prohibiting the behavior they lack any guidelines or directives on *how* to drink. Thus on an individual level drinking can result in serious consequences in such cultures. Bales cites as an example the American East Coast Indian tribes whose leaders attempted to impose prohibition when the tribes were first introduced to alcohol. Without stable attitudes about how to handle drinking, the "drunken comportment"—to use MacAndrew and Edgerton's term—of those who did drink was often devastating in its results.[55]

(b) Ritual attitude—alcohol is usually consumed in rigorously defined situations, especially religious ceremonies. The attitudes toward drinking and the behavior related to drinking are clearly understood. Bales uses as an example orthodox Jews who drink regularly, but in a highly regulated manner, during religious services. This group has an extremely low rate of problem drinking.

(c) Convivial attitude—this is closest to what is commonly referred to as *social drinking*. Alcohol is a means of setting people at ease and producing congeniality in group settings; it is a symbol of social unity and good will.

(d) Utilitarian attitude—this refers to drinking that serves personal rather than social interests. This includes drinking for medical purposes—to get over a hangover, for example—and for purposes of forgetting one's troubles, of gaining courage to face difficult situations, and so on. Such an attitude, according to Bales, can often evolve from convivial attitudes and is the one attitude most likely to result in drinking problems.

3. *The extent to which a culture provides suitable substitutes for easing tensions.* According to Bales a third factor contributing to problem drinking is the lack of substitutes for alcohol by which persons can relieve their tensions. He does not specify what such substitutes might be in the United States. However, it is probably safe to speculate that, were it not for the use of other psychoactive drugs, both legal and illegal, the amount of problem drinking in this country might be even greater.

As Bales insists, individually these factors are likely to have little explanatory value; they must be considered in concert. Even then, however, the Bales model admittedly provides only the barest outline of the complex issue. Nevertheless, it will probably be a similar model that will prove to be the most fruitful means of explaining problem drinking.

ALCOHOL AND CONFLICT

We mentioned earlier that a formula involving deaths by cirrhosis places the number of "alcoholics" in the United States at 5.5 million, or *slightly less than 3 per cent* of the total population. From the standpoint of the concept of problem drinking, Don Cahalan's data from the national survey show the impact of alcohol to be still more widespread.

> Depending upon where one puts the cutting point on scores, one can represent the adult population as having a high rate of problem drinking

(since 43 percent of men, 21 percent of women, and 31 percent of the total reported having some degree of one or more of the eleven types of problems [e.g., problems with relatives, employment, the law and so on over drinking] during the three preceding years) or as having a relatively low rate (almost six of ten men and eight of ten women reported having none of these [problems]).

One out of six American male adults have at least a moderate potential problem of getting intoxicated fairly often; two out of five men and 15 percent of the women appear to have at least some psychological dependence upon alcohol; and 12 percent of men and 8 percent of women said they had had something of a health problem associated with their drinking within the past three years.[56]

By whatever standard, alcohol unquestionably has an adverse impact upon great numbers of Americans. But the deviant status of alcohol use has been the subject of diverse ethical and political definitions. There is wide consensus that *some* control over the drug is necessary; for example, intoxicated persons should not be allowed to drive, and kindergarteners should not sip Bloody Marys during recess. But the nature and extent of such control are issues upon which interest groups differ.

The most visible evidence of interest group influence can be seen in the changing policy toward those whose dependence on alcohol has brought them to public, or at least official, attention. Traditionally, public drunkenness has been treated as a legal problem—intoxicated individuals were subject to arrest and confinement. For some, those without other resources, this policy frequently caught them in a revolving door of repeated arrests, incarcerations, releases, and rearrests accompanied by increasing loss of self-esteem, employability, and hope.[57] With the growing influence of the *disease* concept of alcoholism, medical and hospital groups moved to include the alcoholic as their responsibility. In an unprecedented action in 1956 the American Medical Association (A.M.A.) decided by formal vote that "Alcoholism must be regarded as within the purview of medical practice."[58]

The position of the A.M.A. is perhaps best illustrated by the following statement by Dr. Marvin A. Block, who at the time was chairperson of the A.M.A.'s Committee on Alcoholism.

Today the physician is equipped to help care for these sick people [alcoholics]. . . . Doctors can prescribe drugs to alleviate physical symptoms. In physical complications from excessive drinking, proper diet, vitamins and drugs can be used to restore the patient physically and usually he can return to his former physical fitness. When underlying psychological reasons can be discovered to account for the patient's escape into alcoholic oblivion, corrective therapy can be applied. Anxieties due to insecurity in financial, domestic or physical matters may be alleviated by psychotherapy. In his relationship with the physician, the alcoholic may be relieved of fears that have no foundation in fact, thus obviating the need for escape through alcohol. . . .

It must be remembered that alcoholism is a disease, that habitual excessive drinking is an illness which the physician is ready to treat. His advice should be sought early. As with other diseases, the earlier it is detected and treatment begun, the greater the chance for recovery and happy living.[59]

As we discussed in detail previously, there is no agreement over whether the disease concept of alcoholism represents anything more than a decision not to punish offenders. The decriminalization of public drunkenness offenders certainly is a humane step, but whether the groups advocating treatment rather than jail can deal with the alcohol problem more effectively is a matter of conjecture.

Historically, however, the most intense conflicts have arisen over what should be done about alcohol rather than the alcoholic. Interest groups have actively sought to reduce the perceived costs of drunkenness by employing variations of the four "models of social control" suggested by Edwin M. Lemert.

1. *A system of laws and coercive controls making it illegal to manufacture, distribute, or consume alcoholic beverages.* [For the purpose of convenience we shall refer to this model as *prohibition.*]
2. *A system of indoctrination of information about the consequences of using alcohol—thus leading to moderate drinking or abstinence.* [This we shall call *education.*]
3. *Legal regulation of the kinds of liquor consumed, its pecuniary cost, methods of distribution, the time and place of drinking, and its availability to consumers according to age, sex, and other socioeconomic characteristics.* [In other words, *regulation.*]
4. *Substitution of functional equivalents of drinking.* [*Substitution.*][60]

The experience of the United States with the *prohibition* model had its origins in the formation of local temperance societies in the early nineteenth century. The events that led from these humble beginnings to nationwide prohibition were extremely complex, but it is generally recognized that the Eighteenth Amendment forbidding the manufacture and sale of alcoholic beverages was symbolic of more than disputes over drinking.[61] Drinking as a problem emerged when *abstinence became a symbol of the middle class.* According to Joseph R. Gusfield:

The ethic which supported temperance and the temperance movement was associated with the rise to dominance of the middle classes in American life. Temperance became obligatory behavior for all who sought to operate within the major social institutions. If sobriety in all areas of life is demanded by family, employer, and friend, then the young man should at least preserve his reputation if he wishes to "strive and succeed." The character valued by a dominant class is supported by the rewards which it obtains and the punishment which its [absence] entails.

As social classes rise and fall, as new classes emerge and contend for power and status, the status value of styles of life are called into question. Because it has been a significant status symbol, drinking has been an issue through which status struggles have been manifested.[62]

After the Civil War the drinking reform movement emerged as a national political issue. Organizations such as the Woman's Christian Temperance Union (W.C.T.U.) and the Anti-Saloon League were established to educate the uninformed about the dangers of drinking and to pressure legislatures into enacting prohibitory legislation. The Anti-Saloon League, for example, was largely responsible for such laws as those excluding alcohol from Army posts, prohibiting its sale to Indians, and excluding advertising of liquor from the U.S. mails.

The philosophies of these and similar organizations were closely tied in with political philosophies and the spirit of reform existing at the turn of the century. It was a period of trust-busting, child labor legislation, movements to gain voting rights for women, regulation of the food industry, increased unionization, and progress in the area of human rights generally. The temperance movement was part of this climate of reform; it was interested in solving the problems of lower-class urban workers by enabling them to reach perfection in terms of middle-class, small town society. Abstinence from alcohol was seen as a crucial step toward that state of perfection.

A *dry*, writing in 1930, sums up the rationale of those pushing for prohibition shortly after the turn of the century.

They wanted [prohibition] for social reasons, for economic reasons, for political reasons, for moral reasons; they wanted it in order to reduce poverty, in order to minimize the squandering of incomes, in order to eliminate at least one of the causes of the birth of weak, sickly, handicapped children. Finally, they desired it in order to banish the saloon, the most efficient agency for the breeding of sin, vice, political corruption, infamy, and moral turpitude extant. In short, the people demanded prohibition as an initial step toward cleansing and purifying the national envionment; as an essential factor in rendering America a safe place in which to rear children and to foster families.[63]

Buoyed by such ideals, these moral crusaders (or "moral entrepreneurs"—Howard S. Becker's term discussed in Chapter 3) gained political strength as various temperance groups became more unified and organized, more skilled at obtaining funds, and more adept at influencing the election of politicians who favored the temperance cause. Many citizens were sympathetic to the general humanitarian goals of the drys, although these voters did not necessarily favor prohibition itself. However, the opposing wets had neither the organization nor a positive program to offer as an alternative.

Alcohol increasingly became a focal point of conflict after the turn of the century because the temperance movement began to abandon its general reform interests and became more politically and economically conservative. The reason, according to Gusfield, was that the ideal upon which the movement was based—the rural, Protestant, native, middle class—was being threatened by the influx of Catholic and Jewish immigrants who were swelling the ranks of the urban working class. The more general humanitarian concerns of temperance groups declined in favor of pushing national prohibition. This brought about a polarization of conflicting interest groups.

> The segregation of temperance from other movements, at the same time as it became a dominant issue in politics, fostered the polarization of status groups in American life. That segregation was both a manifestation and an enhancing force in pitting the urban, secular, immigrant groups against the rural, Protestant, and native middle classes. As the power of the church member led to victory after victory for prohibition in state and local campaigns, the wets were pushed into greater organization. After the Eighteenth Amendment was passed, the status struggle was in full force. The dominance of the middle-class style of life was symbolized in Prohibition. It became the focal point for the political and social ambitions of American status groups.[64]

The period of the "noble experiment," as prohibition is sometimes called, began in January of 1920, one year after the ratification of the Eighteenth Amendment. The machinery for administering prohibition was the Volstead Act, which defined an intoxicating beverage as one containing one half of one per cent, or more, alcohol. Many reasons are suggested for the failure of the Volstead Act, including an absence of adequate enforcement facilities and the failure to make the purchaser as well as the seller guilty of a crime.[65] But *lack of popular support* remained the constant that undermined prohibition in the United States. Add to this the factors of organized crime with its corrupting influence on government officials, a general lack of aggressive enforcement, and the growth of organized opposition to the Eighteenth Amendment. Disillusionment with Prohibition finally doomed it; the Twenty-first Amendment repealing prohibition was ratified in 1933.

Another prohibition movement in the near future is extremely unlikely, if only because total abstinence has become less acceptable at all levels of society. The dry middle class, which served as a basis for temperance in the past, has eroded away. Again, we quote Gusfield:

> With the rise of a corporate economy of large-scale organizations, a new middle class of salaried white-collar workers, managerial employees, and professionals has developed. The styles of life of such groups contrast with those of the middle class of small enterprisers, independent farmers, and free professionals. The new middle class is less likely to adhere to old

middle class values. In an economy of surplus and in an atmosphere of organizations, mastery over other men supplants mastery over things and over the self as character virtues. Ability to "get along with others," to be tolerant, and to express solidarity are prized to the detriment of the complex of old middle class virtues.[66]

None of the other models of alcohol control suggested by Lemert have been as systematically implemented in the United States as prohibition. *Education* is attempted. It takes a variety of forms ranging from high school programs alerting students to the dangers of drinking to public service advertisements placed by organizations such as liquor manufacturers and distributors. An example of the latter is an ad paid for by the Distilled Spirits Council of the United States. A photo of a man refusing a drink is headlined: "It's all right to offer someone a drink. It's all wrong to insist." The ad goes on to say: "It's a friendly social custom to offer guests a drink. But there's a difference between hospitality and pressuring."

The effectiveness of any educational program is unknown. Lemert doubts that the education model can succeed in a society where drinking habits are highly diverse and learned not from formal educational agencies but from family and friends.[67]

The closest the contemporary United States comes to a model of control over drinking is in the area of *regulation*. There are a multitude of laws regarding the manufacture, sale, and taxation of alcoholic beverages. But the net effect is only to make alcohol somewhat inconvenient to obtain and expensive—approximately half of what you pay for a bottle of liquor is taxes. Such regulations do nothing to alter the values concerning drinking; they simply increase the complexity of the mechanism by which alcohol reaches its user.

The final model of social control suggested by Lemert involves *substitution,* or an equivalent for drinking. This, of course, is consistent with Robert F. Bales's claim that rates of problem drinking are related to a culture's provision of alcohol substitutes for easing tensions in its members. One can conceive of a situation where this approach would be feasible—providing a wide variety of recreational facilities to an isolated military installation, for example. It is difficult, however, to imagine an entire society such as the United States embarking on a program to systematically supply or encourage substitutes such as marihuana. To further complicate matters we do not even know what might be effective and satisfactory substitutes.

Thus the questions raised by problem drinking remain unanswered. The move away from the labeling of lower-class drunks as criminals may be a step in the right direction, but altering the labeling from legal to medical is not in itself a solution. Until values concerning drinking are changed, alcohol will continue to be a drug that adversely affects the lives of millions.

Heroin

For most people the *drug problem* means heroin. Unquestionably heroin is a far more potent drug than alcohol: its euphoric effects are greater, the human system is capable of building an extremely high tolerance of heroin, and the likelihood of developing patterns of physical dependence and continual use is very high. Yet, as we shall see, most problems associated with heroin result not from the drug itself, but from policies surrounding the drug's regulation.

The raw material of heroin is opium, which is simply the dried juice of the unripened seed pods of the opium poppy. Opium's effects were known at least as early as 4000 B.C. to the Sumerians, living in what is now Southern Iraq, who called the opium poppies "joy plants." In 1803 the chief active ingredient of opium was isolated. It was called *morphine*, appropriately named after the Greek god of dreams, Morpheus, because it proved to be the greatest pain reliever the world had known. But it was discovered that the use of morphine, like opium, resulted in drug dependence; and a search was undertaken for a substitute. One result was the development of *heroin*, a derivative of morphine, in 1898. Heroin proved to be an extremely potent drug—it increases the strength of morphine two or three times (heroin actually turns into morphine once in the body), and its effects are particularly rapid when it is injected by hypodermic needle. But it too results in dependence; today heroin is regarded as having no unique medical qualities and is outlawed in most countries.

No satisfactory substitute has yet been found for the medical qualities of morphine. Opium poppies are cultivated in various areas throughout the world to supply the pharmaceutical market, but about 40 per cent of the total production of opium reaches illicit markets to supply opium smokers or for conversion into heroin. Up until 1973 most of the heroin reaching the United States originated in the poppy fields of Turkey. After harvest either the opium itself or the morphine base, which reduces the raw opium volume tenfold, moved into Western Europe, especially France. There it was converted into heroin in small, mobile laboratories. The heroin was then smuggled into the United States, either directly into New York City or indirectly by way of Canada, Mexico, or through various Latin American countries into east coast ports.[68]

The Turkish-French heroin flow slowed considerably as a result of law enforcement pressures on French traffickers and Turkish restrictions on the growing of poppies. But Turkey lifted its restrictions in 1974, so the volume from that part of the world may increase. In the meantime, Mexico has become the leading heroin supplier to the United States by increasing its share of the market from 20 to 60 per cent in the last five years. Regardless of its source, once heroin is in the United States it goes through a series of dealers who progressively dilute it before it reaches its ultimate user. The product, which the user injects into her or his arm, is from 2 to 7 per cent pure heroin, depending upon available supply.[69]

All of this sounds very complex and risky, and it is, but only insofar as distribution is concerned. Opium itself is rather cheap and its conversion into heroin is basic and inexpensive. It is the illegality of the product that makes the distribution complex and expensive. Risks must be taken and compensated for. The profits made for servicing the United States market are sizeable, as illustrated by Table 8-4.

TABLE 8–4
MARKET PRICES OF HEROIN REACHING THE UNITED STATES *

	$ Per Kilogram (2.2 lbs.)
Price paid Turkish farmer for opium	$22
Wholesale price for heroin in Marseilles, France (raw opium reduced in volume by a ratio of 10:1)	$5,000
Border price for heroin in New York City	$10,000
Wholesale price for heroin in New York City	$22,000
Retail price for heroin in New York City (If sold as pure heroin; the user's dose is about 5 per cent)	$220,000

* Derived from Cabinet Committee on International Narcotics Control, *World Opium Survey 1972* (Washington, D.C.: U.S. Department of State, 1972), p. 34.

Obviously, heroin users in the United States are paying an extremely inflated price for their drugs. But the demand for heroin remains relatively inflexible; prices can be escalated without diminishing the volume of sales.

Late in 1961, a critical shortage of heroin, an event which came to be known as the "panic," occurred in New York. According to some, this "panic" is largely responsible for the inflated cost of maintaining a habit today. Because the substance was in such short supply, dealers cut the quality of the dose many times and therefore increased the amount of the drug needed and the amount of money necessary to buy it. Yet, even with the inflated price and deflated quality, dealers experienced little difficulty in disposing of their supplies. . . . The cost of maintaining a habit was said to have increased to ten times what it had been only twenty years before.

The inflationary cost of heroin, however, did not disappear with the passing of the panic, and recent estimates of the daily cost of supporting a habit have ranged from $20 to $100, fluctuating according to availability and location.[70]

In short, it is apparent that some heroin users are willing to pay any price for the drug. This suggests something of the nature of heroin dependence; the motivations toward heroin use are particularly strong, and intensified or compulsive use is extremely difficult to alter. To better understand the nature of heroin dependence—the process of being hooked—let us explore what the drug does.

HEROIN AS A DRUG

As indicated earlier, heroin is a depressant—it is particularly effective in blocking pain; it creates drowsiness, lethargy, and an inability to concentrate. By themselves these effects scarcely explain dependence, however. Heroin use as a habit can be discussed only in terms of three factors characterizing persons' experiences with the drug: the *initial impact* or *rush*, the *euphoria* or *high* or *nod*, and the *withdrawal symptoms*. The initial impact is experienced when heroin is injected into a vein. This sensation has been variously described as ranging from a sudden flush of warmth in the stomach to a huge orgasm. The rush is followed by a more prolonged state of euphoria known as the *high* or *nod*. It is in this phase that one may attain a sense of well-being and a loss of anxiety. The following statements by occasional heroin users convey their impressions of the high:

> "It gives you a real warm, mellow feeling . . . puts everything at ease and relaxes your nerves."
> "It's the ultimate in escape. Nothing bothers you."
> "Life passes swiftly as if you're in a dream."
> "Stimulates the freedom of my ideas."
> "It's like a steambath." [71]

Although these effects seem to be identifiable, first experiences with the rush and the high may be anything but pleasurable. In reality, some persons have feelings of fear and sickness instead. *The reason is that positive responses to the effects of heroin are neither automatic nor inherent in the chemical properties of the drug. One's responses are learned.* Most first experiences with heroin occur in the company of others who encourage a favorable interpretation of the drug's effects.[72] This influence may counteract even the most distasteful initiation to heroin. Erich Goode provides us with this description of one woman's first shot, taken with her boyfriend:

> I am truly surprised that we both didn't die that very first night. I was more physically miserable than I had ever been before. The whole night was spent vomiting. The thing that surprises me is that we didn't forget heroin right then and there. It was horrible! But we later decided that our dear friend had given us too much. So I decided to give it another chance. . . . My friends were all doing it, and it had become a question of prestige within our small group.[73]

But learning to enjoy the euphoric effects of heroin is only the first step in the process of becoming hooked. The individual must also decide whether he or she should continue use and risk joining the ranks of those for whom heroin becomes an absolute need. Does a person *decide* to become dependent on heroin? Apparently not. Instead, the decision is that he or she will be immune from such a fate.

> The individual user never believes he himself will become addicted. Perhaps we see here the same mechanism that allows a soldier on a battlefield to surge forward and continue fighting while he sees soldiers around him dying from wounds. One can be firmly set in the belief that the self is inviolable, unique, and not subject to suffering, accident, or death. . . . One no more decides to become an addict than one decides to die on the battlefield.[74]

Although group influence and the euphoric effects play important roles in the initiation and continuation of heroin use, the state that is commonly known as addiction—or in our terminology, intensified or apparently compulsive dependence—is created in large part by the factor of *withdrawal symptoms*. The reader will recall from the first table in this chapter that heroin is characterized by both *tolerance* and *physical dependence*. The first of these terms refers to the consequence of continued drug use whereby the person becomes accustomed to its effects and in order to experience the euphoria requires steadily larger doses. But as the regular user increases the dosage the body adjusts to the drug and now requires it for normal physical functioning. Should the user abstain, certain physical symptoms occur until the body adapts to the new state.[75] These are the withdrawal symptoms and include yawning, runny nose, perspiration, fever, chills, vomiting, and so on. As we mentioned earlier, the severity of the symptoms may be influenced by psychological factors, but generally the intensity of the symptoms is related to the strength of the dosage to which the body has adjusted. Apparently there is no limit to the degree of tolerance that can be developed; however, the degree of physical dependence, as measured by the intensity of the symptoms, is limited.

If there is such a thing as an invariable sequence in becoming hooked on heroin we are ignorant of it. However, for most cases the process probably approximates that suggested by Troy Duster and it goes something like this. The individual first tries heroin usually on the spur of the moment. The introduction takes place in a group of friends if the individual is a male, but a female is more likely to be introduced by someone with whom she has an intense emotional relationship, a husband or a lover. After the first or subsequent attempts the person decides that the experience of the drug is both physically (the rush) and emotionally (the high) pleasurable. After using the drug the novice notices a slight headache or nausea, but it quickly disappears. The same result occurs after the next few experiences. The user connects the symptoms with the drug, but they are considered a very small price to pay. The user erroneously concludes that this minor discomfort is all that withdrawal will involve. Thus he or she feels clearly insulated from becoming addicted.

This continues for a few months until the user begins to recognize that the original dosage is no longer supplying the wanted effect. But this is no problem; the dosage can be increased and the only inconvenience will be that the headaches and nausea will be a little stronger. But the sequence intensifies. The dosages get larger and the symptoms progress to vomiting, hot flushes, diarrhea, and so on. Now the user begins to take the drug to get relief from the symptoms, and is hooked.[76]

The progression described above is not inevitable; people do use heroin on an occasional basis for years without becoming involved in the dependence spiral. However, the high potential of heroin for extreme dependence cannot be denied. From this fact has arisen a controversy over the degree to which euphoria and withdrawal symptoms contribute to extreme forms of heroin dependence. For over a quarter of a century the prevailing sociological view was that proposed by Alfred R. Lindesmith. According to Lindesmith there is a definite distinction between the heroin *user* and the *addict*. This distinction entails what he calls a "reversal of effects":

> In the beginning phases of addiction, the pleasurable effects of drugs, other than those that occur at the time of injection, tend to diminish and vanish. As this occurs, and as withdrawal distress increases, the psychological significance of the doses changes. Whereas they at first produced pleasure, their primary function becomes that of avoiding pain, that is, withdrawal. The addict seems to continue the use of the drug to avoid the symptoms which he knows will appear if he stops.[77]

For the addict then, according to Lindesmith, all that heroin provides is the rush and the avoidance of pain; the high of euphoria is gone. A more recent interpretation of this matter by William E. McAuliffe and Robert A. Gordon casts doubt on Lindesmith's contention. They find evidence that even among hard core addicts, euphoria remains a positive factor reinforcing continued use of the drug.[78] If such persons have just enough drug to avoid withdrawal they will be satisfied with that. However, should a larger supply be available they will use it to obtain positive effects beyond merely feeling normal. McAuliffe and Gordon suggest it is this ability of all addicts to enjoy euphoria that recruits others to try heroin and to continue use even after any initial unpleasant results.

> Their own enjoyment, in turn, leads these recruits to continue use until they themselves become physically dependent. Once dependent, the promise of euphoria holds the addict to his habit, and the pursuit drives up his tolerance, increases the high overhead cost of his addiction, and

depletes his legitimate resources. If he remains determined to pursue euphoria at a maximum level in the face of these developments, rather than contenting himself merely with avoiding the abstinence syndrome, he must commit himself more completely to the life-style of the criminal addict.[79]

According to the McAuliffe-Gordon thesis continued heroin use involves a complex interrelationship of two goals: avoidance of withdrawal symptoms and re-experiencing the pleasures of the drug. The relative importance of each of these goals doubtlessly will be subject to further controversy and research. Whether Lindesmith or McAuliffe and Gordon is more accurate in their assessment, one fact remains incontrovertible: the incentive to continue the use of heroin is great.

HEROIN USE AND DEVIANCE

It is impossible to discuss heroin use as deviant behavior without considering the historical context of the heroin laws. But before we do that, let us briefly indicate some facts about dependence. *First, heroin has a high potential for creating dependence, and no effective means of ending that dependence has been found.* There is considerable reason to believe the adage, "Once a junkie, always a junkie," because the proportion of those who succeed in kicking the habit permanently through any form of therapy is miniscule.[80] An indication of the official recognition of this fact is the movement toward treatment programs involving either the *substitution* of legal, cheap, but addicting drugs such as methadone, or the provision of *maintenance* doses of heroin itself. More will be said about these alternatives later; suffice it to say here that nothing else has worked: jail, hospital, psychotherapy, or therapeutic communities. If anything can be said to halt heroin dependence it is age; many users simply quit on their own when they reach their mid-thirties.[81] The reason for the relationship between advancing age and termination of heroin use is unclear. Possibly it has nothing to do with a waning desire for the drug; rather there may be a growing weariness with the continuing risks of the habit—financing and finding fixes, concern about overdoses, and the dangers of arrest and incarceration. Whatever the reason it is evident that junkies can and do quit, but therapy is seldom responsible.

Second, in comparison with other psychoactive drugs, heroin is physiologically harmless. This may come as a surprise to those who have read newspaper horror stories about overdoses and heroin-related deaths. And many are undoubtedly familiar with the popular image of the addict as a dirty, skinny person with rotten teeth and running sores. In reality, as psychoactive drugs go, heroin is one of the safest—prolonged use results in no disease or damage to organs or cells.[82] There are some minor short-term effects for persons under the drug's influence: diminished sexual potency, menstrual irregularities, constriction of pupils, constipation, and excessive sweating. In the long run, cigarette smoking and alcohol drinking are far more dangerous than heroin—they can kill, heroin cannot.

Furthermore, if the user's primary motivation is to avoid withdrawal distress, he or she can take just enough of the drug to do that and can still behave quite normally; that is, the user can work, drive, and think lucidly, even while using very large dosages. Such would not be the case for the user of alcohol, however. Relatively large doses of alcohol decrease one's mental and physical effectiveness regardless of experience with the drug.

But how does the claim of the harmlessness of heroin square with claims that people die from "heroin abuse?" There is no doubt that the death rate among users is high, but the cause of death is not the drug itself but the *conditions under which its users must live.*[83] Try to imagine the situation if you were a junkie. You have a habit you cannot afford because the illegality of the drug has driven the price beyond what you can earn. Much of your time is spent getting funds, one way or another. Who can worry about food? Further, you are forced to purchase drugs about which you have no guarantee as to their quality or composition. They could even be laced with arsenic—a practice not unknown in the drug world. Finally, you take a fix with a needle a friend has had wrapped in his dirty handkerchief. Now you settle back to enjoy yourself until you have to worry once more about where the next fix will come from—if you should live so long.

Such conditions lead to many deaths caused by complications arising from malnutrition, tetanus, hepatitis, pneumonia, and gangrene. What about overdose? Does heroin kill in that instance? Of course, one can take too much of nearly any drug, including aspirin. If a nonuser should take a dose of heroin equivalent to that used by someone with a high tolerance, death would surely result. Because of the illegal nature of the product there is no quality control or standardization of the amount of heroin in any dose. It is entirely possible for even a long-term user to purchase a dose that is too powerful for his or her system to handle.[84] Thus the danger of heroin stems not from the drug itself, but from the conditions that its illegality creates.

Third, most criminal activities of heroin users stem not from the drug use itself, but from attempts to find means of obtaining the drug. One study of ex-addicts in New York City revealed that only about four per cent of the funds used to purchase heroin were obtained from legal sources; all the rest came from selling heroin (45 per cent), shoplifting (12 per cent), prostitution (16 per cent), burglary (10 per cent), and so on.[85] In cities having high numbers of users (New York,

Chicago, and Washington) it is estimated that half of all property crimes are committed by addicts.[86] Even if these figures should be inflated, it is impossible to overlook the relationship between heroin dependence and property crime. Even among the most vehement heroin enemies it is generally conceded that violent personal offenses by users are unlikely. Users usually wish to get their fixes with the least amount of trouble; if they achieve euphoria their aloofness from their surroundings makes them uninterested in anything else—sex included. Among dealers it is a different story. In the struggle for markets, cutthroat competition is often carried to its most literal extreme.

Even an individual with a relatively low-cost daily habit—say $20—still needs $7,300 per year. This figure is well beyond the means of most users, who are concentrated in big-city slums where the average family income is less than half that amount. To further complicate matters, stolen merchandise is not convertible into its real cash value. If a person must steal to support a habit, he or she must take property amounting to between 2½ to 5 times the actual cost of the habit.[87] That $100 portable TV set that was ripped off from you will pay for one or two fixes; of course, somebody is also getting a bargain-priced set, if that is any consolation.

Fourth, there is some indication that heroin use may be decreasing. As we continually remind readers, statistics concerning any form of deviant behavior must be viewed with extreme suspicion. This is especially true of heroin use. Heroin itself does not cause death—as in the case of cirrhosis from alcohol—and importers naturally do not publish reports on their business volume. Consequently, one can easily become involved in a numbers game in which "the experts" provide greatly varying figures. For example, in 1971 and 1972 estimates of the number of addict-users in the United States ranged from 300,000 to 560,000; for New York City alone they ranged from 150,000 to 600,000.[88]

When there are such disparities in the estimates of existing addicts, to suggest trends involves a good deal of guesswork. There does seem to be agreement among experts that by 1974 heroin use had at least stabilized, if not actually decreased. As President Nixon announced in September, 1973: "We have turned the corner on drug addiction in the United States." [89] This claim is based on an apparent decrease of use among black males in large cities.

Black males from poor urban neighborhoods are definitely the one group that is greatly overrepresented among heroin addicts. Nearly 80 per cent of persons undergoing treatment for addiction are black males, and perhaps as many as 15 per cent of all black males use heroin.[90] It is speculated that among this group there is increasing disenchantment with heroin—it is no longer considered as cool as it once was and is seen as a symbol of political oppression whereby white society keeps blacks under control.[91]

Some decrease in heroin use represents a shift to methadone and cocaine. This means that in some instances the number of drug users has not changed; only their drugs have changed.

On the other hand, there is evidence that decreased heroin use in large cities is being offset or even exceeded by its increased use in cities under half a million population. In short, heroin use may be breaking out of the big-city ghettos and spreading into the hinterlands. Whether heroin use will remain a lower-class phenomenon or diffuse into the white middle class is a matter of speculation. There is a precedent for its spread to the middle class; marihuana use was once confined to lower-class minority groups. We shall say more about marihuana later in this chapter.

HEROIN AND CONFLICT

It should be clear from the above discussion that the inherent dangers of heroin are few. Aside from the likelihood of dependence and the possibility of harm occurring to one because of an inability to react while under its euphoric influence, heroin scarcely seems to deserve all the excitement surrounding its use, especially in a society already heavily saturated with psychoactive drugs. But the history of official policy aimed at heroin control is one of overreaction and heavy-handedness. That history is an excellent example of interest group influence and the process by which behavior becomes labeled as deviant.

"Thou shalt not use heroin" is not one of the Ten Commandments; it is a legal philosophy that developed to solve a problem. The origins of that problem date back to the mid-nineteenth century. Opiates were easily available then; physicians wrote prescriptions for them; they were available in drug, grocery, and general stores; and they could even be ordered through the mail.[92] Countless patent medicines containing opium could be purchased for a variety of symptoms ranging from teething problems of children to coughing and menstruation. Toward the end of the century the use of morphine was even encouraged by physicians as a substitute for alcohol on the theory that morphine was considerably less dangerous.[93]

Of course, the possibility of dependence upon opiates was recognized, and in some circles their use was regarded as immoral. But the *reaction* against dependence was in no way like that of today.

Employees were not fired for addiction. Wives did not divorce their addicted husbands, or husbands their addicted wives. Children were not taken from their homes and lodged in foster homes or institutions because one or both parents were addicted. Addicts continued to participate fully in the life of the community. Addicted children and young people continued to go to school, Sunday School, and college. Thus, the nineteenth century avoided one of the most disastrous effects of current narcotics laws and attitudes—the rise of a deviant addict subculture, cut off from respectable society and without a "road back" to respectability.[94]

There was, then, a tolerance for addicts. They were not viewed as a menace to society, nor is there any evidence that they were a menace. In fact, the typical addict of the nineteenth century was a middle-aged, middle-class female. What happened? Why did the addict suddenly become a criminal?

The first law concerning opiates in the United States was a municipal ordinance against opium dens passed in 1875 in San Francisco. Evidently the law had little to do with the hazard of opium but was race oriented.[95] Opium smoking was introduced in the United States by Chinese who were imported to work on railroad construction crews. Their opium dens were at first tolerated, but as the Chinese began to pose a threat to the white labor market, and when the dens presumedly began to attract "respectable" whites, toleration evaporated. Several cities besides San Francisco adopted similar ordinances, and Congress progressively increased the tariff on opium prepared for smoking. In 1909, the importation of smoking opium was prohibited altogether. The passage of the law apparently had little to do with concern over the Chinese addict population in the United States, but was the result of a curious combination of prejudice against the Chinese in general, and a desire to obtain diplomatic good will with China, which was waging its own war against opium use.[96]

In the meantime, other legislation was being enacted to curtail the indiscriminate availability of opiates despite great pressures by the patent medicine interests. The keystone of U.S. policy toward heroin was embodied in the Harrison Narcotics Act passed in 1914. The principal factor contributing to the law's passage was an obligation to honor commitments made two years before at the Hague Convention, where several countries had agreed to limit the trade and production of opiates to medical and scientific purposes in order to solve the opium problems of the Far East, particularly China.

The Harrison Act was not prohibitionary. It was basically a tax law requiring persons handling or manufacturing opium products to register, pay a fee, and keep records of their transactions. There was no mention of addiction; patent medicines could still contain small portions of opiates, including heroin; and, more important, physicians could prescribe larger quantities. Thus, two powerful interest groups that had been actively lobbying to control the scope of the bill were satisfied. The drug industry was able to avoid control of many of its medicines, and physicians were assured that their professional activities would not be tampered with.[97]

But the interest groups had not reckoned on the power of the enforcement agencies and the climate of the times. What started out as a revenue act to control the nonmedical use of opiates evolved into a weapon to suppress addiction.

The enforcement of the Harrison Act—since it was a revenue act—was the responsibility of the Treasury Department. Its Narcotics Division, which eventually became the Bureau of Narcotics, in the very earliest days of the act made clear its intent to eliminate drug addiction by forbidding any nonmedical prescriptions of opiates; that is, it refused to recognize the legality of providing an addict with drugs to maintain her or his habit. By harassment, through complicated regulations and arrests, the division quickly discouraged the medical profession.[98] Less than nine months after the effective date of the Harrison Act, this editorial comment appeared in *American Medicine:*

> Narcotic drug addiction is one of the gravest and most important questions confronting the medical profession today. Instead of improving conditions the laws recently passed have made the problem more complex. Honest medical men have found such handicaps and dangers to themselves and their reputations in these laws . . . that they have simply decided to have as little to do as possible with drug addicts or their needs. . . . The druggists are in the same position and for similar reasons many of them have discontinued entirely the sale of narcotic drugs. [The addict] is denied the medical care he urgently needs, open, above-board sources from which he formerly obtained his drug supply are closed to him, and he is driven to the underworld where he can get his drug, but of course, surreptitiously and in violation of the law. . . .
>
> Abuses in the sale of narcotic drugs are increasing. . . . A particular sinister sequence . . . is the character of the places to which [addicts] are forced to go to get their drugs and the type of people with whom they are obliged to mix. The most depraved criminals are often the dispensers of these habit-forming drugs. The moral dangers, as well as the effect on the self-respect of the addict, call for no comment. One has only to think of the stress under which the addict lives, and to recall his lack of funds, to realize the extent to which these . . . afflicted individuals are under the control of the worst elements of society.[99]

What had been a medical problem, if a problem at all, had become a legal one; patients became criminals practically overnight. In a very few years an organized underground for black market drugs was in operation, and crimes began to be connected with drug use. In the meantime, the Narcotics Division solidified its position by 1. launching a public information campaign labeling drugs as a crucial factor in a crime wave and as an evil to be stamped out at any cost, and 2. undertaking a series of court cases in order to broaden the division's powers.[100]

Exactly how much influence the division had on public opinion is impossible to say. It does seem that the nation was ripe for altering its previously tolerant attitudes toward drug users.[101] It must be remembered that the Harrison Act was passed at a period that included the First World War, the emergence of Prohibition, and increasing nationalistic tendencies fanned by growing fears of anarchism and communism. This was a period of reform and re-evaluation of whatever was seen to threaten the social structure. It was a time of social crisis; a time to confront forces disruptive of the old order, including the proponents of alcohol, drugs, and radical ideas. It is no coincidence that in 1919 the mayor of New York City appointed a single committee to investigate two problems: heroin use among youths, and bombings by revolutionaries.[102]

Though its activities did decrease public tolerance of drug users, the Narcotics Division's strength stemmed mainly from its success in securing Supreme Court decisions favorable to the division's interpretation of the law. In a series of decisions between 1919 and 1922 the court ruled that a doctor could not prescribe enough drugs to maintain the addict. The user thus could not legally obtain drugs unless he or she were undergoing institutional treatment for drug dependence. A later decision was to modify the court's earlier decisions. In the so-called Linder Case of 1925 the court held that addiction was a disease and that a physician acting in good faith could administer moderate amounts of a drug to relive withdrawal symptoms.[103] In practice, however, the Narcotics Division studiously ignored the implications of the Linder decision and for decades carried on an enforcement policy consistent with the earlier decisions. As Charles Reasons concludes:

> By focusing upon judicial decisions, rather than Congressional action, the Narcotics Division circumvented the strong lobbies of physicians and pharmacists and was able to create a whole new class of criminals, i.e., the addicts. The Treasury Department drew up its regulations based upon these early decisions, instructing doctors when and when not to give narcotics. The judgment had been made that addiction was essentially not a disease, but a willful indulgence meriting punishment rather than medical treatment. Those invested with enforcing the law and the dominant moral order would prove to be very capable in maintaining such an approach.[104]

Thus a law that began as a revenue measure gave birth to an agency that turned the law into an instrument of moral crusade. In the process a new criminal was created. Unfortunately, the process did not end there. The agency became larger, and its budgets greater. More and more anti-drug legislation was passed at state and federal levels with increasingly harsher punishments. In the 1930s the agency was influential in creating still another class of criminals—those using marihuana.

Marihuana

Compared to heroin, marihuana is a subject much nearer, and perhaps dearer, to readers' hearts. If statistics and personal observation have any relevance to the real world, there should be little question that many of you have risked arrest and imprisonment (if not eternal damnation and curvature of the spine) by using marihuana at least once. In 1972, the National Commission on Marihuana and Drug Abuse found that over half—55 per cent to be exact—of persons aged eighteen to twenty-one had tried marihuana; among all psychoactive drugs it ranked third in popularity, next to alcohol and nicotine.[105]

The source of marihuana is the Indian hemp plant, *Cannabis sativa*, which provides not only a drug, but rope fiber and other useful by-products.[106] The drug is prepared by drying and chopping the leaves and flowering tops of the plant. Another more potent drug, known as *hashish*, is produced from drying the resins of the hemp plant. The potency of both marihuana and hashish varies greatly according to the type of seed and the source of the plants. For example, a significantly stronger preparation can generally be obtained from plants grown in Mexico as compared to those in the United States. Usually marihuana and hashish are smoked in the United States; however, they can be eaten blended in food or drinks.

As with alcohol and opium, marihuana has a long history. There is some evidence it may have been used as a medicine around 2700 B.C. in China. There is extensive documentation of its widespread use for its psychoactive effects in Asia and Africa by 500 B.C. Later, the Moslems readily accepted the drug as a substitute for forbidden alcohol. The hemp plant was introduced in South America by either Spaniards or African slaves in the early sixteenth century; in 1611 it was brought into what is now the United States by settlers of Jamestown, Virginia, who used it solely for its fibers. Thereafter it was widely cultivated for its fiber and other products until the late nineteenth century, when it was replaced by superior substitutes. Today, the plant grows practically everywhere in the world, and tens of thousands of acres in the United States are infested with a wild variety.

MARIHUANA AS A DRUG

In some literature you will find marihuana classified as a mild hallucinogen, but recent writings classify it as unique.[107] When smoked, the drug passes quickly into the bloodstream. The immediate physical effects are minimal; an increase in pulse rate and reddening of the eyes are the most obvious.[108] Like other psychoactive drugs, marihuana most noticeably affects the mental processes and the motor responses directed by those processes. The extent of impairment of these processes is related to the size of the dosage and past experience with the drug. Even with moderately large dosages the impairment is minor, however, and experience with the drug apparently enables a user to compensate to improve motor responses. The National Commission on Marihuana and Drug Abuse concludes:

> The immediate effect of marihuana on normal mental processes is a subtle alteration in state of consciousness probably related to a change in short-term memory, mood, emotion, and volition. This effect on the mind produces a varying influence on cognitive and psychomotor task performance which is highly individualized, as well as related to dosage, time, complexity of the task and experience of the user. The effect on personal, social and vocational functions is difficult to predict. In most instances, the marihuana intoxication is pleasurable. In rare cases, the experience may lead to unpleasant anxiety and panic, and in a predisposed few, to psychosis.[109]

In general, the drug has none of the physical dangers so prominent in the other drugs we have discussed. There is no evidence that there is a lethal dose of marihuana. It does not produce *physical dependence* and is not likely to result in *tolerance*—although some tolerance does occur with very heavy, very long-term use, which is exceptional in the United States. Regarding long-term physical harms that might result, the evidence varies from month to month as often contradictory research results are released. The commission found "little proven danger" from experimental or intermittent use, and this conclusion remains unchallenged. The greatest area of debate concerns more frequent use. But even here the evidence is contradictory and inconclusive. All of the following recently have been attributed to prolonged use of marihuana: brain damage, lowered resistance to disease, birth defects, lung damage, sterility, and impotence. But, as Consumers Union concludes:

> Out of all of these studies . . . a general pattern is beginning to emerge. When a research finding can be readily checked—either by repeating the experiment or by devising a better one—an allegation of adverse marijuana effects is relatively short-lived. No damage is found—and after a time the allegation is dropped (often to be replaced by allegations of some other kind of damage due to marijuana).
> If the test procedure is difficult . . . independent repeat studies are not run in other laboratories. So these allegations of damage continue to be cited in the scientific literature and in the lay press. Then they, too, are eventually replaced by fresh allegations of marijuana damage.[110]

The absence of physical dependence removes one important factor leading to dependence on the drug, but the psychological effect—euphoria or the intoxication referred to by the National Commission—is capable of creating psychologically dependent persons or potheads. However, the commission found that the proportion of individuals who used the drug on at least a daily basis is very small. Although constant use of the drug can create lethargy, even heavy users often maintain interest and participation in a variety of activities ranging from athletics to reading and work.[111] Heavy users appear to be more interested in the personal effects of the drug rather than using it as a social experience with others, and they appear to be generally more withdrawn. But whether heavy marihuana use causes social isolation, or vice versa, has yet to be proven.

Marihuana, like alcohol and heroin, is largely a *social* drug. For the great majority of users their *introduction* to and *continued use* of the drug occur within a group context. Friends and/or relatives provide encouragement, guidance, and a spirit of companionship, making the experience worthwhile.[112] According to Howard S. Becker, the process of becoming a marihuana user involves three steps:

1. Learning the technique of producing the effects. One must discover the correct manner of smoking or the effects of the drug will not appear.
2. Learning to recognize the effects and connect them with the drug. Some sensations, such as feeling hungry or elated, are not always perceived as stemming from the drug; one must learn what the high is.
3. Learning to enjoy the effects of the drug. At first, the sensations are not automatically perceived as pleasant; reassurances that all is well can come from the group.[113]

In addition, the initiate acquires from the group the verbalized motives necessary to overcome any reluctance to try something that is illegal and about which he or she may have learned all kinds of horrible consequences. As Becker points out, in order to become a regular user it is not enough to learn to recognize the drug's effects. One must also set aside fears and conceptions of morality. The group can help one to do this.

> A person will feel free to use marihuana to the degree that he comes to regard conventional conceptions of it as the uninformed views of outsiders and replaces those conceptions with the "inside" view he has acquired through his experience with the drug in the company of other users.[114]

MARIHUANA USE AND DEVIANCE

From what we have already discussed about marihuana it should be clear that it is a relatively harmless drug. It is unlikely to create dependence and there appear to be few, if any, organic consequences associated even with consistent use. In terms of hazards to the individual it ranks well below the legal psychoactive drugs such as alcohol and nicotine. Because dependence does not develop, there is no need for the individual to resort to property crimes to support the habit. Although some users feel the drug enhances sexual behavior, there is no evidence that it contributes to sexual aggressiveness, nor does it contribute to other forms of aggressiveness or violence. What does that leave as far as crimes are concerned? In the words of the commission: *"The only crimes which can be directly attributed to marihuana-using behavior are those resulting from the use, possession or transfer of an illegal substance."* [115]

However, one claim about the relationship between marihuana and deviance is less easily disposed of—the claim that marihuana use leads to the use of heroin or other more dangerous drugs. As one publication of the Bureau of Narcotics stresses:

> It cannot be too strongly emphasized that the smoking of the marijuana cigarette is a dangerous first step on the road which usually leads to enslavement by heroin. . . .
> *Most* teenage addicts started by smoking marijuana cigarettes. *Never let anyone persuade you to smoke even one marijuana cigarette. It is pure poison.* [116]

There is no question that studies comparing marihuana users with nonusers find that users are more likely to use heroin.[117] But it is one thing to say that persons who use marihuana are more likely to try heroin; it is quite another to say that marihuana use leads inexorably to heroin use. Consider first that both coffee drinkers and aspirin takers are more likely to use illegal drugs—in fact, any user of any drug, legal or illegal, is more likely than a nonuser to use any other drug. As Goode puts it:

> Individuals who use drugs tend to be selectively recruited from segments of the population that are already oriented toward the use of drugs. In this sense, there is a kind of drug-taking "disposition." Thus, even before we examine whether the effects of marijuana per se have anything to do with "causing" the use of more dangerous drugs, it is necessary to start with the question of whether the population characteristics of those who use marijuana might be correlated with those of individuals who use other drugs, to see whether dangerous drug users might not be selectively recruited out of the larger marijuana-using group.[118]

Goode also points out that the criminal status of marihuana use also serves to isolate users to some degree from conventional society and incorporates them into a drug-taking subculture with its particular norms and verbalized motives supporting all kinds of drug-taking. It is possible, suggests Goode, that removing the illegal status of marihuana would decrease the number of persons turning to heroin because it would neutralize the influence of the criminal drug-using subculture.

MARIHUANA AND CONFLICT

Word about marihuana first emerged in the legislative halls as early as 1911 during hearings on what was to result in the Harrison Act of 1914.[119] It was then suggested that marihuana be subject to the same controls as opiates and cocaine because some experts believed it to be habit forming. But the drug industry was firmly opposed; it used the drug in corn plasters and animal medicines, and the drug scarcely seemed to pose a threat that would warrant restrictions. Consequently, marihuana was not included in the 1914 legislation.

But fears over marihuana were building. Rumbles of concern came from California where large numbers of immigrants from India were believed to be initiating whites into the habit. But those most feared were the Mexican migrant laborers in the Southwest. Murder, mayhem, and rape, to say nothing of the corruption of children, were all attributed to the influence of the weed. During the Depression when jobs were scarce Mexicans were even less welcome; the problem of marihuana and the problem of Mexican immigration became one. A member of one patriotic society, the American Coalition, connected things this way:

> Marijuana, perhaps now the most insidious of our narcotics, is a direct by-product of unrestricted Mexican immigration. Easily grown, it has been asserted that it has recently been planted between rows in a California penitentiary garden. Mexican peddlers have been caught distributing sample marijuana cigaretes [sic] to school children. . . . Our nation has more than enough laborers.[120]

Political pressure mounted for federal prohibition of marihuana. In 1936 a Colorado newspaper editor addressed this plea to the Bureau of Narcotics:

> Is there any assistance your Bureau can give us in handling this drug? . . .
> I wish I could show you what a small marijuana cigarette can do to one of our degenerate Spanish-speaking residents. That's why our problem is so great: The greatest percentage of our population is composed of Spanish-speaking persons, most of whom are low mentally, because of social and racial conditions.
> While marijuana has figured in the greatest number of crimes in the past few years, officials fear it, not for what it has done, but for what it is capable of doing. They want to check it before an outbreak occurs.
> Through representatives of civic leaders and law officers of the San Luis Valley, I have been asked to write to you for help.[121]

In addition to marihuana's association with a powerless minority group, myths about the effects of the drug were considerably elaborated. By 1936, for example, 68 per cent of all crimes committed in New Orleans were attributed to marihuana users. A propaganda campaign had been launched, with the support of the Bureau of Narcotics, to warn the unsuspecting public about the "Marihuana Menace" and its role as a "Killer Drug."

An illustrated poster found in trains, buses, and street cars:

BEWARE! Young and old people in all walks of life! This marihuana cigarette may be handed to YOU by the *friendly stranger*. It contains the Killer Drug Marihuana in which lurks MURDER! INSANITY! DEATH!—WARNING! Dope Peddlers are shrewd! They may put some of this drug in the teapot or in the cocktail or in the tobacco cigarette.

A pamphlet issued by the International Narcotic Education Association:

Prolonged use of marihuana frequently develops a delirious rage which sometimes leads to high crimes, such as assault and murder. Hence marihuana has been called the "killer drug." The habitual use of this narcotic poison always causes a very marked mental deterioration and sometimes produces insanity. . . .

While the marihuana habit leads to physical wreckage and mental decay, its effects upon character and morality are even more devastating. The victim frequently undergoes such degeneracy that he will lie and steal without scruple; he becomes utterly untrustworthy. . . . Marihuana sometimes gives man the lust to kill unreasonably and without motive. Many cases of assault, rape, robbery, and murder are traced to the use of marihuana.[122]

By 1937 the evil dimensions of this new drug enemy had become clear: not only was it used by Mexicans, but blacks and lower-class whites were becoming interested in it. Furthermore, the image of the drug as a killer had become too terrifying to ignore any longer. That year another revenue bill, the Marihuana Tax Act, became law. An extremely high tax was placed on the drug, and responsibility for the law's enforcement was assigned to the Bureau of Narcotics. Another class of criminals had been created.

Drug Control: The Great American Flop

In baseball the player with three strikes is out. But after three failures in trying to stop the use of alcohol, opiates, and marihuana, the United States government often stands at the plate convinced it can gain victory by smashing the hell out of the problem. Unlike the ballplayer, who adjusts to the peculiarities of various pitchers and who tries to put past experience to use, many U.S. legislators subscribe to a single-minded philosophy—if you don't hit it the first time, you're not swinging hard enough.

With the exception of Prohibition, which was finally repealed, the approach has been unvaried. Pass a law; if that does not work make the sentences harsher, get more policemen, get better detection devices, loosen up the law to make arrests easier, and so on. Whatever you do, refuse to recognize that making some behaviors criminal does not prevent them.

After 1937, drugs did not become a legislative issue again until the early 1950s. Then the short-memoried lawmakers were amazed to discover that organized crime was profiting from drugs. Furthermore, there was some suspicion that communists were also involved in the drug traffic in an attempt to corrupt American youth.[123] The answer, of course, was to "get tough." There followed a series of new federal and state laws of increasing severity aimed at both heroin and marihuana use. Most states, in fact, made no distinction between the two drugs. But the laws changed nothing. According to all estimates, drug use, especially marihuana use, continued to rise and presumably threatened the great heart of America: the white middle class. The 1966 Annual Report of the Bureau of Narcotics complained:

> The dangerous rise in illicit marihuana traffic and the increased use of marihuana and narcotic drugs by college age persons of middle and upper economic status became more evident at the close of 1966. These facts present a new challenge which must and will be met for the welfare of the country.[124]

By 1970 the laws had reached their extreme in severity. Here are some of the penalties one could receive for marihuana offenses. In Alabama first offense for possession meant no less than five years, the second offense ten to forty years; in Illinois, first-sale offense meant ten years to life; in Louisiana, for those over twenty-one possession meant at least five years at hard labor; first-sale offense drew ten to fifty years hard labor; in Rhode Island first-sale could get you twenty to forty years; in Utah the life sentence was possible for a first-sale offense; and in Texas a judge could give life for a first-possession offense.[125]

To some degree 1970 proved to be a watershed year. Some law enforcement authorities began to recognize that marihuana use was continuing to grow despite the harsh penalties. Furthermore, that growth appeared greatest among the more powerful interest groups—the white middle and upper classes. Indeed, drug use by college students was approaching 50 per cent. Relatives of some of the most powerful families in America were being arrested for smoking the damnable weed. (None of these were sentenced to anything approaching five years at hard labor, in case you might have wondered.) There was also evidence that nearly two thirds of the armed forces in Vietnam had smoked marihuana at some time.[126] Clearly, marihuana was here to stay, and the first indication that the federal government recognized this was President Nixon's signing into law of the Comprehensive Drug Abuse Prevention and Control Act, which actually *reduced* penalties, especially those for possession of marihuana.

Since then some states and municipalities have also reduced penalties. Oregon has a maximum penalty of $100 for possession of less than one ounce of marihuana; Alaska, California, Colorado, and Maine have enacted laws making the possession of small amounts of marihuana in one's home a civil offense rather than a crime, punishable by a small fine; in Ann Arbor and Ypsilanti, Michigan, local ordinances set the penalties at $5. Several other states and communities have similar legislation pending. But in practice the decriminalization trend has yet to be reflected in national arrest statistics: in 1971 there were 225,828 arrests on marihuana charges, in 1973 arrests nearly doubled—to 420,700.[127]

The legal attempts to crush drug use have left their marks, some humorous, others outright tragic. One of the more humorous attempts to stop drug traffic was "Operation Intercept," an attempt to seal off the Mexican border to marihuana smuggling in 1969. Billed as "the nation's largest peacetime search and seizure operation by civil authorities," it employed hundreds of extra border guards, pursuit planes, specially installed radar facilities, and torpedo boats. Within a few days it had immediate impact: it tied up border traffic for miles, irritated hundreds of individuals who were forced to strip nude, and aggravated the Mexican government, at whose request the operation was terminated in twenty days. The more long-term effect was to encourage the importation of stronger marihuana than the Mexican variety from other parts of the world such as North Africa and Vietnam. Operation Intercept also encouraged more serious efforts to grow and harvest the domestic product.[128] The operation did create a marihuana shortage in the United States, but the shortage was only temporary because the higher prices attracted more sellers into the market. Operation Intercept was a failure by any measure, and an expensive one at that.

More tragic results have followed efforts to make arrests easier for police by such devices as the *no-knock law* provided for in the Comprehensive Drug Abuse Act of 1970. This provision allowed special warrants enabling officers to enter private premises without warning, on the assumption that they must do so to prevent pushers from destroying evidence while the officers were still pounding on the doors.

After the law was passed, however, dozens of violent and mistaken assaults on innocent persons and their homes were carried out by narcotics officers.

The following are only two of the more publicized cases. In both instances the officers were subsequently cleared of any wrongdoing because no criminal intent could be established. The first concerns two separate incidents by the same agents.

Shabbily-clad, unshaven [narcotics agents] barged in on two houses [owned by Mr. and Mrs. Giglotto, and Mr. and Mrs. Askew] without federal no-knock authority, let alone ordinary search warrants required by the fourth amendment. . . . Sworn testimony indicates that they kicked in the doors without warning, while shouting obscenities and threatening the inhabitants with drawn weapons. The Giglottos and Askews were understandably terrified. They were forced to stand idly by while their homes were ransacked and their lives threatened. At no time during the raids did the agents satisfactorily identify themselves as federal narcotics agents or explain the nature of their authority. When they discovered that they had raided the wrong premises, they simply left—no apologies, no explanations, no offers to fully compensate for the damage done.

On April 24, 1972, a total of 19 agents, including five Bureau of Narcotics and Dangerous Drug agents, two federal chemists, nine sheriff's deputies, and an Internal Revenue Service agent moved in on [Dirk] Dickenson's mountain retreat near Eureka, California. The purpose of the raid was to seize a cabin in which there was thought to be a "giant lab" producing illegal drugs. After arriving on foot with dogs and by air in borrowed helicopters, agents assaulted the cabin with handguns and rifles. Reports indicate the agents were not in uniform and failed to identify themselves. Mr. Dickenson, unarmed, frightened, and confused, ran toward the woods and a federal agent fatally shot him in the back. No "giant lab" was found.[129]

"Overzealous agents," say some observers of these actions; "shades of Nazi Germany," say others. Regardless of which explanation you prefer, this kind of activity is just one legacy of the attempt to deal with drugs through the criminal law. Although the no-knock law was repealed in 1974, the criminal approach to drug problems will always threaten the integrity of our society. The laws create a criminal class who must rely on illegal sources for drugs. This means high prices and high profits for those willing to take the risk. High profits mean greater ability to further corrupt the agents of law enforcement. The incorruptible thus must become "overzealous" to overcome their frustration at trying to destroy a problem that defies solution.

Who loses? Everybody—almost. There is the honest taxpayer who must (or should) wonder about the incredible resources expended (such as for blocking entire borders) only to be told that the drug problem is getting worse, and that certain rights must be temporarily relinquished—the right not to have your door kicked in, your phone tapped, or your suitcase searched. As the sign says at airport Customs Bureau stations: "Patience Please, a Drug-Free America Comes First." [130] There is the law enforcement system that must expend its energies on behavior that does not endanger others, but exposes officers to corrupting influences that can discredit the entire system. There is the user who pays too much and risks too much. Finally, there is the dealer—part of the great service industry that keeps the user supplied, the law enforcement system in action, and the profits rolling in. The dealer is the only person who does not lose.

Abraham S. Blumberg nicely sums up the American drug experience to date.

> It has by now become quite evident that the continued employment of a legalistic-criminal enforcement model in attempting to manage the drug problem will result in the further erosion of our constitutional system and the further corruption of our enforcement agencies. The exorbitant profits that are made possible by the illicit markets created by our drug laws insure the total failure of drug prohibition, in the same manner that we failed to banish the use of alcohol under the Eighteenth Amendment. The enormous profits that are assured for those engaged in the distribution of the prohibited drugs, make it an attractive enterprise regardless of the criminal sanctions that may be imposed. The consequences of [harsh] drug laws . . . simply tend to impoverish the quality of life for the rest of us, but nevertheless afford a relatively acceptable degree of risk to those who traffic in drugs or have a need to use them. Historically, that is the substance of the impact of our drug laws.[131]

There is some recent evidence that approaches other than criminal are being considered. Although on the one hand a state like New York is still passing harsh laws—a 1973 statute requires judges to impose life prison terms on those convicted for either selling or possessing various amounts of certain drugs—on the other hand, in the same state attempts are being made to remove the drug user from the legal system. Because it is assumed that the dependent user will continue to rely on drugs, there is increasing approval of maintenance programs in which users can take drugs to avoid withdrawal symptoms.

Today, the only maintenance programs having widespread official acceptance involve *methadone*, a synthetic drug similar in chemical structure to heroin and morphine. Taken orally, methadone produces little euphoria, but does replace the missing heroin in the human system, thus halting withdrawal symptoms. The body acquires a tolerance for methadone just as it does for heroin, but there is a difference; the drug is *legal* and therefore cheap. In short, methadone users are still drug-dependent, but they can abandon the criminal subculture so necessary to continuing heroin use, and can take their places in respectable society—at least that is the goal.[132]

There are several problems with methadone maintenance programs, which need not concern us here.[133] Suffice it to say that methadone is not the answer for all or even nearly all heroin users. Now even *heroin maintenance* is being seriously discussed as an alternative. This type of program, which has been the British approach for many years, will also not be the ultimate answer to the drug problem. But heroin maintenance, like methadone maintenance, should bring many users back into the normal world once more. Then perhaps the many myths about drug dependence can be dispelled at last.

NOTES

1. National Commission on Marihuana and Drug Abuse, *Drug Use in America: Problem in Perspective* (Washington, D.C.: Government Printing Office, 1973), p. 9.

2. Erich Goode, *The Drug Phenomenon: Social Aspects of Drug Taking* (Indianapolis: Bobbs-Merrill, 1973), p. 39.

3. Ibid., p. 39.

4. There is considerable debate on what constitutes a realistic classification of psychoactive drugs insofar as human use is concerned. Practically every author on the subject has his or her own system. For example, see Goode, *The Drug Phenomenon*, pp. 8–9; Ronald L. Akers, *Deviant Behavior: A Social Learning Approach* (Belmont, Calif.: Wadsworth Publishing, 1973), p. 68; William Bates and Betty Crowther, *Drugs: Causes, Circumstances, and Effects of Their Use* (Morristown, N.J.: General Learning Press, 1973), pp. 6–10; and Joel Fort, *Alcohol: Our Biggest Drug Problem* (New York: McGraw-Hill, 1973), pp. 172–177.

5. Goode, *The Drug Phenomenon*, p. 13.

6. Richard Jones, " 'Up' on Psilocybin," *The Harvard Review*, 1 (Summer 1963), as cited in *In Their Own Behalf: Voices from the Margin*, 2nd ed., eds. Charles H. McCaghy, James K. Skipper, Jr., and Mark Lefton (Englewood Cliffs, N.J.: Prentice-Hall, 1974), pp. 68–69, 71.

7. Goode, *The Drug Phenomenon*, p. 10.

8. Paraphrased from Richard R. Lingeman, *Drugs from A to Z: A Dictionary* (New York: McGraw-Hill, 1969), pp. 244–245.

9. The discussion is based on National Commission, *Drug Use in America*, pp. 120–140.

10. Bureau of Narcotics and Dangerous Drugs, U.S. Department of Justice *Drugs of Abuse* (Washington, D.C.: Government Printing Office, 1972), pp. 2, 4.

11. National Commission, *Drug Use in America*, pp. 13–14.

12. Ibid., pp. 20–23.

13. Ibid., pp. 50–59.

14. The discussion is based upon Norman Taylor, *Narcotics: Nature's Dangerous Gifts*, rev. ed. of *Flight From Reality* (New York: Dell Publishing, 1963), pp. 67–95. Also see Fort, *Alcohol*, pp. 43–48.

15. Taylor, *Narcotics*, pp. 74–75.

16. National Institute of Mental Health, *Alcohol and Alcoholism: Problems,*

Programs, and Progress, rev. ed. (Rockville, Maryland: National Institute of Mental Health, 1972), p. 4.

17. Morris E. Chafetz and Harold W. Demone, Jr., *Alcoholism and Society* (New York: Oxford University Press, 1962), p. 9, cited in Craig MacAndrew and Robert B. Edgerton, *Drunken Comportment: A Social Explanation* (Chicago: Aldine Publishing, 1969), pp. 6–7.

18. Charles H. McCaghy, "Drinking and Deviance Disavowal: The Case of Child Molesters," *Social Problems,* **16** (Summer 1968), pp. 43–49.

19. MacAndrew and Edgerton, *Drunken Comportment,* pp. 13–135.

20. Ibid., pp. 165, 172.

21. *The Gallup Opinion Index,* June, 1974, Report No. 108.

22. Statistics derived from *Crime in the United States, 1973, Uniform Crime Reports* (Washington, D.C.: Government Printing Office, 1974), p. 121.

23. *Crime in the United States, 1970, Uniform Crime Reports* (Washington, D.C.: Government Printing Office, 1971), p. 122.

24. National Institute of Mental Health, *Alcohol and Alcoholism,* p. 11.

25. Jack West, "Drunk Loses 'Home' After 396 Arrests," *Arizona Republic* (Phoenix), March 18, 1974, pp. 1–2.

26. President's Commission on Law Enforcement and Administration of Justice, *The Challenge of Crime in a Free Society* (Washington, D.C.: Government Printing Office, 1967), p. 236.

27. Robert A. Voas, "Alcohol As an Underlying Factor in Behavior Leading to Fatal Highway Crashes," in *Proceedings of the First Annual Alcoholism Conference of the National Institute on Alcohol Abuse and Alcoholism,* ed. Morris E. Chafetz (Washington, D.C.: National Institute of Mental Health, 1973), p. 330.

28. National Commission, *Drug Use in America,* pp. 192–193.

29. This discussion is based on Charles S. Lieber, "Medical Complications of Alcoholics," in *Proceedings of the First Annual Alcoholism Conference,* pp. 3–5; and Lawrence K. Altman, "Baboon Experiment Shows Alcohol, Not Poor Diet, Causes Liver Damage," *New York Times,* January 22, 1974, p. 41.

30. *Metropolitan Life Statistical Bulletin,* **55** (July 1974), pp. 2–4.

31. For a book with this as its major theme, see Fort, *Alcohol.*

32. For descriptions of people living on skid row see: Howard M. Bahr, *Skid Row: An Introduction to Disaffiliation* (New York: Oxford University Press, 1973); James P. Spradley, *You Owe Yourself a Drunk: An Ethnography of Urban Nomads* (Boston: Little, Brown, 1970); Samuel E. Wallace, *Skid Row As a Way of Life* (Totowa, N.J.: Bedminster Press, 1965); and David Levinson, "Skid Row in Transition," *Urban Anthropology,* **3:**1(1974), pp. 79–93.

33. Bahr, *Skid Row,* p. 103.

34. This discussion is based on Earl Rubington, *Alcohol Problems and Social Control* (Columbus, Ohio: Charles E. Merrill Publishing, 1973), pp. 50–52.

35. E. M. Jellinek, *The Disease Concept of Alcoholism* (New Haven, Conn.: Hillhouse Press, 1960), p. 35.

36. Ibid., pp. 37–38.

37. This discussion is based on Robin Room, "Assumptions and Implications of Disease Concepts of Alcoholism," (paper delivered at the 29th International Congress on Alcoholism and Drug Dependence, Sydney, Australia, February 2–14, 1970).

38. Derived from E. M. Jellinek, "Phases of Alcohol Addiction," in *Society, Culture, and Drinking Patterns,* eds. David J. Pittman and Charles R. Snyder (New York: John Wiley & Sons, 1962), pp. 356–368.

39. Room, "Assumptions and Implications," p. 12.

40. E. Mansell Pattison, "Comment on 'The Alcoholic Game,' " *Quarterly Journal of Studies on Alcohol,* **30** (December 1969), p. 953. There are several discussions of alcoholism as a disease but some of the best are Claude M. Steiner, "The Alcohol Game," *Quarterly Journal of Studies on Alcohol,* **30** (December 1969), pp. 920–938, with comments by Ben J. Doreshtov, Solomon Machover, Humphry Osmond, Griffith Edwards, Dale C. Cameron, and E. Mansell Pattison, pp. 939–956; David Robinson, "The Alcohologist's Addiction: Some Implications of Having Lost Control over the Disease Concept of Alcoholism," *Quarterly Journal of Studies on Alcohol,* **33** (December 1972), pp. 1028–1042, with comments by Robert A. Moore, Peter B. Dewes, Matthew P. Dumont, and Robin Room, pp. 1043–1059; and Don Cahalan, *Problem Drinkers* (San Francisco: Jossey-Bass, 1970), pp. 1–17.

41. This discussion is suggested by Cahalan, *Problem Drinkers,* pp. 10–14.

42. Thomas F. A. Plaut, *Alcohol Problems: A Report to the Nation by the Cooperative Commission on the Study of Alcoholism* (New York: Oxford University Press, 1967), pp. 37–38.

43. Robert F. Bales, "Cultural Differences in Rates of Alcoholism," in *Drinking and Intoxication: Selected Readings in Social Attitudes and Controls,* ed. Raymond G. McCarthy (Glencoe, Ill.: Free Press, 1959), pp. 263–277.

44. For collections of the various studies see: McCarthy, *Drinking and Intoxication,* and Pittman and Snyder, *Society, Culture, and Drinking Patterns.*

45. Richard Jessor, Theodore D. Graves, Robert C. Hanson, and Shirley L. Jessor, *Society, Personality, and Deviant Behavior: A Study of a Tri-Ethnic Community* (New York: Holt, Rinehart, and Winston, 1968).

46. The terminology and discussion of these variables have been purposely simplified for the benefit of the undergraduate student. For a precise explanation see ibid., pp. 50–115, 233–331.

47. This resulted in a description of patterns of drinking behavior. See Don Cahalan, Ira H. Cisin, and Helen M. Crossley, *American Drinking Practices: A National Survey of Behavior and Attitudes* (New Brunswick, N.J.: Rutgers Center of Alcohol Studies, 1969).

48. Cahalan, *Problem Drinkers,* pp. 27–34.

49. Ibid., pp. 81–85.

50. Ibid., pp. 141–142.

51. Edwin M. Lemert, "Sociocultural Research on Drinking," in *Human Deviance, Social Problems, and Social Control,* ed. Edwin M. Lemert, 2nd ed. (Englewood Cliffs, N.J.: Prentice-Hall, 1972), pp. 207–217.

52. For a discussion and test of this approach see Sharon C. Wilsnack, "The Needs of the Female Drinker: Dependency, Power, or What?" in *Proceedings of the Second Annual Alcoholism Conference of the National Institute on Alcohol Abuse and Alcoholism,* ed. Morris E. Chafetz (Washington, D.C.: National Institute of Mental Health, 1973), pp. 65–83.

53. For discussions of this approach see David C. McClelland, "Drinking As a Response to Power Needs in Men," and Ozzie G. Simmons, "Discussion: Alcohol and Human Motivation," in Chafetz, *Proceedings of the Second Annual Alcoholism Conference,* pp. 47–64 and 84–91 respectively.

54. Bales, "Cultural Differences."

55. For a detailed discussion concerning how types of norms are related to deviant drinking behavior see Ephraim H. Mizruchi and Robert Perrucci, "Prescription, Proscription and Permissiveness: Aspects of Norms and Deviant Drinking Behavior," in *Approaches to Deviance: Theories, Concepts, and Research Findings,* eds. Mark Lefton, James K. Skipper, Jr., and Charles H. McCaghy (New York: Appleton-Century-Crofts, 1968), pp. 151–167.

56. Cahalan, *Problem Drinkers,* pp. 36, 38.

57. For the classic study of this process see David J. Pittman and C. Wayne Gordon, *Revolving Door: A Study of the Chronic Police Case Inebriate* (New York: Free Press, 1958).

58. National Institute of Mental Health, *Alcohol and Alcoholism,* Public Health Service Publication No. 1640 (Washington, D.C.: Government Printing Office, n.d.), p. 6.

59. Marvin A. Block, *Alcoholism Is a Disease,* pamphlet distributed by The National Council on Alcoholism, Inc., reprinted from *Today's Health* (n.p., n.d.), pp. 6–8.

60. This discussion is based on Edwin M. Lemert, "Alcohol, Values, and Social Control," in *Human Deviance, Social Problems, and Social Control,* 2nd ed., ed. Edwin M. Lemert (Englewood Cliffs, N.J.: Prentice-Hall, 1972), pp. 112–122.

61. This discussion is based on Raymond G. McCarthy and Edgar M. Douglass, "Prohibition and Repeal," in *Drinking and Intoxication,* ed. McCarthy, pp. 369–383; and Joseph R. Gusfield, "Status Conflicts and the Changing Ideologies of the American Temperance Movement," in *Society, Culture, and Drinking Patterns,* eds. Pittman and Snyder, pp. 101–120.

62. Gusfield, "Status Conflicts," p. 103.

63. Byron C. Kirby, "The Logic of Prohibition," *Scientific Temperance Journal,* **39** (1930), p. 1, as cited in *Drinking and Intoxication,* ed. McCarthy, p. 383.

64. Gusfield, "Status Conflicts," p. 113.

65. McCarthy and Douglass, "Prohibition and Repeal," pp. 377–379.

66. Gusfield, "Status Conflicts," p. 114.

67. Lemert, "Alcohol, Values, and Social Control," pp. 115–116.

68. This discussion is derived from Cabinet Committee on International Narcotics Control, *World Opium Survey 1972* (Washington, D.C.: U.S. Department of State, 1972).

69. Gary Hoenig, "The Infinite Resilience of Drug Abuse," *New York Times,* February 9, 1975, Section 4, p. 16; and Nicholas Gage, "Latins Now Leaders of Hard Drug Trade," *New York Times,* April 21, 1975, pp. 1, 32.

70. National Commission, *Drug Use in America,* p. 174.

71. Douglas H. Powell, "A Pilot Study of Occasional Heroin Users," *Archives of General Psychiatry,* **28** (April 1973), pp. 587–589.

72. There is little consistency in descriptions of exactly what feelings are experienced by persons using heroin for the first time with or without their knowledge, and by persons who have used it for long periods. Furthermore, the means of using the drug also seems to influence the perceived effects. For example, injecting heroin under the skin rather than mainlining it into the veins appears to preclude the experience of the rush. The discussion concerns only mainlining and is drawn from the following sources: Edward M. Brecher, *Licit and Illicit Drugs* (Mount Vernon, N.Y.: Consumers Union,

1972), pp. 12–15; Alfred R. Lindesmith, *Addiction and Opiates* (Chicago: Aldine, 1968), pp. 23–45; William E. McAuliffe and Robert A. Gordon, "A Test of Lindesmith's Theory of Addiction: The Frequency of Euphoria Among Long-Term Addicts," *American Journal of Sociology,* **79** (January 1974), pp. 795–803; and James V. Delong, "The Drugs and Their Effects," in *Dealing With Drug Abuse: A Report to the Ford Foundation,* eds. Patricia M. Wald, Peter Barton Hutt, et al. (New York: Praeger, 1972), pp. 78–85.

73. Erich Goode, "The Criminology of Drugs and Drug Use," in *Current Perspectives on Criminal Behavior: Original Essays on Criminology,* ed. Abraham S. Blumberg (New York: Alfred A. Knopf, 1974), p. 172.

74. Troy Duster, *The Legislation of Morality: Law, Drugs, and Moral Judgment* (New York: Free Press, 1970), pp. 70–71. See also Alan G. Sutter, "The World of the Righteous Dope Fiend," *Issues in Criminology,* **2** (Fall 1966), p. 191.

75. Delong, "The Drugs and Their Effects," pp. 81–84.

76. Duster, *The Legislation of Morality,* pp. 69–75.

77. Lindesmith, *Addiction and Opiates,* pp. 31–32.

78. McAuliffe and Gordon, "A Test of Lindesmith's Theory of Addiction," pp. 795–840.

79. Ibid., p. 831.

80. For a discussion of the failures of various programs see Brecher, *Licit and Illicit Drugs,* pp. 64–89.

81. M. Snow, "Maturing Out of Narcotic Addiction in New York City," *International Journal of the Addictions,* **8** (December 1973), pp. 921–938.

82. For discussions on this point, see Brecher, *Licit and Illicit Drugs,* pp. 21–32; Goode, *The Drug Phenomenon,* pp. 40–44; and Delong, "The Drugs and Their Effects," pp. 71–85, 116.

83. For a discussion of drug-related deaths see T. Premkumar, Walter Cuskey, and Johannes Ipsen, "A Comparative Study of Drug-Related Deaths in the United States," *International Annals of Criminology,* **11**:2 (1972), pp. 501–527.

84. There is also the theory that overdoses among addicts are actually very rare. The argument is that such deaths are actually caused either by the adulterants used in the heroin or by the interaction of heroin with other drugs being used at the same time, for example, alcohol. See Brecher, *Licit and Illicit Drugs,* pp. 101–114.

85. John F. Holahan and Paul A. Henningsen, "The Economics of Heroin," in *Dealing with Drug Abuse,* eds. Wald, et. al., pp. 292–293.

86. Goode, "Criminology of Drugs," p. 186.

87. National Commission, *Drugs Use in America,* pp. 175, 161–163, 165.

88. James M. Markham, "Heroin Addict Numbers Game," *New York Times,* June 6, 1972, p. 42; and Markham, "Youths Rejecting Heroin, but Turn to Other Drugs," *New York Times,* December 12, 1972, pp. 1, 34.

89. Except where noted this discussion is based on Leon Gibson Hunt, *Recent Spread of Heroin Use in the United States: Unanswered Questions* (Washington, D.C.: The Drug Abuse Council, Inc., 1974).

90. Ibid., p. 16; see also Patricia M. Wald and Peter Barton Hutt, "The Drug Abuse Survey Project: Summary of Findings, Conclusions, and Recommendations" in *Dealing With Drug Abuse,* eds. Wald, et al., p. 4.

91. Markham, "Youths Rejecting Heroin," pp. 1, 34.

92. The history of drug control legislation is discussed in Brecher, *Licit and Illicit Drugs,* pp. 3–63; Alfred R. Lindesmith, *The Addict and the Law* (Bloomington, Ind.: Indiana University Press, 1965); David F. Musto, *The American Disease: Origins of Narcotic Control* (New Haven, Conn.: Yale University Press, 1973); and Charles Reasons, "The Politics of Drugs: An Inquiry in the Sociology of Social Problems," *Sociological Quarterly,* **15** (Summer 1974), pp. 381–404.

93. Brecher, *Licit and Illicit Drugs,* pp. 8–11.

94. Ibid., pp. 6–7.

95. Ibid., pp. 42–44; and John Helmer and Thomas Vietorisz, "Drug Use, the Labor Market, and Class Conflict," (paper presented at the annual meeting of the American Sociological Association, New York City, August, 1973).

96. Musto, *The American Disease,* pp. 5–6.

97. Reasons, "The Politics of Drugs," pp. 393–394.

98. Musto, *The American Disease,* pp. 121–128.

99. Editorial Comment, *American Medicine,* **21** (O.S.), **10** (N.S.) (November 1915), pp. 799–800, cited in Brecher, *Licit and Illicit Drugs,* p. 50.

100. Donald T. Dickson, "Bureaucracy and Morality: An Organizational Perspective on a Moral Crusade," *Social Problems,* **16** (Fall 1968), pp. 149–151.

101. Musto, *The American Disease,* pp. 132–134, 244–249.

102. Ibid., p. 134.

103. Linder v. U.S., 268 U.S. 5 (1925).

104. Reasons, "The Politics of Drugs," p. 398.

105. National Commission, *Drug Use in America,* pp. 63–65.

106. For histories of marihuana see Brecher, *Licit and Illicit Drugs,* pp. 397–430; and Allen Geller and Maxwell Boas, *The Drug Beat* (New York: McGraw-Hill, 1969), pp. 3–42.

107. Delong, "The Drugs and Their Effects," p. 97.

108. This discussion is based on National Commission on Marihuana and Drug Abuse, *Marihuana: A Signal of Misunderstanding* (Washington, D. C.: Government Printing Office, 1972), pp. 49–66.

109. Ibid., p. 59.

110. Edward M. Brecher and the editors of *Consumers Reports,* "Marijuana: The Health Questions," *Consumers Reports,* **40** (March 1975), p. 149.

111. National Commission, *Marihuana,* pp. 37–41.

112. For statistics concerning the circumstances of first use see National Commission on Marihuana and Drug Abuse, *Marihuana: A Signal of Misunderstanding. The Technical Papers of the First Report of the National Commission,* vol. II, (Washington, D.C.: Government Printing Office, 1973) pp. 949–950.

113. Howard S. Becker, *Outsiders: Studies in the Sociology of Deviance* (New York: Free Press, 1963), pp. 41–58.

114. Ibid., p. 78.

115. National Commission, *Drug Use in America,* p. 159 (italics mine).

116. U.S. Treasury Department, Bureau of Narcotics, "Living Death: The Truth About Drug Addiction," (Washington, D.C.: Government Printing Office, 1965), cited in *Marihuana,* ed. Erich Goode (New York: Atherton Press, 1969), p. 66.

117. This discussion is based on Goode, *The Drug Phenomenon,* pp. 44–48. See also National Commission, *Marihuana,* pp. 45–49; and Stanley E. Grupp, *The Marihuana Muddle* (Lexington, Mass.: D. C. Heath, 1973), pp. 101–111.

118. Goode, *The Drug Phenomenon,* pp. 47–48.

119. This discussion is based on Musto, *The American Disease,* pp. 216–229; Geller and Boas, *The Drug Beat,* pp. 23–33; Brecher, *Licit and Illicit Drugs,* pp. 410–421; Becker, *Outsiders,* pp. 135–146; Dickson, "Bureaucracy and Morality," pp. 151–156; and Charles E. Reasons, "The 'Dope' on the Bureau of Narcotics in Maintaining the Criminal Approach to the Drug Problem," in *The Criminologist: Crime and the Criminal,* ed. Charles E. Reasons (Pacific Palisades, Calif.: Goodyear Publishing, 1974), pp. 144–155. These authors, although more or less in agreement on most matters of fact, differ greatly in their interpretations. The principal point of contention concerns the role of the Federal Bureau of Narcotics. Was its agitation for legislation an independent action or a response to pressures outside the Bureau? The author is in no position to resolve this problem; the discussion presented here represents a combination of these differing interpretations.

120. *New York Times,* September 15, 1935, cited in Musto, *The American Disease,* p. 220. For a discussion of the Mexican labor glut as instrumental in the crusade against marihuana, see Helmer and Vietorisz, "Drug Use."

121. Musto, *The American Disease,* p. 223.

122. Geller and Boas, *The Drug Beat,* pp. 24–26.

123. Reasons, "The 'Dope' on the Bureau of Narcotics," p. 147.

124. Ibid., p. 148.

125. Brecher, *Licit and Illicit Drugs,* pp. 419–420.

126. Ibid., pp. 423–426.

127. "Marijuana: The Legal Question," *Consumers Reports,* **40** (April 1975), p. 265.

128. Brecher, *Licit and Illicit Drugs,* pp. 434–450.

129. Senator Charles H. Percy, "The Legacy of No-Knock: Drug Law Enforcement Abuse," *Contemporary Drug Problems,* **3** (Spring 1974), pp. 5–8. See also Andrew H. Malcolm, "Violent Drug Raids Against the Innocent Found Widespread," *New York Times,* June 25, 1973, pp. 1, 22.

130. Percy, "The Legacy of No-Knock," p. 8.

131. Abraham S. Blumberg, "The Politics of Deviance: The Case of Drugs," *Journal of Drug Issues,* **3** (Spring 1973), pp. 106–107.

132. For a complete description of an ideal methadone program see U.S. Department of Justice, *Methadone Treatment Manual* (Washington, D.C.: Government Printing Office, 1973).

133. For discussions of some of these problems see Sidney Cohen, "Methadone Maintenance: Trick or Treatment?" *Human Behavior,* **2** (January 1973), pp. 22–25; Walter R. Cuskey and William Krasner, "The Needle and the Boot: Heroin Maintenance," *Society,* **10** (May–June 1973), pp. 48–49; Allan Parachini, "The Money in Methadone," and " 'Since When Has It Been Against the Law to Make Money?' " *Village Voice,* April 18, 1974, pp. 5–10, and April 25, 1974, pp. 26–28; and James V. Delong, "The Methadone Habit," *New York Times Magazine,* March 16, 1975, pp. 16, 78–80, 86–92.

9
MENTAL DISORDERS

In the last chapter we discussed how people use psychoactive drugs to alter their perception of the environment. Whether you are under the influence of alcohol, heroin, marihuana, or a host of other similar drugs, events and people around you may take on character and meanings incomprehensible to those not experiencing the same euphoria. Jokes that seem absolutely hilarious to you draw nothing but groans from others; statements of profound significance for all humanity are regarded as trivial by those same individuals; or the reversal of these experiences might occur. In short, drug users see, hear, and feel differently from nonusers.

But being different in both perceiving and responding to one's surroundings is not limited to drug users. And when this difference becomes obvious and cannot be attributed to drugs or some other logical source, we become uncomfortable. For example, supposing your boy or girl friend, after a few drinks, finds everything you say to be extremely funny—he or she develops a giggling fit lasting most of the night. That is understandable and a good time is had by all. But the next morning your "Hi" results in gales of laughter; "What's so funny?" really breaks up your friend; and "Are you crazy or something?" has him or her rolling on the ground in uncontrolled mirth.

When people act inappropriately for rea-

311

sons we cannot readily explain—and perhaps they cannot explain either—we put them into the crazy-or-something category. No doubt most readers have had personal experience with someone so classified. Your great-aunt Minnie talks to herself a lot, and your father says she is "nuttier than a fruit cake." Your neighbor Waldo Jones refused to get out of bed and go to work for one whole week; he finally went to a rest home to cure his nervous breakdown. And your best friend's mother was always screaming about people not appreciating her—she is taking some drugs and is much calmer now.

We are, of course, talking about behavior now most frequently referred to as *mental illness* or *mental disease.* It was once *madness, craziness,* and *insanity.* Today the first two are considered unflattering, and the third is strictly a *legal* term implying a lack of responsibility for one's behavior. Whether a person is or was insane is a decision made by courts—in most cases, juries—and the basis for the decision varies from one jurisdiction to another. Most federal courts, for example, have adopted the following definition, which incorporates the term *mental disease:*

> A person is not responsible for criminal conduct if at the time of such conduct as a result of mental disease or defect he lacks substantial capacity either to appreciate the criminality (or wrongfulness) of his conduct or to conform his conduct to the requirements of law.[1]

Despite its widespread use, however, the term *mental illness* (or *disease*—the words are used interchangeably) is highly controversial. We shall elaborate on some of this controversy later, but for now the reader should be aware that *the term has no precise, objective definition.* Instead, it is usually discussed in the context of highly relative concepts such as "lack of social adjustment" and "deviations from normality." [2] Thus the illness is defined in terms of norms, ethics, and law. It is a matter of *social definition* as to whether the behavior in question will be acceptable to whoever makes such judgments.

Thus, to say that certain behavior is evidence of an illness tells us nothing about its *cause,* but there is an important implication for the *social reaction* toward the behavior. Specifically, the sufferers of the illness become patients who may go to a hospital or doctor for treatment rather than to a jail, church, or other institution designed to change people's behavior.

No evidence exists, however, that most of what is called mental illness is any more a medical issue than is alcohol dependence or any other form of deviance discussed in previous chapters. Thus for purposes of consistency and clarity we shall usually refer to mental *disorder* rather than mental *illness.* The substitution is not entirely satisfactory, but it is less likely to be misleading about what is known about the source of the behavior, and it focuses on the effects of the behavior as perceived by those reacting toward it.

What Is Mental Disorder?

This is a difficult question to answer concisely. There are so many possible kinds of behavior regarded as disorders, and each may have varying degrees of impact on an individual's social interaction. Some writers would include practically all types of criminal behavior, ranging from theft to homicide. We shall attempt to remain within the generally accepted boundaries of what constitutes mental disorder; our purpose is not to be encyclopedic but to provide the reader with some idea of the range of behaviors coming to the attention of psychiatrists, clinical psychologists, and mental hospitals.

It is important at the outset to distinguish between two categories of mental disorder: that associated with *physical disorders of the brain* and that *not* so associated. The first category, usually called *organic disorders,* are clearly medical problems. The brain has been affected by any of a variety of factors such as syphilis, encephalitis, tumors, lead poisoning, lack of proper nutrition, exposure to carbon monoxide, head injuries, and general deterioration resulting from age.[3]

The symptoms associated with the forms of organic brain disorder are not important to our discussion, but one historical footnote is relevant. The first scientific advances in the study of mental disorders, made in the late nineteenth century, concerned the link between brain damage by syphilis and a disorder known as *paresis.* Because a form of brain damage was found to underlie one kind of disorder there emerged in the early twentieth century the dominant belief that all disorders could ultimately be connected with brain pathology. Thus, the field of medicine gained an early and firm foothold as the discipline possessing expertise concerning mental disorders.

But it soon became apparent to researchers that most disorders failed to display connections with any organic problem, be it brain damage or any other physiological factor. Such disorders are usually called *functional disorders* and are assumed to stem from psychological rather than physical sources. The following is an abbreviated classification of the major functional disorders and their associated symptoms.

1. Personality Disorders. This is a grab-bag category. The behaviors range from apparently trivial conduct to serious criminal acts, and from being transient and situational to long-term. This category

represents more than any other the importance of ethics and social norms in defining what constitutes mental disorder. James C. Coleman's textbook in abnormal psychology designates the following disorders as stemming primarily from "faulty development": stuttering, nail-biting, tics, bed-wetting after age three, psychopathic personalities, criminality and juvenile delinquency, and deviant sexual behavior. The latter includes impotence, prostitution, rape, masturbation when it "interferes with the establishment of normal heterosexual relations," homosexuality, sadism, and child molesting.[4] (Later in this chapter we shall discuss in detail how the assumption that deviant sexual behavior results from personality disorder has dramatically influenced the official reaction toward sex offenders.)

2. Neuroses. These disorders are generally considered to be among the less serious. Persons exhibiting the symptoms usually do not experience gross hallucinations and they are not likely to be hospitalized. The key factor in neuroses seems to be *anxiety*. Worry about one's health, job, and so on may result in chronic fatigue; tremors; excessive fears (phobias) of particular situations such as heights, storms, crowds, or certain animals; and compulsions such as incessant handwashing to avoid germs. These symptoms are essentially means of dealing with anxiety—they are *defense mechanisms* whereby individuals attempt to isolate themselves from problems.

3. Psychoses. These are the disorders that most people associate with being institutionalized. The man who thinks he is Napoleon, and the woman who gets instructions from Russian agents hidden in electric outlets belong in this category. Most psychoses fall into two main groups:

(a) Schizophrenia. Of the serious disorders, this is considered the most common.

More than 2 million Americans at one time or another have suffered from the tragic mental disorder of schizophrenia. Half of the Nation's beds in mental hospitals are now occupied by schizophrenic patients. It is estimated that 2 per cent of the population will have an episode of schizophrenia some time during their lives; in certain social settings—the urban slum, for example—the prediction rises to 6 per cent, or more than one in twenty persons.[5]

That which is labeled schizophrenia comprises a wide range of possible behavior. It is thus possible that two persons can be diagnosed schizophrenic and exhibit few common characteristics. Consequently schizophrenia itself is subdivided into various types such as simple, hebephrenic, and paranoid. We will not burden the reader with descriptions of these types, if only because psychiatrists themselves are inconsistent in designating who is what kind of schizophrenic. However, the following are considered some of the more exaggerated indicators of some form of schizophrenia: hallucinations (hearing a dead mother who keeps whispering); delusions (believing one's insides are rotting away); extreme apathy (total lack of animation, even to the point of remaining in whatever position one is placed); incoherent and illogical speech ("I am a fampus from whom all slugus reeks. Flibater me. Scratch delineation in case of emergency"); paranoia (the belief that someone is out to get one); inability to concentrate; extreme but nameless fears; and extreme childishness (giggling, and so on).

(b) Manic-Depressive Behavior. This is a type of psychosis involving wide fluctuations in mood, ranging from great elation, excitement, and activity to deep despair and listlessness. The individual may have delusions about suffering from incurable diseases, for example. Hallucinations may also occur. Psychiatrists believe that manic-depressives have a tendency toward suicide in the depressive state.

The symptoms described above seem obvious enough, particularly those of the psychoses. But in practice, the symptoms displayed by individuals are seldom so clear-cut and magnified; thus the diagnoses of patients usually turn out to be very hit-and-miss affairs. Psychiatrists can agree neither on who should be diagnosed as what nor on what the visible symptoms really mean.

A reliable diagnostic system has eluded psychiatry since the [very] first systematic efforts. Psychiatrists using a given diagnostic system still find themselves in disagreement, both about *how* to label a particular patient and *what* the label signifies. Traditionally, diagnostic systems have depended on the patient's presenting signs and symptoms; yet their significance to his past life or eventual outcome has been difficult to establish. Moreover, the reported signs and symptoms often vary according to the observer's theoretical stance and depth of knowledge. Further complicating the diagnostician's task is the fact that "presenting" signs and symptoms are changeable; a patient who was initially seen as a simple schizophrenic, for example, may look paranoid or hebephrenic [a type of schizophrenia characterized by silliness] after more intensive scrutiny.[6]

Diagnoses in psychiatry are akin to one physician telling you that your malady is a case of appendicitis while another disagrees, saying you have a broken leg. Although this analogy may be slightly far-fetched, the state of diagnostic consistency does not inspire confidence in statistics that purport to describe the distribution of mental disorder. It is apparent that we really know little about the *behaviors* of those "2 per cent of the population who will have an episode of schizophrenia" or about those "schizophrenics" occupying half the mental hospital beds.

If the serious disorders—the psychoses—defy adequate diagnosis, one would easily conclude that even less is known about the less dramatic forms. One study attempting to measure the extent of mental disorder of any type was conducted in Manhattan (the study is usually referred to as the Midtown Manhattan Survey). The study's method was to diagnose a random sample of adults through interviews. By interpreting claims of restlessness and nervousness among other behaviors as symptoms of disorder, the researchers arrived at some startling conclusions: only 18 per cent of the sample was mentally well, 23 per cent had marked or worse symptoms of disorder, and the remainder had moderate or mild symptoms.[7] When the great majority of a city's residents are found to be in need of psychiatric help, one can only wonder what has really been measured—the extent of disorder or the researchers' opinions about city dwellers?

But even recognizing that diagnostic procedures are inconsistent, misleading, and lacking in explanatory value, we must recognize the fact that countless persons behave in ways that are translated as signs of mental disorder. On occasion this process of defining behavior may be initiated by the individuals themselves; many persons commit themselves to mental hospitals or clinics, consult various types of mental health professionals, or periodically attend group therapy sessions, ranging in purpose from getting to know your body better to improving emotional outlooks on growing old, getting a divorce, enjoying sex, and tolerating idiotic co-workers.

Of interest here, however, is the majority of "mentally ill" persons who are defined as such by others. They seek help only after encouragement or pressure to do so and, in many cases, they are forced to submit to various control and treatment measures because their behavior has been perceived as inappropriate. Thus the question, "How does behavior—whatever it may be—become interpreted as a sign of mental disorder?" does not refer to diagnostic procedures, but rather to the labeling process preceding diagnosis.

> The early definitions of mental illness, especially in middle-class populations, are likely to take place in the groups within which the person primarily operates; evaluations are made by family, fellow employees, friends, and employers. If symptoms appear and are not recognized as such by members of the individual's more primary groups, it is unlikely that he will become accessible to psychiatric personnel unless his symptoms become visible, and disturbing enough to lead to his commitment to some treatment center by external authorities. . . .
>
> The basic decision about illness is usually made by community members and *not professional personnel.*[8]

The Medical Model

Thus the matter of definition or labeling plays a role in determining whether an individual will be treated as someone suffering from a mental disorder. But how significant a role? This is a crucial question because it pinpoints the distinction between the two major approaches to mental disorder. Our discussion thus far has dealt with the approach usually called the *medical model*. Most simply stated, this model assumes that certain behaviors are symptomatic of a disease and, depending upon one's particular theoretical orientation, that the disease stems from either organic causes (e.g., the lack of certain chemicals in the brain is currently being explored as a cause of schizophrenia) [9] or psychological causes.

The role of labeling (social reaction to the individual) is considered minimal within this model. The individual's symptoms are considered as invariable and inevitable as those of someone suffering from whooping cough or athlete's foot. Although some observers may or may not recognize the symptoms, or may pretend not to recognize them, the symptoms—or the diseases—are not appreciably affected by social reaction to the sufferer. In short, the individual experiencing mental disorder is seen as acting within a social vacuum. This model can be illustrated by the following axioms underlying the psychiatric conception of schizophrenics:

1. Schizophrenics differ fundamentally from the rest of humanity; their experiences—the images, delusions, and logic—are so unreal that others never encounter them except possibly in dreams. Schizophrenics are nearly inhuman, kinds of alien creatures.
2. The schizophrenic disease process progressively strips individuals of all social learning so they eventually have little left of what could be called civilized characteristics.
3. Schizophrenics have no control over their illness. They are weak and ineffective; consequently they do not make things happen, things happen to them. [10]

Thus the medical model, by focusing on the individual, portrays the source of mental disorder as almost exclusively *within* the individual. And, in the more serious cases at least, the individual is considered both out of control and out of touch with reality. The patient needs medical help on an individual basis just as surely as if he or she were suffering from a physical disease against which the body was helpless.

But as we suggested earlier, the majority of persons who become mental patients do so because others—particularly friends and relatives—define them as ill. This is not necessarily inconsistent with the medical model, but it does alert us to an important fact: *the symp-*

toms of mental disorder are forms of social behavior defined by others as deviant. In short, we are talking about a social phenomenon—as in drug dependence and crime, the behavior is subject to interpretation by others as to its appropriateness.

If this author were to claim he had spoken with little green men in a flying saucer, what would result? Would he be locked in a rubber room or end up as a highly paid touring lecturer? In our society either would be a possibility; he could be defined as having hallucinations or as discovering a major breakthrough in extraterrestrial relationships. What if your gray-haired grandmother carries on lengthy conversations with God? Is she a candidate for sainthood or for heavy sedation in an institution? Although these examples may seem extreme, they are not as far-fetched as they sound. As behavior becomes less extreme and the reality seems less "unreal," the matter of whether one is disordered becomes even more problematic.

The difficulty in using individual-centered explanations of mental disorder is that the nature of the behavior's deviation from "normal" is ignored. The behavior is labeled inappropriate to specific situations—thus it is a matter of social judgment. To concentrate solely on individuals and their symptoms is to disregard some very striking social factors and reasons contributing substantially to the process of defining those who "need help."

Some Correlates of Mental Disorder

SOCIAL CLASS

Because the disease model is so prevalent the term *epidemiology* is widely used in connection with studies on the social correlates of mental disorder. The term simply refers to the study of the distribution of illnesses.[11] There are many such studies, but we shall review only a few that reveal the most consistent finding: that there is a *definite relationship between social class and diagnoses of serious mental disorder.*

The pioneering study in this area was conducted by Robert E. L. Faris and H. Warren Dunham, who examined the distribution of persons admitted to mental hospitals in Chicago from 1922 to 1934. Using procedures similar to the ecological studies by Clifford Shaw on crime and delinquency (discussed in Chapter 2), Faris and Dunham found that rates of hospital admissions for psychosis were highest for persons residing in the city's center—the area of lowest economic status. As the distance from the city center increased and the status rose, rates of hospitalization fell off.[12] These findings clearly indicated to Faris and Dunham that social factors must play a role in mental disorder, and like Shaw they described those factors in terms of *social disorganization,* stating that the areas characterized by conflicting cultures and breakdowns in old normative structures also produced the greatest proportion of mental disorders.

> In these most disorganized sections of the city and, for that matter, of our whole civilization, many persons are unable to derive sufficient mental nourishment from the normal social sources to achieve a satisfactory conventional organization of their world. The result may be a lack of any organization at all, resulting in a confused, frustrated, and chaotic personality, or it may be a complex but unconventional original organization. In either case there is a serious divergence from the conventional organization which makes communication and understanding impossible and, for that matter, makes any form of co-operation difficult. It is just this type of unintelligible behavior which becomes recognized as mental disorder.[13]

The next study of major significance was that of August B. Hollingshead and Frederick C. Redlich in New Haven, Connecticut in 1950. Unlike Faris and Dunham, whose sample contained only those hospitalized and whose judgment about social class was based on area of residence, Hollingshead and Redlich drew as their sample all patients in public and private psychiatric institutions and those under the care of private practitioners but not institutionalized. The gauge of social status was based upon an index including area of residence, occupation, and education. The results confirmed those of Faris and Dunham: *an inverse relationship exists between the occurrence of psychoses and social class.*[14]

Other findings were also of interest. First, Hollingshead and Redlich found that neuroses—the less severe disorders—were concentrated in the *upper* classes. The authors concluded that a neurosis is a "state of mind" involving not only the patient but his or her social status and the therapist as well.

> A diagnosis of neurosis is a resultant of a social interactional process which involves the patient, the doctor, and the patient's position in the status structure of the community.
>
> It seems likely that the most important role in diagnosing "neurosis," is played by the individual who bears the label. Just how and why he accepts this designation is a fascinating question. In a very literal sense, the individual usually decides whether he is neurotic. The old saw, "Anyone who goes to a psychiatrist should have his head examined," is applicable here. The degree to which he accepts or rejects the role he plays or is assigned in his social milieu often determines whether or not he considers himself neurotic or accepts others' appraisal of his being disturbed.[15]

Further, different social classes experience not only *different types* of mental disorder but also *different reactions* toward the disorders. Hollingshead and Redlich found that social class was important even among those diagnosed as psychotic: the higher the social class, the less time spent in hospitals and the more intensive the treatment. Indeed, psychotics of the lower classes were more likely to be confined without treatment or to be treated by lobotomies and various forms of shock administered primarily to control rather than to cure.

Many subsequent studies have explored the relationship between social class and mental disorder.[16] Each is distinctive in its methods of sampling, its measurement of social class, and its criteria of mental disorder. But even after accounting for these variations and after recognizing that psychiatric diagnoses are extremely unreliable, it is inescapable that with decreasing social status there is a greater proportion of individuals who are diagnosed as suffering from some form of serious mental disorder.

The consistency of this finding raises important issues. On one hand one might conjecture that a cultural bias exists: upper class psychiatrists are simply unequipped to interpret some lower class behaviors except in terms of mental disorder. If one, on the other hand, subscribes to the medical model one can only conclude that the lower classes are crazier than the upper. Obviously, however, lower class status per se explains little, especially when you consider that the great majority of individuals in the lower class is as "normal" as are those in the upper class. What is it then about being in the lowest stratum of society that makes one more susceptible to serious mental disorder? As you might guess, there are nearly as many explanations as studies, including the hypothesis that being in the lower class leads to insecurity and an inability to reach one's goals.[17] But no explanation to date has proved really satisfactory.

GENETICS

Ever since the connection between syphilis and paresis was discovered, there has been a continuing search for physiological bases of mental disorder. In other words, there is widespread belief that even the so-called functional disorders have some organic source. However, there is little expectation that the cause of disorders lies solely within the organism or that the relationship will be as direct and simple as syphilis-paresis. Rather, numbers of scientists suspect the existence of physiological conditions that increase the *risk* of or *susceptibility* to contracting disorders.

One of the more consistent research findings supporting this view is the finding that persons biologically related to someone diagnosed as schizophrenic stand an increased chance of also being so diagnosed.[18] There is some evidence, albeit inconclusive, that this result occurs even when the related individuals have had no personal contact. Although the numerous genetic studies have used various types of samples (e.g., parents and their offspring, identical and fraternal twins), the nature of the link between genetic factors and mental disorder remains a mystery. It is not yet clear exactly what is being genetically transferred, and to what degree genetics increases the risk of mental disorder.

> Despite the impressive data that have recently accumulated from a variety of genetic studies, the basic genetic mechanisms for this disorder [schizophrenia] remain enigmatic. That is, we do not know what is inherited or its mode of genetic transmission. . . . Although a variety of genetic theories have been proposed, none have been confirmed, and none have been definitively discredited. Despite the lack of answers to very basic questions, recent genetic studies seem to have had salutary effects on several related issues. They suggest a genetic predisposition to schizophrenia, but at the same time make clear that genes alone are insufficient to produce schizophrenia.[19]

When one tries to connect the unknown genetic factor to the high incidence of disorder in the lower class things get particularly sticky. Is the genetically-induced susceptibility greater in the lower class, or is the susceptibility evenly distributed across classes? Are other factors that trigger the disorders more prevalent in the lower class? These are important questions, but they lack answers.

FAMILY SETTING

Obviously confounding the relationship between genetics and mental disorder is the role of the family in transmitting behavior patterns. Does one learn from relatives (or close non-relatives for that matter) behaviors that eventually become defined as evidence of mental disorder? (This is not to imply that parents must necessarily be diagnosed as schizophrenic themselves, but that something about the family system communicates or creates behavior interpreted as mental disorder.)

Research findings in this area are meager and inconclusive. But some of the variables that show promise are: serious medical problems of the mother; blurring of identities in family roles (father perceives self as similar to mother, child sees self as similar to parent, and parents see selves as similar to child); and the parents' general lack of communication and reasoning skills.[20] But even when such variables seem to distinguish families with schizophrenic children from those without them, a tangled web of questions remains. How do family variables contribute to understanding social class differences in the occurrence of serious mental disorder? Do parental characteristics create the child's disorder or does the development of the disorder bring about certain parental characteristics? And, why do some children in a family become schizophrenic, but others do not?

STRESS

One factor often associated with mental disorder seems more consistent with the social class relationship than either genetics or family: anxiety caused by real or imagined problems and misfortunes. The term most frequently used in describing this factor is *stress*.[21] It is easy to conjecture that for the lowest social class, feelings of economic and political powerlessness alone can create great stress. But a bad situation becomes even more intolerable in the event of serious illness, death of loved ones, loss of employment, family conflict, or any variety of social difficulties and frustrations. In reaction to stress and its attendant anxieties one may become depressed to the point of inactivity. Fatigue and indifference to job, family, and other social obligations result. One may even reach the point of constructing another "reality" that is greatly preferable to the "real" one with all its distress.[22]

Just as in the cases of social class, genetics, and the family, there is evidence that worry and stress are related to the incidence of mental disorder. But again the research is far from conclusive—stress clearly does not invariably result in disorder. The reader may ask, "Why not a theory involving all four factors?" So the reader can be spared the stress of that burden—and whatever consequences it would have on mental health—he or she will be relieved to know that Melvin L. Kohn has developed precisely such a theory.[23]

Restricting his theory to the causes of schizophrenia, Kohn believes that there is sufficient evidence that some persons are genetically vulnerable to mental disorder, and that such persons are disproportionately concentrated in the lower class. However, he argues that most disorders in this class stem not from vulnerability alone, but from vulnerability combined with other characteristics of lower class life.

Kohn claims that lower class persons generally experience stress-producing situations over which they have *less personal control* than those in higher social classes. Their lack of power and money allows them fewer resources for coping with problems of illness, unemployment, and so on. In addition to a lack of control over stressful situations, the impact of the situations themselves may be influenced by *conceptions of reality and self*. This is the area in which the lower class family plays a strategic role in the mental disorder process. Kohn argues that many lower class families transmit a life orientation that is too rigid and limited for dealing with stress. This is not to say that what the family teaches is unrealistic, for the conceptions of reality transmitted to children may be quite consistent with actual experience. If parents know from their own past that there are limited means to deal with stress, there is no reason for their children to learn otherwise.

Kohn has attempted to bring together the research findings concerning the relationships between schizophrenia and class, genetics, family, and stress. In his words:

> The thrust of the argument is that the conditions of life experienced by people of lower social class position tend to impair their ability to deal resourcefully with the problematic and the stressful. Such impairment would be unfortunate for all who suffer it, but would not in itself result in schizophrenia. In conjunction with a genetic vulnerability to schizophrenia and the experience of great stress, however, such impairment could well be disabling. Since both genetic vulnerability and stress appear to occur disproportionately at lower social class levels, people in these segments of society may be at triple jeopardy.[24]

Kohn's theory, of course, remains conjectural at present. Its testability will be a formidable task. Doubtlessly, the several factors interact in highly complex ways, and the influence that each has on the process will be difficult to determine. However, Kohn's scheme does provide us with a framework in which known facts about mental disorder make some sense.

But for many sociologists the really important issues about mental disorder do not concern the whys and wherefores of persons acting as schizophrenics or neurotics. In the context of the medical model there is the lingering problem of the inability to consistently diagnose or label the behavior in question. A related and equally irksome problem is that being "crazy" depends so much on what people happen to think about an individual's behavior. Mental disorder is not like leprosy—either you have leprosy or you don't. With mental disorder, maybe you have it or maybe you don't, depending upon *how you get along* and *with whom you get along*. The many decision processes surrounding the mentally ill person may be only tangential to the degree and disruptiveness of the individual's actual behavior or symptoms. To investigate this decision process we must turn from the medical model of mental disorder to the labeling model.

The Labeling Model

While the labeling model may seem to contradict the medical model in many, if not most, respects, advocates of the labeling model do not totally reject the research hypotheses based on the medical model. Advocates of the two viewpoints clearly disagree, however, over the basic assumptions of the nature of mental disorder. The dispute centers around the *role of social reaction* toward persons who behave in ways considered to be disagreeable.

Those of the medical persuasion minimize the importance of social reaction. They may allow that such reaction can aggravate behavioral difficulties, but they believe that the principal source of the difficulties is a clearly definable disease whose symptoms can become progressively severe and finally require professional assistance. Logically, then, all that is needed is to find the cause of the disease and its cure will be readily available. As our discussion above indicated, the search for cures has concentrated on a variety of factors, but the results scarcely point the way to stopping mental disorder in its tracks. What is needed, argue many, is a completely new approach to the problem, and this is what the labeling model tries to provide.

MENTAL DISEASE AS A MYTH

One of the forerunners of the labeling approach to mental disorder was not a sociologist but a psychiatrist, Thomas S. Szasz. Szasz has directly attacked the fundamental core of the medical model by asserting that mental disease does not exist—it is a myth. The assumption that disorders are evidence of disease stems from the early association of brain damage with certain problems of behavior, e.g., syphilis leading to paresis. Thus the medical profession established itself as having expertise not only in the area of *physical symptoms* and their *physical causes* but also in the area of *behavior,* regardless of whether it was related to physical causes or not. Szasz asserts that it is an error to conceptualize an individual's beliefs or ideas in the same way you would characterize a physical defect. The appropriateness of particular beliefs or ideas is a matter of judgment and communication.[25]

> The concept of illness, whether bodily or mental, implies deviation from some clearly defined norm. In the case of physical illness, the norm is the structural and functional integrity of the human body. Thus, although the desirability of physical health, as such, is an ethical value, what health is can be stated in anatomical and physiological terms. What is the norm, deviation from which is regarded as mental illness? This question cannot be easily answered. But whatever this norm may be, we can be certain of only one thing: namely, that it must be stated in terms of psychosocial, ethical, and legal concepts.[26]

Thus to say, for example, that chronic hostility is a sign of mental illness merely reflects a judgment that people should be kind to each other. How often have you heard, "Anyone who commits suicide must be mentally ill"? This simply indicates that the speaker disapproves of suicide and cannot understand why anyone would disagree with the statement—unless he or she were crazy, of course. According to Szasz judgments about similar normative matters have been entrusted to the psychiatric profession in the mistaken belief that psychiatry is value-free because it "treats disease."

> Remedial action . . . tends to be sought in a therapeutic—or covertly medical—framework. This creates a situation in which it is claimed that

psychosocial, ethical, and legal deviations can be corrected by medical action. Since medical interventions are designed to remedy only medical problems, it is logically absurd to expect that they will help solve problems whose very existence [has] been defined and established on non-medical grounds.[27]

If what we have been calling *mental disorders* are not symptomatic of illness, then what are they? According to Szasz, they are "problems of living": problems of expressing unacceptable ideas and of behaving in unacceptable ways—unacceptable, that is, to those who must interact with the individuals, and perhaps unacceptable even to the individuals themselves. They boil down to "moral conflicts in human relations" that cannot be cured by disposing of an individual malady.[28]

A LABELING THEORY OF MENTAL DISORDER

The reader may recall from our discussion on the labeling perspective in Chapter 3 that the proponents of the perspective attach little significance to the original causes of deviant behavior, particularly if the behavior is tolerated and can be incorporated into an otherwise non-deviant image. This behavior is termed *primary deviance* or *rule-breaking;* it might stem from any one of a variety of causes.

Of principal concern to the labeling theorists are the reactions of others toward persons whose behavior is defined as deviant. This reaction is important because it can reinforce the deviant behavior by limiting an individual's contact with the nondeviant world, and it can impress upon the individual that he or she is the kind of person who becomes involved in such behavior. In short, acquiring a deviant status can set off a career sequence in which the individual ends up in *secondary deviance*—deviant behavior becomes a means of defense, attack, or adjustment to the problems created by social reaction.

The application of this perspective to mental disorder produces quite a different framework from that of the medical model. The emphasis shifts from the individual and his or her problems that cause mental disorder to the issues of how certain behaviors come to be regarded as evidence of disorder, and of how the reaction to the behaviors can lock individuals into careers of being mentally disordered.

A theory of mental disorder based on the labeling perspective has been proposed by Thomas J. Scheff. Scheff states his theory in propositional form and we shall enumerate the propositions as he presents them. Before we begin, however, two points should be emphasized. First, the reader should not be misled by Scheff's occasional use of the term *mental disease.* Scheff agrees with Szasz that mental disease is a myth, and he uses the term for the sake of convention only. Second, the term *residual rule-breaking* requires some explanation.

The reader may recall from Chapter 3 that Howard Becker makes a distinction between *rule-breaking* and *deviance;* rule-breaking being the violations of norms, and deviance being those behaviors against which there is a social reaction. People "break" rules all the time—they lie, steal, clean their ears in public—but a wide range of behavior is tolerated and, according to the labeling perspective, true deviance depends not only on rules but also on the reaction to their violation. Within a cultural group, rule-breaking behavior is variously classified as crime, bad manners, vice, and so on.

But some rule-breaking behaviors do not fit so nicely into such categories; they are residual behaviors because they defy classification into the normal types of rule-breaking. For example, your friend who is so distracted all the time and does not seem to be listening when you speak to him. Or another friend who gets upset too easily and who seems to be always on the verge of flying off the handle. These behaviors are not consistent with what we think appropriate human conduct should be. But what rules have been broken? It is from this residual category, according to Scheff, that what is called *mental disorder* is drawn. The violations seem so unusual, weird, or inexplicable that they are seen as evidence of a mental problem.[29] Scheff's first proposition concerns the origins of residual rule-breaking.

1. *Residual rule-breaking arises from fundamentally diverse sources.* There are many reasons why persons might hear, see, or otherwise experience the unusual. These reasons include the genetic, family, and stress factors we discussed in connection with the medical model. Others suggested by Scheff include: psychoactive drugs, starvation, fatigue, and deliberate attempts to rebel against the conventional. He cites as an example of the last the French impressionist painters whose colors were seen by some critics as evidence of madness.

2. *Relative to the rate of treated mental illness, the rate of unrecorded residual rule-breaking is extremely high.* This simply means that many people do or imagine culturally inappropriate things, but their behavior goes unrecognized, is ignored, or is rationalized as being eccentric. *Denial* is the term used in the mental disorder literature for this pattern of inattention to or rationalization of unusual behavior.[30]

3. *Most residual rule-breaking is "denied" and is of transitory significance.* In total, this proposition claims that most of what could be labeled as madness are acts of primary deviance. The proposition does have two parts, however. The first concerns the general reluctance of people to shift their judgment of someone they know from "well" to "sick." One can easily get the impression that symptoms of mental disorder will be readily recognized as such. Instead, extraordinary efforts are often made to interpret such behavior as normal. One

study of women whose husbands were diagnosed as mentally disordered found these examples:

> [Some] wives describe their husbands as spoiled, lacking will-power, exaggerating little complaints and acting like babies. This is especially marked where alcoholism complicates the husband's symptomatology. For example, Mrs. Y., whose husband was chronically alcoholic, aggressive and threatening to her, "raving," and who "chewed his nails until they almost bled," interprets his difficulty thus: "He was just spoiled rotten. He never outgrew it. He told me when he was a child he could get his own way if he insisted, and he is still that way." . . .
>
> Many recall their early reactions to their husbands' behavior as full of puzzling confusion and uncertainty. Something is wrong, they know, but, in general, they stop short of a firm explanation. Thus Mrs. M. reports, "He was kind of worried. He was kind of worried before, not exactly worried. . . ." She thought of his many physical complaints; she "racked" her "brain" and told her husband, "Of course, he didn't feel good." Finally, he stayed home from work with "no special complaints, just blah," and she "began to realize it was more deeply seated." [31]

In practice, many do not recognize the symptoms of mental disorder in persons they know until a third party—physician or employer—redefines the situation by suggesting illness as an explanation.

The second part of Scheff's proposition is important because it claims that although persons may exhibit symptoms of mental disorder, it does not necessarily follow that they will develop the full-blown incapacitating characteristics associated with psychoses. But what about the small percentage of residual rule-breakers who do go on to careers of residual deviance? This is the question that the remaining propositions attempt to answer.

4. *Stereotyped imagery of mental disorder is learned in early childhood.* Evidence is meager on this point but the impression is that children soon grasp what is meant by terms such as *crazy,* or *off his rocker,* and what kinds of behaviors are associated with those terms. Once learned, the stereotypes are reinforced throughout life.

5. *The stereotypes of insanity are continually reaffirmed, inadvertently, in ordinary social interaction.* Has anybody ever said to the reader, "I am mad about you"? That is flattering, of course, but it means that the speaker has lost his or her reason. As George Bernard Shaw wrote about marriage:

> When two people are under the influence of the most violent, most insane, most delusive, and most transient of passions, they are required to swear that they will remain in that excited, abnormal, and exhausting condition continuously until death do them part. [32]

We constantly use terms referring to mental disorder in everyday situations: in advertising ("We may be crazy but we have slashed prices to the bone!"); in humor (Asylum inmate to farmer: "What are you going to do with that manure?" "Put it on my strawberries." "I put cream and sugar on mine and they got me in here!"); and in general conversation ("I think Edna is nuts to go out with that weirdo.").

But the stereotypes are not always so innocuous. The notion of mental disorder is often used by the mass media as a kind of explanation of disapproved conduct. How often have you seen headlines similar to: "Police in shootout with ex-mental patient"? This only serves to reinforce our notions about the mentally disordered as being unpredictable and untrustworthy. The common acceptance of the stereotype was clearly demonstrated in the 1972 election, when a vice presidential candidate was forced to resign his nomination after it was revealed he had once been a psychiatric patient. No assurances about his present state of mind could alter the fact that he was seen as some kind of nut.

Thus, while most residual rule-breaking is denied, it is also widely known how the mentally disordered are supposed to act. According to Scheff, the individual begins to stabilize his or her career of rule-breaking once observers decide not to deny the behavior any longer.

> In a crisis, when the deviance of an individual becomes a public issue, the traditional stereotype of insanity becomes the guiding imagery for action, both for those reacting to the deviant and, at times, for the deviant himself. When societal agents and persons around the deviant react to him uniformly in terms of the traditional stereotypes of insanity, his amorphous and unstructured rule-breaking tends to crystallize in conformity to these expectations, thus becoming similar to the behavior of other deviants classified as mentally ill, and stable over time.[33]

6. *Labeled deviants may be rewarded for playing the stereotyped deviant role.* Once a person is labeled as *ill,* there are pressures to accept that fact. For example, the person who voluntarily enters a mental hospital will be complimented for "doing the right thing."

7. *Labeled deviants are punished when they attempt the return to conventional roles.* Once a person is labeled, it is difficult to return to a normal status. People may refuse to allow the individual to resume former responsibilities. Would you want an ex-mental patient to marry your sister, babysit with your children, or shave the back of your neck?

8. *In the crisis occurring when a residual rule-breaker is publicly labeled, the deviant is highly suggestible, and may accept the proffered role of the insane as the only alternative.* It is easy to imagine the confusion, anxiety, and shame you would feel were you to discover that your family wanted you committed to a mental institution. Should you fight it? Or might they recognize something about your behavior that you are unaware of? Is there something really wrong with you?

9. *Among residual rule-breakers, labeling is the single most important cause of careers of residual deviance.* This final proposition clearly separates Scheff's theory from that of the medical model. It is not the "disease" that distinguishes the mentally disordered from others; it is the *reaction* that closes off other behavioral alternatives and forces the individual into the role of the mentally ill.

As you have probably guessed, Scheff's theory has generated some heated debate.[34] No doubt the ultimate explanation of mental disorder lies somewhere between the extremes of the medical and the labeling models. In the meantime, the principal point of contention remains the relative importance of the behavior that precipitates the labeling process, which in turn—according to the labeling approach—*stabilizes* the behavior. In short, is labeling the single most important cause of a career of mental disorder as Scheff claims?

One critic, Walter R. Gove, argues that it is the individual's behavior, not the reaction to it, that is more important:

> The evidence shows that a substantial majority of the persons who are hospitalized have a serious psychiatric disturbance quite apart from any secondary deviance that may be associated with the mentally ill role. Furthermore, persons in the community do not view someone as mentally ill if he happens to act in a bizarre fashion. On the contrary, they persist in denying mental illness until the situation becomes intolerable. Once prospective patients come into contact with public officials, a substantial screening still occurs, presumably sorting out persons who are being railroaded or who are less disturbed.[35]

In response, Scheff claims that most systematic studies lend support to the labeling model.[36] In reality, however, the studies are inconclusive at best and contradictory at worst. For example, one study indicates that length of hospitalization is related more to the family's wishes than to the psychiatric condition of the patient; another study indicates the opposite.[37]

Nevertheless it is difficult to deny that labeling has some significance for careers in mental disorder. One indication of that significance comes from a unique study conducted by D. L. Rosenhan.[38] Eight subjects gained admissions to twelve mental hospitals by claiming they had been "hearing voices." After admission to the hospital—which proved to be remarkably easy—the pseudopatients behaved "normally." Although several of the real patients in the wards had their suspicions, none of the staff did.

> Despite their public "show" of sanity, the pseudopatients were never detected. Admitted, except in one case, with a diagnosis of schizophrenia, each was discharged with a diagnosis of schizophrenia "in remission." The label "in remission" should in no way be dismissed as a formality, for at no time during any hospitalization had any question been raised about any pseudopatient's simulation. Nor are there any records that the pseudopa-

tient's status was suspect. Rather, the evidence is strong that, once labeled schizophrenic, the pseudopatient was stuck with that label. If the pseudo-patient was to be discharged, he must naturally be "in remission"; but he was not sane, nor, in the institution's view, had he ever been sane. . . .

Beyond the tendency to call the healthy sick—a tendency that accounts better for diagnostic behavior on admission than it does for such behavior after a lengthy period of exposure—the data speak to the massive role of labeling in psychiatric assessment. Having once been labeled schizo-phrenic, there is nothing the pseudopatient can do to overcome the tag.[39]

But numerous piecemeal studies are no substitute for a sys-tematic test of the labeling model. No such test has been made, and the degree to which the model will eventually contribute to our un-derstanding of mental disorder remains to be seen.

The Therapeutic State

The debate over the labeling and medical models has far-reaching implications for the entire question of mental disorder as deviance. For example, if the labeling model is the more accurate, the rela-tionship between disorder and social class could be explained thusly:

> It is probable that societal reactions cause more lower-status persons to be hospitalized than higher-status persons. Lower class persons are more apt to have contact with official agencies (jails, welfare organizations, etc.) through which the hospitalization process is often initiated; also, once in contact with such agencies, a lower-class person may be more apt to be hospitalized than a person of higher status. In addition, with decreases in status, tolerance for aberrant behavior may be lower and the need to hos-pitalize may be greater; a family's *economic* ability to tolerate nonproduc-tive persons decreases with socio-economic status.[40]

This interpretation views the reaction toward mental disorder as relative to social class, but still appropriate: not only may the individ-ual profit from hospitalization but also her or his family may be re-lieved of an intolerable burden. One can imagine a situation in which an individual's excessive behavior comes to the attention of impartial authorities who diagnose and recommend treatment. The individual goes to a hospital much as he or she would for gall stones, is appro-priately treated, and returns to the community cured to the benefit of all concerned.

The reality, however, is much harsher than the ideal. We must ask some cold questions. In practice, how is mental disorder defined? What happens to individuals who are labeled mentally disordered? We will not, of course, attempt to answer these questions for the en-tire range of persons labeled as suffering from mental problems, if only because the available data prohibit such an ambitious project. In keeping with the conflict theme of this book, we will limit ourselves to those cases in which differential power and coercion are exercised in what has become known as the *therapeutic state.*

CONFLICT AND STIGMA

Aside from the courts, police, and other agencies designed to implement law, few are more powerful than psychiatrists in their ability to impose and judge standards of conduct.[41] Courts and the police deal with that which is illegal and use as their criteria the written law. Psychiatrists are certified to define mental illness and use as their criteria standards of what constitutes normal conduct. Illegal conduct is subject to punishment such as fines and imprisonment; illness is subject to . . . what? Let us begin with an example of one of the lesser consequences—loss of employment.

In 1969 a New York City high school teacher, Miss Francine Newman, disagreed with her principal over his choice of chairperson for her department. The dispute got so hot that the principal ordered her to get a "medical." It was actually a psychiatric examination. Her first examination began with the psychiatrist setting his alarm clock. He then asked her questions about the dispute, why she had flunked a large number of students four years before (she had been following administrative orders), to add and subtract some numbers, who was the president of the United States, and was she unhappy over being unmarried and without children. The alarm went off and she was dismissed from the examination—and from her job.

Since then Miss Newman has been examined by several medical doctors and psychiatrists who found her mentally fit to teach, but a re-examination by another psychiatrist paid by the school system still resulted in a flunk. As of this writing Miss Newman has not been reinstated.[42]

About one hundred New York City teachers a year are forced to take psychiatric examinations. No doubt many are for the purpose of ascertaining behavior patterns that would jeopardize children's learning or well-being, but many—if not most—are an exercise in power to end conflict.

> The forced psychiatric examination is employed to cow teachers, whip them into line, and, when necessary, to get rid of them. The treatment invariably depends on the extent of conflict between a teacher and principal. For instance, it's common for a principal to threaten a teacher with "a medical" when she fails to conform. "A medical" is classroom shorthand which the teacher clearly understands. It means she's going to be sent to the Board to let its psychiatrists look her over. Often the warning is enough. But if it doesn't do the trick the principal makes good on the threat. Chances are the teacher will pass the test and will return to her

classroom a much chastened individual, grateful she didn't wind up with the stigma of being declared mentally incompetent.[43]

The very fact that one must undergo a psychiatric examination may in itself be a threat to one's identity, however. In an interview survey about fifteen years ago, Derek L. Phillips found that rejection of mentally disordered individuals depended to a high degree upon the type of assistance they sought out.[44] Phillips presented his interviewees with hypothetical cases describing the behavior of individuals with four types of disorder, and one case who was "normal." He also included statements about the kind of help these cases might seek: no help, clergyman, physician, psychiatrist, and mental hospital. He questioned the degree to which the interviewees would be willing to tolerate relationships with such cases. Among his conclusions were these:

> Not only are individuals increasingly rejected as they are described as seeking no help, as seeing a clergyman, a physician, a psychiatrist, or a mental hospital, but they are *disproportionately* rejected when described as utilizing the latter two help-sources. This supports the suggestion . . . that individuals utilizing psychiatrists and mental hospitals may be rejected not only because they have a health problem, and because they are unable to handle the problem themselves, but also because contact with a psychiatrist or a mental hospital defines them as "mentally ill" or "insane."
>
> Despite the fact that the "normal" person is more an "ideal type" [than a "real" person would be], when he is described as having been in a mental hospital he is rejected more than a psychotic individual described as not seeking help or as seeing a clergyman. . . . Even when the normal person is described as seeing a psychiatrist, he is rejected more than a simple schizophrenic who seeks no help.[45]

However, there is recent evidence that the stigma of the mental disorder label may be moderating. For example, in 1974, Stuart Kirk published the results of a questionnaire study whose design was similar to that employed by Phillips. Using community college students rather than a more general sample, Kirk found that actual *behavior,* regardless of the label attached to it, had the greatest influence on the degree of social rejection. Kirk admits some methodological problems with his study—e.g., the use of sophisticated college students— but his findings nevertheless call into question the impact of being labeled *mentally ill.*[46]

Whether or not certain behavior may encourage social rejection independent of the labels employed, it is inescapable that being called "mentally ill" or "in need of a shrink" may have vastly more serious consequences than other reactions. Being wicked or untrustworthy might result in stigma and isolation, but being "mentally ill" threatens not only one's reputation but also one's freedom.

INVOLUNTARY HOSPITALIZATION

Any political state has means by which it deals with persons who, for one reason or another, are defined as troublesome. The most obvious means is the criminal justice system with its laws, enforcement agencies, courts, and places of punishment. Although everyone is aware that persons can lose their freedom by being convicted and sentenced to a penal institution, many do not realize that persons can also lose their freedom without ever being accused of a criminal act. Furthermore, that loss of freedom can be permanent. Under the criminal code, the length of one's sentence is clearly specified, and the state may not restrain a person any longer. But persons are also deprived of freedom without any notion of when, or whether, release will ever come. For what reason? For being "mentally ill."

What we are referring to is the detention of persons, against their will, in mental institutions—what we will call *involuntary hospitalization*. This is the subject of a complex and intense debate, and at its heart lies the philosophy of the *therapeutic state*.[47] This term indicates a belief that society must be defended from dangerous and disruptive individuals, not by punishment, but by *treatment*. This philosophy embraces not only persons who might be or become involved in criminal behavior but also all sorts of suffering, disorganized, or "sick" individuals whose ailments prevent them from leading happy, productive lives. Furthermore—and this is the point upon which most debate centers—the proponents of the therapeutic state hold that these individuals should receive treatment whether they want it or not.

> The goal of the Therapeutic State is universal health, or at least unfailing relief from suffering. This untroubled state of man and society is a quintessential feature of the medical-therapeutic perspective on politics. Conflict among individuals, and especially between the individual and the state, is invariably seen as a symptom of illness or psychopathology; and the primary function of the state is accordingly the removal of such conflict through appropriate "therapy"—imposed by force, if necessary.[48]

Although it is tempting to applaud the benevolent goal of the therapeutic state—the elimination of conflict and unhappiness—its apparent humanitarianism becomes suspect once you examine its assumptions and possible consequences. If you are to propose a treatment approach you must assume that you can recognize, diagnose, and treat the diseases in question. We have already seen that the recognition of mental disorder is a normative decision, and that diagnosis is anything but an exact science. As for treatment, it is obviously difficult to "treat" behavior that may or may not be a sign of illness depending on who is making the judgment.

But if you are satisfied that it is possible to recognize, diagnose, and treat certain problems, what would be the consequences if you were to put your conclusions into practice? What would you do with persons such as Barry Goldwater, who has been diagnosed as "paranoid schizophrenic"; Woodrow Wilson, "very close to psychosis"; or Jesus Christ, "a born degenerate" and "paranoid"? [49] They and thousands of other unfortunates would need treatment, of course. The more trouble they might cause with their strange ideas, the more imperative would treatment become.

Goldwater, Wilson, and Christ were not forced into mental hospitals, but tens of thousands are every year. In 1972, the most recent year for which reliable data are available, nearly 404,000 patients were admitted to state and county mental hospitals. About 170,000 or 42 per cent of these patients were committed involuntarily. [50] The critics of the therapeutic state argue that too frequently involuntary hospitalization is used as a *means of social control* that deprives individuals of their liberty without constitutional safeguards. It is probably easier in our society to have troublesome individuals committed to a mental hospital than to have them placed in jail. The reason is that in the eyes of psychiatrists and the law, mentally "ill" persons are seen as incapable of choice, and that is how they are often handled. For example, the following situation existed in New York until 1973:

> The standard civil commitment procedure . . . does not require or authorize a judicial hearing prior to commitment. Commitment for 60 days is generally based on the certificate of two physicians, who do not have to be psychiatrists. And *emergency* commitment for 30 days can be based on nothing more substantial than the unsworn and perhaps fraudulent allegation of a layman, unsupported and unconfirmed by any doctor, and unexamined, either prior or subsequent to commitment, by any court. . . .
>
> The emergency, or 30-day, patient has very few rights. If he requests release, he can be held for 10 days and then administratively converted from emergency to non-emergency status and held for an additional 60 days. Only after he has been converted does he have the right to request judicial review, and that review, when it comes, will be limited to the need for his *retention*. It will not examine the legality or propriety of his emergency commitment. [51]

A 1973 New York law placed more responsibility for commitment procedures in the hands of the courts, but the extent to which the courts protect individuals from the therapeutic state remains to be seen. Past research clearly indicates that legal safeguards for persons being committed do not provide the protection one would anticipate. For example, Florida law requires that the individual be notified that proceedings have been initiated. One study in that state reveals that the court considers notification to have been made if the notice is signed by any person over the age of fourteen living in the household of the person to be committed.[52] Furthermore, the signing of the notification waives or relinquishes the right of the individual to a court hearing in order to challenge the allegations. Not surprisingly, most commitment procedures are initiated by relatives, and the notifications subsequently signed by relatives. Thus, from the outset the degree of legal involvement is minimal. The rest of the procedure is strictly *medical:* the individual is examined by physicians to ascertain mental competence, and the physicians' decision is rarely disputed by the court.

Although it is true that psychiatric examinations can be used as threats and that legal procedures involving mental competency hearings are often only loosely followed, the reader may still wonder: Are not psychiatrists doing a conscientious job by restricting involuntary hospitalization to only the really serious cases? Such a question can be answered only within the context of what involuntary hospitalization is. It is *imprisonment;* it provides a *stigma* that is probably more damning than incarceration in a real prison is; and the sentence is *indeterminate.* One's release may occur one day after commitment, months or years later, or only when one is carried out in a box. To whom should we assign this fate of involuntary hospitalization?

In the psychiatric literature sometimes simply being psychotic is a sufficient reason, but predominately the criterion is mental illness creating danger to oneself or others.[53] To accept this last criterion, which concerns the interests of society, we must make an important assumption: namely, that psychiatrists know enough about the dynamics of a disorder to predict what it will induce a person to do. If only that were so. In reality, *there is no evidence that psychiatrists possess any special ability to predict that any person will commit a dangerous act.* Therein lies the major problem of the therapeutic state: persons are committed not on the basis of what they *have done,* as those going through the criminal justice system are, but on the basis of what they *might do.* And no body of knowledge is capable of forecasting an individual's behavior.

Bruce J. Ennis and Thomas R. Litwack, who investigated the ability of psychiatrists to predict and diagnose behavior, claim:

> In summary, training and experience do not enable psychiatrists adequately to predict dangerous behavior. Rather, such predictions are determined by the time and place of diagnosis, the psychiatrist's personal bias, social pressures, the class and cultures of the respective parties, and other extraneous factors. Finally, even if psychiatrists could accurately determine which persons are mentally ill, that determination would not assist them in predicting dangerousness because . . . there is no correlation between mental illness and dangerous behavior. To the contrary, the mentally ill may even be less dangerous than the population as a whole.[54]

To further complicate matters, evidence indicates that the relationship between diagnosed mental disorder and dangerous behavior is relatively low. Studies have consistently shown that mental patients have a much lower arrest rate for crimes, especially serious crimes, than the rest of the population. In short, you would be safer in a society where the mad were loose and the sane were locked up. Ennis sums up the findings this way:

> Mental illness does not cause dangerous behavior; it inhibits dangerous behavior. Mental patients may plot and scheme, they may threaten injury to themselves or others, but rarely do they follow through. The most common characteristic of mental patients is an inability to organize their lives and assert themselves. And that characteristic makes them *less* dangerous than people who are more aggressive and, hence, more "normal."
>
> True, some mental patients are dangerous—though it is more likely to be in spite of the mental condition than because of it.[55]

But predictions of dangerousness are too frequently not even an issue, and persons are involuntarily hospitalized without the possibility of future violence even being considered. On what bases then are people committed? A study by Scheff, conducted in a state noted for its progressive psychiatric practices, found that in order for involuntary hospitalization to be *legally* imposed, the individual had to be judged dangerous to self or others, or severely mentally disordered.[56] However, in the *majority* of commitments (63 per cent), the individuals were considered neither dangerous nor severely disordered. Scheff concludes that psychiatrists tend to overlook strict legal criteria because they presume that an illness must exist (one physician is quoted as saying, "If the patient's own family wants to get rid of him you know that there is something wrong,"), that there is an element of danger in all mental disorder, and that treatment will help the individual.

For all the good intentions embodied in the therapeutic state, it is in practice a system of ethics and moral judgments about human conduct. Such terms as *diagnosis* and *treatment* provide the system with a scientific-medical guise for evaluating behavior and imposing controls over that deemed inappropriate. The impact of this model on society is difficult to gauge and criticize in many cases. Thousands of persons do engage in forms of behavior that are disrupting and distressing to their own lives and those of their loved ones. Whether effective or not, the treatment approach at least gives some comfort because it seems humane.

Nevertheless, the therapeutic state is as much a result of *interest group pressures* as are drug laws and other rules governing human conduct. The history of the developing therapeutic state is long and complex, and involves many interest groups claiming to have scientific relief for everything from insanity to delinquency and alco-

holism.[57] Psychiatric interest groups have been particularly successful in exerting their influence in the area of sex offenses.

SEX PSYCHOPATH LAWS

No concept in psychiatry is subject to more disagreement than that of
the *psychopath*. Yet around this concept an entirely new means of
handling some criminals has evolved. Twenty-eight states and the District of Columbia have enacted statutes commonly known as *sex psychopath laws*. These laws lack uniformity in many respects, but they
share to some degree the following characteristics and assumptions:

1. There are special types of persons whose mental condition is such
   that they lack control over sexual impulses or have propensities
   toward commission of sex crimes. The laws usually designate these
   persons as "sexual psychopaths," "sexually dangerous persons,"
   or "mentally disturbed sex offenders." They are not considered
   seriously ill, but as suffering from some sort of personality disorder.
2. In most states those persons affected by the laws have been convicted of some sex crime, usually rape or child molesting. However, in a few states all that is necessary for the application of the
   law is the possibility that the individual was "sexually motivated,"
   regardless of the type of crime committed.
3. In most states, after the court finds the individuals guilty of a
   crime, they are required to undergo examination to ascertain
   whether they are psychopaths. In some states, however, persons
   may be found psychopathic before being found guilty. Then they
   must be "treated" for a condition that supposedly caused them to
   commit acts that they may not be guilty of! Furthermore, in states
   which allow a preconviction commitment, the "cured" or "improved" psychopaths may still have to stand trial and serve a penal
   sentence after their release from treatment.
4. Those found *not* to be psychopathic are sentenced under the ordinary criminal code and receive a prison term or probation. Those
   adjudged psychopathic are subject to *indeterminant confinement*
   and are not to be released until "cured." Such confinement is not
   viewed as a criminal sentence because the individuals are to receive "treatment." Thus the usual constitutional safeguards are
   considered unnecessary. The possible paradoxes are endless: for
   example, the violent rapist could be "cured" in a matter of weeks,
   but someone who exposed himself to elderly ladies could spend
   the rest of his days behind bars. Such bizarre decisions are made
   possible by the therapeutic state, where persons are committed
   not on the basis of what they *have done*, but on the basis of what
   they *might do*.[58]

Nicholas N. Kittrie sums up the situation:

> Like a Kafka-esque character, the psychopath is a man to whom no clear-cut social standards are applicable. He suffers from a disputed mental disorder. He is indefinitely committed for an offense, often unproved, that would impose only a mild sentence on others. To secure release, he must be cured of a condition that is not clearly definable and that some say is not treatable. Finally, his return to society depends upon ambiguous conditions.[59]

The reader can see that sex psychopath laws place a great deal of power in the hands of psychiatrists. Unfortunately, that power has no valid basis. One could at least sympathize with the approach of these laws if there were evidence that: 1. dangerous sex offenses by individuals could be predicted; and 2. once predicted such offenses could be averted by treatment. There is not one shred of evidence that psychiatrists can do either. Strange as it may seem to the reader, there has not been a single study to indicate whether any of the many sex psychopath programs have either reduced recidivism rates among those treated or affected serious sex crime rates in any way.

One of the outstanding instances of the inability to predict is the case of Edmund Kemper. An outline of his career is enlightening.

1. 1964: at age fifteen Kemper murders two grandparents, telephones mother and sheriff about it.
2. 1964–69: he is committed to Atascadero State Hospital, a California institution for the criminally insane. In 1969 he is released as "cured."
3. 1972: he initiates proceedings to have his past criminal records sealed; this involves being examined by psychiatrists. He murders and dismembers two teenage girls. Three days later court-appointed psychiatrists declare him sane and no longer a danger to society. Before the year is gone, he kills two more girls.
4. 1973: Kemper kills three more girls and his mother. He phones the police again; at least *he* knows he is dangerous to society. A number of psychiatrists subsequently admit they have no means of predicting Kemper's behavior. One says, "Most of this work is a matter of an educated guess, plain common sense." [60]

Thus some psychiatrists themselves admit they cannot predict even the most blatant and bizarre offenses. Yet, psychiatrists impose "treatment" for an unlimited time upon thousands of men whose behavior is far more trivial and, in all likelihood, far more unpredictable. With such flimsy expertise at its command, how did the psychiatric profession attain such power in the criminal justice system?

Edwin H. Sutherland has analyzed the spread of sex psychopath laws. In tracing the enactment of the laws between 1937 and 1949 Sutherland finds a relatively well-defined sequence of events and patterns of interest group influence.

1. *A state of fear develops in the public.* The sources of this fear may be diverse, but generally involve a combination of scare stories in the mass media concerning the thousands of sex fiends on the loose, and the actual occurrence of spectacular sex crimes. The sex murders of children are particularly effective in producing hysteria. Sutherland found, however, that the degree of hysteria was seldom related to any unusual increase in sex offenses as reflected by the statistics. In short, the "sex crime wave" was artificially produced.
2. *The public reacts toward the fear.* A "something-has-to-be-done" syndrome develops. The mass media are flooded by all kinds of suggestions, including castration, the suppression of pornography, and life sentences without parole for sex offenders. Of course, a great deal of pressure is placed on legislative bodies, whether local or state.
3. *A committee is appointed.* It is the job of this group to determine the "facts," to sort through the sundry recommendations, and to come up with legislative recommendations. It is at this stage that the psychiatric profession arrives with its "expertise." Sutherland found that in many cases, psychiatrists were represented on the committees—in Minnesota, for example, all but one member of a governor's commission were psychiatrists. In other cases, psychiatric associations acted as pressure groups on the committees to pass psychopath laws.[61]

As special laws applying to sex offenders developed, the psychiatric profession had several advantages in making recommendations. It was a period when a great deal of confusion existed as to what should be done, "enlightened" methods of handling offenders were favored over more punitive measures, and the public was willing to accept the notion that sex offenders were mentally disturbed— especially when the "scientific" medical profession told it so.

Sex psychopath laws were proposed in the name of science, and, despite opposition by some prominent psychiatrists, legislators accepted them with little critical appraisal. Thus the treatment of the sex criminal as a patient became another facet of the therapeutic state.

As we stated above, there is no evidence one way or the other concerning the success of these laws. But there seems to be at least tacit admission of failure among the very persons responsible for the execution of the laws. If tried and true methods of altering sexual conduct ever existed—as psychiatrists who pushed for the laws claimed— after more than twenty years there should be no need for constant experimentation with an incredible array of therapies. For example, in Connecticut and Wisconsin sex offenders watch slides, and when erotic pictures are shown an electrical shock is delivered to their genitals. In New Jersey, there are group therapies where offenders participate in video-taped sessions in which they alternate between badgering each other, hugging each other, and screaming. In California, rapists are taught sexual techniques to improve relationships with their wives. In Washington, there is a program in which offenders simply treat each other.[62]

Often the "cures" are impossible to differentiate from torture. For example there are the painful electric shocks mentioned above. In another example, a California prison has been experimenting with a notorious drug—Anectine. A measure of its power is indicated by the facts that it is used by South American secret police to interrogate political prisoners, and that its use has been outlawed as a war crime.

> According to Dr. Arthur Nugent, chief psychiatrist at Vacaville and an enthusiast for the drug, it induces "sensations of suffocation and drowning." The subject experiences feelings of deep horror and terror, "as though he were on the brink of death." While he is in this condition a therapist scolds him for his misdeeds and tells him to shape up or expect more of the same. Candidates for Anectine treatment were selected for a range of offenses: "frequent fights, verbal threatening, deviant sexual behavior, stealing, unresponsiveness to group therapy programs." Dr. Nugent told the San Francisco *Chronicle*, "Even the toughest inmates have come to fear and hate the drug. I don't blame them, I wouldn't have one treatment myself for the world." Declaring he was anxious to continue the experiment, he added, "I'm at a loss as to why everybody's upset over this." [63]

Apart from their potential use to control inmates, do these methods—and many others currently being used—"cure"? Do some? Do none? Who knows? The last question is easiest to answer: nobody knows. All we know for certain is that "sex psychopaths" and all other types of prison inmates will continue to be used as psychiatric guinea pigs as new "treatments" are invented and imposed under the therapeutic state.

Conclusion

It is obvious that satisfactory answers to the questions about mental disorder are rare and highly controversial. What is the range of the behavior? Can it be defined without reference to ethics, morality, or a psychiatrist's particular view of reality? Is it simply residual deviance, problems of living, or is it symptomatic of some underlying, yet undiscovered, illness? We are aware that certain factors appear to be related to the occurrence of the behavior—but are the correlations merely reflections of differential social reactions toward similar behaviors? What role does social reaction play in locking persons into careers as mental patients?

More relevant for the theme of this book are these issues. Does the therapeutic state hold the promise of eventually alleviating the personal and economic costs of mental disorder? Or is it simply another means by which the more powerful interest groups exert control over the less powerful? These are all crucial questions to which we have no answers. But as Saint Jerome wrote, "It is worse still to be ignorant of your ignorance."

NOTES

1. This is the test proposed in the American Law Institute's *Model Penal Code* as cited in Herbert Fingarette, *The Meaning of Criminal Insanity* (Berkeley: University of California Press, 1972), p. 13.

2. David Mechanic, *Mental Health and Social Policy* (Englewood Cliffs, N.J.: Prentice-Hall, 1969), pp. 1–33.

3. The classification is based on Committee on Nomenclature and Statistics of the American Psychiatric Association, *Diagnostic and Statistical Manual of Mental Disorders*, 2nd ed. (Washington, D.C.: American Psychiatric Association, 1968), pp. 32–46.

4. James C. Coleman, *Abnormal Psychology and Modern Life*, 3rd ed. (Glenview, Ill.: Scott, Foresman, 1964), pp. 352–415.

5. Louis A. Wienckowski, "Foreword," National Institute of Mental Health, *Schizophrenia: Is There an Answer?* (Washington, D.C.: Government Printing Office, 1972), p. iii.

6. Loren R. Mosher, John G. Gunderson, and Sherry Buchsbaum, "Special Report: Schizophrenia, 1972," *Schizophrenia Bulletin*, 7 (Winter 1973), p. 17. For reviews of studies concerning the inconsistencies of psychiatric diagnoses see Donald Conover, "Psychiatric Distinctions: New and Old Approaches," *Journal of Health and Social Behavior*, 13 (June 1972), pp. 167–180; David Mechanic, "Problems and Prospects in Psychiatric Epidemiology," in *Psychiatric Epidemiology*, eds. E. H. Hare and John K. Wing (New York: Oxford University Press, 1970), pp. 3–22; and Bruce J. Ennis and Thomas R. Litwack, "Psychiatry and the Presumption of Expertise: Flipping Coins in the Courtroom," *California Law Review*, 62 (May 1974), pp. 699–711.

7. Leo Srole, Thomas S. Langner, Stanley T. Michael, Marvin K. Opler, and Thomas A. C. Rennie, *Mental Health in the Metropolis: The Midtown Manhattan Study* (New York: McGraw-Hill, 1962), p. 138. For a critique of this study see Frank E. Hartung, "Manhattan Madness: The Social Movement of Mental Illness," *Sociological Quarterly*, 4 (Summer 1963), pp. 261–272.

8. David Mechanic, "Some Factors in Identifying and Defining Mental Illness," *Mental Hygiene*, 46 (January 1962), pp. 67, 69.

9. Boyce Rensberger, "Study Finds Clues to Schizophrenia," *New York Times*, May 5, 1972, p. 8.

10. Paraphrased from Benjamin M. Braginsky, Dorothea D. Braginsky, and Kenneth Ring, *Methods of Madness: The Mental Hospital As a Last Resort* (New York: Holt, Rinehart and Winston, 1969), pp. 31–33.

11. For a review and sampling of the major studies in this area see Stephan P. Spitzer and Norman K. Denzin, eds., *The Mental Patient: Studies in the Sociology of Deviance* (New York: McGraw-Hill, 1968), pp. 85–190.

12. Robert E. L. Faris and H. Warren Dunham, *Mental Disorders in Urban*

Areas: An Ecological Study of Schizophrenia and Other Psychoses (Chicago: University of Chicago Press, 1939).

13. Ibid., p. 159.

14. August B. Hollingshead and Frederick C. Redlich, *Social Class and Mental Illness: A Community Study* (New York: Wiley & Sons, Inc., 1958).

15. Ibid., p. 237.

16. For a brief review of the major social class studies see Melvin L. Kohn, "Social Class and Schizophrenia: A Critical Review and a Reformulation," *Schizophrenia Bulletin,* 7 (Winter 1973), pp. 60–79. Although there is little debate over the concentration of diagnosed severe disorders in the lowest social class, the pattern of the relationship of class and disorder among the higher classes is less clear. For a discussion of this issue see William A. Rushing, "Two Patterns in the Relationship Between Social Class and Mental Hospitalization," *American Sociological Review,* 34 (August 1969), pp. 533–541.

17. For examples see Rema Lapouse, Mary A. Monk, and Melton Terris, "The Drift Hypothesis in Socio-economic Differentials in Schizophrenia," *American Journal of Public Health,* 46 (August 1956), pp. 978–986; and Srole et al., *Mental Health in the Metropolis,* pp. 194–200.

18. For a discussion of such studies see John G. Gunderson, Joseph H. Autry III, and Loren R. Mosher, "Special Report: Schizophrenia, 1974," *Schizophrenia Bulletin,* 9 (Summer 1974), pp. 24–27.

19. Ibid., p. 27.

20. Ibid., pp. 27–30.

21. For a more detailed discussion of stress and mental disorder see Marshall B. Clinard, *Sociology of Deviant Behavior,* 4th ed. (New York: Holt, Rinehart and Winston, 1974), pp. 601–608.

22. For a discussion on a similar but more elaborate sequence of stress and mental disorder see Lloyd H. Rogler and August B. Hollingshead, *Trapped: Families and Schizophrenia* (New York: John Wiley & Sons, 1965), pp. 410–412.

23. The following discussion is based on Kohn, "Social Class and Schizophrenia," pp. 69–75.

24. Ibid., p. 74.

25. The original discussion of this notion is found in Thomas S. Szasz, "The Myth of Mental Illness," *The American Psychologist,* 15 (February 1960), pp. 113–118. A revised version appears in a later work, Thomas S. Szasz, *Ideology and Insanity: Essays on the Psychiatric Dehumanization of Man* (Garden City, N.Y.: Doubleday & Co., 1970), pp. 12–24.

26. Szasz, *Ideology and Insanity,* p. 15.

27. Ibid., p. 17.

28. Szasz's notions of "problems of living and conflict" seem particularly relevant to cases in which persons with "wrong ideas" about ethics, crime, and politics are simply designated "ill" and locked up "for their own protection." However, Szasz assigns more rationality and deliberateness to other kinds of disorders than even his sympathizers can tolerate. For example, see Thomas J. Scheff, *Being Mentally Ill: A Sociological Theory* (Chicago: Aldine Publishing, 1966), pp. 55–64.

29. The discussion is drawn from Scheff, *Being Mentally Ill,* pp. 31–101.

30. Elaine Cumming and John Cumming, *Closed Ranks: An Experiment*

in Mental Health (Cambridge, Mass.: Harvard University Press, 1957), pp. 91–108.

31. Marian Radke Yarrow, Charlotte Green Schwartz, Harriett S. Murphy, and Leila Calhoun Deasy, "The Psychological Meaning of Mental Illness in the Family," *Journal of Social Issues,* **11**:4 (1955), cited in *Deviance: The Interactionist Perspective,* 2nd ed., eds. Earl Rubington and Martin S. Weinberg (New York: Macmillan, 1973), pp. 37–38.

32. George Bernard Shaw, Preface to *Getting Married* in *The Collected Works of Bernard Shaw* (New York: William H. Wise, 1930), vol. 12, p. 201.

33. Scheff, *Being Mentally Ill,* p. 82.

34. In addition to the later articles cited below in note 36 see Walter R. Gove, "Societal Reaction As an Explanation of Mental Illness: An Evaluation," *American Sociological Review,* **35** (October 1970), pp. 873–884; and Ronald Akers, "Comment on Gove's Evaluation of Societal Reaction As an Explanation of Mental Illness," and Gove's reply in *American Sociological Review,* **37** (August 1972), pp. 487–490.

35. Gove, "Societal Reaction," p. 882.

36. Thomas J. Scheff, "The Labelling Theory of Mental Illness," *American Sociological Review,* **39** (June 1974), pp. 444–452. Also see Walter R. Gove, "The Labelling Theory of Mental Illness: A Reply to Scheff"; Robert L. Chauncey, "Comment on 'The Labelling Theory of Mental Illness' "; and Thomas J. Scheff, "Reply to Chauncey and Gove," *American Sociological Review,* **40** (April 1975), pp. 242–257.

37. James R. Greenley, "The Psychiatric Patient's Family and Length of Hospitalization," *Journal of Health and Social Behavior,* **13** (March 1972), pp. 25–37; and Walter R. Gove and Terry Fain, "The Length of Psychiatric Hospitalization," *Social Problems,* **22** (February 1975), pp. 407–419.

38. D. L. Rosenhan, "On Being Sane in Insane Places," *Science,* **179** (January 19, 1973), pp. 250–258.

39. Ibid., pp. 252–253.

40. Rushing, "Two Patterns in the Relationship Between Social Class and Mental Hospitalization," pp. 539–540.

41. For a brief discussion of this issue see Seymour L. Halleck, *The Politics of Therapy* (New York: Science House, 1971), pp. 99–117.

42. The discussion is derived from Joe Haggerty, "Board of Education's Psychiatric Exams: New York City, USSR?" *Village Voice,* June 6, 1974, pp. 5–10.

43. Ibid., p. 5.

44. Derek L. Phillips, "Rejection: A Possible Consequence of Seeking Help for Mental Disorders," *American Sociological Review,* **28** (December 1963), pp. 963–972.

45. Ibid., pp. 968–969.

46. Stuart A. Kirk, "The Impact of Labeling on Rejection of the Mentally Ill: An Experimental Study," *Journal of Health and Social Behavior,* **15** (June 1974), pp. 108–117. For comprehensive reviews of studies on attitudes toward the mentally disordered, see Judith Rabkin, "Public Attitudes Toward Mental Illness: A Review of the Literature," and Dolores E. Kreisman and Virginia D. Joy, "Family Response to the Mental Illness of a Relative: A Review of the Literature," both in *Schizophrenia Bulletin,* **10** (Fall 1974), pp. 9–33 and 34–57.

47. Much of this debate is embodied in and represented by the works of

Thomas S. Szasz. In particular see his works *Law, Liberty and Psychiatry: An Inquiry into the Social Uses of Mental Health Practices* (New York: Macmillan, 1963); and *Ideology and Insanity*. See also Halleck, *The Politics of Therapy*, pp. 99–173; and Nicholas N. Kittrie, *The Right to Be Different: Deviance and Enforced Therapy* (Baltimore: Penguin Books, 1971).

48. Thomas S. Szasz, "Crime, Punishment, and Psychiatry," in *Current Perspectives on Criminal Behavior*, ed. Abraham S. Blumberg (New York: Knopf, 1974), p. 277.

49. Szasz, *Ideology and Insanity*, p. 120.

50. William J. Mitchell, "The Insanity Verdict: Who Is Dangerous, Who Is Sick?" *New York Times*, June 1, 1975, Section 4, p. 20.

51. Bruce J. Ennis, "Mental Commitment," *Civil Liberties*, No. 264 (October 1969), p. 3.

52. Sara Fein and Kent S. Miller, "Legal Processes and Adjudication in Mental Incompetency Proceedings," *Social Problems*, **20** (Summer 1972), pp. 57–64.

53. Szasz, *Law, Liberty and Psychiatry*, pp. 45–46; and Halleck, *The Politics of Therapy*, pp. 157–173.

54. Ennis and Litwack, "Psychiatry and the Presumption of Expertise," p. 733; see also pp. 711–716.

55. Bruce J. Ennis, *Prisoners of Psychiatry: Mental Patients, Psychiatrists, and the Law* (New York: Harcourt Brace Jovanovich, 1972), p. 225.

56. Scheff, *Being Mentally Ill*, pp. 128–155. For a discussion of similar studies see Scheff, "The Labelling Theory of Mental Illness," pp. 448–450.

57. Kittrie's *The Right to Be Different* is a comprehensive discussion of the rise of the therapeutic state.

58. The discussion is based on Alan H. Swanson, "Sexual Psychopath Statutes: Summary and Analysis," *Journal of Criminal Law, Criminology and Police Science*, 51 (July–August 1960), pp. 215–235; Aldo Piperno and Clifford E. Simonsen, "A Social-Legal History of Sexual Psychopath Laws—Beyond Sutherland" (paper presented at the Southern Conference on Corrections, Florida State University, 1973); and Kittrie, *The Right to Be Different*, pp. 169–209.

59. Kittrie, *The Right to Be Different*, p. 191.

60. "8 Murders Laid to a Californian," *New York Times*, October 21, 1973, Section 1, p. 44.

61. Edwin H. Sutherland, "The Diffusion of Sexual Psychopath Laws," *American Journal of Sociology*, **56** (September 1950), pp. 142–148.

62. This and other therapies mentioned here are discussed in Wayne Sage, "Crime and the Clockwork Lemon," *Human Behavior*, (September 1974), pp. 16–25; Michael S. Serrill, "Treating Sex Offenders in New Jersey," and R. V. Denenberg, "Sex Offenders Treat Themselves," both in *Corrections Magazine*, **1** (November–December 1974), pp. 13–24, 53–64; and William E. Cockerham, "Behavior Modification for Child Molesters," *Corrections Magazine*, **1** (January–February 1975), pp. 77–80.

63. Jessica Mitford, *Kind and Usual Punishment: The Prison Business* (New York: Alfred A. Knopf, 1973), p. 128.

10 SEXUAL DEVIANCE: PROSTITUTION AND HOMOSEXUALITY

Sex is the most fun you can have without laughing.

Anonymous

Whether sex is a laughing matter depends upon your perspective. The dirty joke is certainly a universal form of humor, but sexual behavior is a very serious business to most of us and to the societies in which we live.

Obviously humans possess many unique characteristics setting them apart from the rest of living things. No other animal has reached our proficiency in language, art, or war, for example. So too, in our sexual practices we are far more diverse and imaginative than any other species in the animal kingdom. But human societies also impose many restraints that define "acceptable" sexual behavior. In the United States the general convention, and usually the law, limit sexual partners to those of the opposite sex, unrelated by blood, and beyond a certain age. Further, it is generally accepted that sexual relationships should involve no more than two partners who are married or, at least, deeply in love. What a couple may do in the sex act is also restricted: certain "unnatural" acts must be avoided or engaged in only as preludes to the "natural" act.

Essentially, however, what is labeled as

deviant sexual behavior generally does not differ in *form* from normal behavior, but in the *conditions* under which the behavior occurs. No matter whether the behavior is genital-genital, oral-genital, or anal-genital the distinction between deviant and non-deviant sex concerns questions of whether it is premarital, extramarital, comarital, and questions concerning the implied rewards, degree of emotional attachment, the frequency, the choice of partner, and so on. Thus what homosexuals and prostitutes—the subjects of this chapter—do sexually is not basically different from what anyone else does. But the conditions under which they do it make their activities illegal, subject to social disapproval, or both.

In a handful of states, such as Connecticut, Illinois, and Ohio, what goes on behind closed doors is of minimal legal concern; privacy must be maintained, and the participants must be unrelated, of legal age, and not subject to coercion. However, in most states the law limits who goes into and what goes on in bedrooms. But even if the law remains unenforced—which is usually the case—there are powerful social pressures acting to constrain one's sexual behavior. Any departure from sexual "normality" is best kept as secret as one can make it. For example, in Illinois it is doubtful that a self-proclaimed homosexual could successfully run for governor. He or she might be "legal," but still "queer" to most of the voters.

A textbook in deviant behavior could concentrate on any number of conditions in which sexual activity takes place. Consistent with our theme we concentrate on the two which are most obvious to the public and which have resulted in overt interest group conflict: prostitution and homosexuality.

Prostitution

The harlot's cry from street to street
Shall weave old England's winding sheet.
                                        William Blake

John: How did a nice girl like you get into a
business like this?
Whore: Just lucky I guess.
                                        Anonymous

There is a world of difference between Blake's belief that prostitution foretold the downfall of England, and the tired old exchange between a prostitute and her customer. But the contrast is an accurate representation of opposing beliefs about the so-called oldest profession. On the one hand are those who argue that prostitution is a social evil that spreads disease and promotes other forms of crime, as well as being degrading to women. On the other hand are those who claim that prostitution is not only inevitable in society, but also that it performs a valuable service; whatever ills accompany it are not inherent but stem from the way society treats prostitutes.

Regardless of which position one takes, proof is difficult. Despite all the ink expended on the question of prostitution, almost no one has dealt with an indispensable cause of prostitution—the customer or *john*. Although it is a truism that prostitution is impossible without customers, you would never guess it from the great mass of writing on the subject. The research deals primarily with questions of who enters the business, why and how they enter it, and their perceptions of themselves and the business. Consequently, the findings leave one with the impression that prostitution is a consensual act between two parties, only one of whom is deviant. Johns are fleeting shadows not only to prostitutes, but to researchers as well.

The outstanding exception to this generalization is the work of Alfred C. Kinsey and his associates.[1] In the 1940s a sample of 5,300 white males were interviewed at length about their sexual behavior. Kinsey found that males go to prostitutes primarily because they provide easy and certain sexual outlet, they are cheaper than dates with non-prostitutes, the sexual contacts involve no later responsibilities, and prostitutes provide services difficult to obtain from other women: bondage, oral or anal intercourse, and so on.

Kinsey found that 69 per cent of the white male population have had some experience with prostitutes. Although one's first impression may be that this figure is high, Kinsey points out that males having repeated contacts with prostitutes were very exceptional in his sample. In fact, homosexual contacts accounted for more male sexual behavior than did contacts with female prostitutes. Kinsey claims that the attention given prostitution is highly disproportionate to its social significance.

> The world's literature contains hundreds of volumes whose authors have attempted to assay the social significance of prostitution. For an activity which contributes no more than this does to the sexual outlet of the male population, it is amazing that it should have been given such widespread consideration. . . . The extent of the attention which the subject still receives in this country today is, as we have shown, all out of proportion to its significance in the lives of most males, and this makes one skeptical of using the older literature as a source of information on the place of prostitution in past generations. . . . Certainly the older accounts would make it appear that prostitution was much more important in the life of the male who lived any time between the dawn of history and World War I than we have evidence of its having been since then.[2]

Of course, as the reader already knows, any issue is as socially significant as powerful interest groups care to make it. That is why, as indicated in Chapter 8, a half million heroin addicts are more socially significant than six million alcoholics. Nevertheless, Kinsey's comment is worth keeping in mind, because it is based upon the best available data—even though the findings are thirty years old and applicable to whites only. The data's relevance is increased if one speculation is valid: that the proportion of men visiting prostitutes has remained constant since the 1930s.[3]

Regardless of whether the amount of prostitution has remained constant or varied in one direction or the other, works on the subject continue to be published. Few, if any, portray prostitution as a trivial matter. This excerpt from a recent journalistic account of prostitution in New York City is representative.

> This country supports between 200,000 and 250,000 prostitutes, more than any other nation in the Western world. To a Chinese they probably all look alike: floating mouth and disembodied hands that promise release without exacting emotion, consumers of the desperate semen backed up inside society's castoffs. In short, they are in the unidentified body prints left on the sheets after 10 million different acts of prostitution every week in America.[4]

CONTEXT OF PROSTITUTION

What is prostitution? This is not as easy to answer as it seems because there are many variations. For example, a woman agrees to be sexually available if a man shows her a good time for one evening; no money is transferred to the woman. Is she a prostitute? For another example, a male hires a woman to beat him with a whip. He has an orgasm but she never undresses or is even touched by the man. Did an act of prostitution occur? If you answered yes to either or both of these questions you will be uncomfortable with the definition suggested by two prominent students of the subject, Charles Winick and Paul M. Kinsie:

> [Prostitution] can generally be defined as the granting of nonmarital sexual access, established by mutual agreement of the woman, her client, and/or her employer, for remuneration which provides part or all of her livelihood.[5]

Little would be gained by muddying the waters of definition any further, but the reader should be aware that sex and its sale occur in many forms. But whatever its form, all prostitution seems to have the following in common:

1. *Activity that has sexual significance for the customer.* This includes an entire range of behavior from actual sexual intercourse to cases in which the prostitute simply screams obscenities at the customer until he is satisfied.
2. *Economic transaction.* Whether the sellers earn part or all of their livelihood is inconsequential; something of economic value, which

may or may not be currency, is exchanged for the activity, usually just prior to the service.

3. *Emotional indifference.* The behavior is limited to an exchange of service for economic consideration. The participants may or may not be strangers, but their interaction in this instance has nothing to do with affection for one another.

Before describing the contexts in which prostitution occurs, a frequent misconception should be cleared up: namely, that being a prostitute means being a female. There are *male prostitutes,* a small proportion of whom live off the earnings and gifts of females. Such males are commonly called *gigolos* and can be considered prostitutes to the extent that their services go beyond companionship into sexual activity.

A far more common form of male prostitution involves *male customers.* Research on this form is scarce and mainly of recent origin, so the relevant literature is skimpy. The discussion that follows will deal primarily with females, but will refer to male prostitution wherever information exists.

Up until 1939, much of American prostitution flourished within *brothels*—popularly known as *whorehouses* or *cathouses.* These were buildings where, under the management of a *madam,* the women ate, slept, and carried on their business. Typically, half the women's earnings went to the madam to pay for room, board, and other services provided by the house. The number of girls ranged from two to sixteen per house; and the houses themselves ranged from the sleazy to the luxuriously furnished, the latter having their own dance bands and bars and catering to well-to-do businessmen and politicians.[6]

In major cities brothels were often clustered in specific areas known as *red light districts.*

> The phrase "red light" seems to have had its origin in Western railroad construction camps, where prostitutes outnumbered other women by as many as fifty to one. A brakeman visiting a prostitute would hang his red signal lamp outside her tent so that a dispatcher looking for the men to make up a crew could easily find him. On a busy night, a number of such tents that were close together became known as a red light district.[7]

The most famous of such districts were the Barbary Coast in San Francisco and Storyville in New Orleans. In the first decade of this century, Storyville contained as many as 230 brothels within its 36 square blocks.

Because the red light districts and their brothels were so obvious, they were also vulnerable when interest group wrath built up against prostitution. As we shall discuss later, public agitation against the "social evil" destroyed brothels as a major aspect of prostitution by 1939. Only Galveston, Texas maintained a red light district of any consequence into the 1960s. Prostitution, of course, was not eliminated in the process. Today, the contexts in which it occurs are extremely varied, limited only by the imaginations and ingenuity of the women and their customers.[8]

Brothels and their madams have not completely disappeared. But the houses are generally much smaller and less conspicuous than in the past. Today, the women are not likely to reside in the house at all, and many of the houses are simply apartments where women report regularly or whenever the madam phones them about a customer. This last arrangement is sometimes referred to as a *call house*.

The most obvious contemporary brothels are in Nevada—the one state that leaves the legality of prostitution up to county discretion. Only two counties, those containing Reno and Las Vegas, have prohibited prostitution; in the other fifteen, prostitution flourishes. For example, Winnemucca, a town of five thousand population, has five brothels with an average of five women in each.[9]

One new development is the brothel catering to homosexuals. David J. Pittman found several in large cities; they are small, lodging one or two males with another fifteen or more living outside.[10] The customers are typically affluent white professionals and businessmen, a large proportion of whom are married.

With the decline of brothels, prostitution often became a matter of individual entrepreneurship. Thus the *call girl*, and recently the *call boy*, assumed prominence. The call prostitutes' modes of operation differ greatly, but the ideal situation from the standpoint of the prostitutes is the ability to be highly selective in their clientele. New customers are accepted only after referral and recommendation by current customers or by other trusted prostitutes. It is also considered preferable to serve as a date for the customer in a package deal involving sex only after an evening of dinner and nightclubbing. In fact, many firms hire call girls to entertain visiting businessmen. As you might surmise, such call girls are often college graduates or from middle class backgrounds; they are attractive, articulate, well-dressed, and well paid: $150 plus expenses is rock bottom for an evening's fun. A call girl can clear over $1,000 a week. If she works the bachelor party or orgy circuit she makes that in an evening.

In addition to these aristocrats of the trade there are other call prostitutes available through advertisements in sex-oriented tabloid newspapers, such as *Screw* in New York and *San Francisco Ball*. The following are representative ads.

> I am an exceptionally beautiful blue-eyed blonde, willing and eager to share my beautiful soft white curves with you. . . . Exceptionally conservative in appearance. Hotel or Residence.

"Boy Next Door." I am 24, have blue eyes, brown hair, am 5'11" and weigh 147 pounds. My body is lean, hard and well defined from hours in the gym and on a surf board. Because of my good clean wholesome looks I have been billed as the "boy next door" in several underground flicks and have appeared in several publications. I am versatile and cooperative.

Schools's [Sic] Open! Geri and her friends announce the opening of their private classes in English Therapy. We'll teach you how to be a full-fledged slave. Only serious applicants will be accepted. Call promptly for an appointment.

Another context in which prostitutes and customers make contacts is the bar. Many bars employ women primarily to push drinks. These *B-girls* (bar-girls) approach customers with such come-ons as, "Want to buy me a drink, honey?" Once a customer assents, the woman encourages him to drink more himself or to upgrade the proceedings by ordering champagne. Ordering champagne in these places is a costly mistake usually committed only by the extremely gullible or extremely drunk—prices for a nonvintage New York brand will be upwards of thirty dollars. Usually, however, the customer drinks what he wants while the woman gulps some low-alcohol concoction (sometimes ordered as sloe gin) at two dollars a crack, on which she receives a commission.

The role which prostitution plays in the B-girl's occupation varies greatly. Some bar owners prohibit it, though the girls may make after-hours arrangements at their own risk. In other cases, prostitution is an integral part of the job. In the crasser establishments customers may be masturbated under the table, but generally the couple retires to a room on the premises or to a nearby hotel.

The closest counterpart to the B-girl among male prostitutes is the *bar-hustler* (*hustling* is a slang term for prostituting). He is not employed by any establishment, but systematically patrols homo-sexual bars in search of customers.

The institution that has grown most rapidly as a context for prostitution is the *massage business*. In midwestern cities the blatant advertisements seen in *Screw* and *San Francisco Ball* will not receive an enthusiastic legal reception; but prostitutes can avoid difficulty by advertising as masseuses in the yellow pages and in weekly "what's happening in ————" magazines.[11] These *dial-a-massage* services are provided at a motel or at the customer's residence.

Most prostitution in the massage business occurs in the *massage parlors*, which have sprung up nationwide within the past decade. Practices and advertisements vary, but a common theme is the storefront advertisement promising a body rub or massage. This may be embellished as the local authorities permit: e.g., "half hour topless, $15, bottomless, $20." Once in the massage room the customer must further bargain for any services over and above an actual massage. The massage parlor is a particularly safe gimmick for prostitutes because there is nothing illegal about advertising and giving massages, and solicitation for the sex act is left to the customer who has already spent some money. Because the prostitutes themselves need not solicit, they avoid arrest. If a police officer solicits, that is deemed *entrapment,* and the arrest is illegal.

The massage parlor in the United States has reached its finest flower on Forty-second Street in Manhattan, where one establishment has nine massage rooms, each with a different fantasy theme ranging from the Hall of Caesar with its "seductive slave girl" to the House of the Geisha, and from the Western Bordello to the completely mirrored Infinity Room.

Before turning our attention to one of the oldest but still most common types of prostitution, *streetwalking,* it should be evident from the discussion so far that prostitution is found in practically any situation where potential customers exist. Historically, roving armies had their *camp followers.* Today prostitutes are found near military installations, major trucking stops, and large-scale construction projects such as the Alaskan pipeline. The more transient males—those just passing through—can go where prostitutes are found rather than vice versa. Prostitutes can be easily located in any large city behind the facades of nude photo clubs, sexual therapy schools, sauna baths, and, of course, massage parlors. In short, despite its illegality, prostitution thrives wherever a demand exists. To meet this demand, new means of accommodating customers are often devised. One of the most recent occurred in Portland, Oregon, where a woman installed a massage parlor in a motor home recreation vehicle. She says,

> We'd eventually like to go statewide. . . . The [motor homes] are so versatile that you can virtually go to the fisherman on the bank of a river and if he doesn't catch any fish he can just climb aboard and relax.[12]

Despite all the innovations, *streetwalkers* remain a constant staple in the world of prostitution. They probably outnumber all others in the business and are at the bottom of its social ladder. According to Gail Sheehy, three types of street hookers can be found in New York City.

1. *Daytimers.* These are the classiest of the street trade, comprised of white out-of-work models and actresses and suburban housewives supplementing their husbands' incomes. They work office buildings for contacts with executives at no less than sixty dollars a *trick* (sex act; the term may also refer to the john or customer).
2. *Early evening girls.* Usually through by eleven o'clock, these are

full-time independent professionals who work in and around hotels, especially during conventions. They may make as much as $300–400 per evening.

3. *All the rest of the streetwalkers.* This includes the old, the very young, the tough, the desperate, the unattractive, and any others not fitting into the other categories. They work far into the night and try to turn as many tricks as possible before the stream of customers simply runs out.[13]

It is this last and largest category with which we shall be primarily concerned in the following discussion. The reader should bear in mind, however, that within this type there are many variations. For example, female impersonators or *drag queens* (males whose dress and voice imitate females') perform oral sex on customers who never suspect that their sexual partner is a male. And then there are both men and women who use prostitution primarily as a device to mug or rip off their customers, either by picking their pockets or by more forceful methods. While prostitution per se may be a victimless crime, it unquestionably provides the vehicle for many property crimes.

BECOMING A PROSTITUTE

Almost no one is interested in how men become johns, but everyone is eager to investigate how women becomes whores. One of the oldest explanations is that women are *forced* into the profession, a practice usually known to the public as *white slavery,* a curious term implying that only whites are compelled into the profession. The usual fantasy about white slavery in the United States involves the gullible country girls who, arriving at big city train and bus stations, are accosted by slick-talking pimps and lured into brothels. There the girls are repeatedly raped and beaten until their spirit and sense of decency are broken.

Unquestionably, violence is part of the prostitute's world, particularly if she becomes involved with a pimp. But, as will be seen later, beatings by pimps are usually a means of raising production efforts or establishing who is boss. The degree to which women are initially forced to prostitute themselves seems minimal. There are exceptions, of course. One pimp told a *Time* magazine reporter how teenaged runaway girls are initiated.

> You've got to find out if they've got problems, if they're smart enough to say they are 18 when cops make a bust . . . My partner's finding out everything about her. If she sniffs coke [cocaine], he'll give her that. She's in a beautiful crib [apartment], like a penthouse almost. It's heaven on earth—until tomorrow. Tomorrow the respect thing starts. A few blows.

Some ass kicking. You've got to stomp her ass a few times to let her know where you're coming from. You've got to set the rules, make her show respect. . . . If she makes it through tomorrow, the process will take three days. We'll get her a wig, some clothes, then put $10 in her pocket and see if she tries to run. You watch her close, maybe send another girl out with her. If she turns her first trick and comes back smiling, you've got her.[14]

But girls are not the only possible targets of force in the world of prostitution. There are also the *chickens,* boys in their early teens who are hired out to customers known as *chickenhawks.* Many chickens, ranging in age from eleven to fourteen, are self-employed streetwalkers selling their wares for ten dollars for about ten minutes' work. But some become the property of pimps who entice them with a variety of promises. Once a boy works for a pimp, attempts to leave are discouraged by beatings and torture. A reporter for the *Village Voice* tells about one recruiting technique in New York City.

Since the most requested commodity by chickenhawks is a new face, the pimps are always looking for new boys. The pimps stand like vultures around the Port Authority Bus Terminal waiting to descend on runaways. A young boy needs only to get off the bus, a knapsack on his back, walk a few confused steps in the big city, before a nice man will offer him a free meal and a place to stay. Too often the boy accepts. By that night the boy has been broken in. He becomes the victim of what is called on the street the rape artist. The boy is beaten. Perhaps he is drugged. And he's working. All the money he makes goes to the pimp. All the child receives is a few meals and enough pills to keep him too stoned to resist. He is now part of the stable, a chicken sold from john to john until the pimp tires of him.[15]

It would be misleading for the reader to conclude, however, that most prostitutes, either female or male, are initially forced into their professions. It is probably safe to assume that such coercion occurs in only a small minority of cases. This still leaves us with the important question. *Why do people voluntarily become prostitutes?*

Because prostitution is deviant behavior, this question is seldom asked with the same disinterest surrounding such questions as why people become morticians, bookkeepers, truckdrivers. Just as these individuals provide desired services, prostitutes provide services for a fee. True, they sell—actually rent—their bodies, but so do boxers or football players with all their expertise for the task at hand. What if we were to reply that persons become prostitutes because they are following the capitalistic dictum of making the most money with the least effort in the shortest period of time? This would probably not satisfy those expecting a statement about unhappy formative years, disturbed personality, low I.Q., and so on. All these and a host of other possibilities have been investigated over the years, but no research conclusions come close to explaining the incredible variety of persons engaged in the profession, ranging from junkies to suburban housewives to persons like Sally Stanford, an ex-madam who is now a successful restaurateur and politician in Sausalito, California.[16]

From the limited amount of research on the backgrounds of prostitutes, there emerges a set of three experiences common to a majority of the women engaged in the occupation on a full-time basis. These career contingencies do not answer why specific women enter the occupation, but they do point to factors that make prostitution—for these women, at least—a logical behavioral alternative.[17]

1. Early and frequent promiscuous sexual experiences. By early we mean from ten to thirteen years of age at the time of first sexual intercourse. Promiscuous is more difficult to define without sounding moralistic, but there appears to be a pattern of sexual experiences with several men, often after the briefest of acquaintanceships, during a short period of time. Some women, for example, had jobs as waitresses and dated customers. Or as school girls, sexual intercourse was a standard aspect of dating, whether the date was the ninth or the first.

The reader should bear in mind that this pattern of sexual experience may not necessarily distinguish women who become prostitutes from some of their peers who do not. Nevertheless, the pattern facilitates entry into prostitution because experiences of frequent and casual sexual behavior are already established.

2. Acquiring verbalized motives favorable to prostitution. With few exceptions it appears that becoming a prostitute involves associations with persons who encourage undertaking the career. These associations may be with prostitutes or with pimps who extol the life as fast and glamorous, a life of expensive clothes, independence, and excitement. In short, there is social support that neutralizes any misgivings or doubts about *selling it* rather than *giving it away.*

In some cases these motives may become quite altruistic. James H. Bryan found among call girls an ideology that prostitution serves as a positive force against crime and unhappiness in society.

> We girls see, like I guess you call them perverts of some sort, you know, little freaky people and if they didn't have girls to come to like us that are able to handle them and make it a nice thing, there would be so many rapes and . . . nutty people really.
> I could say that a prostitute has held more marriages together as part of their profession than any divorce counselor.[18]

Thus, there comes a realization that prostitution is far less shameful than the rest of society cares to believe.

Males who prostitute themselves must deal with motives regarding two deviant identities: being both a prostitute and a homosexual. Adjustments are made in nearly all possible combinations: some hustlers see themselves as both prostitutes and homosexuals, but others see themselves as neither; and still others see themselves as hustlers but not as homosexuals. How can persons sell homosexual activities and disclaim these identities?

The answer to this question can be found in Albert J. Reiss, Jr.'s study of lower-class delinquent boys.[19] Reiss found that, just as with females who become prostitutes, some boys learn from their close associates the advantage of selling sex; as with females it is simply easy money. However, they also learn that "getting a queer"—being paid by a homosexual for services—is not a sign of being either a hustler or a queer so long as certain rules in the relationship are maintained. First, money must be the only goal; seeking sexual satisfaction from the relationship is forbidden. Second, the relationship must be limited to the adult orally stimulating the boy; no other sexual contacts are permitted. Third, no affection between participants may be displayed during the relationship; the service is always to be conducted in an indifferent, businesslike fashion. Fourth, no violence is to be used if the customer conforms to the norms of the situation. (It is possible that violence will occur if the customer does anything that threatens the boy's self-concept as a person who neither hustles nor is a homosexual. For example, calling the boy "cutie" or "sweetie" in front of his buddies is an invitation to disaster.)

3. Recognition of high financial return and restricted alternatives. Any single explanation of why persons enter prostitution would have to involve money. But money per se is not a sufficient explanation, unless one also considers that for most prostitutes other avenues to comparable incomes are unavailable. For the young, uneducated, black, lower-class female, prostitution holds the promise of rewards she could not dream of otherwise. In a couple of hours a day she can bring in a hundred dollars; she could find no other employment so lucrative regardless of how many hours she worked. At the other extreme, a similar situation holds true even for the older, educated white woman. If she possesses both beauty and an attractive personality, prostitution can provide her a greater financial return than any other available work. This is the way one prostitute explains economics as a rational motivating factor:

> Even a call girl could never make as much in a straight job as she could at prostitution. All prostitutes are in it for the money. With most uptown girls, the choice is not between starvation and life, but it is a choice between $5000 and $25,000 or between $10,000 and $50,000. That's a pretty big choice: a pretty big difference. You can say that they're in this business because of the difference of $40,000 a year. A businessman would say so. Businessmen do things because of the difference of $40,000 a year. Call girls do go into capitalism and think like capitalists.[20]

The same woman goes on to explain that women generally, and black women in particular, are restricted in their economic choices; for the poor black woman there may be virtually no choice at all. She continues:

> For white women you usually can't say that there's no choice but prostitution. There is. But the choice itself is a choice between working for somebody else and going into business for yourself. Going into business for yourself and hoping to make a lot of money. There's that choice. Prostitution on those terms is a kind of laissez-faire capitalism.[21]

Gail Sheehy, a journalist, reinforces the argument that the selection of prostitution as a way of living is a matter of rational economic choice:

> It is a silly question to ask a prostitute why she does it. The top salary for a teacher with a BA in New York City public schools is $13,950; for a registered staff nurse, $13,000; for a telephone operator, about $8,000. The absolute daily minimum a pimp expects a streetwalker to bring in is $200 a night. That comes to easily $70,000 a year. These are the highest-paid "professional" women in America.[22]

Of course, prostitution is filled with risks: arrest, disease, violent customers, and the stigma attached by conventional society are some of the more obvious. Yet, for those who can deal adequately with these problems and can remain independent, prostitution emerges as a rational choice of occupational pursuit. For many who enter the occupation, however, the monetary success goals are illusionary. They may earn hundreds of dollars a day but have no personal wealth except the clothes in their wardrobe to show for their efforts. The reason? In their search for financial and personal independence, the women are beguiled into accepting a servitude that deprives them of those very goals. That servitude is personified by the *pimp*.

THE PIMP

Those who profit from prostitution are far more numerous than one might at first imagine. The prostitutes do, of course; but so too do hotel operators, lawyers, bail bondsmen, taxi drivers, physicians, bellboys, and the owners of various outlets for prostitution such as massage parlors, nightclubs, and brothels. But the one individual who profits the most for the least amount of effort is the pimp. As one woman says about her "sweet man":

> He doesn't do *nothing*. But the way he does nothing is *beautiful*.[23]

This sums up one attitude about pimps. But others feel that "scum of the earth" is far more appropriate. There are few livelihoods about which there are such divergent opinions. To some the pimp represents perfect success—he has totally conned the system; to others, he is the basest exploiter of women; and to the prostitutes in his *stable* he is an essential part of their lives. In short, a balanced opinion of pimping is difficult to find.

What does the pimp do? Despite the quotation cited above, the pimp does *something*. He buys the prostitute's clothes and furniture, pays her rent and doctor bills, arranges for bail bond and a lawyer if she is arrested, and provides her with affection and attention. In return, the prostitute turns over all her earnings to him. Whether this is a fair exchange obviously depends upon your perspective.

The world of the pimp is clearly one in which success breeds success. The more material goods the pimp owns, the greater advantage he has in convincing women they ought to join his stable. The more women in the stable, the more goods that can be purchased and the greater discretion the pimp can use in recruiting. Stables vary in size from one to twenty women (usually streetwalkers), but size is not the gauge of a pimp's success. Productivity is. And high productivity is clearly visible: it buys a suede-upholstered Mark IV Lincoln Continental with telephone, chauffeur, and color television; custom-made clothing; a butler; a house in the country; a penthouse in the city; and pedigreed dogs. These are all indicators of the pimp who has made it by "earning" $500 or more a day.

Whether or not prostitutes "need" a pimp is a question well beyond the scope of this discussion. But there is no doubt that many women are convinced they do for several reasons, including business guidance, protection, status among other prostitutes, and emotional stability. The philosophy of the pimp does nothing to discourage this conviction.

The philosophy of black pimps—who clearly dominate the pimping scene for both black and white prostitutes—is described in the work of two anthropologists, Christina and Richard Milner. Part of this philosophy has grown out of black history in which white domination stripped the black male of his respect and manhood. According to the Milners, dominance over women is now a strong source of manly pride for the black.[24] This is reflected in the pimp's view of the nature of man and woman.

> Man embodies the principle of intellect. His natural role is to be the controller, the director, the lawmaker, and the leader. His analytical mind enables him to be coolly in charge and on top of every situation. . . . His innate sex urges may drive him to want many women, whereas a woman wants to capture one man with whom she can be secure. . . . In order for both sexes to achieve happiness, a woman must please her man above all else, "then she will be pleased." . . .
>
> Woman embodies the principles of basic animal biology. She is by nature concerned with obtaining security for herself and her offspring, and with pleasing her man. . . .

> In her pristine state, woman is only half of the completed unit. Without a man she is nothing. Her being is a vessel to nurture the thoughts and the seed which her man implants in her.[25]

But the pimp's preoccupation with masculinity leads to exploitation. He attempts to exploit not only the woman's "need" for security, but the white man's demand for sex. He refuses to sell his manhood by being exploited by women, whites, or the system in general. Instead, he sees himself as working the system's own game: he is simply another exploiter in an exploitive system.

> [Pimps] see society itself as a network of people gaming off [manipulating] each other for money, power, or some kind of ego-gratification. The preacher is a pimp gaming off his congregation, the politician is a pimp gaming off his constituents, the law-enforcement system pimps the lawbreakers, the wife is a [whore] gaming off her husband who is her trick; the employer games off his workers, the Whites pimp the Blacks, and the federal government pimps everybody! . . .
>
> The [pimp] conceives of himself as a small businessman within the capitalist tradition of free enterprise and considers himself to be no more corrupt in his methods than the legitimate businessmen trying to get ahead in a ruthless, competitive, materialistic economy.[26]

Relationships between prostitutes and their pimps vary greatly, so it is impossible to state categorically the real costs and benefits to the women. But there is no question that some relationships are maintained in an atmosphere of terror. In New York City, the standard among many pimps is that their women must return each night with at least $200; if they fall short of this quota the consequences range from being locked out of their apartments to being beaten.[27] (The official pimp weapon is a wire coat hanger wrapped in cotton to minimize bruises.) Furthermore, shootings are not unheard of. One of the jobs of the New York Police Public Morals Squad is to protect prostitutes threatened with mutilation, or worse, from their pimps.[28]

PROSTITUTION AND CONFLICT

Prostitution has attracted the attention of interest groups since the day the first john paid five clam shells to the first hooker. Traditionally, of course, there have been moral crusades to eliminate prostitution as an institution. More recently, feminist groups have been attempting to rescue prostitutes from themselves—particularly those prostitutes who submit to domination by pimps. On the other hand, prostitutes themselves are becoming a more cohesive interest group; they are agitating for their legal rights and telling the feminists to mind their own business. In looking at this evolutionary process, let us first consider the early conflicts over prostitution as an institution.

Throughout the nineteenth century in America prostitution, like opium, was widespread but tolerated. "Respectable" women had their place, and prostitutes had theirs, the brothels and the red light districts of the larger cities. Streetwalkers ran the risk of being arrested but brothels were seldom bothered, with the exception of occasional harassment for money by police and by gangs of ruffians who were forerunners of organized crime. Officials were generally content with the status quo because localized brothels simplified control and regulation.

But the first decades of the twentieth century found the larger American cities caught up in the fever of vice crusades that were inspired by a series of exposés appearing in magazines and books between 1907 and 1910. The revelations about prostitutes were sometimes contradictory, but always negative. Prostitutes were pictured as moronic and immoral producers of numerous children of the same ilk, as weak-willed women enticed by the lure of easy money, as good but gullible innocents forced into white slavery, as a corrupting influence on middle- and upper-class youth, and as the primary cause of the spread of syphilis. In short, society suddenly had a "social evil" on its hands.

To counter this evil a number of educational and lobbying organizations were formed with such names as: American Society of Sanitary and Moral Prophylaxis, American Purity Alliance, and American Federation of Sex Hygiene. The Y.M.C.A., Y.W.C.A. and the Salvation Army also were active in the cause, as were preachers in their pulpits and the Women's Christian Temperance Union. Three years of pressure from such reform groups, and the newspapers forced the Chicago City Council to establish a vice commission in 1910. A year later, the commission submitted its report, headed by the bold-type statement: "Constant and Persistent Repression of Prostitution the Immediate Method: Absolute Annihilation the Ultimate Ideal." [29] The commission conceded that the ultimate ideal could not be achieved until "lust in the hearts of men" was eradicated. It also found little evidence that white slavery was a major factor in prostitution. The commission did report that lack of education and high economic rewards led girls into the occupation. Despite these interpretations, the commission ignored remedying the causes and instead directed its recommendations toward their effect. The report set forth a series of suggestions for legal repression that were to influence state and municipal laws across the country.

It recommended, for example, that "segregated vice," i.e., the red light districts, be abolished; that imprisonment or probation replace fines for prostitution; and that police departments add special morals squads. But misgivings over the first recommendation served to delay implementation of the commission's report. Many feared that abolishment of the red light districts would merely disperse prostitution and make it even more difficult to control. Pressures by the reform groups eventually prevailed, however, and by October 1912, the Chicago brothels were closed. By 1918 approximately 200 more cities had closed theirs. The visibility of the brothels had contributed to their undoing—an era of prostitution had ended.[30]

Few of the reformers really believed that the shutdown of the brothels and the jailing of prostitutes signalled the end of prostitution. Legal repression was only one step in the wider social reform movement that encompassed education, labor, government, and the general rights of all individuals—a reform movement couched in the ideals of the rural, Protestant, native, middle class. These were the same ideals that led to Prohibition and to the laws regulating psychoactive drugs. But the reformers' vision failed.

The reform movement did not eliminate, nor perhaps even diminish, prostitution. But it did alter its context: prostitution went underground, it dispersed, and it migrated to areas where law enforcement permitted concentration as in the old days. Since 1918 the status of prostitution has fluctuated in some areas from openness to stricter laws and back again. Despite the reform movement, for example, Honolulu had legalized brothels from 1920 until 1944; they were first regulated by the military, then by the Honolulu police, and then by the military again during World War II.[31] More recently, New York changed its law two times: up until 1967 the maximum penalty for prostitution was one year; in 1967 it was changed to fifteen days and/or $250; and in 1969 it was again changed to ninety days and/or $500.[32] In practice, however, New York streetwalkers are virtually the only type of prostitutes likely to be arrested, and even then the fines only occasionally reach $300 and the jail sentences five to ten days.[33]

The persistence of prostitution through both difficult and easy times and its reputation as the oldest profession inevitably lead to another question. *Is prostitution inevitable?* The usual sociological answer is yes, and the most quoted sociological explanation of prostitution is that offered by Kingsley Davis. Davis argues that prostitution is not only inevitable but necessary. *Demand* for prostitution, according to Davis, will vary to some degree with the changing availability of free sexual partners. However, there is a relatively constant demand by males for impersonal and impartial sex that wives and lovers do not meet. This demand persists even in the face of greater sexual freedom among females. Examples are the demands of the legions of males who for one reason or another have no immediate sexual access to their female acquaintances (servicemen, construction crews, or truck drivers); those males interested in forms of sex that many females find intolerable; and those males whose appearance, intelligence, or demeanor hinders the obtaining of free sexual partners.[34]

But can prostitution be eliminated at the source of *supply?* No, says Davis, because the demand dictates that women of very ordinary talents can earn far more money through prostitution than the legitimate application of their talents would warrant. This raises a further question. Why do not more women therefore become prostitutes?

> The answer of course is that the return is not primarily a reward for labor, skill, or capital, but a reward for loss of social standing. The prostitute loses esteem because the moral system . . . condemns her. If, then, she refuses to take up the profession until forced by sheer want, the basic cause of her hesitation is not economic but moral.[35]

Davis' theory of the cause of prostitution has recently been challenged by an amorphous interest group for whom prostitution is of great concern: the *feminists.* (The feminist or women's liberation movement is characterized by many organizations and groups, and the following discussion represents an amalgam of discussions from several sources.)[36] The feminist contention is that prostitution is simply another example of the general exploitation of women. Feminists point particularly to the discrimination involved in the law and its application: the prostitute is usually legally regarded as more "criminal" than her customer, and she is far more likely to be prosecuted.

That the prostitute and her john are differentially treated by society cannot be argued. But the feminists view prostitution per se with mixed feelings. On one hand their philosophy dictates that any woman has the right to do whatever she pleases with her body—including selling it. On the other hand, prostitution remains a blatant symbol of the sexism that the feminists are attempting to destroy.

> The presence of prostitution is a crime against all people. It legitimates people treating others as objects to be bought and sold without respect to human dignity; it supports an illegal market place (police payoffs, pimps, drug pushers, etc.) which results in crime and violence; it enforces a one-sided monogamy and it perpetuates racist and sexist attitudes, dehumanizing women and Third World people.[37]

The feminists recommend that all laws against prostitution be repealed, a step that must be taken to end current legal discrimination and to relieve some of the stigma associated with the occupation. The reader should be aware that repealing laws (often referred to as *decriminalization*) is *not* the same thing as *legalization*, whereby the government would impose regulations upon prostitution, including licensing, periodic medical examinations, and so on. The feminists believe that legalization would merely perpetuate prostitution and make a later shift to more respectable employment virtually impossible. How many school systems can you name that would hire a former licensed prostitute as a teacher? Above all, say the feminists, legalization would allow the government to continue the degradation of women—for a profit. Decriminalization, they argue, is the only logical first step in moving away from oppression in a male-dominated society and toward a prostitution-free society.

> As long as sexism and economic oppression persist, the supply and demand for prostitution will continue. Decriminalization will not eliminate prostitution, but it will remove the burden of guilt and the fear of jail from women as we struggle to destroy the social and economic roots of prostitution and the degradation that all women in our society share.[38]

There is yet another interest group that staunchly supports decriminalization but not legalization: *the prostitutes*. But there the similarity between the prostitutes' and the feminists' positions ends. Prostitutes do not agree that they are degraded, underprivileged, and male-victimized. This difference has led to bitter encounters with feminists. The classic confrontation came in Manhattan in January 1972, when the feminists attempted to define their position on how to eliminate prostitution. Prostitutes present in the audience took exception to the notions that their occupation needed elimination and that they were being exploited. The meeting degenerated into a shouting match, including among the highlights, "So fuck off, feminists, and don't call us, we'll call you." Punches were thrown and the meeting ended in a shambles.[39]

Such confrontations are unlikely today, for the common goal of decriminalization of prostitution joins the feminists and prostitutes in an uneasy union. At the same time prostitutes are showing signs of becoming an organized interest group. A recent development is the formation of a prostitutes' union known as *Coyote*—an acronym for "Call Off Your Old Tired Ethics." [40] In conjunction with associated chapters such as ASP (Associated Seattle Prostitutes) and PONY (Prostitutes of New York), Coyote campaigns for an end to discriminatory law enforcement, for the right of prostitutes to use public defenders, and eventually, for the complete decriminalization of prostitution.

Coyote claims a membership of over 3,500 persons and has been instrumental in obtaining some concessions. For example, until February 1974, prostitutes arrested in San Francisco were forced to take tests for venereal disease, after which they were required either to take a penicillin shot or to remain in jail for three days until test results were available. Coyote, with the help of the American Civil Liberties Union, obtained an injunction against the quarantine system after the health department conceded that the practice was unnecessary: the incidence of venereal disease is easily as high among people twenty to twenty-four years old as among prostitutes.

But whether the more powerful groups in society will soon be ready to permit total decriminalization of prostitution is doubtful. At the moment the mood seems to be one of guarded tolerance. There is little doubt that today the visibility of the prostitute is a more important factor in whether she will be arrested than is the fact that she is prostituting. Streetwalking is far riskier than working in bars or massage parlors. Furthermore, arresting hookers is an expensive proposition (no pun intended); in San Francisco the cost per arrest is estimated at $1,200.

Prostitutes may gain more rights in the law enforcement process, but the laws themselves will probably remain. As the District Attorney of Manhattan indicated, "I think we ought to keep the laws on the books so that we will have the reserve power to do more if we need to." [41] It seems unlikely, however, that any major crusade against prostitution, similar to that of the first decades of this century, will occur. Instead, there will be only occasional minor skirmishes when prostitutes become excessively visible or too closely related to other forms of crime.

Decriminalized or not, is prostitution inevitable? The feminists argue that the elimination of sexual biases will eliminate prostitution, but the existence of male prostitution belies that claim. Davis' interpretation is probably closer to the truth. As long as sex is fun, the free supply is limited, and financial rewards substantial, prostitution, both male and female, will persist.

Homosexuality

In the Book of Genesis, Lot must discourage some men of Sodom from trying to seduce his male guests, who are actually disguised angels. In order to get the Somodites off the premises Lot offers them his two virgin daughters for the night. The men are not interested. There are two remarkable aspects to the story of Lot: first, the low regard Lot has for his daughters—placing their sexual integrity beneath that of two guys who wander in off the plain; second, the abhorrence of homosexuality expressed in the Old Testament. Thomas S. Szasz puts the story in a contemporary context:

> The episode in Sodom is undoubtedly the earliest account in human history of the entrapment of homosexuals, a strategy widely practiced by the law enforcement agencies of modern Western countries, especially those of the United States. In effect, the men of Sodom were entrapped by the two strangers, who in truth were not travelers but angels, that is to say, God's plain-clothesmen. These agents of the Biblical vice-squad wasted no time punishing the offenders: ". . . they struck with blindness the men who were at the door of the house [Genesis 19:11]." The angels then warn Lot of God's plan to destroy the wicked city, giving him time to flee with his family. God's terrible punishment follows: "Then the Lord rained on

Sodom and Gomorrah brimstone and fire from the Lord out of heaven; and he overthrew those cities, and all the valley, and all the inhabitants of the cities, and what grew on the ground [Genesis 19:24–25]." [42]

Thus Sodom gave its name to homosexuality. The term *sodomy*, in its most precise sense, refers to anal intercourse with a human or a beast; in practice, however, the term also designates oral-genital contacts or fellatio. Statutes prohibiting the behavior are often far from exact in their wording. They are, however, highly *moralistic*; in addition to sodomy other legal terms include: "crime against nature," "unnatural intercourse," and "abominable and detestable crime against nature." No other legislation describes forbidden behavior in such righteous language. In 1973 the Supreme Court upheld a Florida law concerning "the abominable crime against nature, either with mankind or beast" because persons could "reasonably understand" what was prohibited. [43] Legislators and judges may know what such terms are all about, but imagine the perplexity facing a legal scholar visiting from Mars—particularly if the visitor feels that shaking hands is perverted.

HOMOSEXUALITY AS DEVIANCE

The tenor of the legal language surrounding sodomy reflects the Judeo-Christian tradition of severely condemning homosexual behavior. The fate of the Sodomites was mirrored in the penalties imposed in Christian Europe from the middle ages until the eighteenth century: flogging, castration, stoning, and burning alive. But the eighteenth century marked a turning point as European nations began liberalizing their laws. Today, the majority of nations have no restrictions against homosexual conduct between consenting adults in private; the nations having such restrictions assign lesser penalties than can be imposed in the United States. [44]

Sanctions against homosexuality in the United States are among the harshest in all modern societies. In the majority of states sodomy between consenting adults can draw maximum penalties ranging from ten years to life imprisonment. Contrast this to the maximum penalty of five years in European countries. However, two qualifications must be added. First, *there is a trend toward abolishing the sodomy statutes*. The first state to do so was Illinois in 1962. Connecticut was next in 1971, quickly followed by six other states. Second, *the enforcement of the statutes is rare*. Does this mean that sanctions against homosexuality have ended? Hardly. Instead, police rely on statutes of lesser severity to deal with homosexuality. Martin S. Weinberg and Colin J. Williams describe the legal control this way:

These statutes proscribe solicitation, disorderly conduct, lewd and lascivious behavior, and vagrancy, all of which are used ostensibly to control the homosexual's sexual behavior and the public pursuit of sexual partners. Often the "disorderly conduct" laws are used to arrest persons for acts for which no other punishment is provided in the code. "Lewd and lascivious behavior" provisions are used to punish acts which range from dancing and hand holding to more explicit sexual behavior. "Vagrancy" laws are a convenient catchall used in a variety of instances to harass homosexuals. It should be noted that most homosexuals are charged on misdeameanors rather than felony offenses not only because these laws are easier to apply but also because it is easier to get a conviction on a misdemeanor charge with its lesser penalties.[45]

Thus the homosexual fears arrest not because of the possible severity of his sentence—chances are that it will be either a fine or probation—but because of the consequences of the publicity: loss of employment and humiliation before his straight friends and family. Even if these consequences are of no concern, police harassment remains an inconvenience. It is an imposition on persons doing nothing more than thousands of other males trying to find a sexual partner. The only difference is the sex of the quarry.

Despite such harassment and its consequences, the degree of reaction toward homosexuality has clearly moderated in American society. Today there exists an ambivalence toward homosexuality as deviant behavior. There is a trend toward decriminalizing the behavior, and little official effort is made to impose heavy sanctions even when they are available. This tempering of legal reaction is consistent with the mixed attitudes toward homosexuality among the general public. Two Harris polls conducted in 1965 and 1969 showed a decline from 70 to 63 per cent of the population who believe homosexuality to be harmful.[46] A 1970 survey by the Institute for Sex Research found that approximately 60 per cent of the public did not favor decriminalizing homosexual behavior.[47] However, a 1973 poll in Virginia indicated that the general population is more accepting of homosexuality than of either prostitution or marihuana use.[48] Only about 21 per cent of the sample felt that imprisonment was necessary for consenting adults involved in homosexual acts; for prostitution and possession of marihuana the percentages were 35 and 48 respectively. The mean prison sentences recommended were: .93 years for homosexuality, 1.57 for prostitution, and 2.18 for marihuana.

This mixed bag of survey results can be used to "prove" that: 1. the majority of the American public is against homosexuals, or 2. an increasing proportion of persons are more tolerant of a behavior that can get a person locked up for decades. This author suggests that the latter interpretation is more relevant to the future of homosexuality in

America. Both research and personal accounts indicate that revealing oneself as a homosexual to parents or friends (coming out) often generates far less negative reaction than anticipated.[49] This is not to say that involvement in homosexual behavior entails no dangers, but clearly much of the severe official reaction is a thing of the past. Within the last two decades a greater toleration of sexual freedom in general, as well as pressures from homosexual interest groups, have created a social climate in which sexual proclivities are losing their significance as targets for law enforcement. As in prostitution, the single factor most jeopardizing the homosexual is his visibility. His likelihood of trouble with the law increases if he frequents public lavatories in search of quick sex; if he dresses as a female, particularly if he also prostitutes himself; or if he has the misfortune to be drinking in a homosexual bar when police raid it as a public nuisance. In short, for most homosexuals today arrest has become less of a threat than other forms of social reaction.

Reactions toward homosexuals fall into four general categories:

1. *Police harassment.* No adequate statistics on police practices toward homosexuals are available. No doubt the practices vary from city to city and in relationship to local police priorities concerning the homosexual "problem." For this discussion we will rely on a study conducted in Los Angeles County between 1962 and 1965.[50]

The reader will notice that the category is labeled police *harassment,* not police *enforcement* or some other less opinionated term. The choice is deliberate. In many cases police action against homosexuals is not preventive; that is, uniformed police do not openly patrol areas about which complaints may have been registered. Instead the police often rely on clandestine methods to catch persons in illegal acts and even to entice them to commit such acts.

A frequently used device is the *decoy.* The decoy is a plain-clothesman whose purpose it is to provide homosexuals with the opportunity to commit a "crime." The decoy's success depends upon his ability to conceal that he is a policeman and to convince homosexuals that he is not just a straight citizen who would take offense at being solicited. Thus the decoy dresses and acts the way he thinks homosexuals do. He hangs around public lavatories and gay bars being friendly. It is this friendliness that arouses a great deal of controversy. The decoy's "act" does not involve simply reading graffiti on lavatory walls, but ranges from a big smile to prolonged conversation to fondling his own genitals. Decoys have even been used in public baths where they run around in the nude.

The decoy is not a method of preventing or detecting crime (although decoys occasionally make arrests when observing a sex act).

Rather, the decoy is presumed to be a safeguard against homosexuals who might solicit the outraged public. But the presumption is fallacious:

> Since the decoy operates to apprehend solicitors, it is difficult to argue that he is a victim or that he is outraged by the proscribed conduct, particularly when he engages in responsive conversation or gestures with the suspect. In fact, complaints to the police regarding lewd solicitations are infrequent. . . .
>
> Empirical data [in the Los Angeles study] indicates that utilization of police manpower for decoy enforcement is not justified. Societal interests are infringed only when a solicitation to engage in a homosexual act creates a reasonable risk of offending public decency. The incidence of such solicitations is statistically insignificant. The majority of homosexual solicitations are made only if the other individual appears responsive and are ordinarily accomplished by quiet conversation and the use of gestures and signals having significance only to other homosexuals. Such unobtrusive solicitations do not involve an element of public outrage.[51]

A second method used to catch homosexuals is that of *secret observation*. This can involve hidden observation posts with peepholes, two-way mirrors, hidden television, and still cameras.[52] One of the more blatant examples of this method occurred in Mansfield, Ohio. There police set up a 16 mm movie camera behind a two-way mirror to record events in a public lavatory. After filming a sex act the police radioed colleagues outside to stop the offenders and obtain their names as part of police routine. No arrests were made at that time so as not to alarm future offenders. Over a two-week period sixty-five acts were photographed. When the trap was finally sprung the police had evidence and obtained convictions on men of all degrees of respectability, ranging from teachers and other middle-class individuals with no criminal record, to drifters. The purpose was clear; to round up as many sex "perverts" as possible regardless of their lack of threat to the public safety.

The use of such methods is probably decreasing because of the expense, the man-hours required, and the greater judicial and public suspicion of hidden surveillance techniques. In 1975 in Philadelphia, for example, a Federal District judge ruled that it was illegal for police to conduct secret surveillance of public restroom stalls because they are private domains although in public places. The case concerned police who drilled holes in restroom ceilings and observed occupants of the stalls.[53]

A third method, what we will call *routine harassment,* is used much more extensively. This entails a wide variety of campaigns: checking personal identifications in an area or bar every half hour, frequent checks on gay bars for violations of health or fire regulations, questioning customers as they enter and leave gay bars, crackdowns on jay-walkers in gay areas, and of course the garden variety raid for lewd conduct, drunkenness, public nuisance, or whatever might be applicable in the statute books.

2. Blackmail. As one might suspect, the legal consequences and social stigma attached to homosexuality make it a form of behavior particularly susceptible to blackmail. The most spectacular case in recent times involved a highly organized extortion ring that operated from about 1956 to 1966.[54] Its victims were college professors, college deans, famous entertainers, businessmen, a congressman, and high ranking military officers in the Pentagon. In its ten years the ring collected millions of dollars from over a thousand victims. One, a wealthy school teacher, was relieved of $120,000. The method involved a young gang member who would lure the target into a compromising situation. Then, either the victim would be overpowered and his money and identification papers stolen, or a phony policeman would interrupt the proceedings threatening arrest and exposure. A deal was worked out and payment was later made.

While bogus police may commit blackmail, there is some evidence that most blackmailing is done by real police as a result of decoy operations.[55] (Incidentally, the ring mentioned above was headed by a former Chicago policeman.) In these instances the victim simply pays off the policeman who threatens arrest. All together, perhaps as many as 15 per cent of all homosexuals have been blackmailed by someone.[56]

3. Danger. Homosexuals face threats not only from legal action and from extortion but from tangible physical danger as well. Among some individuals *queer-baiting*—locating and beating up homosexuals—ranks with professional football as a national pastime. Probably only the most serious cases of such beatings ever reach police records because of the victim's reluctance to elaborate on why he was the target.

Even when legal restrictions on homosexuality are relieved, the homosexual seeking sex in out-of-the-way places jeopardizes his safety. In the summer of 1973 a group of hustlers passing themselves off as gay began to systematically mug their homosexual customers.[57] When the gang was finally arrested police found some fifty wallets with identifications still in them. The police wrote nonincriminating letters to all, but not one victim attempted to recover his property. One journalist observer interprets the current scene in New York this way:

> Once the enemy in the Village was the cop, not the mugger. Since the advent of the gay liberation movement, however, the boys with nightsticks

have taken a more liberal attitude toward homosexual sex (still illegal in New York State), and the boys with knives have moved in to terrorize. . . . The desire for anonymity which characterizes sex . . . can be equated with the fear of being "found out" via the missing wallets. Rather a sweeping statement, maybe, but the truth is that many homosexuals also equate thrills with guilt and shame. Sex for some is settling down with a sweetie in Brooklyn Heights and raising French poodles. For others it's the games. While others opt for thrills and fantasy.[58]

4. *Discrimination*. In the early 1950s, Senator Joseph R. McCarthy accused the State Department of harboring communists and homosexuals—the assumption being that disloyalty and perversion are one and the same thing. This kind of simplistic equation exists today as well, and homosexuals are often excluded from certain employment categories because they are seen as untrustworthy at best and dangerous at worst. One public opinion survey found:

> Substantial majorities of the respondents agree that homosexual men should be allowed to work as artists, beauticians, florists, and musicians, but almost equally substantial majorities do not believe they should be permitted to engage in occupations of influence and authority. Three-quarters would deny to a homosexual the right to be a minister, a school teacher, or a judge, and two-thirds would bar the homosexual from medical practice and government service.[59]

Up until 1969, a homosexual could automatically be barred or dismissed from government employment purely on the basis of his sexual inclinations. Today, a government agency must prove that homosexuality actually will or does interfere with the agency's efficiency. However, the military still bars homosexuals from entrance and dismisses those found within its ranks, giving them a less than honorable discharge.[60] Furthermore, homosexual immigrants are denied entrance into the United States, and aliens already here can be deported—all on the basis of a law excluding admission to those "afflicted with psychopathic personality, epilepsy, or mental defect." [61]

In summary, being identified as a homosexual is not as hazardous as it was a mere decade ago, but sexual preference remains a criterion by which society distinguishes the normal from the deviant.

HOMOSEXUALITY: CONDITION OR BEHAVIOR?

The reader may have noticed that the discussion so far has focused on males. Female homosexuality (sometimes referred to as lesbianism) also exists, of course. It is not our intent to minimize the impact that homosexuality has on the lives of females, but an apparently one-sided discussion is difficult to avoid for two reasons. First, as we shall see, the prevalence of known female homosexuality is far lower. Second, female homosexuality elicits much less public reaction. This is partly due to its low visibility, if only because the public often refuses to acknowledge its existence among females. Two women can openly embrace, kiss, and live together for years, beyond suspicion or concern. Insofar as official response is concerned, it is rare for females to be arrested for homosexual activities. This is not to say that females who openly profess homosexuality will not experience discrimination and exclusion, but they are usually able to have sexual liaisons with decidedly less risk and censure than males are.

Now to the question posed previously. Is homosexuality a *condition* or a *behavior?* The answer is important because it has an effect on the related question of cause. If homosexuality is a condition like smallpox or green hair, then we should embark on an examination of what makes homosexuals different from heterosexuals. But to substantiate that homosexuality is a condition, we must make some other assumptions. We must assume, for example, that a clearcut distinction exists between homosexuals and heterosexuals. Further, we must assume that we know about, or at least can find, a factor or factors other than sexual preference that cause this distinction: character defect, chemical imbalance, genetic predisposition, family problems, and so on.

The first clue that homosexuals are essentially indistinguishable from others comes from anthropological studies of primitive societies. Researchers have found that in the majority of such societies homosexuality is considered normal and acceptable. In a few, participation in homosexual activities is not even a matter of preference, but rather a duty. In others, the same activity is vigorously condemned.[62]

> It seems that in different communities every shade of attitude has prevailed, from severe condemnation, through various shades of indifference, to institutional recognition. Where homosexual conduct was said not to exist at all this probably indicated that strong pressures had been brought to bear against its open manifestation. On the other hand, no primitive society, not even the most permissive, has accepted the open practice of exclusive homosexuality as a permanent way of life by large numbers of adults.[63]

Even considering the last qualification it is evident that the deviant nature of homosexuality is a matter of social definition and of degree. Even more damning to the notion of homosexuality as a condition is the *variability of commitment* to the behavior. If homosexuality is a condition, one would assume that someone either has it or does not. Alfred C. Kinsey describes the condition approach this way:

> A great deal of the thinking done by scientists and laymen alike stems from the assumption that there are persons who are "heterosexual" and per-

sons who are "homosexual," that these two types represent antitheses in the sexual world, and that there is only an insignificant class of "bisexuals" who occupy an intermediate position between the other groups. It is implied that every individual is innately—inherently—either heterosexual or homosexual.[64]

Life would certainly be considerably simplified if we could divide the population so nicely. But Kinsey, in studying the sexual histories of white American males, discovered that the behavior of many was not an either-or proposition. There are those who have been exclusively homosexual or heterosexual in their preferences throughout life. However, a considerable proportion have combined both preferences. Some were involved in one type during one part of their life, and involved in the other at another time. Still others were involved with both sexes at the same time—the same year, month, week, day, or even moment.[65]

Consider these examples. Individual A is married, has three children, and enjoys regular intercourse with his wife. But he occasionally stops in a public lavatory (known as a "tearoom" among homosexuals) for fellatio.[66] Individual B has exclusively homosexual contacts between the ages of 15 and 23, gets married, and never has another homosexual contact. Individual C has exclusively heterosexual contacts until he goes to prison; there he engages in homosexuality; after his release he returns to exclusive heterosexuality. Which of the above are homosexual and which heterosexual? And which has to be explained?

Kinsey found that only four per cent of the male white population are *exclusively homosexual throughout their lives.* Yet 37 per cent of the population have had at least *one homosexual experience to the point of orgasm* between adolescence and old age. If one also includes homosexual attraction that does not involve an orgasm, Kinsey finds that *50 per cent* of the population have had some homosexual experience during their adult life. For white females the percentages are: exclusively, less than two per cent; at least one experience to point of orgasm, 13 per cent; and some experience, 28 per cent.[67] (A word of warning is necessary here. These statistics are often used to indicate the prevalence of homosexuality. The large number of prisoners in the sample, the exclusion of black subjects, and other sampling biases make this a dubious conclusion. However, the data are strong enough to show that a sharp distinction between homosexuality and heterosexuality is impossible to make.)

The reader may argue that just as one swallow does not make a summer, one homosexual arousal does not make a homosexual. And if Kinsey's work is read carefully, one discovers that the great majority of males have no homosexual contacts after age twenty. If homosexuality is a condition, then it is tempting to suggest that most males outgrow that condition just as they outgrow acne. But the analogy does not satisfy the fact that there are varying degrees of commitment to both homosexuality and heterosexuality depending upon time, place, and many other circumstances.

As we shall soon see, there is absolutely no distinguishing factor that explains variations in sexual behavior or sexual preference. So compelling is the notion that homosexuality is strictly a *matter of behavior* that some sociologists have suggested that there really is no such thing as a *homosexual*. One such suggestion comes from Edward Sagarin:

> There is no such thing as a *homosexual*, for such a concept is a reification, an artifically created entity that has no basis in reality. What exists are people with erotic desires for their own sex, or who engage in sexual activities with same-sex others, or both. The desires constitute feeling, the acts constitute doing, but neither is being. Emotions and actions are fluid and dynamic, learnable and unlearnable, exist to a given extent for a limited or longer period of time, but are constantly in a state of change, flux, development, and becoming.[68]

Sagarin's point is well taken, especially when you consider that for most people sexual behavior is but a portion of their everyday activity. To describe someone accurately you would have to call him or her an accountant-reader-drinker-homosexual-tennis player-heterosexual-movie buff-good dresser-avid watcher of "Hawaii Five-O." Also to the point is a study that found in many societies in which homosexuality is permitted, there may be a great deal of homosexual behavior, but no one is known as a *homosexual*.[69] The reason there are homosexuals in our society is because a part—and usually a very small part—of their behavior is forbidden. Imagine what might occur if tennis playing came to be considered deviant. Persons who happened to play tennis, whether annually or daily, would be treated as *tennis players*. Behind their backs they would be called "net nuts" and "court creeps." Folklore about the disgusting differences between *singles* and *doubles* would arise. And, of course, researchers would embark on projects to ascertain how these "deviants" differed from the "normal" professional football watchers.

HOMOSEXUALITY AND CHOICE

As we mentioned earlier, the question of whether homosexuality is a condition or a form of behavior must be resolved before the issue of cause can properly be considered. If it is a condition then it is logical to seek out factors that both cause homosexuality and distinguish persons with the condition from those without it. As you might suspect, the search for such distinctions has been a failure. Science's inability to find a single difference is nicely summed up by one very frustrated citizen:

> I have said I think homosexuals cursed, and I am afraid I mean this quite literally, in the medieval sense of having been struck by an unexplained injury, an extreme piece of evil luck, whose origin is so unclear as to be, finally, a mystery. . . . If I had the power to do so, I would wish homosexuality off the face of the earth. . . . Cursed without clear cause, afflicted without apparent cure, they are an affront to our rationality, living evidence of our despair of ever finding a sensible, an explainable, design to the world.[70]

But those searching for causes do not give up easily. Despite numerous fruitless endeavors, the quest continues unabated.[71] There is little point in even listing the vast array of variables once investigated. But brief mention should be made of those that most frequently make the headlines as probable causes.

The question the author most frequently hears is, aren't homosexuals born that way? This, of course, refers to a *biological condition* in general and a *genetic condition* in particular.[72] Biological positivists have long thought that homosexuality would eventually be linked to heredity, but the evidence is nonexistent. With the discovery that some individuals possess statistically abnormal chromosome arrangements (e.g., XYY—see our discussion in Chapter 1), it was suspected that certain arrangements might make persons more vulnerable to homosexuality. Studies to date indicate that no arrangement of chromosomes can be linked to sexual preference.

The most recent biological factor to be investigated is the level of the male sex hormone *testosterone*.[73] Preliminary findings on small samples indicate that low levels of the hormone are found in males who are predominantly or exclusively homosexual throughout their lives. However, the exact relationship between the hormone and behavior is cloudy for two reasons. First, researchers admit that homosexual behavior may cause changes in hormone levels, not vice versa; and second, researchers find that administering the hormone increases sex drive but does not alter sexual preference.

Whereas some scientists continue to seek biological explanations for homosexuality, others have concentrated on parent-child relationships as the cause. The precise character of the relationship that presumably creates homosexuality depends upon which theorist you are reading. Generally, it involves some combination of a mother who is domineering, seductive, over-indulgent, and possessive; and a father who is indifferent, distant, weak, and ineffectual. In a review of studies prior to 1968 Evelyn Hooker concluded:

> The evidence from these and many similar studies does not support the assumption that pathological parent-child relations are either necessary or sufficient antecedents or determinants of adult homosexuality. The evi-

dence does indicate, however, that some forms of familial pathology appear to be associated with increased vulnerability of some individuals to homosexual development, and it suggests that psychopathology is more frequently associated with homosexuality in these individuals.[74]

A study reported in 1974 compared the parental backgrounds of over 300 males who were either exclusively or predominantly homosexual to those of males who were predominantly or exclusively heterosexual. Although the author, Marvin Siegelman, found that fathers of homosexuals tended to be more rejecting and distant, the presence of protective and demanding mothers was not indicated by the data. Siegelman also found that the more masculine types of homosexuals had had relationships with their fathers similar to the heterosexuals' relationships. Siegelman concludes that his study shows no cause-and-effect relationship between parental behavior and sexual preference, and he doubts any such relationship exists.[75]

Until it is proven otherwise, one can only conclude that it is more accurate to view homosexuality as a *choice of behavior* rather than as a condition. One can with some justification abandon the notion *homosexual* because it implies the existence of a specific type of individual whose differences from the rest of the population go beyond his or her sexual preference. Among homosexual interest groups the preferred term is *gay*. However, that term has its own set of drawbacks. In the author's contact with the so-called gay community, he could find little agreement on the precise meaning of the term. Some felt that it referred strictly to varying degrees of homosexual contacts; others refused to discuss the term in the context of sexuality. To the latter, gay connoted a full-blown philosophy of life, love, justice, and freedom; sex entered the picture only to the extent that one's love and respect for someone else should be expressed in its totality, and that might involve sex regardless of the gender. Because *gay* seems to be as arbitrary and inexact as *homosexual*, we will defer to convention and use the terms interchangeably.

If commitment to homosexuality is a matter of choice, the next logical question is, how does one learn to make that choice? Part of the answer lies in a statement by Kinsey and his associates.

> The data indicate that the factors leading to homosexual behavior are (1) the basic physiologic capacity of every mammal to respond to any sufficient stimulus; (2) the accident which leads an individual into his or her first sexual experience with a person of the same sex; (3) the conditioning effects of such experience; and (4) the indirect but powerful conditioning which the opinions of other persons and the social codes may have on an individual's decision to accept or reject this type of sexual conduct.[76]

The import of the first factor is that all humans have the capacity to be sexually stimulated by the same sex—this is particularly evident in those societies in which homosexual activities are normal occurrences. The accident mentioned in the second factor refers to where one finds oneself in the enormous range of social situations. One could be seduced at an early age by an admired adult; one might be a member of a gang that encourages obtaining easy money by "getting queers"; one might find strong emotional ties transcending mere friendship with another adolescent; or one could be committed to an institution in which homosexual activity is the only sexual activity available outside of masturbation.

Regardless of the context in which initial homosexual experiences occur, continued involvement and eventual commitment to homosexuality depend upon at least two other contingencies: the degree to which the behavior is *defined as pleasureable,* and the degree to which socially imposed *inhibitions* against repeating the behavior can be overcome. For those involved in heterosexual behavior, the latter is unlikely to be a problem. Even if the first contact is regarded as a crass, fumbling, and generally disgusting experience, there is social encouragement to try and try again until you get it right.

There is some evidence that, for young males anyway, the pleasure of the initial homosexual act may be doubly reinforced by images accompanying subsequent masturbation. According to Ronald L. Akers this reinforcement occurs in the following pattern:

> The boy who has had a satisfying homosexual experience is more likely to think of other boys when masturbating, and if he does, masturbatory pleasure serves to condition him toward sexual excitation by other males. . . .
>
> Through both direct reinforcement and reinforcement through masturbatory imagery, then, the homosexual experience may be repeated. Each time that it results in positive outcomes, the probability of repeating it increases. Rewarded repetition and practice enhance the ability to attain pleasure from the homosexual acts of mutual masturbation, fellatio, and anal intercourse. Inhibitions toward homosexuality continue to decrease. Depending on how frequent and how pleasurable simultaneous heterosexual experiences are, each succeeding successful homosexual episode increases the probability of further homosexual involvement.[77]

However, breaking through inhibitions surrounding the sex act is but a step toward becoming gay. Many individuals engage in homosexual behavior but maintain a concept of themselves as *straight.* We have already mentioned the young males who prostitute themselves, whose inhibitions are dulled, initially at least, by the desire for easy money but who remain detached from a homosexual self-concept. A study of tearooms indicates that many males frequent them to experience fellatio because of perceived sexual needs but restricted outlets.[78] They use public restrooms searching for service they either cannot find at home or cannot otherwise afford. This free, impersonal means of obtaining an orgasm does not threaten their masculine self-image.

Homosexual behavior unaccompanied by a homosexual self-concept may also be found in prisons. Those who play the male role in such situations are known as *wolves* or *jockers*. Their behavior is considered by themselves and by their peers to stem from sexual deprivation. Any hint of effeminacy or emotional attachment to partners is studiously avoided.

> The wolf or jocker plays the stereotyped "male" role in sexual activity. He views himself, and needs to be viewed by his fellow inmates, as "a man"; and within prison to be "a man" and still engage in homosexual acts one must present an image of exaggerated toughness and unequivocal masculinity. The jocker, by consistently wielding force over or raping his sexual partners, maintains for himself and others a perception of his behavior as basically masculine under the circumstances. The more violence that surrounds his sexual acts, the closer the jocker comes to actually engaging in an emotionless act of rape, thereby escaping both homosexual anxiety and the imputation of "queerness" by his peers.[79]

Total acceptance of homosexual conduct and of an identity as homosexual or gay obviously entails the removal of any lingering doubts about one's position in the sexual world. In the gay vocabulary this process is termed *coming out*. (Like the term *gay*, *coming out* has no exact definition. Its meaning ranges from the first homosexual act, to the identity change from hetero- to homosexual, to the public acknowledgement of one's homosexual identity. We shall use it in the sense of *identity change*.) As we have consistently stressed throughout this book, acceptance of a deviant self-concept involves the learning of *verbalized motives* that justify the behavior in the face of negative social reaction.

A study by Barry M. Dank found that coming out occurred in several contexts, usually through association with self-admitted gays, but also through contacts with sympathetic straight persons and through reading.[80] From these situations the individuals found the knowledge and support necessary to make their decision. The following are some examples of comments by Dank's gay subjects.

> I met a lot of gay people that I liked and I figured it can't be all wrong. If so and so's a good Joe, and he's still gay, he can't be all that bad. . . . I figured it couldn't be all wrong, and that's one of the things I learned. I learned to accept myself for what I am—homosexual.

> I knew that there were homosexuals, queers and what not; I had read some books and I was resigned to the fact that I was a foul, dirty person, but I wasn't actually calling myself a homosexual yet. . . . I went to this guy's house and there was nothing going on, and I asked him, "Where is some action?" and he said, "There is a bar down the way." And the time I really caught myself coming out is the time I walked into this bar and saw a whole crowd of groovy, groovy guys. And I said to myself, there was this realization, that not all gay men are dirty old men or idiots, silly queens,

but there are some just normal-looking and acting people, as far as I could see. I saw gay society and I said, "Wow, I'm home." [81]

If the previously learned connotations of homosexuality can be rejected, the meaning of the concept can be transformed from negative to positive. The individual can thus find a new identity and accept his behavior and himself as normal. This does not necessarily mean the gay has solved all his problems connected with sexual orientation. Although he does experience relief, release from tension, and a feeling of belonging, the coming out period also often involves a *crisis of femininity*. [82] The range of possible homosexual adaptations runs from the ultra-masculine types—complete with leather jackets, boots, and motorcycles—to dressing in *drag* or masquerading as females. Those who adopt the latter roles may undertake careers as female impersonators (one of the best known examples is an entertainment group known as Les Cockettes) or become prostitutes for unwary males. The vast majority of gays fall somewhere between these extremes, but those just coming out may still be confronted with the decision of where their niche on the continuum is to be.

Regardless of the behavior he eventually adopts, the gay generally enters a social network that continues to positively reinforce his self-concept. It insulates him from the stigma and reactions that threaten him on the outside, provides the appropriate verbalized motives for homosexual behavior, and eases anxieties and guilt feelings over such behavior. This network is variously call the homosexual or gay *community*. [83]

To the straight individual, the community's most obvious indicator is the gay bar. The bar serves as a meeting place for strangers with similar sexual interests and, of course, as a social center for friends. But beyond the bar the community embraces networks of friends, residences, and organizations where gays are free from the sexual and social restraints of conventional society and where they can find both social acceptance and sexual partners. Incorporation into this community represents the final step in becoming—and remaining—gay.

The gay community also contains females, of course. Although research on this point is meager, it is clear that females constitute a very small minority of the community, including gay females and straight females who enjoy associating with gay males. Among gay females, only a minority have extended contact with the community. [84] Among the reasons suggested for this lack of participation are the facts that females are generally less sexually active than males and that gay females have less social visibility. Furthermore, females become gay through a process of emotional involvement leading to sexual contacts; for males the process is likely to be reversed. The following is one coed's description of the beginning of her coming out process.

> I would look at her in the dining room like I just wanted to eat her up and this went on for some time. And she was very tense and I was just kind of ecstatic and I felt loved. I really felt like I'd really blossomed and I just felt just beautiful and just wonderful. And then one day, I heard the word "lesbian" and it suddenly began to dawn on me what society thought of and labelled what I was feeling. . . . The one thing you want to scream to the world about has to be absolutely hidden because they can't see it that way. There's some rule that says that I was supposed to fall in love but not with a girl.[85]

The lesser visibility, the greater likelihood of long-term emotional involvements, and lower sexual promiscuity mean that gay females have less need for the protection and other services provided by the gay community.

HOMOSEXUALITY AND CONFLICT

Up until about 1948 homosexuality was a word rarely heard or seen in print. Few if any American universities would have permitted a lecturer to stand before undergraduates and discuss the subject. In the dormitories and fraternities discussions centered around sex, but sex was sex—none of this distinction between *hetero* and *homo*. Today campus newspapers carry classified advertisements for roommates that specify gay or straight. Beyond academia, there are newspapers and magazines for gays; there are dances, parades, societies, fairs, religious services, and discussion groups—all involving people who barely seemed to exist less than thirty years ago. What happened?

Although it may be too early to place the so-called homosexual liberation into accurate historical perspective, it is quite remarkable that a deviant group has radically altered its position in society after being so persecuted for so long. A student of the gay liberation movement, Edward Sagarin, suggests three contributing factors.

1. Changing social climate. Following World War II attitudes toward all forms of sexual behavior became more permissive. It was easier to discuss pregnancy, illegitimacy, venereal disease, and practically anything about sex than before. The change heralded a toleration of a wider variety of sexual activities and interests.

2. Growing personal anonymity. Increasing geographic mobility and urbanization separated more and more persons from the social control exercised by family, neighborhood, and community. The United States was becoming a nation of strangers, thus providing the homosexual with an atmosphere both more convenient and more safe for his sexual pursuits.

3. *The Kinsey Report.* We have already mentioned Kinsey and his associates' work in conjunction with prostitution and homosexuality. The import of Kinsey's first publication in 1948, which surveyed American male sexual behavior, is difficult to overestimate. The report dealt with every aspect of sexual behavior, which was shocking enough; but even more stunning were the findings that millions of males were exclusively homosexual and millions more predominantly homosexual during a significant portion of their lives. For the first time many homosexuals recognized they were not alone—indeed they began to see themselves as one of the largest minority groups in the United States.[86]

Circumstances were ripe for the formation of interest groups. The first were unpretentious local discussion groups, but 1950 saw the beginnings of a national organization, the Mattachine Society, named after medieval court jesters who told the truth while hiding behind masks. There followed a proliferation of homophile organizations for both males and females. It was soon discovered, however, that common sexual preference does not equate with unity of organizational goals. The organizations remain highly diverse: some are primarily social; others are educational, religious, or research-oriented; and still others are active in agitating for legal changes to give gays increased civil rights.

Homophile organizations are thus diverse, and many suffer from instability as well. Probably the majority of those formed since 1950 have collapsed. The reasons are many, but ideological conflicts over goals and means toward goals have taken their toll by separating many of the organizations into factions that often splinter off to form other groups. Despite such problems among its organizations, the liberation movement has shown remarkable resiliency.

The movement's greatest ideological turbulence began in 1969 with the formation of the Gay Liberation Front (G.L.F.). The late 1960s were a period of radical fervor and activity by militant blacks, feminists, and anti-Vietnam War groups. G.L.F. members, impatient with trying to produce change within the system, felt a close alliance with revolutionary rhetoric and with any minority that appeared to be oppressed.[87] But the death of radicalism among youth in general moderated the G.L.F. philosophy. Today many of its members can be found in the Gay Activist Alliance (G.A.A.) in New York City, which is more directly involved in homosexual matters rather than general radical causes. The G.A.A.'s activities range from confronting political candidates on their stand toward homosexuality to sit-ins at firms whose employment practices discriminate against gays.[88]

It is impossible to determine just how important a role gay organizations have played in overcoming the discrimination suffered by homosexuals. The conflict is not over, but several events in 1974 alone indicate how much traditional discrimination against homosexuals has been eroded.

In 1974 it was estimated that between 200 and 250 college campuses had officially recognized homosexual student groups, conferring on them all the rights and privileges of the more traditional Pershing Rifles and the Accounting Club. In many cases, if not most, recognition resulted from court actions brought by gays against the schools.[89]

In 1974 gays successfully pressured broadcasting stations to cancel television programs which gays found offensive. One show dealt with a lesbian crime ring; another concerned a fourteen-year-old boy who was raped by his science teacher while on a field trip.[90]

In 1974 the American Psychiatric Association voted to drop homosexuality from its list of mental disorders—a position it had occupied for nearly a hundred years. One group which lobbied for the change was the Gay Task Force, an organization formed in 1973 to "work for the liberation of gay people and a change in public attitudes."[91]

By 1974 a number of city governments had enacted legislation to protect gays from discrimination in employment, housing, and public accommodations. These cities include Washington, D.C., Minneapolis, Seattle, Berkeley, and Ann Arbor.

The gay liberation movement has not enjoyed entirely smooth sailing, however, especially in the matter of influencing legislation. In Boulder, Colorado, anti-discriminatory legislation was approved by the city council but rejected in a referendum, two to one, by one of the largest voter turnouts in the city's history. And legislation was defeated in 1974 in New York City, a gay stronghold. The confrontation between the groups attempting to influence the New York City Council's vote was a classic one. On one side were the homosexuals, represented by a group calling itself the Ad Hoc Coalition of Gay Organizations. On the other side was the Roman Catholic Archdiocese of New York. It was the Sodomites versus God all over again. And, as in Genesis, God won.

The gays had been working on passage of the bill since 1971; by 1974 success seemed likely if not assured. But as voting time neared, the Archdiocesan newspaper ran a front page editorial calling the proposal "a menace to family life." Because the legislation would have prohibited discrimination against teachers for their sexual orientation, the paper warned that contact with homosexuals "could harm persons in their formative years."

It was then that other interest groups, including the city's firemen's association, were alerted and aroused. A torrent of mail poured into

the council, mainly from war veterans' organizations, Holy Name Societies, and other churchmen, including rabbis who sent Biblical in-
junctions against homosexuality. With election time nearly at hand,
councilmen had to struggle mightily with the dilemma of whether the
legislation involved civil rights for a minority or official acceptance of
a sexual orientation. The bill lost twenty-two to nineteen.[92]

Conclusion

As the reader has undoubtedly deduced by now, the decades after
the turn of the century were a period of national purification. Reform
groups struggled to realize a dream in which America turned from its
course of moral pluralism and became a homogeneous nation of
hard-working, sober, family-loving, church-going Christians. We were
to be a nation of great cities with small town virtues. Reform groups
fought all kinds of social evils, both real and imaginary, ranging from
meat packers selling rotten beef to young girls being forced into sexual bondage. And, of course, they believed—as all moral crusaders
believe—that solutions were close at hand. Depending upon the evil
in question and upon the philosophy of the reformers, the solutions
might be religious, scientific, or legal.

The reformers' ideals were never realized. Their solutions were inadequate to the task: neither the bluntness of the criminal law nor
the benevolent tyranny of the therapeutic state did much to deter
drinking, drugging, homosexuality, or price-fixing. Today, though we
are still a long way from being able to explain why persons engage in
behavior that comes to be labeled deviant, we are closer to recognizing that our reactions toward such behavior can often result in un-
foreseen consequences.

Some of these consequences stem from the fact that in our economic system *virtue* is often indistinguishable from *evil*. As we have
seen earlier in discussing verbalized motives, everyone who is paid
for supplying a demand, however illegal, views him or herself as a
capitalist. Every demand produces its own set of entrepreneurs who,
for a price commensurate with the risk, will supply the product or
service.

Risk is a key term here. It seems logical that practically any form of
behavior involving rational choice could be substantially diminished if
the risk level were high enough. In reality, however, raising the risk
often only encourages more entrepreneurs: those who protect the
risk takers while exploiting them. Thus for the drug users, the prostitutes, and the homosexuals law enforcement vacillates from tolerance
to crackdown to blackmail. Risks vary from one day to the next and

seldom remain high enough to discourage the seeking of pleasure, profit, or both. In short, the law is simply not as effective in altering behavior as many would hope.

Perhaps frustration over the law's lack of effectiveness is one reason many of the sexual "evils" once so vigorously condemned are declining as legal issues. More likely that lack of effectiveness has contributed to the dissipation of power of those interest groups who would force all Americans into a mold based on some unrealistic ideal. There have been too many shattered dreams, too many failures.

Today, the sexual deviants have become the reformers. They are the moral crusaders exposing the problems to be solved by legislation. By their lobbying efforts they have made more visible the necessity of creating a climate tolerant of varying life styles and greater personal freedom. Opposing groups appear to be content with the status quo, or capable only of fighting occasional rear guard actions. For example, the Catholic Church in New York City rallied its forces at the last minute to prevent, by a narrow margin, homosexuals from being legally permitted to teach; and the voters in Boulder turned out en masse to reverse a city council decision on job rights for gays.

Certainly, life for homosexuals and prostitutes can still be very difficult in some communities. But a delicately balanced toleration is more the rule than the exception, if the deviants can avoid becoming political footballs at election time and can maintain a low profile in their sexual activities so as not to arouse public moral indignation. Perhaps a decision in Boston exemplifies the current situation. In that city an area has been set aside to contain and to limit pornography shops and strip joints. Fittingly called the Combat Zone, it recalls the days of red light districts; sexual deviation is isolated, visible, and tolerated.

Caution must be exercised in interpreting present trends. When certain interest groups exert their influence while competing groups are impotent, or perhaps indifferent, this does not imply a reorientation of basic public attitudes. The *drys*, for example, won their legislation but not public acceptance. At best for the present, gays and hookers can hope for increased legal rights and decreased legal harassment. Public acceptance may have to await another time.

NOTES

1. Alfred C. Kinsey, Wardell B. Pomeroy, and Clyde E. Martin, *Sexual Behavior in the Human Male* (Philadelphia: W. B. Saunders, 1948), pp. 595–609. See also Charles Winick and Paul M. Kinsie, *The Lively Commerce: Prostitution in the United States* (Chicago: Quadrangle Books, 1971), pp. 185–209.

More recently there has been a study of 1,242 johns who patronized call girls. The researcher obtained her data on the transactions and sexual practices by observing through peepholes, one-way mirrors, and at doors left ajar. Because the base fee for the girls' services was $50, the sample is unrepresentative of the population of johns. Martha L. Stein, *Lovers, Friends, Slaves . . . The Nine Male Sexual Types: Their Psycho-Sexual Transactions with Call Girls* (New York: Berkley Publishing, 1974).

2. Kinsey et al., *Sexual Behavior in the Human Male,* pp. 605–606.

3. Winick and Kinsie, *Lively Commerce,* p. 5.

4. Gail Sheehy, *Hustling: Prostitution in Our Wide-Open Society* (New York: Delacorte Press, 1973), pp. 82–83.

5. Winick and Kinsie, *Lively Commerce,* p. 3.

6. For an account of a high class New Orleans brothel, see Stephen Longstreet, *Sportin' House* (Los Angeles: Sherbourne Press, 1965).

7. Winick and Kinsie, *Lively Commerce,* p. 132.

8. The discussion is based on Donald J. Black, "Forms and Reforms of Whoredom: Notes on the Sociology of Prostitution and Moral Enterprise," Center for Research on Social Organization, University of Michigan, 1966 (mimeographed); and Winick and Kinsie, *Lively Commerce,* pp. 131–184.

9. Roger M. Williams, "The Oldest Profession in Nevada—and Elsewhere," *Saturday Review—World,* September 7, 1974, p. 9. For a description of an illegal contemporary brothel in a medium-sized city, see Barbara Sherman Heyl, "The Madam As Entrepreneur," *Sociological Symposium,* **11** (Spring 1974), pp. 61–82. See also Robert M. Castle, "Ash Meadows: A Fly-In Brothel," in *Deviance: Field Studies and Self-Disclosures,* ed. Jerry Jacobs (Palo Alto, Calif.: National Press Books, 1974), pp. 41–51.

10. David J. Pittman, "The Male House of Prostitution," *Trans-action,* **8** (March–April 1971), pp. 21–27.

11. For a discussion of prostitution in Middle America, see James P. Sterba, "Prostitution Is Flourishing in Rich Exurban Market," *New York Times,* June 9, 1974, Section 1, p. 55.

12. Ibid.

13. Gail Sheehy, *Hustling,* pp. 30–32.

14. "White Slavery, 1972," *Time,* June 5, 1972, p. 24.

15. Howard Blum, "The Gay Underground: Boys for Sale," *Village Voice,* February 8, 1973, p. 83. See also "White Slavery, 1972," *Time.*

16. For Stanford's autobiography see Sally Stanford, *The Lady of the House* (New York: G. P. Putnam's, 1966).

17. The discussion here represents an amalgamation of the following studies: James H. Bryan, "Apprenticeships in Prostitution," *Social Problems,* **12** (Winter 1965), pp. 287–297; Nanette J. Davis, "The Prostitute: Developing a Deviant Identity," in *Studies in the Sociology of Sex,* ed. James M. Henslin (New York: Appleton-Century-Crofts, 1971), pp. 297–322; Diana Gray, "Turning-Out: A Study of Teenage Prostitution," *Urban Life and Culture,* 1 (January 1973), pp. 401–425; Robert E. Kuttner, "Poverty and Sex: Relationships in a 'Skid Row' Slum," *Sexual Behavior* (October 1971), pp. 55–63; and Winick and Kinsie, *Lively Commerce,* pp. 38–57. For a discussion of a similar deviant career path, see James K. Skipper, Jr. and Charles H. McCaghy, "Stripteasers:

The Anatomy and Career Contingencies of a Deviant Occupation," *Social Problems,* **17** (Winter 1970), pp. 391–405.

18. James H. Bryan, "Occupational Ideologies and Individual Attitudes of Call Girls," *Social Problems,* **13** (Spring 1966), p. 443.

19. Albert J. Reiss, Jr., "The Social Integration of Queers and Peers," *Social Problems,* **9** (Fall 1961), pp. 102–120. See also Martin Hoffman, "The Male Prostitute," *Sexual Behavior* (August 1972), pp. 16–21.

20. Kate Millett, *The Prostitution Papers: A Candid Dialogue* (New York: Avon Books, 1973), p. 55.

21. Ibid., p. 56.

22. Sheehy, *Hustling,* p. 104.

23. Ibid., p. 6.

24. Christina and Richard Milner, *Black Players: The Secret World of Black Pimps* (Boston: Little, Brown, 1972), pp. 178–271 passim. For other discussions of the pimp, see Susan Hill and Bob Adelman, *Gentleman of Leisure* (New York: New American Library, 1972); Gray, "Turning-Out," pp. 416–418; and Winick and Kinsie, *Lively Commerce,* pp. 109–120. The "bible" of pimps is Iceberg Slim, *Pimp: The Story of My Life* (Los Angeles: Holloway House, 1969). Parts of this work dealing with the pimp's philosophy are reprinted in Charles H. McCaghy, James K. Skipper, Jr., and Mark Lefton, *In Their Own Behalf: Voices from the Margin,* 2nd ed. (Englewood Cliffs, N.J.: Prentice-Hall, 1974), pp. 287–299.

25. Milner and Milner, *Black Players,* pp. 178–179, 182.

26. Ibid., pp. 243–244.

27. Lesley Oelsner, "World of the City Prostitute Is a Tough and Lonely Place," *New York Times,* August 9, 1971, pp. 31, 33; and Tom Buckley, "Where Prostitutes Solicit Determines Arrest Chance," *New York Times,* December 14, 1974, p. 44.

28. Howard Blum, "The Bed Patrol," *Village Voice,* April 4, 1974, pp. 1, 28–31.

29. The Vice Commission of Chicago, *The Social Evil in Chicago* (1911), cited in Eric Anderson, "Prostitution and Social Justice: Chicago, 1910–15," *Social Service Review,* **48** (June 1974), p. 211.

30. The discussion is based on Anderson, "Prostitution and Social Justice," pp. 203–228; Black, "Forms and Reforms of Whoredom"; and Kay Ann Holmes, "Reflections by Gaslight: Prostitution in Another Age," *Issues in Criminology,* **7** (Winter 1972), pp. 83–101.

31. Winick and Kinsie, *Lively Commerce,* p. 223.

32. For discussions of legal changes see Pamela A. Roby, "Politics and Criminal Law: Revision of the New York State Penal Law on Prostitution," *Social Problems,* **17** (Summer 1969), pp. 83–109; and Roby, "Politics and Prostitution: A Case Study of the Revision, Enforcement and Administration of the New York State Penal Laws on Prostitution," *Criminology,* **9** (February 1972), pp. 425–447.

33. Buckley, "Where Prostitutes Solicit," p. 44.

34. The most recent statement of Davis' theory is the source of this discussion. Kingsley Davis, "Sexual Behavior," in *Contemporary Social Problems,* 3rd ed., ed. Robert K. Merton and Robert Nisbet (New York: Harcourt Brace

Jovanovich, 1971), pp. 345–351. For a brief recent critique of Davis' approach see Dorie Klein, "The Etiology of Female Crime: A Review of the Literature," *Issues in Criminology,* **8** (Fall 1973), pp. 19–21.

35. Davis, "Sexual Behavior," p. 347.

36. See especially: Women Endorsing Decriminalization, "Prostitution: A Non-Victim Crime?" *Issues in Criminology,* **8** (Fall 1973), pp. 137–162; and Kate Millett, *The Prostitution Papers,* pp. 81–85, 93–99.

37. Women Endorsing Decriminalization, "Prostitution," p. 160.

38. Ibid., p. 161. For a debate between two males on removing legal barriers to prostitution see Robert Veit Sherwin and Charles Winick, "Debate: Should Prostitution Be Legalized?" *Sexual Behavior,* January 1972, pp. 66–73.

39. Sheehy, *Hustling,* pp. 197–200; and Millett, *The Prostitution Papers,* pp. 18–26.

40. The following discussion is based on Maurica Anderson, "Hookers, Arise!" *Human Behavior,* (January 1975), pp. 40–42; and "Call Me Madam," *Newsweek,* July 8, 1974, p. 65.

41. Buckley, "Where Prostitutes Solicit," p. 44.

42. Thomas S. Szasz, *The Manufacture of Madness: A Comparative Study of the Inquisition and the Mental Health Movement* (New York: Harper & Row, 1970), p. 162.

43. Fred Barnes, "Justices Uphold Sodomy Laws," *Washington Star-News,* November 6, 1973, p. A–7.

44. Donald J. West, *Homosexuality* (Chicago: Aldine Publishing, 1967), pp. 72–84; and Council on Religion and the Homosexual et al., *The Challenge and Progress of Homosexual Law Reform* (San Francisco: The Council, 1968), pp. 10–19.

45. Martin S. Weinberg and Colin J. Williams, *Male Homosexuals: Their Problems and Adaptations* (New York: Oxford University Press, 1974), p. 23.

46. "Public Tolerance Is Little Changed," *New York Times,* October 21, 1969, cited in Gilbert Geis, *Not the Law's Business? An Examination of Homosexuality, Abortion, Prostitution, Narcotics and Gambling in the United States* (Washington, D.C.: National Institute of Mental Health, 1972), pp. 38–39.

47. Eugene E. Levitt and Albert D. Klassen, Jr., "Public Attitudes Toward Homosexuality: Part of the 1970 National Survey by the Institute for Sex Research," *Journal of Homosexuality,* **1** (Fall 1974), p. 40.

48. Personal correspondence with Charles W. Thomas and Robin J. Cage.

49. Weinberg and Williams, *Male Homosexuals,* pp. 183–186, 276–278. For personal accounts of favorable reactions from the straight community see Merle Miller, *On Being Different: What It Means to Be a Homosexual* (New York: Random House, 1971); and John Murphy, *Homosexual Liberation: A Personal View* (New York: Praeger Publishers, 1971).

50. Jon J. Gallo et al., "The Consenting Adult Homosexual and the Law: An Empirical Study of Enforcement and Administration in Los Angeles County," *UCLA Law Review,* **13** (March 1966), pp. 647–832; see especially pp. 686–742. For up-to-date reports on police activities against homosexuals see recent issues of *The Advocate,* published biweekly and available, depending on the reader's location, in pornography shops and the more liberal newsstands.

51. Gallo et al., "The Consenting Adult Homosexual," pp. 698, 795–796.

52. Council, *Challenge and Progress,* p. 21.

53. "Court Bans Spying in Public Toilets," *Toledo Blade*, March 16, 1975, Section 1, p. 21.

54. Council, *Challenge and Progress*, pp. 28–29; and Geis, *Not the Law's Business?* pp. 31–32.

55. Laud Humphreys, *Tearoom Trade: Impersonal Sex in Public Places* (Chicago: Aldine, 1970), pp. 89–90; and West, *Homosexuality*, pp. 89–90.

56. John H. Gagnon and William Simon, "Homosexuality: The Formulation of a Sociological Perspective," *Journal of Health and Social Behavior*, 8 (September 1967), p. 181.

57. This discussion is based on Arthur Bell, "Mayhem on the Gay Waterfront," *Village Voice*, January 13, 1975, p. 5.

58. Ibid.

59. Levitt and Klassen, "Public Attitudes," p. 32.

60. Colin J. Williams and Martin S. Weinberg, *Homosexuals and the Military: A Study of Less Than Honorable Discharge* (New York: Harper & Row, 1971).

61. For a discussion of this law and the celebrated case in which the Supreme Court confirmed the exclusion of homosexuals see Szasz, *The Manufacture of Madness*, pp. 242–259.

62. West, *Homosexuality*, pp. 17–21.

63. Ibid., p. 21.

64. Kinsey et al., *Sexual Behavior in the Human Male*, pp. 636–637.

65. Ibid., pp. 636–657.

66. For a discussion of the types of individuals frequenting public restrooms for sexual purposes see Humphreys, *Tearoom Trade*, pp. 111–129; and Laud Humphreys, "Impersonal Sex and Perceived Satisfaction," in *Studies in the Sociology of Sex*, ed. James M. Henslin (New York: Appleton-Century-Crofts, 1971), pp. 351–374.

67. Alfred C. Kinsey, Wardell B. Pomeroy, Clyde E. Martin, and Paul H. Gebhard, *Sexual Behavior in the Human Female* (Philadelphia: W. B. Saunders, 1953), pp. 474–475.

68. Edward Sagarin, "Survey Essay: The Good Guys, the Bad Guys, and the Gay Guys," *Contemporary Sociology*, 2 (January 1973), p. 10.

69. Mary McIntosh, "The Homosexual Role," *Social Problems*, 16 (Fall 1968), pp. 182–192.

70. Joseph Epstein, "Homo/Hetero: The Struggle for Sexual Identity," *Harper's Magazine*, 241 (September 1970), pp. 43, 151.

71. A concise, though somewhat dated, summary of various explanations of homosexuality may be found in West, *Homosexuality*, pp. 151–215.

72. This discussion is based on John Money, "Sexual Dimorphism and Homosexual Gender Identity," *Psychological Bulletin*, 74:6 (1970), pp. 425–440.

73. Boyce Rensberger, "Homosexuality Linked to Hormone Level," *New York Times*, November 18, 1971, p. 41.

74. Evelyn Hooker, "Homosexuality," in *International Encyclopedia of the Social Sciences*, vol. 14, ed. David L. Sills (New York: Collier and Macmillan, 1968), p. 224.

75. Marvin Siegelman, "Parental Background of Male Homosexuals and Heterosexuals," *Archives of Sexual Behavior*, 3 (January 1974), pp. 3–18.

76. Kinsey et al., *Sexual Behavior in the Human Female*, p. 447.

77. Ronald L. Akers, *Deviant Behavior: A Social Learning Approach* (Belmont, Calif.: Wadsworth Publishing, 1973), pp. 159–160.

78. Humphreys, "Impersonal Sex," pp. 362–372.

79. George L. Kirkham, "Homosexuality in Prison," in *Studies in the Sociology of Sex*, ed. Henslin, p. 345.

80. Barry M. Dank, "Coming Out in the Gay World," *Psychiatry*, **34** (May 1971), pp. 180–197.

81. Ibid., pp. 185, 187.

82. Simon and Gagnon, "Homosexuality," p. 182; and Weinberg and Williams, *Male Homosexuals*, pp. 158–159.

83. This discussion is based on Maurice Leznoff and William A. Westley, "The Homosexual Community," *Social Problems*, **3** (April 1956), pp. 257–263; Evelyn Hooker, "The Homosexual Community," in *Perspectives in Psychopathology* (New York: Oxford University Press, 1965), reprinted in *Sexual Deviance*, eds. John H. Gagnon and William Simon (New York: Harper & Row, 1967), pp. 167–184; Nancy Achilles, "The Development of Homosexual Bars As an Institution," in *Sexual Deviance*, eds. Gagnon and Simon, pp. 228–244; and Carol A. B. Warren, *Identity and Community in the Gay World* (New York: John Wiley, 1974).

84. This discussion is based on William Simon and John H. Gagnon, "The Lesbians: A Preliminary Overview," in *Sexual Deviance*, eds. Gagnon and Simon, pp. 251–263.

85. G. A. Vanderbelt-Barber, "A Lesbian Comes Out," in McCaghy et al., *In Their Own Behalf*, p. 176.

86. Edward Sagarin, *Odd Man In: Societies of Deviants in America* (Chicago: Quadrangle Books, 1969), pp. 81–84.

87. Edward Sagarin, "Sex Raises Its Revolutionary Head," *The Realist*, **87** (May–June 1970), reprinted in *Deviance, Conflict, and Criminality*, eds. R. Serge Denisoff and Charles H. McCaghy (Chicago: Rand McNally, 1973), pp. 174–190.

88. The discussion draws upon Sagarin, *Odd Man In*, pp. 84–110; and Laud Humphreys, *Out of The Closets: The Sociology of Homosexual Liberation* (Englewood Cliffs, N.J.: Prentice-Hall, 1972), pp. 50–126.

89. Iver Peterson, "Homosexuals Gain Support on Campus," *New York Times*, June 5, 1974, pp. 1, 32.

90. Les Brown, "NBC-TV Yields to Homosexuals over Episode of 'Policewoman,' " *New York Times*, November 30, 1974, p. 51; and John J. O'Connor, "Pressure Groups Are Increasingly Putting the Heat on TV," *New York Times*, October 6, 1974, Section 2, p. 19.

91. Harold M. Schmeck, Jr., "Doctors for Shift on Homosexuals," *New York Times*, May 9, 1974, p. 25; Peter Kihss, "8 Psychiatrists Are Seeking New Vote on Homosexuality as Mental Illness," *New York Times*, May 26, 1974, Section 1, p. 32; and "Psychiatric Unit Upholds Stand That Homosexuality Isn't Illness," *New York Times*, June 1, 1975, Section 1, p. 42.

92. This discussion is based on John Darnton, "Furor Clouds Vote Today on Homosexuals' Rights," *New York Times*, May 23, 1974, pp. 1, 26; and Maurice Carroll, "Council, by 22–19, Defeats Bill on Homosexual Rights," *New York Times*, May 24, 1974, pp. 1, 20.

Epilogue

A few parting comments are in order for the reader who has remained with us to the end. It should be apparent by now that *deviance* is not simply a violation of norms or an act of rule-breaking, but is also the result of a decision process that determines accountability, or the extent to which rule-breakers are deemed answerable for their conduct. By this point the reader should be ready to handle such questions as: "Is it deviant in America to threaten the lives of silver-haired grandmothers?" The answer should be: "It depends."

If a poor, uneducated individual takes pot shots at old women, the chances are good, but not perfect, that he or she will be severely dealt with. But the chances are slim that anything will happen to the well-to-do businessperson who supplies contaminated food products to rest homes. If anything does happen, it is likely to be merely a fine or a reprimand. Of course, there are laws against both behaviors. Both individuals are rule-breakers and they both jeopardize lives, but all persons are not equal before the law. Some are more deviant than others.

A theme of this book has been the relationship of interest groups to deviance. The most obvious instances are those in which groups create deviance by influencing the rule-making process—examples here are the laws prohibiting the use of alcohol, heroin, and marihuana. Generally in these cases one interest group's law proves to be another interest group's burden. But direct conflict over whether a specific behavior is good or bad, or whether it should be curtailed by law, is only part of the picture. Conflicts also occur over the ways in which rule-breaking should be handled.

The reader may recall that there is an ongoing dispute over how to deal with the connection between homicide and the ready availability of handguns. Unquestionably, the pro-gun people are as appalled as anyone over the rising homicides rates, but their priority of values places individual freedom and the feeling of security that guns give ahead of concern over the toll guns take. Similarly, businesspersons may express concern over the fraud and deceit found in the business community, but resist the imposition of harsh penalties for such behavior. The reasons for this resistance are less important than the result: namely, that business offenders retain an immunity from being identified as common criminals. Thus businesspersons, operating behind the facade of respectability, find it easier to maintain and promote their own brand of dishonesty.

This differential treatment—the refusal to call some thieves what they are, thieves—suggests another aspect of interest group influence on deviance. This aspect concerns the labels that are imposed on deviants. Just as legislators formulate the criminal code and the rules governing the conduct of business, organizations whose purview is health formally "legislate" diagnoses. For example, in 1956 the American Medical Association voted to declare alcoholism a disease. The vote occurred in spite of a complete lack of any compelling scientific documentation that a disease such as alcoholism actually exists. Although interest groups are responsible for manufacturing disease, they can, by the same token, undo those labels. Witness the 1974 decision —again by a vote—of the American Psychiatric Association that homosexuality is *not* an illness.

Curious as a poll on disease may be, the action by the A.P.A. represents a general trend in the United States toward official toleration and delabeling of several traditional forms of deviance. Within the past decade "deviant" interest groups and civil rights organizations have become increasingly vocal and more effective in lobbying for changes in legislation. The results have been liberalized laws concerning such behavior as abortion, sodomy, marihuana use, and prostitution. Even large-scale heroin maintenance programs for addicts may become routine in the near future. In short, deviant behavior that does not directly endanger others is being normalized. Interest groups have been active and effective on the other side of these same issues, of course, but the success of liberalizing campaigns—and even the public debate of the issues involved—would have been impossible just a few years ago.

This growing political awareness and power among traditionally weak interest groups is not limited to deviants. Other groups are concerned with such broad categories as the poor and the consumers, and have assaulted the activities of respectable deviants in their suites. The morality of politics, the legal system, and business are undergoing close scrutiny and criticism; questions are being asked about the price being paid by society in the name of efficiency, expediency, and profits. This is not to say that the economically powerful have their backs to the wall. But never before in American history has the individual citizen had so many legal rights to counteract the excesses of the powerful against the weak and the gullible; never before has business felt the need to be so defensive.

It is becoming increasingly apparent that the real weakness of America lies not with its addicts and homosexuals, or even with its gun-wielding murderers and robbers. It lies with the moral pretension and hypocrisy of some of its controllers and policy-makers. These persons are the *new* deviants and the targets of the new reformers, who in championing the rights of the weak and disadvantaged have become the conscience of the United States.

Name Index

Subject Index